ROUTLEDGE LIBRARY EDITIONS:
HUMAN RESOURCE MANAGEMENT

Volume 34

MEASUREMENT OF HUMAN RESOURCES

MEASUREMENT OF HUMAN RESOURCES

Edited by
W T SINGLETON AND P SPURGEON

Routledge
Taylor & Francis Group
LONDON AND NEW YORK

First published in 1975 by Taylor & Francis Ltd

This edition first published in 2017
by Routledge

4 Park Square, Milton Park, Abingdon, Oxon OX14 4RN
605 Third Avenue, New York, NY 10017

Routledge is an imprint of the Taylor & Francis Group, an informa business

British Library Cataloguing in Publication Data
A catalogue record for this book is available from the British Library

ISBN: 978-1-138-80870-6 (Set)
ISBN: 978-1-315-18006-9 (Set) (ebk)
ISBN: 978-0-415-78601-0 (Volume 34) (hbk)
ISBN: 978-0-415-78603-4 (Volume 34) (pbk)
ISBN: 978-1-315-22802-0 (Volume 34) (ebk)

Publisher's Note
The publisher has gone to great lengths to ensure the quality of this reprint but points out that some imperfections in the original copies may be apparent.

Disclaimer
The publisher has made every effort to trace copyright holders and would welcome correspondence from those they have been unable to trace.

Measurement of human resources

Edited by
W T Singleton & P Spurgeon

Based on papers presented to a symposium held in Lisbon, June 1973, and sponsored by N.A.T.O.

ALERE FLAMMAM

Taylor & Francis Ltd. London 1975

First published 1975 by Taylor & Francis Ltd,
10/14 Macklin Street, London WC2B 5NF.

ISBN 0 85066 068 8

Printed and bound in Great Britain by
William Clowes & Sons, Limited
London, Beccles and Colchester

Distributed in the United States of America
and its territories by Halsted Press
(a division of John Wiley & Sons Inc)
605 Third Avenue, New York, N.Y. 10016.

Contents

Preface

The North Atlantic Treaty Organization is commonly regarded as a defence organization in the military sense but there is also a civil content in the objective of safeguarding the civilization of the member states. For civil purposes the member states are Belgium, Canada, Denmark, France, Federal Republic of Germany, Greece, Iceland, Italy, Luxembourg, Netherlands, Norway, Portugal, Turkey, the United Kingdom and the United States of America.

One form of non-military co-operation within N.A.T.O. is that which originates in the science committee. This committee, which first met in 1958, has the purpose of strengthening the scientific resources of member countries by helping them to improve their own scientific efforts and also by improving international co-operation. This is done through Science Fellowships, Advance Study Institutes, Research Grants and Programme Development. This last activity involved supporting areas where it is thought that small sums of money invested in special programmes might have a catalytic effect. 'Human Factors' is currently regarded as one such area, as a consequence there has been a series of conferences within this topic, one of these was a conference held at Lisbon in June 1973 with the title 'Utilization of Human Resources'. There were scientists present from Australia, Belgium, Canada, Denmark, France, Germany, Greece, Netherlands, Norway, Portugal, Turkey, U.K. and U.S.A. This book contains papers which were read at this conference, the purpose of the meeting is described and evaluated in the Introduction and Conclusion.

The origin of the meeting can be traced to a discussion one evening in Birmingham in 1971 between Professor Kay then at Sheffield University and myself. We were talking about the development of Applied Psychology generally and I mentioned my interest in taxonomic problems. I thought that weaknesses in this area were the basic obstacle to the development of both theory and practice for many apparently different areas of applied psychology. For example, occupational guidance and ergonomics are usually regarded as very different kinds of applied psychology but progress in both depends on improved classification schemes for jobs in relation to people and for people in relation to jobs. Professor Kay suggested and later supported the idea that this might make a suitable topic for a N.A.T.O. meeting.

Once the proposal had been accepted I invited two of my colleagues from the Aston Applied Psychology Department, Ray Taylor and Peter Spurgeon, to join me in trying to formulate these ideas more precisely. Some of this thinking is reflected in the introduction which follows. Unfortunately Ray Taylor had to leave the group because of pressure of other duties, by this time we were also involved in actually organizing the conference. Most of the administration connected with this complex task was done by Peter Spurgeon and my secretary, Miss Anne Love. In these matters the experience of Mr. Bayraktar of the Scientific Affairs Division of N.A.T.O., Brussels was of great help to us.

Once it had been agreed that the Conference should be held in Lisbon we became dependent on the advice and help of Professor da Fonseca of Lisbon University, Faculty of Medicine. He suggested that the Conference should be held at the Gulbenkian Foundation Conference Centre in Lisbon and this proved ideal for the purpose.

During the Conference arrangements were in the hands of Professor da Fonseca and Miss de Serpa from Lisbon and Peter Spurgeon and Miss Anne Love from Aston.

I am grateful to all these individuals and, of course, to all the participants for what proved to be a most valuable and satisfactory experience in academic and social terms.

W.T. Singleton,
Applied Psychology Department,
University of Aston in Birmingham.

October 1973.

Introduction

W. T. Singleton and P. Spurgeon

We start, as does every scientist and technologist these days, with an acknowledgement that the resources of the world are not unlimited. This was known and agreed even in the days when it was thought that the earth was flat but it has not mattered until very recently. The difference now is that the demands on these resources are approaching the available capacities. There are two reasons for this: world population is rising rapidly and the aspirations of almost all the individuals within this population are also rising.

The preferred activity level of the human race is such that there are not enough physical resources, that is not enough materials and not enough space. The long term remedy is to reduce the world population but there is no acceptable way of doing this in the short-term. So we have literally to learn to live with this large population and we are not, at present, going about it in a very sensible way.

Nations which are regarded as developed are simultaneously pursuing contradictory policies of on the one hand providing every person with the right to work and play as he pleases yet on the other hand, steadily increasing output and expectations per person. Producing more and requiring more both imply greater use of the limited world resources. As social scientists and technologists it is not our job to solve the problems of the world. It is, however, our responsibility to devise models, methods and techniques which will increase everyone's understanding of 'what the human race is up to' (Mitchison, 1962).

Even if world resources were infinite there would still be many very difficult problems at the national, regional or community level. These stem from the fact that the rate of technological advance has risen beyond the rate at which individuals can or will change their skills and customs. There are problems of redundancy alongside problems of labour shortage within any one community. For example, in most advanced countries there is a severe shortage of managers regarded as capable of controlling modern organizations co-existing with extensive unemployment amongst middle-aged executives. Similarly there are, at any one time, gross differences in utilization of labour between areas which have concentrated on particular kinds of production. For example, the North of England which in the past has concentrated on industries such as mining, heavy engineering and cotton decays with high unemployment, while Southern England with electronics, light engineering and commercial activities flourishes and even has labour shortages. When such imbalance occurs should we try to move the people or try to move the jobs? There is no simple answer, almost certainly the optimum remedy is to encourage something of both but how much or what kind and when? Again we need models, methods and techniques so that proposed solutions can be generated and evaluated without too much of the trial and error which is so costly in both human and economic terms.

In general, given scarcities or instabilities or both the well-proved scientific response is measurement leading to description and understanding which makes possible prediction and control. All sciences and technologies are involved in this exercise. The physical scientists and engineers are concerned with serving the basic human needs of energy, materials and communication facilities. The contribution of the biologists lies in the complementary activities of providing methods of restricting population growth by contraception while sustaining existing populations with food supplies and protection against disease. There is a group of para-sciences including statistics, geography and economics which serves the policy makers directly by providing theories and data relevant to the decisions which have to be made in terms of the two resources of space and wealth. Finally there is a fourth group which includes human and social sciences concerned with the core of the whole problem, the people or the human resources. They also must attempt to advance knowledge so that prediction and adjustment become possible. This book is concerned with this last group. There are many who would reject this approach on the grounds that it is potentially dangerous, in that it may be seen (incorrectly) as implying the manipulation of one group by another. In their view it is better to remain ignorant and to allow some form of uncontrolled interplay of interests to prevail. From this standpoint it is better to tolerate waste and inequity rather than to allow the possibility of the development of an organized social system. This was a tenable argument until recently but it is no longer feasible for the reasons mentioned earlier. The combination of demanding populations and limited resources at all levels from the world scale to the regional scale is such that disaster is the only alternative to understanding and control. In short, we must develop the human sciences and technologies. This is not necessarily a gloomy prospect. It has often been pointed out, e.g., Singleton 1967, that the freedom of the individual remains, predictions of human behaviour are inherently probabilistic and there will always be enough slack in the system to enable the individual to determine his own destiny.

Unfortunately the sciences and technologies which should be contributing in this area are at present primitive and fragmented. Although the problem is recognizable intellectually it is extremely difficult to propose, recommend or encourage adaptive action. One step in the right direction is to try to facilitate communication between the relevant disciplines, in the hope, not only of improving recognition of areas of overlap but perhaps also of mutually catalysing development. These were the aims of the conference.

The disciplines involved are those concerned with increasing the 'human resource'. This can be most readily understood in terms of the contribution by individuals to the 'wealth' of the community, both quantitatively and qualitatively. It may be seen in the knowledge and well-being of individual members. Educationalists might argue that the education system should be directed to the development of individual potential. This is a tenable, indeed a self-evidently valid point of view in general terms but it is not susceptible to any great precision of definition. It leaves unspecified what we mean by development or what is the desirable direction of development, clearly there is not going to be very much agreement about these matters. There is less confusion about the concept of 'wealth' as a totality of resources which in itself is desirable for the community generally. There may be argument about whether it is worth the difficulty of acquiring and there will certainly be argument about how it should be distributed but there cannot be much disagreement about the desirability of having it and having more of it if possible. It has often been pointed out that the difficulties about sharing out the wealth of the community ought to be easier when there is more to share and all are spared the agony of deciding between almost equally desirable alternatives, e.g., more money for old-age pensioners or more money for new hospital buildings. The remedy is to generate more wealth so that we can do both. This is not to imply that money is the universal unweighted measure of the wealth of a community. Good hospitals, police services and education services for example are indicators of wealth in the general sense. Within these specialized services the problems of choosing between alternatives also applies. For example, with a given number of high quality teachers how should they be distributed between helping sub-normal children and increasing the wealth generating potential of gifted children? These questions are not dealt with in this book. Instead we concentrate on the equally important problems of how total human resources may be moulded to increase the community's capacity to meet these alternative goals. This book is about increasing wealth on the assumption that fundamentally it comes from the intelligent effort of skilled responsible individuals.

The first activity devoted to the generation of skilled responsible individuals is within the educational system so that education is the first of our relevant disciplines. The different individuals must then be helped to make their own decisions about how each wishes to contribute to the community by work and thus occupational guidance or counselling is a relevant discipline. At this stage the needs of the individual become secondary to the needs of the community and selection and placement are further relevant disciplines. After placement there is often a phase of developing and directing the individual towards a more specific kind of work which is called training. The work itself must be designed for maximum efficiency and so also must be the system within which working activities are integrated towards specific objectives, e.g., particular services or kinds of products. Thus work design and system design are relevant disciplines. Finally the human resource within a community is relatively fixed, it cannot be increased or decreased deliberately except over a very long time scale. It follows that the overall care of the resource must be considered and this is what man-power studies are about.

The relevant disciplines therefore are man-power studies, education, training, selection, placement, guidance, work design and system design. These are separate disciplines in that each one has its own disciples, that is for each there is a group of professional people who earn their living by studies and actions in the particular area. The group identity is defined by the problem area and it is preserved and developed by the models, methods and techniques which the expert in a particular field is required to accept and to know about.

It is dangerously easy to underestimate the differences between disciplines. Any long education and training is likely to have permanent effects on an individual, not only on the way he thinks and the models he uses to think with but also in his assessment of the relative importance of particular facets of a given problem. It follows inevitably that when two individuals from different disciplines get together it requires enormous goodwill and intellectual effort to communicate across the boundaries set by their academic peers.

This is perhaps the reason why pure human sciences so easily become sterile. A psychologist or an educationalist is always tempted to think within his own field and talk only with his own colleagues because life then becomes comfortable and reassuring. Walking round and round in a circle can take just as much effort as making progress in a straight line and the two are indistinguishable to those of narrow vision. The universities are full of such intellectual ostriches.

The remedy is to look at real problems. These never fall neatly within the boundaries of academic disciplines and the investigator is forced to recognize that his particular discipline is not self-sufficient. His problems and also his techniques and theories must overlap with those of other specialists. It is within these areas of overlap that the discrepancies and inconsistencies appear which are the basis of progress.

These overlaps and differences occur in the academic world and in the community generally. For instance there are differences in objectives which result in different ethics. For example, there is a discrepancy between the educational system which broadly aims to develop the individual and the working system which attempts to utilize his abilities for the benefit of the community. There is the danger that those who have no experience outside the educational system may live an isolated and protected life, developing value structures inappropriate to exterior work systems. They communicate these values to those individuals in their charge who will mostly have to transfer from education to work; predictably the effects for many are traumatic, with consequent patterns of job instability, dissatisfaction and ineffective use of human potential. There is often an essential trade-off between pairs of disciplines which have relevance to one problem. For example, the matching of workers and work by improved work design (usually called ergonomics) is the complement of the same matching starting from the other side which aims to improve the worker by guidance and training (usually called occupational psychology). In a given instance there has to be decisions of how much money and expertise to invest in the adjustment from the two sides until the best match is achieved.

All the disciplines under discussion are concerned in one way or another with the appraisal of the individual. Thus, one would expect that the principles underlying methods of measuring man would be commonly agreed and at least some of the techniques should be the same. At present this is not so. Even when the techniques appear to be the same, their aims and procedure can have very little in common. For example, most university graduates go through two sets of interviews at about the same time. Oral examination by academic examiners and selection procedures by employers. The differences are so great and have existed for so long that most people, even the victims, no longer ask questions about why this is so. These operational differences are reflected in specialist differences. That is, those concerned with either the theory or practice of measuring the impact of an education or training on an individual don't talk very much to those involved simultaneously in guidance and selection for the same individuals. To give one instance of a similarity which is an obstacle to progress, most disciplines have accepted too readily the example and standards of measurement set by the physical sciences. It is nice to have numbers but just because of their power and acceptability their validity in the context of any man-centred problem must be scrutinized ruthlessly. Before we can have reliable numbers we must have valid classification systems, that is when we say we have a number of something we must be very clear about what this class of things is, and how it differs from other classes in the context of the particular problem. For example, to say that a particular unit has x men and y women may seem clear and unambiguous but it is of no consequence unless we understand how men differ from women in terms of their contribution to and their expectations from whatever that unit is doing. The beginnings of measurement are in classification and in all fields we currently need more sensitive taxonomies. Rather less attention to number gathering and rather more attention to underlying taxonomies might be a better strategy at the present time.

Having discussed the importance of overlap we might reinforce the case by attempting to demonstrate the consequences of the current lack of overlap. That is, what has gone wrong because the disciplines stay too isolated. For this purpose each discipline can be considered separately.

Education in most advanced countries is currently in serious philosophical and practical difficulties at least partly because it has attempted to be self-sufficient and to ignore its relationship to other facets of society. The concept of education as development of the individual runs into difficulties if these 'developed' individuals find that the community generally has no place for them. That is they cannot get jobs and their skills and interests match no apparent need in the community. The educational system must take some account of man-power planning at the national level. In considering job requirements it often emerges that intellectual qualities are relatively trivial compared with factors such as carefulness and reliability, this throws into some doubt the obsession within education on the narrow assessment of intellectual achievement by examinations. At the technical level the rigid separation of education and training has probably adversely effected both disciplines in that developments in one take too long to penetrate the other yet both are based on learning processes. The teacher is a person doing a job but the methods of teacher assessment and development make no acknowledgement of the possible overlap with similar problems of assessment in other occupations, e.g. industrial managers. New questions arising from attempting to introduce democratic decision processes into the running of schools and universities have their parallels in 'industrial democracy' and local government but again there seems to be little cross-fertilization.

Training has developed largely on the basis of concepts from the experimental psychology of human skill such as 'knowledge of results' and from learning theories which have resulted for example in the various kinds of teaching machines. The emphasis on performance has led to the relative neglect of the individual and individual differences and has also resulted in a concentration on manual skills or at least perceptual motor skills. There has been less progress in training for social skills or for attitudes as distinct from skills. This bias might not have been so strong if the training specialists had talked more to educationalists and to guidance specialists. Training objectives have also been confused by the perpetual problem of who should pay. Should it be a matter for the particular organization although in fact good training increases the risk of losing an asset in the form of a person by improving that asset or should it be the community on the grounds that skilled individuals are the basic asset of any community? This problem can only be considered effectively in a very wide context.

Selection and placement are highly dependent on the assessment criteria used within education and training and it is not unreasonable to ask the educators and trainers to take this into account in designing these assessment procedures. The complementary problems of the needs of the individual and the needs of the system are not so difficult to reconcile in that the person is likely to be more effective in meeting system requirements if he also meets his personal requirements. Nonetheless there are overriding economic restraints which have to be reconciled with the aspirations of persons.

Selection and placement have their clear priority of system needs over individual needs but this priority is reversed when we come to guidance. Nevertheless both points of view remain if guidance is to be realistic. The sheer size of the guidance problem in a society where children are unlikely to follow careers in which the family has experience has not been fully appreciated. It is of great complexity and it is required on an enormous scale. Thus inevitably it must become more technically orientated, e.g., by making greater use of computers. To do this it becomes increasingly dependent on progress in related fields such as training and work design.

In work design and ergonomics there has been a shift in recent years from simple criteria such as short-term productivity to the wider concerns of individual needs. This is partly an ethical matter with a swing to increasing concern for individuals but it remains primarily an economic matter. It is uneconomic to design jobs which people are not willing to do or at least are not willing to do for very long. However, it is not good design to concentrate on matching a job to the interests of a person while omitting to consider the problem of matching the work space to the anatomy of the person. Job design remains anatomical and physiological as well as psychological.

Man-power studies is another area which must necessarily be impersonal but not too much so. Even in a relatively small country such as Britain there are 25 million working people and they must be treated in large groups if we are to grasp the total problem. However, there is all the more reason why the techniques of accumulating data should be sensitive to psychological parameters as well as to statistics and economics.

After looking at the difficulties in such detail it may seem surprising that the modern state survives, that people survive and often flourish within it and that the human scientists and technologists appear to be making some sort of contribution. The reason perhaps is that in any community there is a multiplicity of adjustment mechanisms working through localized feed-back systems. If there is any kind of overall plan it is bound to be crude and temporary with means and ends continuously modified by each other. The whole thing depends on intelligent and reasonable people both working the systems and as customers of the systems. The matching which goes on at all levels and between all kinds of demands can be roughly divided into two kinds, global and individual.

Global matching involves the policy of the community as expressed in legal, fiscal and other mechanisms. Although responsibility for decisions remains mostly with elected representatives both local and national, there is increasing dependence on the advice of experts. Supplementing these global processes there is individual matching also increasingly dependent on expert advice. It is

Figure 1. The manpower utilization problem. Seen as the matching at individual and global levels of the distribution of job factors and the distribution of personal factors. The factor at the tail of each arrow is modified by the processes in the box to match the factor at the head of the arrow

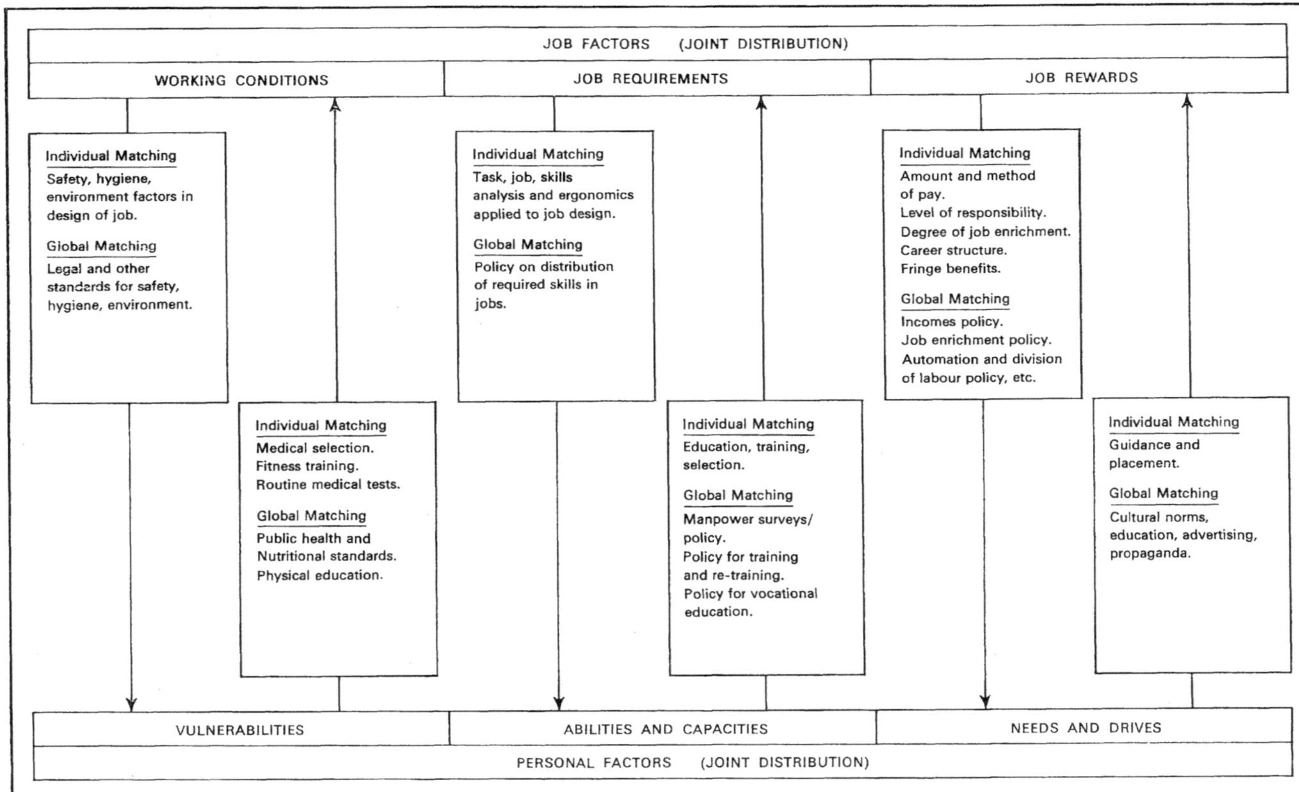

obviously important that all these experts should be scientifically and technically competent. The overall matching problem for manpower utilization is between a population which has needs, drives, capacities, abilities and vulnerabilities and a corresponding set of jobs which have conditions, requirements and rewards. The processes available to achieve the matchings are shown in Figure 1.

All these processes depend for expertise on the separate disciplines already discussed (Figure 2). These disciplines in turn depend on what ideally should be a unitary body of knowledge concerned with human resources.

Figure 2. Areas of study

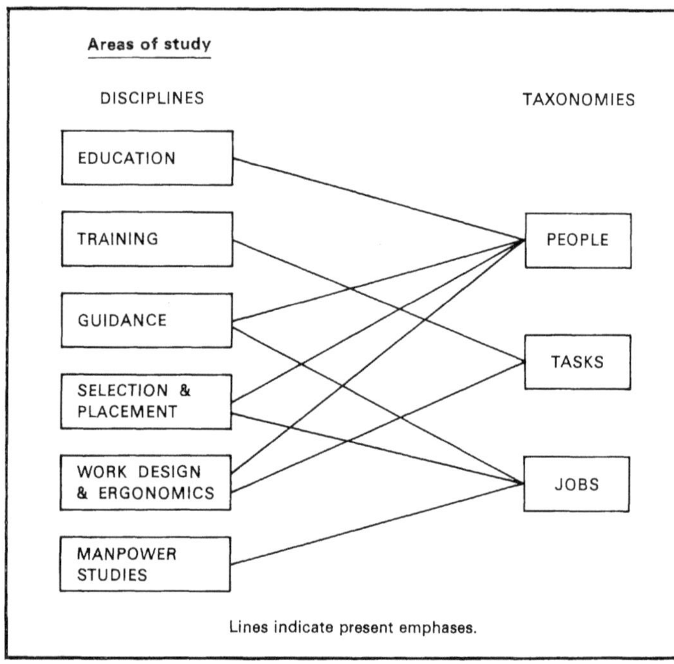

There is a need for a technology which will be concerned with developing and implementing improved practice. Some of this will be specific to the presently accepted separate disciplines but there is a common theme which depends on analysis. This starts at both ends, the jobs and the people. Behind the analysis there must be some taxonomies, that is some methods of classifying variables which meet the twin criteria of being academically sound and of being practically useful. Behind the taxonomic problem there is a problem of metrics, that is of measuring units and scales which are appropriate to people and jobs (Figure 3). This last one has already been discussed and appraised in another book (Singleton *et al.*, 1971). The core of the present book is the problem of taxonomies but it cannot be treated alone. It is only by attempting to use taxonomies in the solution of real problems that their advantages and limitations appear. Thus, it is assumed that progress will be made by a kind of leapfrogging or an

Figure 3. Levels of study

METRICS	Development of scales and units
TAXONOMIES	Classification
ANALYSIS	Study of activities as practised
TECHNOLOGY	Developing and implementing improved practice

iterative process. We cannot attempt to deal with a real problem without having some theoretical concepts which will focus our thinking, on the other hand such concepts can only be refined by application to real problems. As a further complication we must at present attempt to function sometimes within a traditional discipline and sometimes across disciplines. These were the sort of variables we had in mind in attempting to determine the structure of the conference and the book. For the conference we tried to incorporate this model of parallel theoretical and practical progress by having the mornings devoted to surveys of what is known and the afternoons to what is being done. Apart from introductory and concluding sessions there were three days available and it was intended that the first should concentrate on taxonomies, the second on methods of analysis, and the third on applications. Inevitably the individual contributions strayed across these boundaries and with the benefit of hindsight from the conference the structure of the book is different.

The first section concentrates on taxonomies but thereafter there are three sections concerned respectively with the development, use and planning of human resources. Each section begins with survey papers and ends with case-studies. There is one paper (by Bainbridge) in the book which was not presented at the Conference. We invited this contribution after the Conference on the grounds that it makes a unique contribution to the analysis problem and it provides an excellent illustration of the complexities of human behaviour.

One final point is worthy of considerable emphasis. We are concerned with people and with their activities both individually and globally. Our objective is the efficient use of human resources. Efficiency does not imply robotic control and impersonal manipulation of individuals. It means the best possible utilization and the criteria of 'best' are both the needs of society and the needs of each individual within society.

As a kind of summary of this rather involved introduction it seems appropriate to quote the original statement of the aims and format of the conference and the introduction to the programme.

The problem of matching human resources (abilities and aspirations of individuals) with the needs of the community (the jobs which have to be done) is one which every country has in common. The techniques for doing this depend on the technology of specialists in areas which range from manpower studies through education, training, selection, placement and guidance to work design. Each of these separate disciplines has its own methods of analysing and behind this implicitly or explicitly there are conventions for classifying the variables, that is taxonomies. These in turn depend on assumptions or hypotheses about measuring various aspects of people, that is on metric problems. It is suggested that since each of these separate disciplines is making a different approach to what is essentially the same problem (that is the measurement of human capacities, abilities, attainment and aspirations) then they ought to be able to learn a great deal from each other.

References

MITCHISON, N. (Ed.), 1962, *What the Human Race is up to* (London: Gollancz).
SINGLETON, W.T., 1967, Macro-ergonomics. *University Quarterly*, **21**, 2. 199–204.
SINGLETON, W.T., FOX, J.G. and WHITFIELD, D. (Eds.), 1971, *Measurement of Man at Work* (London: Taylor and Francis).

Section 1

Taxonomies of Resources

Professor Gagné received graduate training as an experimental psychologist, and several years ago developed an interest in educational psychology. His continuing research has been in the fields of human learning and memory. He has held positions in several universities, and in organizations conducting research in the behavioural sciences. His present position is as Professor of Educational Research, Florida State University, Tallahassee, Florida.

1:1

Taxonomic problems of educational systems

Robert M. Gagné

Introduction

In common with other systems that serve the needs of nations, educational systems are generally considered to have certain purposes, which are often referred to as educational goals. These goals in turn are usually related to an even broader set of purposes which reflect the aims of a particular society or nation. As a nation develops, national goals may undergo some changes, at least in their relative priorities. Such changes may occur, for example, when a nation becomes more highly industrialized, or when new natural resources are discovered. Still other kinds of changes take place when new means of achieving national goals are put into effect, such as the use of machines to accomplish goals which once required great numbers of men. Since changes of these and other varieties occur with some frequency and often over relatively brief periods of time, there is naturally a concern that educational goals continue to remain compatible with the more broadly defined societal goals.

The need for periodic revision of educational goals, to insure their alignment with national aims and priorities, is widely recognized. If agriculture becomes mechanized, the society needs fewer farmers, and the continued training of large numbers of people with agricultural skills may yield undesirable social consequences. If industrialization has attained the level at which the hours of work per week are diminished, account must be taken of the human activities which are to fill the remaining time. It is not surprising, therefore, to find that most countries of the world, whatever their stage of economic development, devote considerable effort, at least at intervals of several years, to the alignment of educational aims and national goals.

The purposes of a society are served by a number of systems, such as communication systems, transportation systems, commerce systems, banking systems and so on. Education is one of these systems. Yet education not only involves people, but also seeks to change them. It has the purpose of developing within each individual person those learnable capabilities which make it possible for him to function effectively within his society.

How does one translate the goals of a society, comprising the goals of social systems, into goals for individual development? It is the answer to this question which generates one of the major requirements for a taxonomic system of educational goals and objectives. Somehow, the broad aims of a society must be related to activities that the human adult person can perform, and these in turn to certain *capabilities* that he comes to possess. Some of these capabilities, of course, are inborn, as in the case with seeing, hearing or digesting food. But by far the greatest number of capabilities which can serve man-in-society are learned, and thus become the proper focus of interest for an educational system.

Deriving educational goals and objectives

Many efforts have been made, and continue to be made, to derive educational goals and objectives from broader societal purposes. Sometimes these efforts are conducted by formally established national commissions, representing the various sectors of a society. Often, the problem of defining educational goals becomes a central interest of educational philosophers. Frequently, too, educational scholars address this question in books dealing with the topic of 'curriculum design'. To review these writings in a thorough and systematic sense would be too great an undertaking for present purposes. Reference may be made to encyclopedic treatments of the problem (Ammons, 1969; Downey, 1971).

It appears that two major lines of derivation for educational goals can be distinguished. While these two are never entirely independent of each other, they do represent differences in emphasis, which usually lead to somewhat different conclusions. One of these routes may be called *societal*, reflecting its emphasis on goals of the society or nation; while the other may be termed *educational*, emphasizing goals reflecting individual needs, or those of man-in-society. In either case, derivation of educational goals proceeds in a number of steps—one cannot proceed immediately from the statement of a national goal to the inference that students need to learn to convert fractional numbers to decimals. Accordingly, whichever of these routes is followed, there are a number of different *levels of specificity* to be considered.

These two sources of derivation of educational goals, and some nine levels of specificity which can be distinguished, are displayed in Table 1. First, I should like to discuss briefly the first six of these levels of analysis. Following the *Societal* emphasis, there are national goals, which lead to system goals (health care), which lead in turn to manpower goals exemplified by the need for teachers, or lawyers, or farmers, or whatever. The followers of this route usually skip the next level, and the implications of this will be pointed out in a moment. One can then proceed to Level 5, the identification of human activities engaged in by particular manpower types, such as 'repairing electric motors'. Identification of these activities leads in turn to curriculum goals, such as a course in 'electric motor repair', or in 'typing'.

Consider now the second derivation route, called *Educational*. This begins with a statement expressing the purpose that man-in-society will 'lead a useful and happy life'. In doing so, one segment of his life will be devoted (Level 2) to the 'worthy use of leisure' (Commission on the Reorganization of Secondary Education, 1918). Although one segment identified at this level is bound to be 'pursuing an occupation', it is nevertheless common for the followers of this derivation route to pay little attention to the next level, which reflects the goals of a variety of occupations. Instead, the tendency is to skip to Level 4, which identifies certain general human functions, like 'social communication', 'maintaining physical fitness', or 'engaging in civic enterprises'. From such functions,

Table 1. Levels of specificity in the derivation of educational goals and objectives

Level	Source of Derivation: Societal	Source of Derivation: Educational
1	*National Goals.* Example: improve standard of living	*Man-in-Society Goals.* Example: lead a useful and happy life
2	*Social System Goals.* Example: a system of health care	*Life Segment Goals.* Example: worthy use of leisure
3	*Manpower Goals.* Example: teacher	(*Roles and Jobs*)
4	(*Human Functions*).	*Human Functions.* Example: social communication
5	*Human Activities.* Example: repairing electric motors	*Human Activities.* Example: following directions in completing an application
6	*Curriculum Goals.* Example: typing	*Curriculum Goals.* Example: social studies
7	*Human Capability Categories.* Example: intellectual skills	
8	*Broad Objectives.* Example: knowledge of the origins of World War I	
9	*Instructional Objectives.* Example: constructs a sentence with a dependent clause	

more specific human activities can be derived, exemplified by 'following directions in completing a job application'. And further, these activities can be used to imply, at the next level, the need for courses in social studies, or mathematics, or language.

The consequences of omitting levels of analysis

What happens when certain levels of analysis are omitted in deriving educational goals? Consider first the *Societal* route, and the implications of omitting Level 4, concerned with the identification of human functions. It is of course possible to proceed directly from the manpower requirement 'teacher' to the specific activities of a teacher, such as grading examination, or from 'appliance repairman' to 'repairing electric motors'. But when this is done, much of the general functioning of a teacher as a person in society, as opposed to the tasks performed by the teacher on the job, is simply neglected. A teacher is a member of a school, and has many functions to perform which derive from such membership. He is also a member of a community, and of other organizations in that community. He functions as an individual in many roles, and has many personally valuable interests to pursue.

Thus it is evident that to overlook the many kinds of human functioning of the person who is a teacher, or the person who is an electrical appliance repairman, is to infer the human activities he needs to perform from too narrow a base. The result is that educational goals—curriculum goals—also come to be too narrowly defined. Many difficulties and inadequacies follow. A distinction arises between 'academic' and 'vocational' education, and important components of curriculum are missed in each case. Vocational education, that is, education for those students who are not going to attend universities, becomes identified with 'training', which although admirably capable of being precise in its objectives, is nevertheless too restricted to serve the needs of students. In particular, what gets left out because of this narrowness is the *general* education of the graduate—the social skills he needs, the knowledge background which will form the basis of his further development, the social attitudes required of a person in a modern technological society. These are serious consequences which continue to plague the design of educational systems which are derived in the manner described.

In deriving goals via the *Educational* route, the neglect of manpower goals at Level 3 tends to lead to inadequacies. A human function like social communication can readily be derived from a life segment such as leisure, and perhaps equally readily from other life segments such as pursuing an occupation or performing as a citizen. However, the omission of Level 3 means that the relative frequency of these functions within jobs and roles is not taken into account. Communication is obviously a high frequency function in many of the roles an individual may assume, and in many of the jobs he may hold. But suppose the human function mentioned was maintaining physical fitness? Important as this may be, its occurrence among jobs and roles is relatively infrequent.

The result of this omission makes exceedingly difficult the determination of priorities in curriculum goals. In the establishment of objectives for the curriculum, it is not uncommon for committees of educators to list an item like 'shows respect for the flag' in a position coordinate to 'reads newspaper articles with comprehension'. Regardless of the absolute importance of both of these objectives, it should be obvious that one is vastly more pervasive among the life activities of the individual than is the other. Yet this fact becomes obvious, only when due consideration is given to the roles and jobs which may be occupied by individuals during their lifetimes.

A related deficiency arising from the neglect of roles and jobs in the pursuit of this route of derivation is the tendency to use nominal designations for curriculum elements. Thus the goal 'social studies' comes to be substituted for a carefully analysed answer to the question 'what social phenomena need to be studied'; similarly, a goal like 'mathematics' comes to serve as an undiscriminating answer to the question 'what kinds of number operations need to be learned?' The omission of consideration of jobs and roles, then, has the typical consequence of making the curriculum goal taxonomy overly general, and often subject to the charge of being *not relevant.*

The derivation of instructional objectives

Attention is now invited to the final three rows of Table 1, describing Levels 7, 8, and 9 of the process of analysis leading to objectives of increased specificity. Whichever route of derivation one follows, he arrives at a point where he must begin to consider *individual human capabilities*, and the *performances* which are made possible by them. Thus the two different lines of analysis come together at this point, and the deficiencies in each of them continue to plague them in all of these subsequent steps. Irrespective of this fact, the common focus of interest at these levels of specificity is on the question of what needs to be *learned*. The derivation process at this point begins to reflect directly the goal of an educational system, which is to facilitate the development of the individual learner.

Curriculum goals like 'typing' and 'social studies' may lead next to the derivation of certain broad categories of human capabilities. Identifying these is a task about which more will be said later. For the moment, these capability categories are illustrated by the phrase 'intellectual skills', by which is meant those learned capabilities which make possible the great varieties of symbol-using which human beings can learn to accomplish. From these categories, it is possible to derive, at Level 8, what have come to be called broad objectives, typically those that represent the expected outcomes of 'topics' within courses of study. The illustrative example is 'knowledge of the origins of World War I'. Another example, representing a different kind of capability, might be 'composing coherent descriptive paragraphs in the native language'.

At the most specific level, Level 9, one arrives at the statement of objectives which are usually referred to as 'behavioural' or 'performance-based'. Much has been written about these kinds of statements (Mager, 1962; Gagné, 1965), and a certain amount of controversy generated (e.g., Popham, 1969). Despite the latter, performance objectives continue to be perhaps the most important and useful tool available to the designer of instruction. They make it possible for him to identify what is learned in terms of observable human performances. This feature permits him to incorporate into instructional design the situations which enable both students and teachers to be confident that the desired learning has in fact occurred.

Kinds of taxonomies

With reference to the derivation of educational goals and objectives, Table 1 indicates twelve kinds of possible taxonomies which are relevant to this task. Naturally enough, the more general categories would find applicability in several other areas of social planning—in the establishment of national priorities, in the estimation of manpower needs, in the description and analysis of jobs, in the determination of career fields. In at least nine out of twelve instances, one can see that the full development of taxonomies would be both feasible and useful.

For the purpose of deriving objectives for an educational system, it is possible to begin the process at any of the first six levels of specificity. For example, one can begin with manpower goals, and assume that these reflect the larger purposes of social systems and national priorities. Alternatively, one can begin the process of analysis with human functions, and assume that these have taken into account the broader goals of life segments and man-in-society. Or, one can begin with subjects of the curriculum, and proceed from this point under the assumption that these subjects adequately represent the more general goals of the educational system. The derivation of educational objectives in fact often proceeds in this way. I have already pointed out the potential distortions which may result from this course of action, when steps in the chain of reasoning are overlooked. But however shaky the foundations, the process of deriving educational objectives can begin at a number of different points.

Taxonomies for educational objectives must at some point focus upon *what is to be learned.* For this reason, it seems to me that Level 7 is of critical importance—a level of specificity which identifies the categories of capabilities that are possible for human beings to acquire. What kinds of entities are these, and how can they be categorized? These are the questions to be considered next.

Varieties of human capabilities

The usual aim of an analysis process in the educational realm is to identify those human performances which are learned as a result of instruction (broadly defined). Objectives for instruction are commonly derived by beginning with certain curriculum goals, or sometimes with even more general statements of human activities, and listing the broad objectives, within which categories of specific instructional objectives can then be further listed. In other words, the categories of Level 7 are often omitted from consideration. For example, it is not uncommon for the specification of objectives to begin with a course like 'third-grade arithmetic'. From this statement one derives a set of categories of broad objectives such as 'solves problems in long division', or 'converts fractional numbers to decimals'. For such a course, the number of broad objectives identified is likely to be in the range of 30 to 50. The ninth level of specificity is then attained by identifying within each of these categories the specific varieties of performance involved in each broad objective. Long division, for example, may be undertaken with whole numbers and decimal numbers, and in a variety of kinds of settings for the presentation of the problems. Accordingly, the total set of specific instructional objectives derived for such a course typically numbers in the hundreds. Although I have used here an example from mathematics instruction, the procedure itself and the general nature of the outcome is not dissimilar in other fields such as reading, science or social studies.

It is my view that this procedure, while it is not inherently unreasonable, creates serious difficulties for the planning of instruction—the enterprise it is supposed to aid. These difficulties arise from the neglect of a taxonomy that is labelled 'Human Capability Categories' in Table 1. Just as the omission of categories of human functions, or of roles and jobs, create problems at the more general levels of analysis, so too does the omission—or relative neglect—of these categories of learned human capabilities cause trouble in the identification of instructional objectives.

The unfortunate consequences of ignoring categories of human capabilities include at least the following:

1. The planning of instruction on the basis of scores of broadly stated instructional objectives, or of hundreds of specific objectives, becomes an enormous task. If all of these objectives are not too much for the human mind to comprehend at one time, then certainly they are too many to deal with in a practical sense. In practice, regardless of good intentions, curriculum designers and teachers tend to throw up their hands in despair over striving to match specific conditions of instruction to each specific objective.

2. The attempt to deal with hundreds of specific instructional objectives often leads to an undue emphasis on those features of description which are non-essential. For example, if a child is learning to identify a printed letter, one statement of the instructional objective may include the phrase 'circles the letter', whereas another may say 'makes a check mark beside the letter'. No one would disagree that, to an external observer, these two statements refer to two different performances. But is the difference between them an essential one?

3. Perhaps the most serious consequence of using specific statements of instructional objectives for instructional planning is that common characteristics of learning, applicable across curriculum categories, are ignored. The conditions for learning a concept like 'isosceles triangle' in geometry are not fundamentally different from the conditions for learning the concept 'dependent

clause' in language study, or the concept 'momentum' in science. The neglect of such common features leads in the extreme to the preservation of the myth that there are substantive differences in the processes of 'mathematics learning', 'language learning' and 'science learning'. These artificial categories only serve to complicate further the task of planning instruction in terms of specific objectives.

In practice, curriculum and course planners often struggle hard against the complexities engendered by hundreds of specific instructional objectives. They try to use categories which will reduce this great number to a smaller number of taxonomic classes of a manageable size. Accordingly, there is a strong tendency to use such verbs to describe human capabilities as 'recognizes', 'understands', 'knows' and 'appreciates'. I need not repeat here the arguments by Mager (1962) and others to the effect that such verbs are ambiguous in their denotation of classes of human performance. It seems to me, as I have written elsewhere (Gagné, 1972a), that the strong tendency to use such verbs for descriptions of human performance reflects a strong need for classes of human capabilities which are at least freer of ambiguity.

Can such relatively unambiguous classes of learned capabilities be found? Table 2 indicates my suggestions of a taxonomy of human capabilities, containing five major categories. Since I have described these in a previous article (Gagné,

Table 2. Characteristics of five major categories of learned human capabilities

Capability	*Learning Conditions*	*Probable Characteristics*
Motor Skill	Practice of movements	Improved by continued practice. Retention high.
Verbal Information	Relating to meaningful context	Improved by more effective 'coding' and rehearsal. Retention subject to alteration and interference.
Intellectual Skill (rules, concepts, discriminations)	Availability of component skills	One-trial learning. Retention high; dependent upon verbal information cues.
Cognitive Strategy	Opportunities for use	Generalized and refined over many occasions. Retention high.
Attitude	Various, including human modelling	Resistant to change and to forgetting.

1972b), I shall only attempt here to summarize their major characteristics, and to show why they may be considered to differ from each other.

The table lists in the first column the names I have suggested for the five major categories of learned capabilities. In the second column are given brief descriptions of the optimal conditions for learning each type of capability, according to the best interpretation I can make of present evidence. The third column lists the characteristics of these entities—what distinguishes them in their learning and in their retention. The amount of evidence on this point is sometimes quite limited; accordingly the word 'probable' is used to indicate the tentativeness of some of these inferences.

Motor skill

The first category is motor skills. These are the capabilities inferred to underlie the execution of performances involving timing and smoothness of muscular movement. As is well known, the learning of motor skills requires practice, that is, the repeating of muscular movements which result in a particular outcome, whether this is driving a golf ball or pronouncing an unfamiliar sound in a foreign language. Motor skills are improved by practice, according to available evidence, virtually without end (Fitts and Posner, 1967). And it is a commonly accepted fact that they are retained very well over long periods of time.

Verbal information

By the phrase verbal information I mean the learning of names, labels, 'facts', and more highly organized units which can be represented in propositional form. Meaningfully organized masses of such information may be referred to as 'knowledge' (in one meaning of that term). It is generally agreed among those who study human learning that the most important condition for learning verbal information is relating the particular fact to be learned to a body of *organized* information which exists within the memory of the learner (cf. Tulving and Donaldson, 1972). Thus, learning of verbal information is improved if the learner undertakes such an activity as internal rehearsal which in turn may have the effect of 'encoding' the items to be remembered so as to insure their more effective storage and later retrieval. The empirical fact of interference among items of learned information has a long history of research (Postman, 1971). In addition, tendencies toward simplification and other kinds of alteration in meaning have often been verified (Bartlett, 1932).

Intellectual skill

The third category, intellectual skills, constitutes a centrally important part of school instruction. These skills are conceived as capabilities by means of which the human being interacts with his environment with the use of symbols. In the early grades of school, they are often spoken of as 'basic skills', and include the manipulation of language in reading, writing and speaking, and the performance of arithmetic operations. Such skills are by no means confined to the early grades, however, since they are elaborated in many kinds of problem solving within all of the subjects of the school curriculum.

The most important condition for learning such skills is the availability in memory of simpler component skills, or prerequisite skills (Gagné, 1970). Thus, the intellectual skill of finding the mechanical advantage of a lever may be acquired most readily if prior learning has established the skills of (1) representing verbal statements of force and distance as symbols; (2) substituting numerical values for variables in a proportion; and (3) solving an equation for an unknown value of a variable. When the prerequisite skills *are* available to the learner, the learning of a new intellectual skill appears to occur quite rapidly, in the manner spoken of by learning investigators as 'insight'. According to such evidence as exists, the retention of intellectual skills is relatively quite good. However, their retrieval from memory may depend upon cues provided by verbal information. For example, an individual may have to have a verbal cue to remember the formula for converting Fahrenheit temperature to the Celsius scale. But once given a suitable cue, he remembers *how* to make the conversion very well.

Cognitive strategy

Cognitive strategies are also skills. They are internally organized skills which govern the learner's own behaviour in attending, learning, remembering and in thinking. A good deal of emphasis on the importance of strategies of thinking as aims of school learning is to be found in the writings of Bruner (1971). 'Teaching students how to think' often appears as one of the most prominent aims in lists of educational goals. Presumably, strategies of learning, remembering, and thinking are learned, although there is some thought that they may be innately determined.

If these heuristic capabilities are learned, it is evident that we know little at present about the conditions that facilitate their learning. Most commonly recommended is the prescription of providing frequent opportunities for their employment. That is to say, teaching students how to think becomes a matter of presenting them with challenging problem-solving situations. This method of instruction, while apparently feasible, is not as satisfactory as might be hoped for. Perhaps increasing knowledge of the nature of cognitive strategies will reveal better ways of instruction. At any rate, under such a regime, strategies appear to be refined and generalized over relatively long periods of time, and also to be highly resistant to forgetting.

Attitude

The fifth category of human capability is attitudes. These are learned dispositions which influence the choices of personal action the individual makes. Thus, a positive attitude toward listening to classical music would be evidenced by choices of such action over other listening activities, whereas a negative attitude would be shown by choices indicating the avoidance of classical music as something to be listened to.

Attitudes are established, or changed through learning, in a number of ways, according to the evidence. Direct reinforcement through success in an activity is often cited as a condition for learning. There are also quite ineffective conditions for changing attitudes, such as communications presenting rational arguments and emotional appeals. The work of Bandura (1969) demonstrates the effectiveness of the technique of human modelling, in which a respected person is observed making the choice of action to be learned, and being rewarded for it. This situation is considered to establish attitudes by what is called 'vicarious reinforcement'. By whatever means they are established, attitudes seem notoriously resistant to change (in a relative sense), and also to forgetting.

These five categories—motor skills, verbal information, intellectual skills, cognitive strategies and attitudes—seem to me to constitute the major forms of learned human capabilities. They are distinguishable from each other in terms of the classes of performance they make possible, the conditions of learning required for their establishment, and to a considerable extent in the characteristics they display in the processes of storage and recall. Five categories make a taxonomy that is very convenient to use, both conceptually and practically.

Deriving instructional objectives

Returning again to a consideration of Table 1, the suggestion is that these categories of human capabilities, shown as Level 7, need to be taken into account in the derivation of instructional objectives. Beginning with whatever curriculum categories one has arrived at in Level 6, the next step in not simply to make exhaustive lists of either broad or specific objectives, but to categorize these objectives as one proceeds. Several advantages result from this method.

1. Consideration of human capabilities helps in the avoidance of trivialities

in instructional objectives. Suppose, for example, one has designed an exercise in elementary science in which the child has examined and learned the names of the four major parts of a flower: petals, sepals, stamen, pistil. He has done this by examining, say, a petunia and a rose. What is the objective of such an exercise? Using varieties of human capabilities makes it possible to see two different possibilities. One is *verbal information*—the child may be expected to learn to name the parts of the flower he has examined, using either the rose, the petunia, or both. The other possibility is that he may be acquiring *intellectual skills*, in this case, *concepts*. If that is so, he should then be able to identify the four parts of a flower in entirely new instances of these concepts, which might be displayed in an iris, or morning glory. The choice between these two possible types of objective implies different choices of how the instruction itself would be designed.

2. A related consequence, implied by the previous example, is the clarification of how to assess the outcomes of learning—how to measure the performance or disposition which has been newly learned. For example, one may readily find, these days, lessons on the evil effects of using certain types of drugs, such as heroin. Irrespective of how such lessons are presented, one needs to ask how he shall assess what has been learned. This involves consideration of the types of human capabilities. Does one wish to know that the learner has acquired certain *information* about drugs? Then the appropriate measure is an information test. Perhaps, in contrast, the expectation is that the learner's *attitude* toward using drugs will be modified by instruction. In that case, the measure of outcome to be used would be one which indicates the learner's attitude, that is, his choices of action.

3. Clarification of instructional objectives also results from the realization that human capabilities possess formal characteristics which are invariant across subject-matter categories. Learning to use a rule (an intellectual skill) for the agreement of subject and verb is a part of instruction in language. Learning to use a rule for the expansion of a binomial expression is a part of instruction in mathematics. Regardless of the obvious differences in content, the learning conditions for the learning of rules are fundamentally the same, and the techniques of measuring what has been learned have common characteristics.

In the derivation of educational goals and instructional objectives, a number of taxonomies are useful, ranging from the most general categories of societal goals to the most specific statements of objectives for courses and lessons. It appears that the omission of consideration of certain kinds of taxonomies, at different levels of analysis, can result in deficiencies of the derivation process. Particularly critical in this respect is the taxonomy which identifies classes of human capabilities, whose categories imply differential treatment of both conditions for learning and methods of assessing learning outcomes. Systematic consideration of these five categories of human capability may be seen to produce substantial clarification of instructional objectives, and thus to contribute significantly to the process of designing successful instruction.

References

AMMONS, M., 1969, Objectives and outcomes. In Ebel, R.L. (Ed.), *Encyclopedia of Educational Research*, 4th Ed., pp. 908–914 (New York: Macmillan).

BANDURA, A., 1969, *Principles of Behavior Modification* (New York: Holt, Rinehart and Winston).

BARTLETT, F.C., 1932, *Remembering* (Cambridge: Cambridge University Press).

BRUNER, J.S., 1971, *The Relevance of Education* (New York: Norton).
DOWNEY, L.M., 1971, Goals of education: History and trends. In *Encyclopedia of Education* (New York: Macmillan-Free Press).
FITTS, P.M., and POSNER, M.J., 1967, *Human Performance* (Belmont, California: Brooks/Cole).
GAGNÉ, R.M., 1965, The analysis of instructional objectives for the design of instruction. In Glaser, R. (Ed.), *Teaching Machines and Programmed Learning, II: Data and Directions* (Washington, D.C.: National Education Association).
GAGNÉ, R.M., 1970, *The Conditions of Learning* (New York: Holt, Rinehart and Winston).
GAGNÉ, R.M., 1972a, Behavioral objectives? Yes! *Educational Leadership*, **29**, 394–396.
GAGNÉ, R.M., 1972b, Domains of learning. *Interchange*, **3**, 1–8.
MAGER, R.F., 1962, *Preparing Objectives for Instruction* (Belmont, Calif.: Fearon).
POPHAM, J., 1969, *Instructional Objectives: An Analysis of Emerging Issues* (Chicago: Rand McNally).
POSTMAN, L., 1971, Organization and interference. *Psychological Review*, **78**, 290–302.
TULVING, E., and DONALDSON, W. (Eds.), 1972, *Organization of Memory* (New York: Academic Press).

Dr. Miller's degrees are in experimental psychology. During the 1950s at the American Institutes for Research he developed technology in systems and human task analysis, engineering psychology, training and personnel subsystem design. At I.B.M. he is currently developing interactive task languages for non-programmers working conversationally with computer terminals. He also teaches management science and organization theory at Union College.

1:2

Taxonomies for training

Robert B. Miller

I. Introduction and point of view

This paper, for the most part, will be an expanding definition of training. So let us start with the traditional statement that training consists of the practices and facilities for getting an individual or a group from some starting competence to some range of criterion competence. A competence is inferred from performance. But performances can only sample from a competence, and never exhaustively sample from it. A competence is indicated by behaviour that is adaptively variable as well as by behaviour that is standardized and predictable. The distinction between training for a competence and training only towards performance goals reflects a difference between organic and mechanistic philosophies about the worker as a person, about the nature of work, and the nature of a work career. Inevitably, what I call an 'organic philosophy' will be reflected in training practices that will differ from those based on a strictly mechanistic (or strictly performance-oriented) objective. If I seem to be turning back the clock of progress about mushy goals versus objective training objectives, this is not my intent. In any event, the distinction is not crucial to this paper, although significant to a later course of action. We should be warned that any definition of training which is grossly incomplete may produce a training technology which will be not only inadequate but potentially misleading on a grand scale.

A summary of my argument runs like this. A taxonomy of training would be an organized category structure derived from a technology of training. We don't have a technology of training. A technology at least implictly relates costs to benefits according to design rules for applying a repertory of resources and reference knowledge in achieving a class of objectives. The creation of design rules requires a specification of the variety and linkages of functions comprising the intended system. The formulation and administration of training is a *design* operation for which we are to construct a technology. A first step therefore consists of identifying and linking the functions which, in the broad sense, permit a map of training functions and decision nodes to be established. Much of this paper is an attempt to structure and relate training functions. These terms must be defined in the context in which they will appear. This paper really talks about the structures of a training technology.

Institutionalized training takes place in a real world consisting not only of potential benefits but also of actual costs. The goodness of training is therefore a relationship between the gain in competence—according to various criteria—acquired by a target set of candidate students and the cost of the facilities (and student time) in the acquisition of that gain in competence. Training value is measured both by its effectiveness against a profile of criteria and by its efficiency. (A logical consequence of this assertion is that a project which shows how to get a given training benefit at a lower cost is as valuable as a project which shows how to increase some training benefit at a given cost.)

Having loosely characterized training and technology, let us do the same for the concept of taxonomy. For our purposes, a taxonomy is more than a mere classification. It is rather a systematic classification with some reference to one or more related theoretical models which together embrace the domain to which the taxonomy is to be applied. The application of a taxonomy to a set of facts or observations results in adding more information to those facts or observations in the sense of revealing patterns, enabling predictions and the giving of guidance to various kinds of action. It is a code for accessing organized information. The Periodic Table in physical chemistry is a classical (but technically inapplicable) example, as are some others in biology.

A better analogy exists in physical medicine. Its applied taxonomy is based on disease entities. The taxonomic characterization, say, of chicken pox, points to diagnostic descriptors for identifying the entity, for distinguishing it from a similar entity (say, small pox) and for selecting treatment and alternative treatments. Correctly naming the entity also enables prediction of what is likely to happen to the patient if he takes the therapy or if he doesn't take the therapy. This is what one would like a training taxonomy to do. (Of course, the content of training consists of functional activities, and not differentiable objects such as disease organisms, therefore the analogy to physical disease is misleading. After all, the taxonomy of *behaviour* pathology is hardly any better off than those of the normative behaviour arts and sciences.) The example of what a taxonomy does for physical medicine may guide our aspirations, even though based on different assumptions.

Presumably, a training taxonomy would be derived from the properties of the phenomena and facilities with which training deals. These consist, on the one hand, of the constellation of adaptive behavioural properties of human learners in the role of students, and on the other hand, the properties of the practices, procedures and facilities which constitute training. Or, rather, we should say it is the *interaction* of these two sets of properties—student learning/performance properties and training practices—which are the subject matter of a taxonomy. A third taxonomic dimension must also be introduced: the characteristics of the competences to be acquired by the student, and their classification. We have therefore, as a requirement for a non-existent theoretical model, the definition and interaction of three sets of variables: (1) learning properties; (2) training procedures; (3) task characterizations.

Attempts to classify learning properties according to a consistent theoretical reference model have not met wide acceptance. Furthermore, the recent developments in studies and conceptual structures by what might be called the 'information modellers' seem to be opening up regions in human learning that have previously been closed by *S–R* and other mechanistic models. Training procedures are still in the process of invention, and fortunately so, thus any reference models could not be comprehensive. Notwithstanding some localized inquiries, efforts by experimental research to discover fundamental task taxonomies have been collapsing, perhaps in favour of a merely 'practical' classification scheme.

The outcome of this introduction should be apparent: we have neither a theoretical nor, as yet, a practical basis for creating (or being logically able to create) a training taxonomy. But let us not despair. The recognition of a false aspiration can lead to the perception of a realistic aspiration. I propose that a realistic aspiration consists of the rational *invention* of a classification scheme that will make more efficient and reliable the selection and application of training resources (actual or potential) to student learning properties for the acquisition of task and career competences. Let us turn first to what an invented training taxonomy should ideally attempt to accomplish. Anticipating the outcome, we shall find that this taxonomy can be useful only if it manifests and communicates the variables in a training discipline or 'training technology'.

Primary purposes for an idealized training taxonomy

The objective for a training taxonomy is to reflect a decision-making model for the selection and application of facilities, procedures and sequencing schedules. The model should link decisions and practices in training to analytic descriptions of the tasks and task objectives which comprise the intended competences of job incumbents after training. It should be clear that a comprehensive and workable discipline must enable the translation of task languages not only into training objectives but also into training specifications and procedures. It would be unwise to assume that *any* form of task description, even objective ones that included very specific performance requirements, would be sufficient for the selection of efficient training regimens. A handbook of operating procedures, which may be one form of task description, may be fairly adequate in describing the performance *content* of a task requirement, but provide little or no guidance to the instructional organization and sequencing of learning experiences for not only that task, but its work and behavioural context. The language of a training discipline, however, should have a reciprocal language in task analysis disciplines.

Additionally, the discipline reflected in a training taxonomy should foster the selection and application of procedures for accomplishing the following activities in some systematic way (Table 1).

II. Survey of taxonomic approaches

The preceding sections have suggested that a training taxonomy should derive from a training technology; and a training technology would consist of an integrated pattern of decisions, practices and facilities (or functions) that are efficiently geared to mate student learner properties, task descriptions and the properties of instructional facilities to generate work competences. The following examples of classifications are intended to suggest the varieties of thought and levels of phenomena proposed by various investigators and practitioners. These examples suggest that some writers classify according to the process of *training* (or learning) and others classify the *products* of learning. Still others characterize and classify according to the tools and devices used. Something may be learned from all of the examples taken as a collection.

1. Reference to education models. Bloom and his associates (1956) published

Table 1. Training Taxonomy: Objectives (*summary table*)

Primary:
1. Pretesting of candidate students (involving the creation of tests to evaluate potential ability in respect of target competencies).
2. Sequencing of blocks of training operations (imposition of modular structure).
3. Selection of training media and devices.
4. Preparation of training content.
5. Testing of student adequacy (at various stages of progress).
6. Selection of training environments.
7. Induction and transfer into job responsibility.
8. Fullest actualization of the student's abilities (ensuring that training procedure develops highest possible potential as well as standard competence).
9. Preparation for competence enhancement (on the 'job' as well as in training).

Secondary (Practical) Objectives:
1. Best use of training resources (incorporating both the student himself as well as external training resources).
2. Standardization of practices (enabling interchangeability and adaptation of resources).
3. Creating and referencing a research data base (an accepted taxonomy would facilitate feedback and guidance for future projects).

> The ultimate criteria for a training discipline are, of course, relative rather than absolute. They consist of training that is efficient according to the cost factors that are considered most important: student time and student ability, or facilities cost; and of training that is effective measured by job performances that sample the student-operators' capabilities.

a taxonomy of educational objectives which still stands as a landmark in breadth of view and of coverage. The entire field of education was divided into three domains: the cognitive, the affective and perceptual-motor skills. The introduction to the cognitive domain contains some useful suggestions on differentiating a taxonomy from a classification structure. From these suggestions, Bloom recognizes that his taxonomy must be an article of faith. His cognitive domains are presented in Table 2.

According to Bloom, the ordering of these categories is, in general, from lesser to greater complexity of accomplishment. But the rationales offered for the

Table 2. Taxonomic Approaches: Education Models

1. *Bloom 1956:* *Cognitive Domain*

Cognitive Domain	
Knowledge	↓ *Increasing complexity*
Comprehension	
Application	
Analysis	
Synthesis	
Evaluation	

2. *Gagné 1970*
   1. Signal learning—(Pavlovian conditioning).
   2. Stimulus responses learning (Skinnerian instrumental conditioning).
   3. Chaining—(sequences of S–R units).
   4. Verbal association—(verbal chains supported by language repertoire).
   5. Discrimination learning—(somewhat similar to type 2).
   6. Concept learning—(common response to class of stimuli).
   7. Rule learning—(chain of two or more concepts in form of 'if A then B').
   8. Problem solving—(two or more rules combine to form higher order rules).

taxonomy has little by way of psychological reference to justify either the differentiations or the sequencing of categories.

More recently Gagné (1970) has proposed a psychological rationale for a set of progressive categories that together comprise a system rationale. He postulates the integration of levels of learned units from relatively simple elements to complex organizations of competence. On page 63 of the reference cited, he offers summary definitions of these categories (Table 2).

Gagné's taxonomy has the advantage of successful empirical applications of these progressions in cognitive behaviour—level 4 and above. By contrast, however, Ausubel (1968) proposes that at least cognitive learning proceeds on the basis of individuation of general conceptual responses into individual procedures and skill elements—or rather that such a progression is more efficient and effective. Decisive experiments on such issues are practically impossible because the training hypothesis must be embedded in some concrete manifestation of training materials. The skill with which the training material, in the instance, is created may readily overshadow the influence of the hypothesized variable. (Furthermore, in the world of practical affairs it is often unwise to treat too literally the definitions of functions intended to stand up against one's colleagues and adversaries in the psychological laboratories. The concern of the latter is essentially with analysis and theory. The traditional criteria of the academician differ from those more pragmatic criteria of cost, and workability and results in practice which concern the training practitioner.)

2. *Reference to behaviour class.* Gilbert (1962) and Mechner (1967) differentiate and formalize three classes of behaviour. For each of these classes, they propose a different instructional technique. These distinctions overlap several of Gagné's categories. They are:

(1) Discrimination.
(2) Generalization.
(3) Chain—a behaviour sequence where each response is the stimulus for the next response.

These categories are intended to apply both to perceptual-motor behaviour and cognitive behaviour. They are similar to Noble's (1969) variables for 'selective learning'.

3. *Reference to training devices.* The list of training devices, or even classes of training device, may be interminable. Those presented in Table 3 may be considered representative.

Perhaps one should add to this list actual demonstration by live operators of the tasks to be performed at various levels of competence, and the working device itself.

4. *Reference to learning context.* It is difficult to retain a systematic basis for these categories. Those shown in Table 3 are in frequent usage with the implication of being alternatives. The categories are of practical importance in that each implies a different cost basis.

5. *Reference to kind of work-related content.* The distinction among the following terms (see Table 3) with respect to their bearing on job-competence is likely to be hazy.

6. *Reference to human abilities.* The massive studies of Guilford (1967) have led to a taxonomy of intelligence, derived at least in part by empirical means from factor analysis. It might be possible to relate the terms and concepts of

Table 3. Taxonomic Approaches: Training Models

Reference to training devices:
1. Instructor and blackboard—not usually in such a list but a useful reference control for alternatives.
2. Demonstration, training aids, graphics.
3. Films, closed circuit TV
4. Procedural trainers.
5. Programmed instruction, book form.
6. Computer assisted instruction.
7. Simulators—usually controlled by a computer, used for aircraft training, business gaining, strategy training.
8. Books, manuals, references.

Reference to learning context:
1. Classroom.
2. Instructional shop or laboratory.
3. On the job—and here the alternatives of self-teaching, managerial supervision, or 'buddy-system'.
4. Remedial—which may be any one or combination of the above.

Reference to kind of work-related content:
1. Job knowledge. (Operationally derived from concretely identified task requirements definitions, or what the instructor considers 'good for the student to know'.)
2. Job skills. Perceptual-motor, procedural, or cognitive, or a combination likely to be directed to 'have mastery' levels of competence.
3. Work habits. Neatness, time-keeping, keeping records, diligence etc.
4. Attitudes. May apply to incentives, 'organizational loyalty', value of work, implications of wastefulness.

this kind of structure to a task description terminology on the one hand, and to the selection and application of training principles and operations on the other. The feasibility is not apparent to this writer. However, an outline of Guilford's structure should be presented. The list is adapted from page 63 of the reference cited; the page is contained in a summary chapter of definitions of these factors.

(1) Operation
  (*a*) Evaluation
  (*b*) Convergent production
  (*c*) Divergent production
  (*d*) Memory
  (*e*) Cognition
(2) Product
  (*a*) Units
  (*b*) Classes
  (*c*) Systems
  (*d*) Transformations
  (*e*) Implications
(3) Content
  (*a*) Figural
  (*b*) Symbolic
  (*c*) Semantic
  (*d*) Behavioural

The structuring of the items into groups and sequences is based on logical grounds, and is not directly derived from the data or procedures used in empirical analysis. It should also be borne in mind that the naming of categories derived from factor analysis is a somewhat arbitrary matter and dependent on the expertise and the insights of the researcher. (These comments are in no way intended as disrespect to the researcher, but rather state a well-known issue in factor analytic disciplines.)

E.A. Fleishman (1962) has derived from extensive empirical studies and factor analytic technique, 'about eleven psychomomotor factors and nine factors in the area of physical proficiency which consistently appear to account for the common variance in such tasks'. He argues that a very large scale study in the factor analytic paradigm would yield a taxonomy that would be useful for establishing and relating educational objectives and learner abilities.

The various proponents of factor analytic studies have not as yet offered an explicit procedural scenario, much less even a partial demonstration, of how to use these—or any other—'factors' in the practical construction of concrete training operations in realistic training situations. Nor have they proposed by what practical means a description of concrete task requirements can be based on, or referenced to, a factor analytic taxonomic base.

To the previous set of classifications I would like to add three more sets with which I feel some identification.

7. *Reference to role of the student.* Although the following distinction is often implicit in various training practices, the failure to make it explicit and to integrate the distinction into practical training technique may forfeit a major potential resource: the capability of the student to serve as his own instructor. The point will be expanded in a later section.

(1) *The student role as passive.* The student is assumed to be cognitively docile to the instructional environment where the content, level of performance, criteria, pace, are controlled by the instructional media imposed on the student. The student may internalize this role, and may even act diligently in this role. But he is essentially 'run by the programme'. Even his 'insights' and 'discoveries' are pre-planned and externally contrived.

(2) *The student role as active.* This may be a matter of degree in actual practice, but presumably the student feels that he maintains the initiative in selecting instructional alternatives, interacting with the learning problem in an exploratory fashion, accepting guidance alternatives rationally rather than in obedience to authority. In order to be effective, the active role requires that the student be skilled not only in 'learning how to learn' but knowledgeable in how he, as an individual, best learns.

8. *Reference to task structure.* All of the following variables are found in any task, or at least at some stages in learning task competence, but some variables are more preponderant in some tasks than in others. This assertion does not necessarily apply to what is found in many task descriptions; it does apply to the performance of tasks in real life environments where contingencies are inevitable. A preliminary cut may distinguish portions of work that consist primarily of 'continuous tracking' from phases of work or tasks that are discrete

and discontinuous in nature. The distinction is important because the engineering psychology literature contains a large body of information intended to be specifically applicable to the learning of tracking tasks. The distinction may be regarded as artificial if one accepts the proposition that although performance may appear to be continuous, behaviour is discontinuous.

Since Miller (1962) has defined and described the following terms elsewhere, they will merely be named here. (See Table 4.)

Table 4. Task Structure Variables

1. Goal criteria, goal image, values, incentives.
2. Scan and detect.
3. Identifications and nomenclature.
4. Decode—encode (assuming direct translation rules).
5. Interpretation.
6. Long term memory for procedures, facts, work and behaviour formats.
7. Short term memory (working memory) for transient operational data.
8. Decision making and problem solving (category structures and cognitive formats).
9. Motor output and organization, potentially dependent on and related to all factors cited above.

This structure is obviously derived from an information processing model of behaviour where the minimum set of functions consist of input, processing, memory and output. The limitations of the information processing model to human competences is the absence of treatment of motor output and its structural and organizing principles. Information may symbolize physical work but it is not in itself physical work.

These factors seem compatible with subdividing (modularizing) a task or work segment into part-task learning at suitable stages of learning a total competence. The classification scheme in the next topic suggests what is meant by 'stages of learning'.

9. Reference to stage of learning. With substantial increases in practice, cues (both external and internal) that were necessary for earlier performance may no longer be necessary, or may substantially change their character. Miller (1953 and 1965) outlined these processes some years ago and is currently extending these concepts. It would seem efficient of training resource to adapt and sequence the content and form of training to these progressive behaviour changes, and where possible to accelerate them. Obviously, all of the content being learned does not proceed at the same time from one learning stage to the next in ordinary unmanipulated learning of a complex task—such as operating a bench lathe, for example. In general, the cost for the preparation and administration of each phase of training tends to increase as one goes down the list. The following division of stages of learning assumes the cognitive participation of the student.

(1) Orientation, indoctrination. Acquisition of task and work goals; criteria of good and bad performance; conceptual 'maps' of goal routes, relationships among task functions; general context in which the task and work is performed. Essentially demonstrational presentation.
(2) Nomenclature and identifications of work objects and situations. Enables the formation of self-instructions or response to external

symbolic instruction. Provides mnemonic support for learning and for learned content. Essentially rote practice with potential for enriched conceptual and perceptual context.

(3) Mediated (self-instructed) response in learning and performing procedures. Student learns to tell himself what to do. Essentially repetitive practice of procedures both symbolically and/or in task situation context. Requires guidance and corrective feedback at both symbolic and physical levels. Low fidelity to situation context permissible with respect either to spatial or temporal or dynamic representations.

(4) 'Automated' response and development of hierarchical control. Essential to skill levels. Response 'automation' applies not only to perceptual-motor skills, but also to decision-making and problem-solving formats of categories and procedures that develop implicitly to classes of more or less standardized situation inputs to the operator. 'Automatic' is a matter of degree and condition. Requires 'simulator' level of instructional presentation and management; timing and pacing relationships important in forcing self-instructed response into 'automatic' response. Response automatization is also forced when operator/student has simultaneous competing demands on attention. The operational act, when automatized, is instigated by the operator's intent or expectation.

(5) Task integration and contingency management. The student must integrate concurrent activities, manage both the information load and response execution loads, distribute attention, anticipate and/or cope with samples from the range of real contingencies (non-'normal' events). Requires the equivalent of full work simulator capabilities, programmable for contingencies. Requires high fidelity in spatial, temporal and dynamic factors.

(6) Strategic performance and high skill level. Every task has potential for optimizing strategies by the operator. The implicit (automatic) or explicit exercise of these strategies characterizes high skill as contrasted with adequate competence. Strategies may potentially be introduced as early as Stage 3—or even Stage 1 as indoctrination and as exercise material or as an achievement aspiration. Exercise of complex conceptual strategies, including situation assessment, in operations imposes considerable cognitive load, so many other parts of task performance should have been automated in behaviour. Learning of strategies requires specialized guidance by instructional facilities.

(7) Transition learning. Presumably from one set of tasks to another which seems different but shares many requirements. Not a 'stage in learning' but an important consideration for the management of training. The problem is too broad for capsule summarization. Within a period of years, most jobs require changes in procedure, rules, values and even goal variables.

10. Reference to specificity of operator performance. An operator's job may consist of a varied collection of tasks. Some of these tasks may best be learned and performed with a high degree of regularity, consistency and lack of deviation from one occurrence or cycle to the next. At the other extreme, some tasks may require a large amount of interpretation, judgement, improvisation and even invention. Where the pressures of cost and efficiency in the training are considerable, one would want to stop at the earliest practicable item in the list below.

(1) Stereotyped performance: exactly the same responses in the same order are made every time to a fixed and limited set of cues and situations that require only simple identification.
(2) Routinized performance: occasional variations in response patterns. Minor contingencies encountered and responded to, but within well defined scope of work.
(3) Formatted performance: a fixed set of situation input variables, and of output variables, and a relatively fixed set of task processing rules, but variations from one work cycle to the next in the values which the input variables may take, and of the selection and combination of applicable rules. Troubleshooting an equipment and other forms of decision making that is restricted to a class of situations are examples. So are repetitive design constructions, sales presentations, run-of-the-mill research—which are governed by strategies as well as by fixed rules.
(4) Improvisational performance: the unusual adaptation of given (limited) resources to the requirements of unique or unusual circumstances.
(5) Inventive performance: embodying the properties and attributes of things and processes in entities that perform functions in a new way; synthesis of an array of elements into a pattern, organization or system; conceptual design.

Obviously these categories are not mutually exclusive: the meaning of one item merges into that of the next, and a task or a work segment may consist of activities some of which are stereotyped and some improvisational.

This list is intended to imply that a training regimen intended to result predominantly in formatted performance should almost certainly take a different pattern, even from its start, than a regimen intended to result in, say, stereotyped performance such as the literal translation of Morse code into English text.

E.E. Miller (1969) of HumRRO has proposed a classification of perceptual-motor tasks which are linked to training strategies. The four classes of tasks are:

(1) Reactive-adjustive (steering a car).
(2) Reactive-selection from a set of responses (typing).
(3) Developmental-procedural (starting a car).
(4) Developmental-skilled performance (batting a ball).

Each of these task classes is defined in transactional terms that are related to a variety of conditions of practice, form of knowledge of results, form of 'prompting', pacing, form of preparation of student for practice and goal clarifications. Miller's analysis of instructional alternatives reveals awareness and sensitivity to the possibilities of the student's active participation in his own learning processes. Miller's structure also reflects HumRRO's active awareness of the importance of behavioural analysis in bridging the gap between a task description consisting of objective performance requirements and the design of training. (The report of Miller's that is cited also contains a summary critique of other taxonomies and an extensive bibliography.)

Comments on the classifications

These categorizations are only a sample of what might be found by exhaustive literature search. Singer's (1972) excellent selection of readings in motor learning has several chapters which describe other 'modules'. Melton's (1964) collection of papers on learning taxonomies contains additional sets of classifications and classificatory procedures. But from all of this diversity, no clear pattern or combination of patterns with direct implications for practical guidance in training seems to emerge. Nor is it likely to. No mere array of names of functions, processes, entities, can produce a discipline or technology of training. Only a model of decision alternatives, supported by rationales and strategies for the selection and combination of alternatives can produce such a discipline. The assignment of names to the alternatives then becomes a matter of secondary importance.

III. Dimensions of the training problem

Let us now shift from the subject of taxonomies to the topic of training technology. Some of the issues presented will reflect the writer's biases about skills, competence, human learning and the nature of work. We are reminded that we seek to define a technology that will enable us to design and administer training with a responsibility both for results and for costs to achieve the results. We must also recognize that the training establishment should be responsive to variety in the mix of student candidates and variety in the processing mix—that is, in what is taught and how it is learned. The training establishment must be able to handle varying loads, so that we should have flexibility in service and minimum set-up time for a given pattern of demand. And demand will always exceed available resources. So while laboratories fiddle, we are in the business of contributing to survival.

The development of any systems technology—such as training should be regarded—is marked by cycles. Within a cycle there are several critical stages, each of which can be identified. A cycle in a technology is entering maturity when it exhibits the following key factors. One is the clarity and simplicity by which the tradeoff criteria in its goals are perceived, so that one knows what one should try to optimize. A second indicator will be the kind and extent of standardization and the rationales for what is to be customized: an attempt to 'over-programme' a facility beyond the state of an application art may have disastrous consequences in reject rates. A third but related indicator of maturity (stability) in a technology is shown by its modularity discipline: the structural entities of construction, servicing and modification. A sophisticated systems technology has well-defined building blocks, usually hierarchical in complexity, with relatively simple interface rules. It is obviously premature to apply such criteria of maturity to training technology, but useful to have clear aspirations.

I would suggest an approach that begins by tentative separation of psychological models from what I will call a technical training management model. The distinction should be useful for analytic purposes. Obviously the outcome must be fused in a synthesis that results in a training design matrix.

The *psychological* model we construct should reflect not only an amalgam of theory of learning, but also a theory of work performance and perhaps even a theory of work—and hopefully we can resolve the antinomies of mechanistic and organic philosophies, and of external control versus autonomy of control as ideal operative principles.

In the technical *management* model of training we will see a structure outlined without a philosophy of operational implementation beyond that of cost-benefit optimization.

Psychological issues in training

A total training system may be governed by a conditioned response model of learning. The model may be very sophisticated. It may result in ingenious procedures for managing the conditions of practice. Practice will be based on circumscribed assumptions about incentives and motivation. The training procedures may be highly effective in embedding prescriptive rules into the student, thus leading to performance which is reliable but not necessarily flexible. The conditioning model will tend to ignore the potential of the student's participative roles in his own cognitive initiatives, or even suppress them if they interfere with planned schedules of training sequence. This model is not likely to generate much interest in the invention of instructional communication content: expressions like 'cognitive map' will be treated as meaningless. A primary objective—and value—of conditioning practices is in apparent control of behaviour and in apparent objectivity. It would seem to be a model most appropriate for students whose cognitive capabilities were relatively low and whose capabilities for self-motivation were neutral or low. This comment is not intended as deprecation but as a realistic recognition of individual differences not only among teachers but also among students.

There is no general name for a concept which implies an alternative to conditioning techniques. I will use the term 'cognitive' in a special sense here to refer (perhaps vaguely) to this alternative. An example of a cognitive practice is the precept that in learning to perform a voluntary act, the human first conceptualizes the act and then attempts to translate this conceptualization into an overt performance. (I am not offering this here as a fact, but as an example of a point of view about learning and behaviour.) It would seem to me that subscribing to the conditioning model would lead to quite a different slant on the entire training operation than that developed from a cognitive model, even though the resulting regimen may of necessity embody practices which are consistent with both models.

A second distinction differentiates, on theoretical and practical grounds, points of view about cognitive learning. There are proponents for building up a competence by the acquisition and integration of component learned elements (Gagné, 1970). Others propose first providing what might be called conceptual maps and overviews which are progressively individuated until a full complement of competences is achieved (Ausubel, 1968).

A third point of distinction is the image of the learner's role in learning as primarily *passive* to programming influences in contrast to the learner as primarily *active* conceptually during the entire learning process, perhaps even when participating in the drill practice of rote materials. By 'active' is meant not only the contribution of the student when an 'insight' is reached in acquiring a concept or principle, but also his initiatives in programming his drill, his own perception and interpretation of performance feedback in the light of his hypotheses about what actions lead to what consequences in his attempts to better his achievements.

All three of these issues have been intentionally dramatized, and probably express more extreme positions than any proponent would care to accept. But the practitioners who follow and implement the proposals of the theorists tend to work from the simplest model they are given, and to apply them without the qualifying context which the wisdom of the technical leader himself might bring to bear.

There is a factor perhaps more important than efficiency in training: the choice within each of these three issues will certainly reflect in the kind of operator that is produced. If it is true that one does what one learns, then an operator for whom reinforcement means 'candy' or approval will work differently from an operator who seeks feedback as an informative corrective signal intrinsic to this task. The operator whose competence is primarily an organization of elements may well have different constraints on generalizing his competence from one tool or situation to unfamiliar ones than the operator whose competence is organized (because it was so acquired) from general schema to component element. And certainly the operator trained as a docile entity to his learning milieu is not very likely to maintain cognitive initiatives to contingencies or changes in his work environment. Surely it is a truism that training inculcates attitudes, values, incentives and adaptive tendencies as well as 'objective performance capabilities'. It was at training schools that probably many of us learned to hate our jobs, or to be excited by them.

The psychology of learning, and therefore the technology of training, has not explicitly recognized, much less adopted or reconciled, these fundamental alternatives in the creating of work competences. The experimental paradigms of learning have assumed the operator to be docile to the treatment and contrived to enhance that docility. Even research into 'learning how to learn' generally assumes a conditioning meta-process. (See Reitman's [1970] excellent critique on strategies of learning.) It is indeed difficult to find investigations in which the learner is deliberately made a partner in developing and applying his own learning strategies in the acquisition of a competence. (Studies in which subjects are encouraged to try to create 'meaningful associations' in nonsense syllable learning exercises are dubiously relevant and of trivial significance to training methodology.) It is quite conceivable that the technology of training must jettison many of the paradigms and findings of traditional psychological research in learning and develop its own reference base of information.

This innovation would properly rest on a different paradigm for inquiry and quite fundamentally different assumptions about the learner and his actual and potential attributes for acquiring competences. The use of the term 'competence' is intended to underline the near-certainty that the concept of what is learned that is expressed as a competence differs from the laboratory concept of the product of learning. As Johnson (1972) puts it, quantity and quality (speed and accuracy) are not sufficient for competence: flexibility to environment, tool, situation and procedure beyond the sample exercises of training is essential to competence. So, too, are capacity for extended, sustained work with minimum fatigue, and work under adverse circumstances such as uncertainty and risk. If the inclusion of these functions implies that motivational factors are intrinsically embedded in a competence, let it be explicitly acknowledged as a fundamental variable in training, and not merely an extrinsic variable to be manipulated in job performance.

This iconoclastic proposal does not imply repudiating the paradigms and findings of experimental research in learning. It does assert that the conventional findings be put into a far broader paradigm that encourages a much larger base for the development of hypotheses and inventions for training and for concepts of competences.

A technical management model of training

I trust the reader will not be intimidated by a picture which will have many parallels with an industrial process, and which borrows from the terminology of industrial operations. An industry must be concerned with the utility of its product and with the costs of the raw materials and of the processing facilities that produce the product. Like the training establishment, an information processing industry is required to change its product as technology changes. Its product has both an inventory of structural formats (hardware, control programmes) and expertise for customizing these formats to classes of demand, and within a class of demand, to the individual customer. Like training, the principal commodity with which it deals is information.

Technical management designs the structure for the operations of the enterprise. In simplest terms this structure is the organization of decisions and processes that translate inputs into output products. Inputs consist on the one hand of raw materials (student candidates) and on the other hand, of specifications for the output product (the trained operator). Technical management organizes the process flow into pathways and decision/action nodes. It also formats the decisions and actions within expedient limits of standardization and compromises with the specialist's expertise. In addition, technical planning attempts to optimize the selection and costs of resources that support the entire operation. Implicit in these functions is the imposition of technical controls on quality and quantity of throughput, and diagnostic sensors for determining processing bottlenecks and causes of rejects.

Cost analysis serves far more than crass objectives of dollar savings. Cost analysis may indeed conclude that not enough is being spent for achieving an objective. And in the context of training, our concern with costs is not necessarily with dollar costs, but primarily with human costs. These can be assessed in terms of training time, level of ability consumed, frustrations both during and after training. These may be more important to conserve than costs in training facilities. Cost analysis in these terms when performed not by accountants but by technical expertise leads to refinement of objectives as well as of means for achieving objectives. It tests the practices of affluence which predisposes acceptance of an operation or facility on the basis of face validity and the assertion: 'It probably can't do any harm and it might do some good.' Cost analysis therefore leads to a differentiation of the essential from the non-essential, and of the important from the trivial. Cost analysis is only bad medicine when it is a purgative that does not differentiate food from waste, and enfeebles the victim.

Cost analysis balanced against benefit analysis, by clarifying objectives and forcing attention on alternatives, can play a constructive (and necessary) role in the development of a technology. I believe this truism applies to training technology, and to developmental research in training technology.

As already observed, one input to the training establishment consists of specifications of a manpower skill requirement: some number of individuals who will emerge with a pattern of operational skills. This input may be expressed well or poorly according to the processing needs of the training model. A second input consists of (*a*) information about the pool of potential recruits for the training and (*b*) the actual candidates that have been selected for training. A third input source may be the potential instructor population.

A thoroughgoing training technology will consist of a decision model for identifying and selecting (on the basis of expertise and judgement if not on the basis of formal rules) appropriate alternatives for each of the following classes of activity for a given set of input conditions and objectives. The alternatives chosen should make up a self-consistent pattern.

Decision formats and alternatives precede each of the following nodes of activity. In general, a decision at an earlier node is part of the assumptions going into the information for a decision at a later node. A decision later in the series may reflect back as a constraint to an earlier decision. Understand that a decision is an attempt to (*a*) secure a relevant benefit and (*b*) do so at relatively low cost.

Job requirements specification. Gathering and preparing job requirements data is usually expensive. Even so, its cost may often not be justified because the information is so poor. Job requirements specifications can take many forms. In some examples functions may be merely named. Other formats may establish performance criteria at various levels of specificity. Still others may extend to the analysis of behaviour structures that appear to underlie effective or ineffective performance. Some specifications may be sufficiently detailed to enable job procedures manuals to be prepared directly from them. The terminology and level of analysis in some cases may facilitate the choice of a training philosophy; in other cases they may obscure the choice. Task description and analysis is another name for job requirements specification. There is no concensus in discipline for the technique or the terminology.

Procedure design, job design, career design. Each of these may derive from a separate set of operations. Procedure design may be supported by psychological considerations that link training and performance. Job design is concerned with the grouping of tasks into what a given man or team is to do. Career design is concerned with a combination of organizational and psychological factors relating to the incumbent's expected ability ceilings and to growth of competence. The psychology of career design is appearing as a major challenge arising from changes in technology and the relationships of job experience to education and training, and to personal motivations.

Selection and pre-testing of candidates. Selection procedures and content should be consistent with the competences established as objectives, and with task procedure design and with training technique. Since in many cases, selection tests tend to be based and validated mainly on training criteria, it is especially important that training be relevant to the intended competence. If such factors as self-instructional initiatives are stipulated for training technique. this requirement should clearly be identified in the selection filter and suitably weighted against other selectors. The pre-testing of candidates to determine existing capabilities for the job should enable selecting the route through training which the individual student will take.

Curriculum development. This is the 'nut' in the entire management and design of training. The art of designing and transmitting the communications of what is to be learned may compensate for limitations elsewhere in the training model. Only the selection of very outstanding student candidates can compensate for gross faults in the design of the training content. Curriculum development must include the separating, sequencing and integrating of the components that make up a competence, and specify those indicators in the student's activity that signal not only the student's progression to a competence but also the remedial operations specifically essential to returning or hastening that progression when the student falters. It is in the development of training content that it would be highly desirable to know how to translate a high degree of communication art from one training context to another: unfortunately, this implies a functional basis for determining when one training context is similar to another on grounds other than specific task content. But since other sections of this paper have been aimed at this consideration, let us move on to them.

Physical facilities. More than perhaps any other factor in management decision-making, the assessment of physical facilities has a strong, tangible cost consideration. The lack of a physically referenced model of what can be learned from what *minimum* facilities, and how each segment of learning can be fitted into progression towards a competence, permits and fosters great extravagances in physical facilities. Costs escalate when functions are added to any device; these costs are reflected in design, fabrication, maintenance, storage and obsolescence. But without clearly identified training alternatives, management may feel that the costs that achieve face validity and 'full simulation' are justified. Obviously, the benefit of a device or training facility must be estimated both on its potential contribution to a competence and the amount of practice time per student that can be justified within the training budget. The question management needs to have answered is: What is the least costly *pattern* of facilities that can be used by n students in a class to achieve a pattern of competences as required by the training objectives? A 'class of facility' may mean an instructor and blackboard, an airplane, a cockpit simulator of an airplane, a cardboard mockup of a cockpit—to identify a few examples.

Training process. This is the management of the training activities and its administrative and technical control. It should be responsive to such realities as failure to get the levels or kinds of ability specified for recruitment of trainees, and to changes in the specification of requirements for the graduates of training. By knowing the respective relationships of (*a*) the content and process of segments in training to (*b*) specific elements in the intended competence, it becomes possible to shift direction midstream with minimum loss. Awareness of the contingencies may also generate a strategy for flexibility that is not unduly costly if the contingencies fail to appear.

Criterion testing. An individual's competence is likely to be a profile of relative strengths and weaknesses. Profiles for all members of a class will compound the problems of cut-off levels for acceptance. Severity and immediacy of demands for trained manpower further complicate decisions about what students can be entrusted with job responsibilities. It is therefore important that criteria provide realistic estimates of what the graduated student can and *cannot* do on the job. With rare exceptions, it is unlikely that a single figure of merit, such as rank in class, will be very informative. Furthermore, since no tests can be exhaustive of job situations, but must necessarily sample from them, tests should be efficient in diagnostic sampling. If years are not allowable for the empirical development of efficient criterion tests, a model of the essential behavioural variables underlying various kinds of task performance is necessary. This is another dimension of training that would be reflected in a taxonomic discipline.

Assignment to jobs. In the real world, it is rare that a person is assigned to precisely the work environment, tasks and tools for which he was trained. It is therefore often necessary to make estimates of the degree of mismatch between a given pattern of proficiencies (of varying levels) with a given pattern of job requirements. The practical implications of the mismatch then need spelling out. Thus the best match may be made between what is needed and what is available, and suitable remedies for the mismatching can be planned.

Transition to jobs. Invariably there is a gap between the training environment in which skills were learned, applied and evaluated, and the actual job situation and its pattern of values. Left unplanned and uncontrolled, these transition periods can be costly in many ways. It may be highly desirable for the training arm to be extended to the operational scene so as to minimize the normal liabilities of transition and to offset the frequent travails and confusions of this period. A discipline for efficient transition management would belong technically, if not administratively, to the training enterprise.

On-the-job follow-up. In order to complete a picture of the domain of training management, we must include structured follow-up activities that will efficiently sample from the performances on the job of ex-students. The purpose of this follow-up is not only for diagnostic data with which to correct any existing model of training assumptions and practices. Since idealized kinds of measurement are impractical in the field of operations, compromises with expedience can best be based on a clear picture of what fewest observations will be most significant.

Training systems design

A pattern of psychological variables and of training operations has been outlined. The proper implications is that all of these variables do comprise a pattern: they interact with each other. The nature of these interactions as well as the many options for choices in the design of training operations demand simplifying models and some optimizing objectives. One such objective is maximum *standardization*, at least of instructional formats. (By standardization I do not mean trivia like layout of curriculum topics!) A second principle for optimizing facilities for complex operations is the minimizing of the number and variety of *modules* which comprise the operational entity. Efficiency must aim at minimum levels of customizing for a given range of potential requirements and demands upon a given inventory of resources in the training establishment. These principles, which guide rational production in industrial enterprises, should also govern the training enterprise. They should certainly be manifest in a rational training design discipline. The terminology for this discipline insofar as it were to apply to its 'modularities' would constitute its 'taxonomy'. Training technology would consist of the rules for creating modules and for relating them to each other in order to achieve a specification of a see of training operations.

The format of a training module

In a well-formalized training discipline, the network of technical management's decisions, outlined in the previous section, would be directed to choices of training format alternatives. A set of alternatives would be available for each choice point. The format structure would identify the set of input variables that enter a given decision point. The data entered into the format for that decision node would then specify, on the basis of formula combined with human judgement, either an existing training module or the characterization of that module. Input variables might be, for example, kind of task (e.g., procedural or continuous; perceptual, interpretive or motor: routinized, formatted or improvisational; and so forth). Other input factors might include the name of the stage of learning; active or passive student role; the temporal relationship of the task to other tasks in performance; stage of learning of concurrent activities, and so forth. The output specifications for the training module might include a cost-referenced range of options in training medium, display and display fidelity, student operated controls and their minimum degree of fidelity, display-control processing and feedback (in kind and amount) and their respective minimum requirements in fidelity to the 'real world' environment of the task. In addition, the format might specify the role of the instructor, the strategy for programming the exercise content, the duration or extent of use of the module in the training, and schedules for interaction of training with other modules in the training programme.

This scheme is an idealization of a production operation. I have no claims of validity for the particular variables I have cited. Although the practical solution does not exist, I am confident that the concept of the solution is eminently practical. It would be not only unnecessary but undesirable to demand a complete set of defining and translating rules in order to have a useful operating guide for large-scale training operations. There must be sufficient ambiguity allowed to remain in the operation to justify continued creativity in design of training at every level.

The guiding philosophy I would propose in seeking for these design procedure formats is that of: 'What's the near-minimum cost for getting a given level of training output from a given input to training?' As I observed earlier, this philosophy not only fosters a critical eye on relevance of resource to objective: it also focuses invention and research on the essential rather than the secondary. The laboratory researcher is not likely to have experience with this philosophy. (An interesting example of an exception is found in a HumRRO study by Grimsley (1969) on low fidelity of simulation in training.)

There will be many for whom this approach will be abhorrent. It will seem to institutionalize a mechanical treatment of training and support bureaucracy rather than expertise and inspiration in training development. I share these fears. On the other hand, a representative sampling of the realities in the design and administration of training today will reveal precious few signs of expertise and inspiration. One may question whether the risk of organized incompetence is worse than the realities of disorganized incompetence. I will sidestep that judgement by referring to the central theme of discussion: If there were to be a systematic discipline or technology of training, what would it look like? I have suggested at least some of the properties of that discipline.

IV. Where do we stand now?

The design matrix proposed in the preceding pages already has precedents, at least in concept. The 'systems approach' applied to personnel subsystems was initiated in the mid-fifties by the U.S. Air Force and one of its instruments was the Qualitative and Quantitative Personnel Requirements Information (Q.Q.P.R.I.) programme. The goal was a general unification and harmonization of the many facets of personnel subsystem design of which training was a major entity. The current status of this programme is described in Headquarters Air Force Systems Command documents (1967) (1969). The procedures are intended to insure systematic flow of requirements information from one manpower agency to another in the development and use of weapons systems. Although elements of a comprehensive technical decision-making matrix for training exists as expertise, a complete and explicit structure as outlined in the previous section of this report awaits the future.

Perhaps the most extensive programmatic, self-consistent developmental and applied effort in training technology is expressed by the 'systems engineering of training' activity at the Human Resources Research Office (HumRRO). This organization serves as the R. & D. arm for training of the U.S. Army. Crawford (1966) briefly outlines the principles of developing training. An official Army regulation prescribes in considerable detail the administration of the procedures for applying the systems engineering for training doctrines. This document identifies practically all of the considerations outlined in a previous section on the 'Technical Management Model of Training'. Recommended policies stress relationships between training value and training cost. The entire philosophy underlines the importance of building in measurement and evaluation not only of the student, but of the effectiveness of the training and its various parts.

As already noted, HumRRO has taken active interest in the development of task taxonomies that can be geared to training strategies. Its continuity of purpose and charter enable consistency of progress. Its intimate relationship with its sponsor provide opportunity for both testing and evaluating its hypotheses, and for integrating its findings into the growth of a discipline. Thus, it has developed rationales for partitioning and sequencing segments of training into modular structures that can have branch points into various specializations growing out of a common knowledge and skill base. Its inquiries are concerned with the varieties and degrees of the 'simulation' of work environments essential to effective learning at various stages in the training process. This concern with the degree and kind of fidelity that is sufficient for a given stage of learning is certainly the single most important cost factor in the entire training enterprise—if one discounts the cost of student time as a necessary overhead expense. Cogan (1967) writes: 'The systems-analytic point of view suggests that critical ingredients in evaluation (of training programmes) are operating system costs and operating system gains, and that the critical check-points in the development process are to be found at the interfaces between training development and the operations system.' This organization is actively creating a master plan for training that embodies training technology.

The American Institutes for Research under contract to the Advanced Research Projects Agency of the Department of Defence has been developing techniques for making consistent the specification of manpower requirements with the specification of manpower resources in the form of capabilities. In the course of this work, it has developed what has promise for taxonomic entities (if not a taxonomy) of human capabilities. These entities have been rather formally defined: they are generally more comprehensive than what is usually considered a task, but less general (and far less vague) than what is generally called a 'duty'. The 'task module' is a basis for organizing the description of a job requirement for purposes of training, evaluation and the characterization of a capability. The standardization of the description of 'task modules' makes a generally useful data base feasible to construct for serving both operational and research purposes. Stephenson (1972) and Miller (1972) have described their respective concepts of the duty module. No systematic naming discipline for classes of duty module has yet been invented, although some taxonomic dimensions have been proposed. The empirical value of the organizing and taxonomic concepts in this research programme await conclusion.

U.S. Naval Training Equipment Center has recently let a contract for a developmental study into a predictive 'model' of education and training parameters intended ultimately to be quantitative. This project may be primarily aimed at assisting the administration of training such as in dollar budgeting, time expectations for the training to a given level of a given number of trainees for a given task or position, time to prepare the training, and so forth. In the course of this exercise, however, it is inevitable that technical training alternatives will appear as nodes or parameters in the model. Suffice to say, this is another example of a 'systems approach' to the manpower training issue.

At Applied Science Associates, Folley and his colleagues have been applying systematic thinking to the actual design of military training programmes with many parallels to the technical decision matrix proposed above. Folley's (1964) report foreshadowed these developments. An encyclopaedic procedural guide by Schumacher and Glasgow (in press) treats in an interlocking fashion the identification of performance requirements; determining critical training objectives; teaching steps for achieving objectives; selecting media: developing instructional materials and evaluating the instructional system. Folley and his group are sensitive to the cost factors in training as well as in getting well-trained personnel.

These examples of tangible military concern with a systematic approach to the development of training disciplines give timeliness to our present aspirations and some realism to our ambitions.

The systems approach to the development of personnel subsystems has recently come into textbook format. De Greene's (1970) first and third chapters in 'Systems Psychology'—of which he is also the editor—outlines philosophies of design and major principles which parallel those I have described.

But despite these signs of receptive mood and these large scale efforts in the military establishment, factors of crucial importance seem to be missing. The glue that holds together the training 'system' and binds it to its personnel interfaces is largely localized, organizational expertise. If Computer Assisted Instruction is that organization's particular interest, training requirements will tend to be equivalent to C.A.I. requirements.

There does not appear to be a generally accepted 'model of learning' that is *comprehensive* and *directive* for the training establishment. This is not to assert that acceptable ones do not exist. These models must not merely represent the attributes of the learner and the learning process, but also be directive—or be translated into directives—of management of training content and training sequencing. I would insist that the model must extend to conditions where the learner was an active cognitive participant in his learning process as well as passively dependent or manipulated by the external training milieu. The model of learning must also represent progressive changes in the mediating and control levels that govern the learner's performance as a function of extended and varying conditions of practice. This aspect of the model would also have to be translated into directives for training.

Secondly, there does not yet seem to be a comprehensive, joined and articulated model of what I have called the technical management of training. This model would be a generalized scenario of the information flow, decision nodes, decision alternatives and alternative actions of the total training operation beginning with the description of manpower requirements and into the activities of selection and training, and to assignment and evaluation of the ex-student on the job. Such a scenario would show what information would be necessary or sufficient at each decision node, and thus establish a basis for consistency in that information. The factual or reference data at each node should enable the selection of an action and facility with a given effectiveness in training at some lowest cost.

Thirdly, there is no substantial movement in either training research or training development that is generating alternatives to the working assumption that the human learner is no more than a programmable mechanism with little or no capability for contributing to his acquisition of competence beyond being 'motivated'. The learner as passive mechanism is of course an image we automatically acquire as researchers in the laboratory and as training specialists in curriculum development. As manpower specialists, our image of the learner is, I suspect, that generally held by parent for the child, the physician for the patient, the missionary for the heathen, the programmer for the reluctant computer. If I dramatize this issue it is to highlight my belief that a massive resource for training technology is being forfeited by default: the potential capability of human learners to participate actively in strategies for their own learning. Excepting my own personal work, I see no R. & D. efforts whatsoever in the direction of self-manipulated and implicit learning strategies and their inculcation into a learner population. Since the learner in the role of student has played dunce to teachers all his life, bringing about change will not be easy. It may not even be generally feasible.

But in any systematic taxonomy of training that is to be anchored both in training benefits and in training costs, the distinction of the learner's role as a passive or active participant should be one important dimension. As we stand now, however, we lack even constructive hypotheses, to say nothing of data, to justify this conclusion which I suspect all of my readers will subjectively share with me.

V. How to get there

A systematic training technology having the properties and capabilities outlined above is not likely to come about through accretion of theories, and of specialized development efforts and practices. A systems problem is solved when the entire domain of the system's functions is bounded. Some tentative ordering of the sequence of major functions is then made. The classes of information necessary and sufficient for the performance of a given function in the series may then be specified, at least loosely. This permits the *problem* to be subsetted into parts with some confidence that the interfaces of the parts can be fitted together later. The various properties of alternative devices and procedures for accomplishing each of the gross functions may then be determined. Where several functions share the same processing or information properties, the definition of a 'module' may arise. And so forth into the analysis and synthesis that creates an integrated technology. (Let us hope there will still be a place for the inspired individual teacher in this new world!).

This kind of architectural thinking requires, I believe, some centralized conceptualization where the elements of the model are harmonized and fused. It cannot be accomplished by ad hoc committees. And only a naive faith can expect that a problem solution will be larger than the problem definition.

Under highly favourable conditions of staffing, however, I think we could put together at least that 20% of the discipline that would cover 80% of technical training management decisions in a couple of years of intensive work. It might take another five years to make it culturally acceptable to the body of theorists, investigators and practitioners in training, and a decade to bring it into general adoption. If the modularities in the design were sound, the system could evolve without collapse by integrating change and expansion. By definition, a system is out-of-date when it is completed because the conditions that inspired it no longer obtain after the seven years required to design and build it and introduce it to cultural acceptance.

A concluding word about the apparatus of technology. Our forefathers taught their sons to hunt and to use the spear and bow. No doubt but that variations in the instructional milieu and the programming of the practice conditions varied widely, as did the forms and conditions of learning feedback. The evidence confirms however that there was at least some statistical level of success in the use of these primitive facilities and procedures. Of course, it was unlikely that the father had a diffident student. Closer to home, we can observe that a boy given his first bicycle will be riding it in minutes if he has seen his friends ride bicycles, and if he is merely left alone with the contrivance. The general function of our technology in training, as in other subject matters, is just to hurry things up a little, and perhaps also to spread the dubious advantages of the few to the responsibilities of the many. At least in prospect this may be progress. On the other hand, perhaps some of us should wonder—on occasion—if we aren't trying to design a herd of elephants to crack a peanut. The proposal in this paper might fit that metaphor. But as of today, I doubt it.

Bibliography

AUSUBEL, D.P., 1968, *Educational Psychology: A Cognitive View* (New York: Holt, Rinehart and Winston).

BLOOM, B.S., ENGLEHART, M.D., FURST, E.J., HILL, W.H. and KRATHWOHL, D.R., 1956, *Taxonomy of educational objectives: the classification of educational goals* (New York: Longmans Green and Co.).

BRIGGS, L.J., CAMPEAU, P.L., GAGNÉ, R.M. and MAY, M.M., 1967, *Instructional Media: A Procedure for the Design of Multi-Media Instruction* (Pittsburgh: American Institute for Research).

COGAN, E.A., 1967, *The Evaluation of Systems-Analytic Training Programs* (Alexandria, Va.: Human Resources Research Office Professional Paper, 29–67).

CRAWFORD, M.P., 1966, *HumRRO Techniques in Course Development* (Alexandria, Va.: Human Resources Research Office Professional Paper, 15–66).

DE GREENE, K.B., Ed., 1970, *Systems Psychology* (New York: McGraw-Hill).

FLEISHMAN, E.A., 1962, The description and prediction of perceptual-motor skill learning. In Glaser (Ed.), *Training Research and Education* (Pittsburgh: University of Pittsburgh Press).

FOLLEY, J.D. Jr., 1964, *Development of an Improved Method of Task Analysis and Beginning of a Theory of Training.* (Pt. Washington, New York: U.S. Naval Training Device Center T.R. NAVTRADEVCEN, 1218–1).

GAGNÉ, R.M., 1970, *The Conditions of Learning* (2nd Edn.) (New York: Holt, Rinehart and Winston).

GILBERT, T.F., 1962, Mathetics: The Technology of Education. *J. Mathetics*, **1**.

GRIMSLEY, D.L., 1969, *Acquisition, Retention and Retraining: Group Studies on Using Low Fidelity Training Devices* (Alexandria, Va.: HumRRO TR69–4).

GUILFORD, J.P., 1967, *The Nature of Human Intelligence* (New York: McGraw-Hill).

HEADQUARTERS AIR FORCE SYSTEMS COMMAND, 1967, *Handbook of Instructions for Aerospace Personnel Subsystems Design* (Washington, D.C.: Andrews AFB: AFSCM 80–3).

HEADQUARTERS AIR FORCE SYSTEMS COMMAND, 1969, *Personnel Subsystems* (Washington, D.C.: Andrews AFB: AFSC DH 1–3).

JOHNSON, N.W., 1972, Skill = Speed × Accuracy × Form Adaptability. In Singer, R.N. (Ed.), *Readings in Motor Learning* (Philadelphia: Lea and Febiger).

MECHNER, F., 1967, Behavioral analysis and instructional sequencing. In Lange, P.C. (Ed.) *Programmed Instruction* (Chicago: National Society for the Study of Education).

MELTON, A.W. (Ed.), 1964, *Categories of Human Learning* (New York: Academic Press).

MILLER, E.E., 1969, *A Taxonomy of Response Processes* (Alexandria, Va.: Human Resources Research Office Technical Report, 69–16).

MILLER, R.B., 1953, *Handbook on Training and Training Equipment Design* (Pittsburgh, Pa.: American Institutes for Research, Wright Air Development Center Technical Report 53–136).

MILLER, R.B., 1965, Analysis and Specification of Behavior for Training. In Glaser, R. (Ed.), *Training Research and Education* (Pittsburgh: University of Pittsburgh Press.)

MILLER, R.B., 1962, Task description and analysis. In Gagné, R.M. (Ed.), *Psychological Principles In System Development* (New York: Holt, Rinehart and Winston).

MILLER, R.B., 1972 (in press), *Theoretical Background to the Design of Duty Modules* (Washington, D.C.: American Institutes for Research and U.S. Army Behavior and Systems Research Laboratory).

NOBLE, C.E., 1969, Outline of human selective learning. In Bilodeau, E.A. (Ed.), *Principles of Skill Acquisition* (New York: Academic Press).

REITMAN, W., 1970, What does it take to remember? In Norman, D.A. (Ed.), *Models of Human Memory* (New York: Academic Press).

SHUMACHER, S.P. and GLASGOW, Z. (in press), *Instructional System Development Handbook* (Wright-Patterson AFB: Air Force Human Research Laboratory).

SINGER, R.N., 1972, *Readings in Motor Learning* (Philadelphia: Lea and Febiger).

SMITH, R.G. Jr., 1967, *An Annotated Bibliography on the Design of Instructional Systems* (Alexandria, Va.: Human Resources Research Office).

STEPHENSON, R.W., 1972 (in press), *A Taxonomical Base for Future Management Information and Decision Systems: A Common Language for Resource and Requirement Planning* (Washington, D.C.: American Institutes for Research and U.S. Army Behavior and Systems Research Laboratory Technical Research Note).

Dr. Fleishman holds degrees in psychology, has been a professor at Yale University and has held a number of senior research posts. He is at present Director of the American Institutes for Research, Washington, D.C. He is also Editor of the Journal of Applied Psychology and is the current President of the Division of Industrial and Organizational Psychology of the American Psychological Association.

1:3

Taxonomic problems in human performance research*

Edwin A. Fleishman

Introduction

A major problem confronting researcher and technologists in human resources is the lack of a generally accepted set of unifying concepts for the systematic description and prediction of human performance. For some years a number of us have felt the need to develop such a set of concepts to help make more dependable generalizations of research results to new tasks. In particular, better ways are needed to generalize research findings from laboratory studies to operational settings and from one experimental situation to another. The essential problem is the need to generalize the effect of some training, environmental or procedural condition, from knowledge of its effect on one task, to its probable effect on some other task. What has been lacking, it is felt, is a system for classifying such tasks which would lead to improved generalization and prediction of human performance (cf. Fleishman, 1967). In particular, what we need is a learning and performance theory which ascribes task dimensions a central role.

It is not too long ago when a favourite distinction in psychology textbooks was between 'mental' and 'motor' tasks or between 'cognitive' and 'non-cognitive' tasks. Such broad distinctions are clearly too all-inclusive for generalizing results obtained on the effect of some learning condition, on a particular task, to the probable effect of this condition on a new task. In a recent project we have examined many different schemes or taxonomies that have been devised for describing tasks (Farina, 1969; Theologus, Romashko and Fleishman, 1970; Wheaton, 1968). Job analysts, for example, have developed highly detailed task analysis systems, but these are probably too specific to particular jobs to help us arrive at general task dimensions applicable across many different tasks and jobs. Other psychologists have proposed categories of tasks in terms of

* Some of the material presented is derived from research supported by the Advanced Research Projects Agency and the Department of the Army Behavior and Systems Laboratory under the Project 'Development of a Taxonomy of Human Performance' (Edwin A. Fleishman, Principal Investigator). Summaries of this work are described in Fleishman, Kinkade and Chambers, 1968; Fleishman, Teichner and Stephenson, 1970; and Fleishman and Stephenson, 1970.

Other work reported was supported at different times by the National Science Foundation, Office of Naval Research, the Army Surgeon General's Office, the National Institutes of Health, the Navy Training Equipment Center and the Department of the Air Force.

broad human functions required to perform them. For example, such categories as identification, discrimination, sequence learning, motor skill, scanning and problem solving are terms which have been used in the literature. However, everything we know about actual correlations among human performances indicates a considerable diversity of functions *within* each of these broad areas.

It is only recently that concerted attempts have been made to explore more intensively some of the issues and alternatives in taxonomic development, and to proceed on a more empirical basis in the evaluation of these alternatives. My purpose here is to review a programme of research that has made at least some beginnings in this area.

Specifically the paper will discuss some general problems in the development of taxonomic systems applicable to descriptions of human performance and tasks. Some alternative approaches and provisional classification schemes developed will be described. Then, some specific measurement and scaling techniques applicable to certain task classification systems will be illustrated and their reliability evaluated. We shall then describe attempts to evaluate the utility and validity of these systems. Finally, specific attempts to apply certain task classification systems to several areas of human performance research will be described. In particular, these areas include effects of drugs, noise, learning procedures, alcohol, and factors affecting vigilance performance.

Some taxonomic issues*

Early in our research programme we reviewed relevant literature bearing on taxonomic approaches and concepts in the behavioural sciences (Wheaton, 1968; Farina, 1969; Chambers, 1969). Our objective here was to sharpen some issues and to illuminate some of the reasons for the slow progress in this area. In our review three issues stood out:

(*a*) The objectives to be served by a particular classification system,
(*b*) The descriptive basis upon which a system is founded, and
(*c*) The methodologies employed to establish and validate a system.

Taking these in turn:

Purpose of classification

Why are we interested in task classification? The question is important because individuals who attempt classification usually do not view the development of such a system, in and of itself, as an end. Rather they view a system of classification as a tool to increase their ability to interpret, predict, or control some facet of performance (Cotterman, 1959). This goal is to be achieved by seeking relationships between that which is classified (e.g., tasks, processes mediating performance, etc.) and selected variables of interest to a particular investigator (e.g., distribution of practice, training regimens, environmental stressors, etc.).

Desiring to establish such relationships, however, the behavioural scientist must initially decide upon one of two objectives. He can elect to develop a system of classification having utility for a very specific and, consequently, limited area (e.g., the classification of tasks with respect to which training methods are most efficacious in promoting high levels of task performance). In this case the objective is oriented toward a particular problem area and is to be achieved by developing a *unique* classificatory system having little utility

* I am indebted to George W. Wheaton of the Taxonomy Project Staff for his contributions to this conceptual phase of research. More extensive treatment may be found in Wheaton (1968).

for other problem areas. Thus, a classificatory system designed to be of aid in the interpretation of training phenomena may contribute relatively little to the interpretation of environmental stressor phenomena.

Or the investigator may look for a system from which a *variety* of applications may stem. He may develop a classification of tasks, and *then* attempt to organize a wide range of data in terms of a general system. For example, he might first classify tasks and *only then* relate stressors, learning principles, training regimens, etc. to each class of tasks in his system. In this case, classification is designed from inception to be general, and to serve a variety of users by aiding in the interpretation, prediction, or control of a broad range of phenomena.

Utilitarian classifications with specific applications

With respect to utilitarian classification systems, those having rather specific applied objectives, classifications dealing with training are most numerous. A number of investigators (Annett and Duncan, 1967; Cotterman, 1959a, 1959b; Eckstrand, 1964; Folley, 1964a, 1964b; Gagné, 1962; E.E. Miller, 1969; and Stolurow, 1964) have proposed systems which will permit the classification of tasks* into sets or categories which are relatively homogeneous with respect to principles of learning, training techniques, etc. The objective of such systems would be to supply training personnel with an explicit rationale for the selection of specific training programmes for specific tasks.

Some human-engineering investigators hope to provide for effective design in complex systems. They would ultimately wish for categories of tasks which remain relatively invariant for principles of design.

Still other investigators (Fitts, 1962; R.B. Miller, 1967) have proposed more comprehensive classification systems, in the sense that they would provide for more than one specific application. Fitts viewed the objective of 'task' classification to be the identification and application of important correlates of learning rate, performance level, and individual differences.

Theoretical classifications with broad applications

Classificatory systems may also be developed, however, as autonomous structures which are only some time later to be related to other variables or 'applied'. In these instances, the classificatory exercise is an integral and inextricable step in the development of theory. The resultant system provides a consistent conceptual framework, the elements of which eventually are to be utilized in the interpretation, prediction or control, of behavioural phenomena. One is not precluded from seeking specific applications for such classifications. The point is that he must not let a specific application dictate the composition and structure of his system.

Learning theorists have been most prolific in these pursuits (Melton, 1964). As yet, no categorization has been proposed which effectively compares, contrasts, and interrelates the various human learning 'categories'. Consequently, we have been unable to formulate a general theory of learning.

The ability theorists have been engaged in analogous work. They have attempted to isolate dimensions of behaviour upon which a general theory of human performance might be based. Guilford (1967) and I (Fleishman, 1964)

* Task in this instance is employed as a generic concept including its physical attributes, human functions, performance requirements, etc.

have been perhaps most explicit in attempting to integrate the ability dimensions identified with the general framework of experimental psychology. In particular, my associates and I have conducted research relating ability dimensions identified in research on individual differences to stages of learning (Fleishman and Hempel, 1954, 1955), stimulus-response relations (Fleishman, 1957), retention (Fleishman and Parker, 1962), part-whole task relations (Fleishman, 1965), effects of drugs (Elkin, Freedle, Van Cott and Fleishman, 1965), etc. This variety of studies was possible because we first attempted to develop a standard and consistent classificatory structure of human abilities and then attempted to test the feasibility of this framework across areas. We will examine this approach later in this paper.

Bases of classification

The next issue, after the consideration of the purposes of representative behavioural classifications, is an examination of the descriptive bases of taxonomy, insofar as they have been stated or can be inferred. Since the subject matter to be classified has generally been the 'task', our concern must focus on the definition and meaning of the concept 'task'. Second, is there general agreement as to the bases upon which task description, differentiation and classification can be accomplished?

Definition of the task

The concept of task has been defined in an almost endless variety of ways. Task definitions vary greatly with respect to their breadth of coverage. At one end of this dimension are definitions which view the task as the totality of the situation imposed upon the subject. For example, this definition would consider ambient stimuli as an integral part of the task. The other end of this dimension is represented by definitions which treat a task as a specific *performance*. In this case, for example, one task could be to 'depress the button whenever the light comes on'. Suffice it to say that very different concepts may underlie definitions falling at either end of this dimension.

This diversity of opinion is also reflected in the extent to which tasks are defined as being external to or an intrinsic part of the subject. Some definitions take into account the propensity of subjects to redefine an imposed task in terms of their own needs, values, experiences, etc. In the grossest sense, these definitions treat a task as whatever it is the subject *perceives* the task to be. Other definitions attempt to define the task in terms of what has been *imposed* upon the subject, be it total situation or a specific performance requirement.

In general, most investigators seem to treat tasks as dynamic entities consisting of interrelated processes and activities. For example, R.B. Miller (1966) states that 'A task is any set of activities, occurring at about the same time, sharing some common purpose that is recognized by the task performer' (p. 11).

We should not attempt to debate about *the* definition of a 'task' as if only one were possible. Rather, we must adopt or *develop* a definition which will serve as an adequate vehicle for classification. An adequate vehicle will permit the derivation of terms which reliably describe tasks and distinguish among them. These derived terms provide the conceptual basis for classification.

Comments on conceptual bases for classification

Every system of classification has as its very foundation a set of terms to be employed in the description and eventual classification of the subject-matter toward which the system is oriented. The investigators whom we have reviewed differ substantially in opinion as to the proper basis for describing and classifying tasks. Each has attempted to coin his own set of terms. And yet, differences of opinion on this issue are not unreasonable when one considers the diversity of objectives and the range of task definitions.

We shall deal with four major conceptual bases underlying task description and classification.

Behaviour Description Approach. In this conceptual approach to task classification, categories or types of tasks are to be formulated based upon observations and descriptions of what operators *actually do* while performing a task. Obviously, many variations on this theme are possible. Overt behaviours such as dial setting, meter reading, soldering, etc., are most often employed.

In spite of the large number of terms available for this approach to task description, relatively few descriptive systems have been developed which are based exclusively on operator behaviours or activities. McCormick (1964) has employed this descriptive approach in his studies of worker-oriented job variables (e.g., handling objects, personal contact with customers), and Fine (1963) uses this approach as a basis for describing worker functions in terms of handling (things), analysing (data) and negotiating (with people).

Are descriptions of each component activity necessary to completely identify the task and reliably distinguish it from others? If each and every activity is not to be included, how are the most 'critical' or 'representative' activities to be chosen—on the basis of frequency of occurrence, duration, criticality, etc.? As noted above, the system has been most often employed in the description of what people do on jobs.

The acceptance or rejection of this (or any other) approach is only possible in light of one's *purpose* in classifying.

Behaviour Requirements Approach. A second approach to 'task' description appears to be increasing in popularity. In this approach emphasis is placed on the cataloguing of behaviours which *should* be emitted or which are assumed to be *required* in order to achieve criterion levels of performance. The human operator is assumed to possess a large repertoire of processes which will serve to intervene between stimulus events and responses. There has been a great deal of interest in codifying the required intervening processes (functions, behaviours, etc.), cataloguing tasks in terms of the types of processes required for successful performance, and then relating the types of tasks which emerge to particular training methodologies.

Gagné and Bolles (1963) and Miller (1967), Eckstrand (1964) and Annett and Duncan (1967) have all discussed or proposed the classification of tasks in terms of required behaviours. Typical of the functions used to describe and differentiate among tasks are scanning function, short-term memory, long-term memory, decision making and problem-solving.

Ability Requirements Approach. The third conceptual basis for the description and classification of tasks, which we call the ability requirements approach (see e.g. Fleishman, 1972) is in many respects similar to the behavioural requirements concept. Tasks are to be described, contrasted, and compared in terms of the abilities which a given task requires of the operator. These abilities are relatively enduring traits or attributes of the individual performing the task. The assumption is made that specific tasks will require certain abilities if performance is to be maximized with respect to established criteria. Tasks requiring similar abilities would be placed within the same category.

The abilities approach differs from the behaviour requirements approach primarily in terms of concept derivation and level of description. The ability concepts are empirically derived through factor-analytic studies, and are treated as more basic units than the behaviour functions and processes. These differences not withstanding, the ability and behaviour requirements approaches to classification proceed in the same manner. Both seek to identify critical aspects of the *individual* intervening between input stimuli and output response.

Task Characteristics Approach. A fourth approach differs from the preceding approaches in terms of the type of task description which is attempted. The task characteristics descriptive approach (see Farina and Wheaton, 1971) is predicated upon a definition that treats the task as a set of conditions which elicit performance. These conditions are imposed upon the operator, and have an objective existence quite apart from the activities they may trigger, the processes they may call into play, or the abilities they may require of the operator. Having adopted this point of view, appropriate descriptive terms are those which focus on the task *per se*. The assumption is made that tasks can be described and differentiated in terms of intrinsic, objective properties which they may possess. These properties or characteristics may pertain to the goal toward which the operator works, relevant task stimuli, instructions, procedures, or even to characteristics of the response(s) or the task content. The obvious problem is the selection of those task components which are to be described, as well as the particular terms or parameters by means of which description is to be accomplished.

This selection will be dictated primarily by the particular task definition which is adopted. We have seen that tasks can be defined in several ways, particularly in regard to: the scope of definition; the extent to which tasks may be treated as objective entities, clearly apart from the operators who perform them; and the extent to which tasks are viewed as processes or structures.

Some methodological issues

Within the scope of this paper we cannot dwell on the more general problems of 'how' to proceed with classification. We shall discuss instead a number of criteria for evaluating such systems.

The requirement for operational definition of terms becomes increasingly critical if the system is to be used by a broad range of specialists. The descriptive terms may be completely unfamiliar to many of these individuals, or even too familiar as in the case of the popular terms 'decision-making' and 'problem-solving'. While homage is paid to the need for operational definitions, few investigators have actually generated such definitions. Also, as a minimum requirement, the descriptors employed in the differentiation and classification of tasks must permit *nominal scaling*. That is, a judge must at least be able to ascertain whether each descriptor applies or does not apply to the particular task being examined.

Also, descriptors must be defined and treated within a system of measurement so that they can be reliably evaluated. No matter what the descriptive bases or the techniques employed in classification, it is essential that descriptor values be assigned reliably.

Another criterion requires that classes within the system be mutually exclusive. In other words, it should be possible to place any given sample of subject matter in one and only one classificatory grouping. If the classification contains a hierarchical structure, then categories on the same horizontal level are required to be mutually exclusive.

Another major criterion concerns the extent to which classification of subject matter is exhaustive. While exhaustive classification is an ultimate objective, it is perhaps unrealistic during initial efforts. It is this continuing search for both mutually exclusive classes and exhaustive classification which seems to lead to the constant revision and modification found in healthy systems of classification.

Another major criterion is that classes are desired which have specific behavioural implications, as with the interest of Annett and Duncan (1967) in classifying 'tasks' so that each category or class of tasks has specific training requirements associated with it. Ultimately, of course, any behavioural classification scheme must make the 'match' between specific categories and behavioural effects. The degree to which the 'match' can be made will determine the predictive power of the system. At one level a statement might concern *whether or not* a particular environmental variable would affect performance. At another and more sophisticated level it might be possible to predict the *direction* and *magnitude* of effect.

A final set of criteria includes efficiency and utility. The taxonomy should promote communication among its users, be they laboratory researchers or technologists.

In our own programme we found it useful to lay out these general issues which have been elaborated elsewhere. In no sense can we say that our subsequent efforts met the rigorous standards called for. However, they at least provide indications of where we fell short and allow for successive iterations toward meeting these criteria.

In the remainder of this paper, we shall illustrate some developments with two provisional systems, one based on the ability requirements approach and another based on the task characteristics approach. We shall conclude with some attempts to link these two approaches.

The abilities approach

Much of what we know today about the categorization of human skills, at least that which is based on empirical research, comes from correlational and factor analysis studies. Such correlational studies are typically carried out in the psychometric tradition and until recently, little attempt has been made to integrate the ability concepts developed there into the more general body of psychological theory. Here the fact of individual differences is exploited to gain insights about common processes required to perform different groups of tasks. Abilities are defined by empirically determined relations among observed separate performances. For example, that individuals who do well in Task A also do well on Tasks B and C but not Tasks D, E, and F implies a common process is involved in performing the first three tasks, distinct from that involved in the last three. To account for these consistencies and distinctions, an ability is postulated.

It has been my feeling, over many years, that research using combinations of experimental and correlational methods, properly conducted, can lead to the development of a taxonomy of human performance which is applicable to a variety of basic and applied problems and that ability concepts may provide an integrative framework.

Elsewhere (e.g., Fleishman, 1962) I have elaborated on the concepts of ability and skill. Briefly, ability refers to a more general capacity of the individual, related to performance in a variety of human tasks. For example, the fact that spatial-visualization has been found related to performance on such diverse tasks as aerial navigation, blue-print reading, and dentistry, makes this ability somehow more basic. The assumption is that the skills involved in complex activities, such as diving, flying an airplane, operating an industrial machine, or playing basketball, can be described in terms of the more basic abilities.

An extensive series of interlocking experimental-factor analytic studies, which we have conducted over many years, has attempted to isolate and identify the factors in common variance in a wide range of perceptual-motor performances. Essentially, this is laboratory research in which tasks are specifically designed or selected to test certain hypotheses, about the organization of abilities in a certain range of tasks. The experimental battery of tests is administered to several hundred subjects, and the correlation patterns examined. Subsequent studies tend to introduce task variations aimed at sharpening or limiting our ability factor definitions. The purpose is to define the fewest independent ability categories which might be most useful and meaningful in describing performance in the widest variety of tasks.

Through our investigation of a wide range of several hundred different tasks, we have been able to account for performance in terms of a relatively small number of abilities. In subsequent studies, definitions of these abilities and their distinctions from one another have become more clearly delineated. Figure 1 gives the labels of 11 perceptual-motor factors which consistently appear to account for the common variance in such tasks. We shall not define all of these here, but extensive definitions of each ability exist with illustrations of the tasks which best measure them (Fleishman, 1964).

Figure 1. Perceptual motor factors identified in factor analytic research. (For detailed descriptions see Fleishman, 1964.)

PERCEPTUAL—MOTOR ABILITIES

- Control Precision
- Multi-Limb Coordination
- Response Orientation
- Reaction Time
- Speed of Arm Movement
- Rate Control (Timing)
- Manual Dexterity
- Finger Dexterity
- Arm-Hand Steadiness
- Wrist-Finger Speed
- Aiming

Perhaps it might be useful to provide some examples of how one examines the generality of an ability category and how one defines its limits. The specification of an ability category is an arduous task. The definition of the *Rate Control* factor may provide an illustration.

In early studies it was found that this factor was common to compensatory tracking, as well as to following pursuit tasks. To test its generality, further tasks were developed to emphasize responses to stimuli moving at different rates, where the tasks were not conventional tracking tasks. For example, the subject had to *time* his movements in relation to stimulus rates, but he did not follow a target. The factor was found to extend to such tasks.

Later studies attempted to discover if emphasis on this ability is in *judging the rate of the stimulus* as distinguished from *ability to respond at the appropriate rate*. Several motion picture tasks were adapted in which the subject was required to extrapolate the course of an airplane moving across a screen. The only response required was on an I.B.M. answer sheet. (At what point did the planes meet? Points 1, 2, 3, 4 or 5?) These moving picture tests, involving only judgements about stimulus rate, did *not* correlate with the group of tasks previously found to measure 'rate control'. Thus, our definition of this rate control ability was expanded to include measures beyond tracking and pursuit tasks, but restricted to tasks requiring the *timing* of an actual adjustive movement to the changing stimulus.

A similar history can be sketched for each ability variable identified and a great number of principles relating task characteristics and abilities measured can now be described.

Abilities predictive of learning

Our subsequent work attempted to use the ability concepts developed to predict various learning measures and other aspects of task performance (e.g., Fleishman and Hempel, 1955; Fleishman, 1957, 1960; Fleishman and Ellison, 1969) with encouraging results. In general, these studies, with a great variety of practice tasks, show that (*a*) the particular combinations of abilities contributing to performance on a task change as practice on this task continues; (*b*) these changes are progressive and systematic and eventually become stabilized; (*c*) in perceptual-motor tasks, for example, the contribution of non-motor abilities (e.g., verbal, spatial) may play a role early in learning, but their contribution decreases systematically with practice, relative to motor abilities; and finally (*d*) there is also an increase in a factor specific to the task itself not common to the more general abilities. Figure 2 gives an illustration of one set of findings. Our work relating abilities to more general performance phenomena led us to feel that this kind of taxonomic system might be worth future development.

Use of tasks standardized by ability measured

As one illustration, we have carried out a number of studies in which 'standardized tasks' representing such ability dimensions have been used in laboratory studies of factors affecting human performance. Such studies have included the effects of stress, diet, anoxia, noise and drugs. With respect to drugs, we are observing the effects of a variety of drugs and dosages on measures of a variety of reference ability tasks. These measures sample the perceptual, motor, sensory and cognitive areas.

Figure 3 gives a few illustrations of these events for a given dosage of the drug scopolamine (Elkin *et al.*, 1965; Fleishman, 1967). As can be seen, we are getting differential effects; that is, some abilities within each area were more affected than others. The absolute performance decrement, time to reach maximum effect and time to recover, depended on the ability measured. For

Figure 2. Comparison of learning curves on a discrimination reaction time task for groups scoring high and low on different ability test measures. (From Fleishman and Hempel, 1955.)

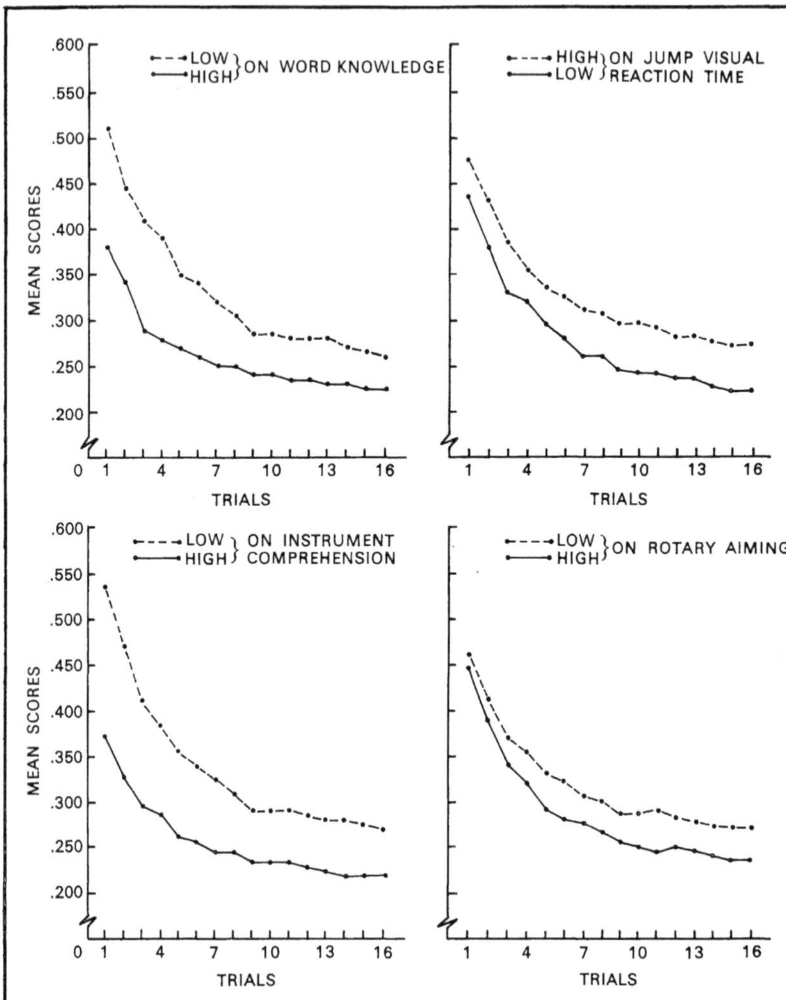

example, the physical abilities of Dynamic Flexibility and Explosive Strength showed only slight effects, whereas the motor abilities of Multi-Limb Coordination and Finger Dexterity showed marked effects. Such findings indicate why the category 'motor skill' is too broad. Similar findings have been found for drugs such as magnesium-pemoline and ritilan (Baker, Geist and Fleishman, 1967).

We are currently conducting similar studies on the effects of different noise stressors (Theologus *et al.*, 1971). The rationale of this programme is that different components of human task performance will be affected differently

Figure 3. Effects of a given dosage of scopolamine in degrading performance on several different tasks involving different abilities. (From Fleishman, 1962.)

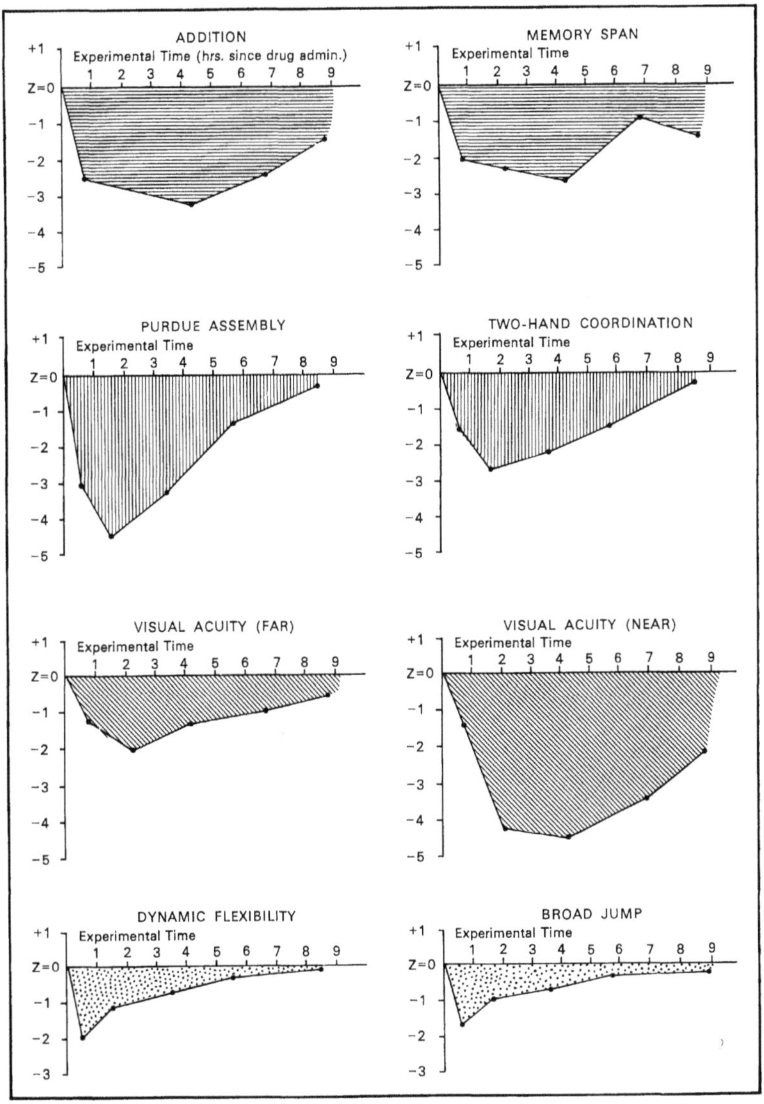

as a function of the type and level of stressor, and that measurement of changes in these components will provide quantitative evaluations of the disruptive effects of the stressor and of man's vulnerability to it.

Time does not permit elaboration of the experimental design and data reduction procedures. We found that intermittent moderate intensity noise (85 dB) is more likely to affect performance on tasks emphasizing some abilities but not others. We also found a significant effect of the random intermittent noise on the mean Reaction Time and the absence of any effect on this measure for the patterned noise of the same intensity. However, on the Rate Control task (tracking), no effect of either type of noise is demonstrated. The results are illustrative of differential effects according to task category.

The feeling was that improved generalizations of research data might be possible if careful specifications of our categories were utilized, and that ability concepts may hold the key.

Methods of estimating ability requirements

A phase of the programme involved extensive reviews of the factor analytic ability literature. Figure 4 gives a summary of the ability categories we eventually worked with. One of the striking findings in this review was the difficulty in moving from the factor analysts' definition to a more operational

Figure 4. Ability requirements for which ability rating scales have been developed. (From Theologus and Fleishman, 1971.)

1. Verbal Comprehension
2. Verbal Expression
3. Ideational Fluency
4. Originality
5. Memorization
6. Problem Sensitivity
7. Mathematical Reasoning
8. Number Facility
9. Deductive Reasoning
10. Inductive Reasoning
11. Information Ordering
12. Category Flexibility
13. Spatial Orientation
14. Visualization
15. Speed of Closure
16. Flexibility of Closure
17. Selective Attention
18. Time Sharing
19. Perceptual Speed
20. Static Strength
21. Explosive Strength
22. Dynamic Strength
23. Stamina
24. Extent Flexibility
25. Dynamic Flexibility
26. Gross Body Equilibrium
27. Choice Reaction Time
28. Reaction Time
29. Speed of Limb Movement
30. Wrist-Finger Speed
31. Gross Body Coordination
32. Multilimb Coordination
33. Finger Dexterity
34. Manual Dexterity
35. Arm-Hand Steadiness
36. Rate Control
37. Control Precision

definition which could be used reliably by observers. A large effort in our programme involved the successive refinement of such definitions to improve the utility of these concepts in describing tasks. A host of different reliability studies have been conducted in which task descriptions have been examined by individuals who rated these descriptions in terms of these 37 abilities. These descriptions have ranged from descriptions of laboratory apparatus to description of jobs. The attempt has been to use the same ability concepts to *bridge the gap in describing laboratory and real world tasks* within the same conceptual framework.

Scaling techniques have been developed which include precise definitions of the abilities, distinctions with other abilities and behaviourally anchored scales (Theologus, Romashko and Fleishman, 1970; Theologus and Fleishman, 1971). Figure 5 gives an example of one such scale. The scale values of the task examples have been empirically determined.

Figure 5. Example of an ability requirement scale (task statements have empirically determined scale values). (From Theologus, Romashko and Fleishman, 1970.)

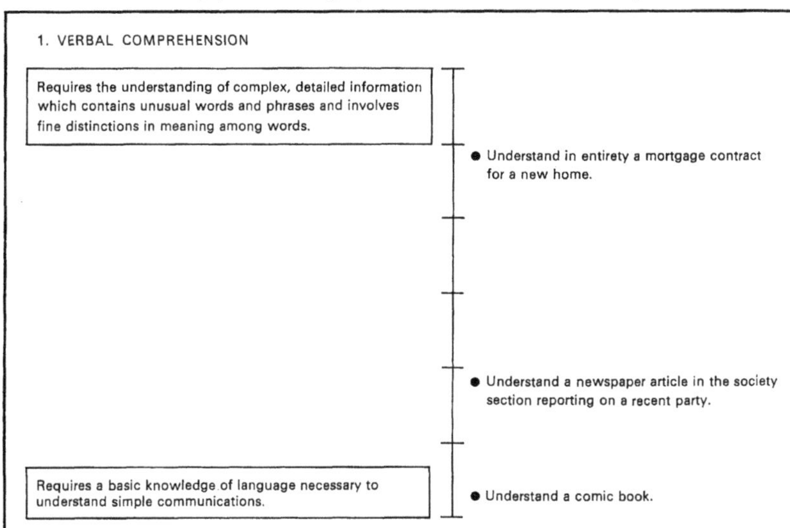

We have examined questions of number of raters needed, training required, etc., with regard to achieved reliability using these techniques when applied to given kinds of tasks. All of the answers are not in, but successful refinements have been made and the scales have been found useful for a number of purposes. A manual including the scales for 37 abilities is now in use. Another method for estimating ability requirements of tasks is in a preliminary state of development. This approach requires the observer to make binary decisions and to follow through a series of minor decisions until the ability definition is reached. Figure 6 gives an example of one such system for one ability area.

Evaluating the utility of ability requirements in classifying tasks

A preliminary evaluation of the abilities taxonomic system was made in terms of its capacity to organize a portion of the data found in the human performance

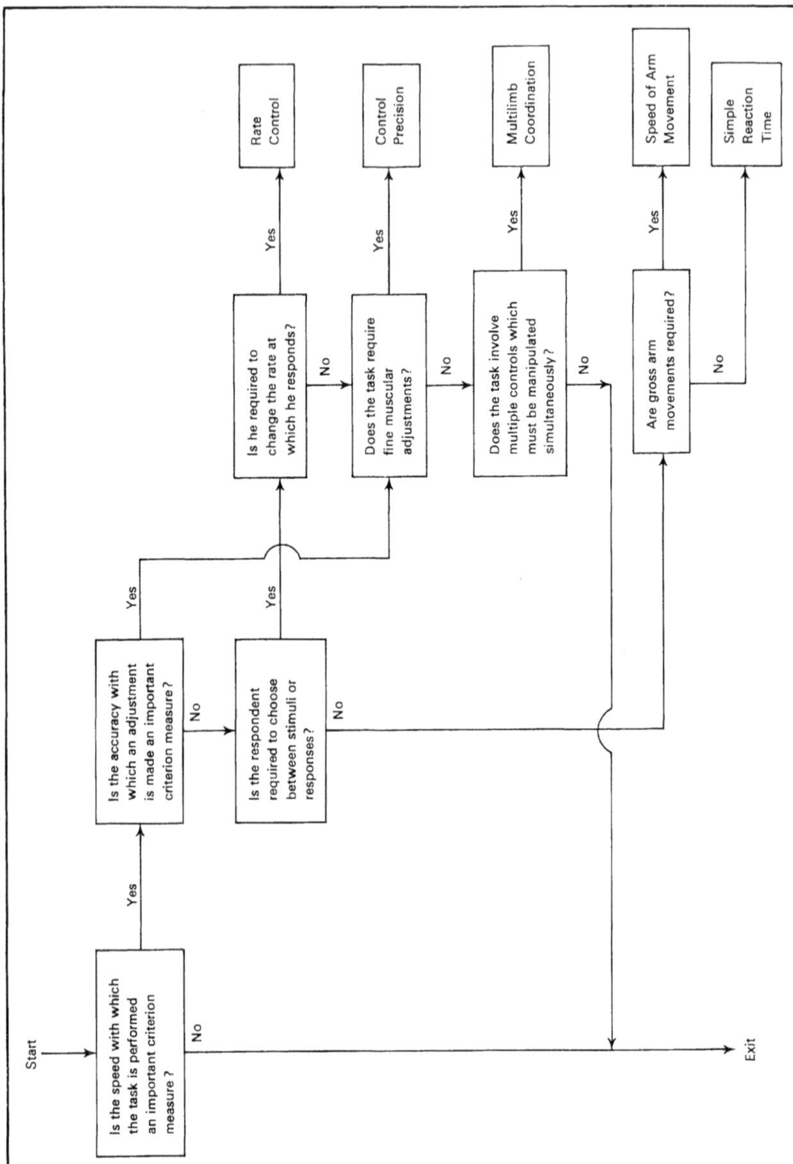

Figure 6. Portion of a binary flow diagram used to make decisions about the relevance of selected perceptual-motor abilities for performing particular tasks. (From Fleishman and Stephenson, 1970.)

literature (Levine, Romashko and Fleishman, 1973). The objective was to examine the feasibility of structuring an area of literature according to the 'abilities' required for task performance. The area of human performance selected for examination was that of sustained attention or vigilance behaviour.

Vigilance is generallv considered to involve a change in the detection of infrequent signals over prolonged periods of time.

The vigilance area was selected for study for several reasons. First, while a variety of different tasks have been used in previous vigilance research, the range of tasks is not as great as in many other areas. Consequently, the number of different abilities involved is not likely to be large and this in turn would reduce the complexity of the evaluation. Secondly, a reasonably large number of studies have been reported on the effects of several selected independent variables on vigilance performance and it is important that enough studies be available to provide a sufficient number of data points within task categories. Thirdly, a common dependent measure is employed in nearly all vigilance studies, i.e., detection accuracy. It is essential to the integration of findings across studies that a common metric be available.

The study was designed to examine (*a*) the extent to which performance in vigilance tasks could be differentiated on the basis of abilities, and (*b*) whether improved generalizations about the effects of independent variables in vigilance performance were possible as a result of such task classifications. Median percent correction detections through the first 90 minutes of the vigil were computed for all studies categorized according to one of the four predominant abilities required for task performance. Scales such as the one in Figure 5 were used to classify tasks in the vigilance literature.

For tasks in which the predominant ability was Perceptual Speed, the performance decrement occurred primarily within the first hour of the vigil and subsequent time in the task led to no further performance deterioration. With tasks involving the predominant ability of Flexibility of Closure, after the initial hour of performance degradation, performance was enhanced with time in the vigil.

The data were next partitioned according to levels of selected independent variables: signal rate, knowledge of results, and sensory mode.

With respect to sensory mode, Figure 7 depicts percent correct detections at 30 minute intervals throughout the first 180 minutes of the vigil. This independent variable was trichotomized into auditory, visual, and auditory-visual redundant categories. Regardless of whether the ability category was Perceptual Speed or Flexibility of Closure, overall performance was superior under auditory conditions rather than visual conditions. Furthermore, the redundant condition was markedly superior to either auditory or visual presentation when the main ability required for task performance was Flexibility of Closure.

The auditory condition revealed a marked differentiation between the relationships describing performance as a function of time in the task for studies involving Perceptual Speed and those involving Flexibility of Closure. For Perceptual Speed tasks a severe performance decrement was obtained with time in the task, up to 90 minutes. Alternatively, there was a very small performance decrement for Flexibility of Closure tasks within the first 90 minutes, and an increment in performance accuracy beyond that time. For the visual condition the function describing performance with time in the task for Perceptual Speed studies was similar to that obtained for the auditory condition. However, the Flexibility of Closure function in the visual condition was almost the reverse of that for the auditory condition.

While the data provided are preliminary and in several instances functions are based upon only a few data points, it is nevertheless possible to infer that

Fig. 7. Median percentage of correct detections as a function of time in the task and ability category for different sensory modes. (From Levine, Romashko and Fleishman, 1973.)

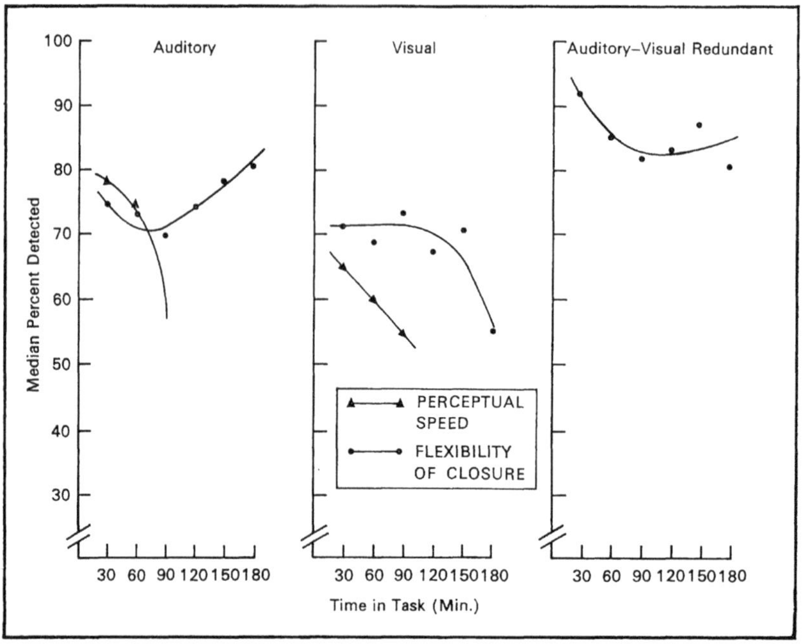

the effects of the independent variables on performance in a vigilance task are in part a function of the class of task imposed upon the subjects. It has been demonstrated that when studies are categorized by abilities required by the task, relationships between performance and time in the task differ markedly as a function of the selected independent variables.

It should be emphasized that despite the differences among specific tasks in terms of equipment, displays, response requirements, etc., the classification system enabled an integration of results and the development of functional relationships that were otherwise obscured.

A more recent study, along these same general lines, was conducted on the effects of alcohol on human performance (Levine, Greenbaum and Notkin, 1973). As before, the attempt was to structure data from the literature so as to (*a*) integrate appropriate disparate and isolated results, (*b*) improve generalizations across experimental studies, (*c*) identify gaps in the existing literature, and (*d*) identify new relationships among independent variables and performance.

The effort was designed, in part, to categorize the existing literature into task groups in order to determine whether alcohol effects differ as a function of different types of tasks. Tasks were grouped together on the basis of the abilities required to perform the task. A preliminary set of abilities was chosen representing the cognitive, sensory-perceptual, and psychomotor domains. Classifying studies with similar abilities into groups or domains should permit relationships between alcohol dosage, time since dosage, and performance to be developed as a function of classes of tasks. The literature on the effects of alcohol upon human performance might, in this fashion, be made more useful and suggest hypotheses which have previously been elusive to researchers.

We have time to present only a few representative results. We investigated dosage as an independent variable in 41 studies (165 tasks).

Figure 8 depicts performance as a function of dosage, with ability categories

Figure 8. Median percent decrement as a function of alcohol dosage and predominant ability for two periods since ingestion. (From Levine, Notkin and Greenbaum, 1973.)

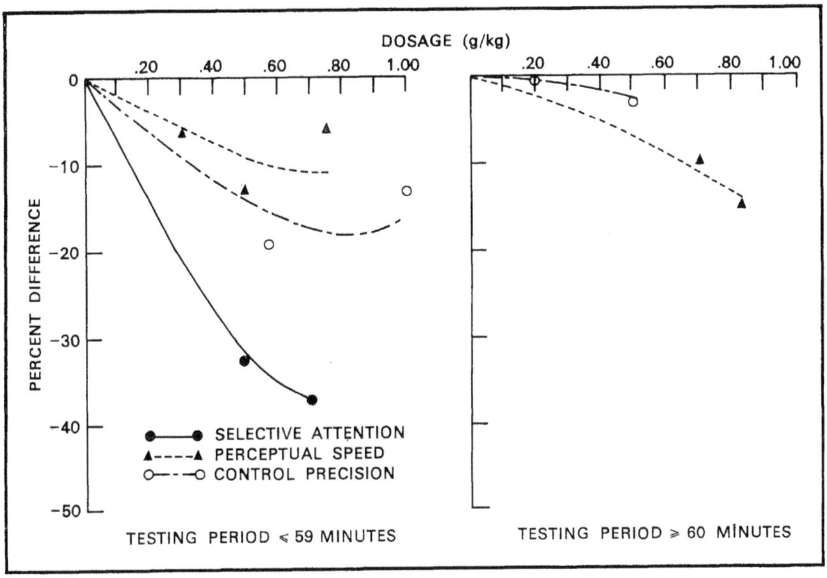

of selective attention, perceptual speed, and control precision. The number of data points here is small and therefore conclusions and interpretations must be made with caution. There is a striking similarity between *Perceptual Speed* and *Control Precision* tasks in terms of their rate of performance deterioration and their asymptotes. There is only a 10% difference between alcohol and non-alcohol treated groups. There is little or no difference between tasks involving the abilities of Perceptual Speed and Control Precision in terms of the relationship of dosage to performance.

This situation is somewhat different, however, for tasks involving Selective Attention. The data suggest that performance on tasks involving this cognitive ability is seriously impaired. Moderate dosages cause marked performance impairment (up to 40% degradation).

Similar analyses were made with time since dosage as an additional independent variable. The data suggest that the curves relating performance to dosage differ as a function of the ability requirements of the task. Further, the effects on performance of length of testing period and time between alcohol administration and the initiation of testing were marked and dependent upon the abilities required by the task. In each case, different functional relationships were evident. Performance deteriorated more rapidly and was impaired to a greater degree when the testing period was less than one hour than when it was one hour or greater. Further, cognitive tasks were most impaired in shorter testing periods but perceptual-sensory tasks were most impaired in longer testing periods. The greatest impact of alcohol upon performance occurred when an hour or more was permitted to elapse between the administration of alcohol and the initiation of testing. Overall, psychomotor tasks appeared to be least impaired by alcohol and perceptual-sensory tasks appeared to be most impaired. Cognitive tasks fell in-between.

Despite differences among the specific tasks in terms of displays, response requirements, performance index, technique of alcohol administration, etc., the categorization of tasks according to ability requirements enabled an integration of results and the development of functional relationships which otherwise were obscured.

These results are preliminary, but we are encouraged that a data base (perhaps computerized) about human performance can be developed, indexed by type of task. We are working on developing such a data base in several areas. From knowledge about a future task's category, we should be able to predict the effect of some learning or environmental variable on the performance of it.

Several other kinds of evaluation have been made. One has involved validating the ability ratings against actual factor loadings obtained on tasks. Such evaluations have lead to further refinements of the scales.

Task characteristics approach

In a second general approach to taxonomic development, our project staff (Farina and Wheaton, 1971) has been working with what has been termed the *task characteristics approach*. As mentioned earlier, this approach attempts to provide for the description of tasks in terms of a variety of task-intrinsic properties including goals, stimuli, procedures, etc. Knowledge of how performance varies, as a result of manipulating the characteristics of tasks (e.g., creating a number of different tasks), might provide a basis for estimating performance on other tasks whose characteristics could be described.

The consequences of the foregoing rationale for development and use of a task descriptive system were explored by constructing an heuristic model of performance. In turn, this model helped specify what was to be described, how description was to be accomplished, and how the task descriptive indices were to be related to performance.

We cannot describe this model in detail here, but during early stages of this approach, consideration was also given to the manner in which the descriptive data provided by the system were to be used in organizing tasks and consequent performance data. This issue was of importance for it was felt that specification of the intended use(s) of the descriptive data would culminate in a set of requirements for the language itself. Two major uses were identified: classification and prediction. Task characteristics data would provide a basis for classifying tasks in terms of their observed similarities and dissimilarities. The descriptive data could also be utilized within a multiple regression context to relate variations in the characteristics of tasks to variations in performance.

The development of task characteristics received initial guidance from a definition of the term 'task' which was devised early in the project. A task was conceived of as having several components with each component possessing certain salient characteristics. These components were: an explicit goal, procedures, input stimuli, responses and stimulus-response relationships.

In order to differentiate among tasks, the components of a task were treated as categories within which to devise task characteristics or descriptors. As previously mentioned, additional requirements were set forth regarding these characteristics. Each had to be applicable to most, if not all, types of tasks so as to avoid the problem of not being able to rate or measure all tasks on a comparable set of dimensions. Each characteristic had to be expressed quantitatively, being scaled in at least an ordinal fashion. Each had to possess an acceptable degree of reliability. Finally, to achieve economy of use, it was desirable that the characteristics require a minimum of training and application time on the part of the user.

Figure 9 clarifies the relationship among the terms 'task', 'task components' and 'characteristics'. Each characteristic was cast into a rating scale format

Figure 9. Conceptual scheme of task characteristics. (From Farina and Wheaton, 1971.)

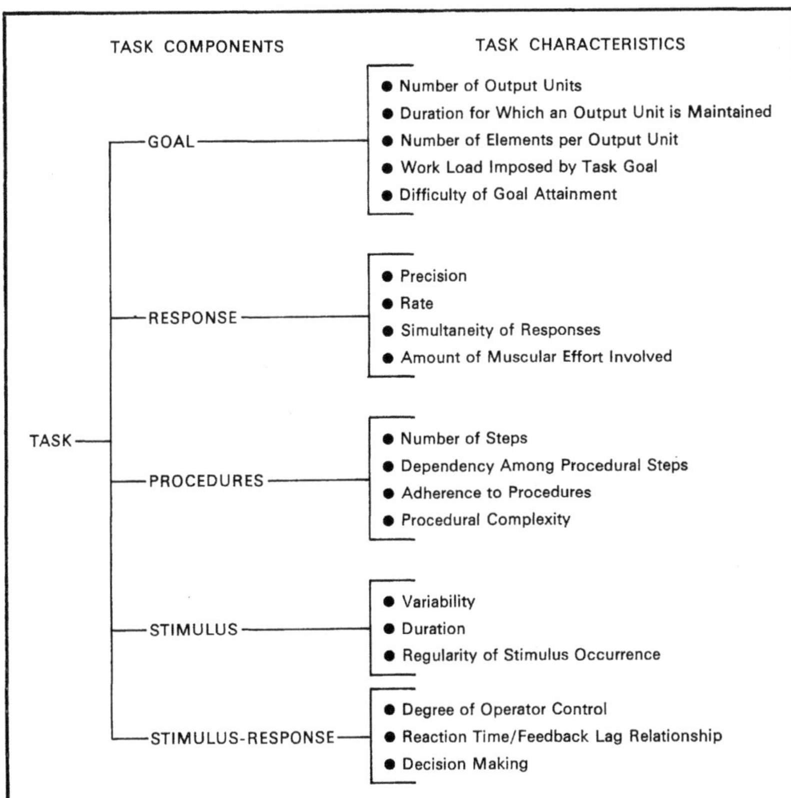

which presented a definition of the characteristic, and provided a seven-point scale with defined anchor- and mid-points along with examples for each point (Smith and Kendall, 1963). A sample rating scale is shown in Figure 10. A set of 19 scales developed were combined into a Task Rating Manual. The original

Figure 10. Example of a task characteristic scale. (From Farina and Wheaton, 1971.)

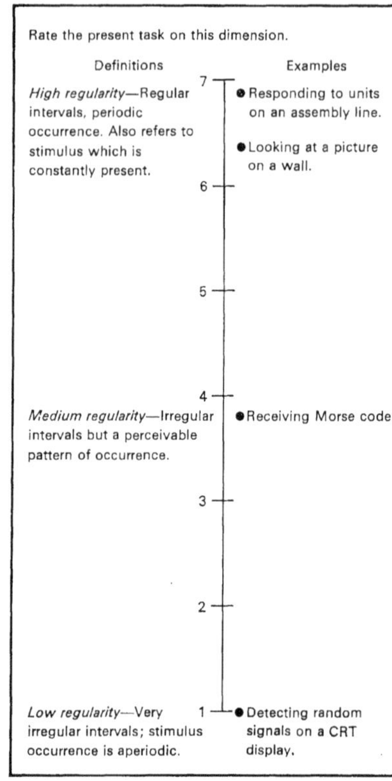

set of scales has undergone changes due to refinement, additions and deletions.

Many different reliability studies have been conducted. Relations between values obtained from three judge groups and larger groups were high and a human factors background by raters was helpful.

Of primary interest here are studies in which ratings of task characteristics have predicted actual task performance. In an illustrative study (Farina and Wheaton, 1971), judges rated 37 tasks on 19 scales. Applying the requirement for a common performance measure, it was found that 26 of the tasks had one measure in common which was designated as the 'number of units produced per unit time'. The 'units' varied and included such things as: number of blocks moved; number of assemblies completed; number of taps made; and number of correct discriminations given. Common to these 26 tasks was the requirement that as many 'units' as possible be produced during specified time periods. Since different amounts of time were allowed for completion of the various tasks (e.g., 25 to 900 seconds), a common time frame was needed to provide a standard basis for comparison. The 'unit time' chosen for this purpose was one second. Therefore, the performance score reported for each task was prorated to obtain the average number of units produced per second.

Since the entire set of 19 rating scales could not be employed, a smaller subset was selected. The six most reliable scales were chosen for analysis. For each of these scales the ratings provided by three judges were averaged to obtain a single value on each scale for each of the tasks. The specific scales employed in the study were:

(1) Stimulus duration (scale #15).
(2) Number of output units (scale #1).
(3) Duration for which an output unit is maintained (scale #2).
(4) Simultaneity of responses (scale #9).
(5) Number of procedural steps (scale #10).
(6) Variability of stimulus location (scale #14).

The multiple correlation coefficient for this analysis (based on four predictors) was $R=0{\cdot}85$ which accounted for 72% of the variance (R^2) in the criterion measure. After a correction in R for small sample bias (Guilford, 1956, p. 399), (cR) was 0·82, still highly significant. It was possible to specify those task characteristics which contributed most to performance.

Several replications of such studies have been completed, the most recent of which have employed more complex training devices (Wheaton and Mirabella, 1973).

This effort has tentatively demonstrated that it is possible to describe tasks in terms of a task-characteristics language which is relatively free of the subjective and indirect descriptors found in many other systems. It has further demonstrated that the task characteristics may represent important correlates of performance. Although more convincing proof of this point must await cross-validation, it was possible to describe subtle differences among tasks and to relate such differences systematically to variations in performance.

Linking abilities and task requirements

We now present a final set of results, relevant to task taxonomy and human performance.

We have encouraging results from studies which indicate that it is possible to build up a body of principles about interactions of task characteristics with ability requirements through experimental-correlational studies in the laboratory. The approach is to develop tasks which can be varied along specified task dimensions, to administer these tasks to groups of subjects who also receive a series of 'reference' ability tasks, known to sample certain more general abilities (e.g., Spatial Orientation, Control Precision, etc.). Correlations between these reference tasks and scores on variations of the criterion task specify the ability requirements (and changes in these requirements) as a function of task variations.

In an earlier study (Fleishman, 1957), subjects were required to press a button within a circular arrangement of buttons on the control panel in response to particular lights which appeared in a circular arrangement of lights on the upper display panel. The correct button depended on the position of the light. Subjects performed under seven different conditions where the display panel was rotated from 0°, 45°, 90°, 135°, 180°, 225° and 270°. These same subjects performed on a series of spatial, perceptual, and psychomotor reference tasks.

We are able to show systematic changes in the ability factors sampled by the criterion task as a function of degree of rotation of the display panel. Progressive rotation of the light panel shifted the ability requirement from Perceptual Speed to two other factors: Response Orientation and Spatial Orientation.

Perceptual Speed was measured in the upright and slight displacement conditions. The other abilities were measured at larger display rotations. Here, individual differences along known ability dimensions are used to explore the relations between tasks and the characteristics of people who can perform the tasks most effectively. Of course, these are problems faced every day by personnel, training, engineering, and systems psychologists.

A study just completed (Wheaton, Shaffer, Mirabella and Fleishman, 1973) has taken us a step closer in applying this paradigm to an operational task. The task used was that of Navy sonar operator. An experiment was developed in which subjects listened to standardized sonar type of signals and background noise, where two task parameters, signal duration and signal-to-noise ratio, were varied. The subjects received a battery of auditory and visually presented ability measures. Would the ability requirements vary as a function of changes in these task requirements?

While the changes were not marked, they were consistent. For example, factor loadings of one auditory perceptual ability factor increased as the background noise increased and as the signal durations grew shorter. Other abilities were not so related to performance. However, loadings on this ability varied according to the type of signals (cargo ships, light craft, warships and submarine), to be identified. As Figure 11 shows, the loadings for the ability

Figure 11. Estimated factor loadings of four types of auditory signals on the auditory perceptual factor as a function of background noise level. (From Wheaton, Shaffer, Mirabella and Fleishman, 1973.)

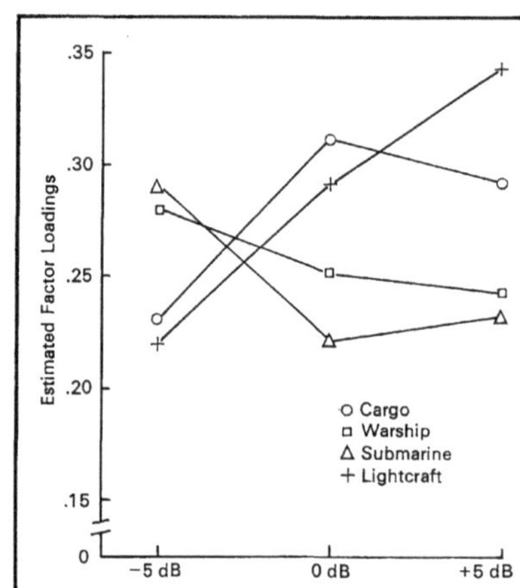

of auditory perceptual speed increased as a function of background noise for cargo and light craft signals, but decreased for warship and submarine signals. This study confirmed the importance of task variables in determining the abilities required to perform effectively on a complex auditory-processing task. Principles derived from this series of studies should provide a basis for translating information about the specific nature of the job or task to be performed into statements about the capabilities which operators should possess in order to perform effectively.

Summary statement

In summary, I have tried to lay out some general issues in taxonomic development, to give some examples of measurement approaches, and methods of evaluation of taxonomic systems. Some studies were shown in which predictions and generalizations about human performance may be enhanced through applications of such task classification systems. Only a beginning has been made, and only tentative conclusions are possible. Hopefully, after such initial probings, more comprehensive programmes can be undertaken.

References cited

ANNETT, J. and DUNCAN, K.D., 1967, Task analysis and training design. *Occupational Psychology*, **41**, 211–221.

BAKER, W.J., GEIST, A.M. and FLEISHMAN, E.A., 1967, *Effects of cylert (magnesium-pemoline) on physiological, physical proficiency, and psychomotor performance measures* (Washington, D.C.: American Institutes for Research).

CHAMBERS, R.M., 1963, Operator performance in acceleration environments. In Burns, N.M., Chambers, R.M. and Hendler, E. (Eds.), *Unusual environments and human behavior*, pp. 193–319 (London: Glencoe).

COTTERMAN, T.E., 1959, *Task classification: An approach to partially ordering information on human learning* (WADC TN 58–374 Wright-Patterson Air Development Center, Wright-Patterson Air Force Base, Ohio).

ECKSTRAND, G.A., 1964, *Current status of the technology of training*, AMRL-TR-64-86, Sept. 1964 (Aerospace Medical Division, Wright-Patterson Air Force Base, Ohio).

ELKIN, E.H., FREEDLE, R.O., VAN COTT, H.P. and FLEISHMAN, E.A., 1965, *Effects of drugs on human performance: The effects of scopolamine on representative human performance tests* (Washington, D.C.: American Institutes for Research).

FARINA, A.J., Jr., 1969, *Development of a taxonomy of human performance: A review of descriptive schemes for human task behavior* (Washington, D.C.: American Institutes for Research).

FARINA, A.J., Jr. and WHEATON, G.R., 1971, *Development of a taxonomy of human performance: The task characteristics approach to performance prediction* (Washington, D.C.: American Institutes for Research).

FINE, S.A., 1963, *A functional approach to a broad scale map of work behaviors*, Sept. 1963. HSR-RM-63/2 (McLean, Virginia: Human Science Research, Inc.).

FITTS, P.M., 1962, Factors in complex skill training. In Glaser, R. (Ed.), *Training research and education* (pp. 177–198) (Pittsburgh: Univ. of Pittsburgh Press).

FLEISHMAN, E.A., 1957, Factor structure in relation to task difficulty in psychomotor performance. *Educational and Psychological Measurement*, **17**, 522–532.

FLEISHMAN, E.A., 1960, Abilities at different stages of practice in Rotary Pursuit performance. *Journal of Experimental Psychology*, **60**, 162–171.

FLEISHMAN, E.A., 1962, The description and prediction of perceptual-motor skill learning. In Glaser, R. (Ed.), *Training research and education* (Pittsburgh: Univ. of Pittsburgh Press).

FLEISHMAN, E.A., 1964, *The structure and measurement of physical fitness* (Englewood Cliffs, N.J.: Prentice-Hall).

FLEISHMAN, E.A., 1965, The prediction of total task performance from prior practice on task components. *Human Factors*, **7**, 18–27.

FLEISHMAN, E.A., 1967, Performance assessment based on an empirically derived task taxonomy. *Human Factors*, **9** (4), 349–366.

FLEISHMAN, E.A., 1972, On the relation between abilities, learning and human performance. *American Psychologist*, **27**, 1017–1032.

FLEISHMAN, E.A. and ELLISON, G.D., 1969, Prediction of transfer and other learning phenomena from ability and personality measures. *Journal of Educational Psychology*, **60**, 300–314.

FLEISHMAN, E.A. and FRUCHTER, B., 1965, Component and total task relations at different stages of learning a complex tracking task. *Perceptual and Motor Skills*, **20**, 1305–1311.

FLEISHMAN, E.A. and HEMPEL, W.E., Jr., 1954, Changes in factor structure of a complex psycho-motor test as a function of practice. *Psychometrika*, **18**, 239–252.

FLEISHMAN, E.A. and HEMPEL, W.E., Jr., 1955, The relation between abilities and improvement with practice in a visual discrimination reaction task. *Journal of Experimental Psychology*, **49**, 301–312.

FLEISHMAN, E.A. and HEMPEL, W.E., Jr., 1956, Factorial analysis of complex psychomotor performance and related skills. *Journal of Applied Psychology*, **40**, 96–104.

FLEISHMAN, E.A., KINKADE, R.G. and CHAMBERS, A.N., 1968, *Development of a taxonomy of human performance: A review of the first year's progress*. (Washington, D.C.: American Institute for Research).

FLEISHMAN, E.A. and PARKER, J.F., 1962, Factors in the retention and relearning of perceptual-motor skill. *Journal of Experimental Psychology*, **64**, 215–226.

FLEISHMAN, E.A. and STEPHENSON, R.W., 1970, *Development of a taxonomy of human performance: A review of the third year's progress* (Washington, D.C.: American Institutes for Research).

FLEISHMAN, E.A., TEICHNER, W.H. and STEPHENSON, R.W., 1970, *Development of a taxonomy of human performance: A review of the second year's progress* (Washington D.C.: American Institutes for Research).

FOLLEY, J.D., Jr., 1964, *Development of an improved method of task analysis and beginnings of a theory of training*, June 1964. NAVTRADEVCEN 1218-1 (Port Washington, New York: USNTDC).

GAGNÉ, R.M., 1962, Human functions in systems. In Gagné, R.M. (Ed.), *Psychological principles in system development* (New York: Holt, Rhinehart and Winston).

GAGNÉ, R.M. and BOLLES, R.C., 1963, A review of factors in learning efficiency. In Galanter, E. (Ed.), *Automatic teaching: The state of the art* (New York: John Wiley & Sons, Inc.).

GUILFORD, J.P., 1956, *Psychometric Methods* (New York: McGraw-Hill).

GUILFORD, J.P., 1967, *Nature of human intelligence* (New York: McGraw-Hill).

LEVINE, J.M., GREENBAUM, G.D. and NOTKIN, E.R., 1973, *The effects of alcohol on human performance: A classification and integration of research findings* (Washington, D.C.: American Institutes for Research).

LEVINE, J.M., ROMASHKO, T. and FLEISHMAN, E.A., 1973, Evaluation of an abilities classification system for integrating and generalizing human performance research findings: An application to vigilance tasks. *Journal of Applied Psychology*, **58**, 149–157.

McCORMICK, E.J., 1964, *The development, analysis and experimental application of worker-oriented job variables*, Final Report; ONR Nonr-1100 (19) (Lafayette, Indiana: Purdue).

MELTON, A.W., 1964, The taxonomy of human learning: Overview. In Melton, A. (Ed.), *Categories of human learning* (New York: Academic Press).

MILLER E.E., 1969, *A taxonomy of response processes* (Alexandria, Va.: Human Resources Research Office Technical Report, 69–16).

MILLER R.B. 1967, *Task taxonomy: Science or technology? in "The Human Operator in Complex Systems"*, 1967 W.T. Singleton, R. Easterly, D. Whitfield (eds): Taylor & Francis.

MILLER, R.B., 1967, *Task taxonomy: Science or technology?* (Poughkeepsie, New York: IBM).

MIRABELLA, A. and WHEATON, G.R., 1973, *Effects of task index variations on transfer of training criteria.* Technical Report (U.S. Navy Training Equipment Center, Orlando, Florida). American Institutes for Research Contract N61339-72-C-0126.

SMITH, P.C. and KENDALL, L.M., 1963, Retranslation of expectations: An approach to the construction of unambiguous anchors for rating scales. *Journal of Applied Psychology*, **47**, 149–155.

STOLUROW, L., 1964, *A taxonomy of learning task characteristics*, AMRL-TD 12-64-2, Jan. 1964 (Aerospace Medical Research Laboratories, Wright-Patterson Air Force Base, Ohio). (AD 433199).

THEOLOGUS, G.C. and FLEISHMAN, E.A., 1971, *Development of a taxonomy of human performance: Validation study of ability scales for classifying human tasks* (Washington, D.C.: American Institutes for Research).

THEOLOGUS, G.C., ROMASHKO, T. and FLEISHMAN, E.A., 1970, *Development of a taxonomy of human performance: A feasibility study of ability dimensions for classifying human tasks* (Washington, D.C.: American Institutes for Research).

WHEATON, G.R., 1968, *Development of a taxonomy of human performance: A review of classificatory systems relating to tasks and performance* (Washington, D.C.: American Institutes for Research).

WHEATON, G.R., SHAFFER, E.J., MIRABELLA, A. and FLEISHMAN, E.A., 1973, *Methods for predicting job-ability requirements:* 1. *Ability requirements as a function of changes in the characteristics of an auditory signal identification task* (Washington, D.C.: American Institutes for Research).

Section 2

Development of Resources

H.J. Butcher, who is Professor of Educational Psychology at the University of Sussex and was formerly Professor of Higher Education at the University of Manchester, is the author of *Human Intelligence* and (with Raymond B. Cattell) of *The Prediction of Achievement and Creativity*. He has edited several books on educational research and educational psychology and is founder-editor of the journal *Research in Education*.

2:1

Use of resources in British higher education (with particular reference to selection and assessment)

H. J. Butcher

If one goes back even less than 20 years, one sees that British universities were in a remarkably privileged position, although it seemed normal enough at that time. Of course, there were great differences between the institutions in this respect and it is possible that the four of which I have had personal experience, i.e., Cambridge, Manchester, Edinburgh and Sussex, did not form a representative sample. The study of differences in environment and atmosphere between different institutions of higher education is still in its infancy, at least in Europe, but one or two such studies have gradually been appearing in Britain. Wiseman, for instance, instituted a quite extensive research in the School of Education at Manchester University that produced a comparison of the perceived atmosphere in all the colleges of education in the Manchester area training organization and also of at least one department in the University. The techniques used were those developed by Pace and Stern (1958) in the U.S.A.

This privileged position may be illustrated by a few examples. In the first place, universities were at that time the only degree-giving institutions. But, since the institution of the so-called Binary system in higher education by the Labour Minister of Education, Anthony Crossland, there are now a considerable number of degree-awarding polytechnics whose degrees are designed to carry equal prestige with those awarded by universities. Another privilege of the universities that has been more recently modified, and one that must be very rare in cross-cultural terms, has been their very considerable support from Government sources of finance combined with an almost complete freedom about how they spend these sums. It is only in the last four or five years that university books have been opened to Government audit. One of the reasons for this change was undoubtedly the growing realization of an undue lack of planning and intercommunication between universities in terms of capital expenditure. Charles Carter, Vice Chancellor of the University of Lancaster, has commented that in cases known to him it would have been more economical to drive certain students to another university by Rolls-Royce every time they wished to use engineering equipment rather than duplicate it in their own, as actually occurred. But in recent years a more rational division of expensive resources and a greater consciousness of the need for cost effectiveness has been enforced to a large degree by the University Grants Committee.

There is also a much greater degree of co-operation and organization between universities in spheres other than the financial. In recent years the Committee of Vice-Chancellors and Principals of British Universities has become a much better equipped and tightly knit committee, providing a reasonable degree of mutual planning and co-ordination between the 40-odd universities and colleges represented upon it. Yet another instance of a more effective use of human resources is the development of the Universities Central Council for Admissions, which processes all applications from would-be students, thus replacing the rather hand-to-mouth and chaotic situation that existed until a few years ago. For several years also, joint deliberations have been proceeding between the Standing Conference on University Entrance representing the universities, and the Schools Council, representing the interests of sixth-formers in secondary schools. The aim of these rather drawn-out deliberations is to produce an agreed and quite radical modification of the existing conditions and qualifications required for entrance to higher education.

Such organizational changes were paralleled in the attitudes of universities and other institutions, especially to research and innovation. Until about 1960 British universities were open to the charge that they carried out research into an enormous variety of topics, into everything under the sun in fact except themselves. An obvious turning point occurred with the publication of the Robbins Committee report (1963) which crystallized a great deal of feeling already in the air, to the effect that enormous expansion was required and with this expansion corresponding changes in attitude. The Committee was not content to take a mere armchair approach but took very seriously the question of accumulating statistical data, which was the prime responsibility of Claus Moser. The forecasts and extrapolations of the Committee about the degree of expansion that would be required to fulfil the growing need for higher education and consequently about the scale of financial support and reorganization that would equally be required seemed bold at the time, but experience has proved that they were in fact on the conservative side. Probably the most significant feature of the Committee's work, however, was not the degree of accuracy of its statistical predictions and graphs but the fact that it represented the first detailed and objective attempt to plan the rational use of human resources in the higher educational system of Great Britain. The Robbins Committee also took within its purview such questions as the rate of wastage and dropout in British universities as compared with corresponding institutions in other countries. In doing so, it reflected a concern that had rapidly been growing subsequent to the publication a few years earlier of a report by Parnell (1951) on 'Mortality and Prolonged Illness Among Oxford Undergraduates'. Parnell's study showed that the suicide rate among Oxford undergraduates was approximately 12 times that in a comparable population of the same age. This report and others induced some university doctors and psychiatrists to clamour for greater provision in terms of counselling and psychiatric services for students. A consequence of this new appreciation was that instead of the student being expected to adapt entirely to the institution, the view came increasingly to be held that there was more responsibility for the institution to adapt to the broadening and changing student population consequent upon expansion.

At about the same time a very different kind of study reinforced these tendencies. Glick and Miller (1956) in the United States published what was probably the first profitability study, or at least the first well-known one. 'A college education is worth a hundred thousand dollars' became the slogan. As a result of studies of this kind, selection and assessment of students began to be seen quite differently. Academic questions now appeared too important to be left to the academics, especially those who had been heads of departments for 30 years or more.

Along with these changed attitudes to student problems came changed attitudes to the social sciences. Chairs of psychology and especially of sociology were scarce until the late fifties, and although universities had prided themselves on their universality, it was quite widely felt that these subjects were not 'disciplines', but at best the dressing up in a new and inelegant jargon of facts and theories that had been known since antiquity under other names.

The complacency and suspicion of innovation was particularly evident in attitudes to research into higher education. It is not unfair to say that universities encouraged research least of all into their own rationale, constitution and methods of selection and assessment. In particular a veil of secrecy tended to be drawn over their power structure and decision-making processes, a veil that to-day is only imperfectly penetrated. Very little has been published in this field until the last two or three years, during which original investigations have been made by Burns, Worsley, Moodie and Lockwood, respectively at the Universities of Manchester, Edinburgh, York and Sussex.

None the less, one should not engage in a diatribe of hindsight against the dark ages before systematic research into higher education and its use of human resources in the United Kingdom got under way. As already implied, the institutions were humane and, within their terms of reference, seriously concerned with their main functions—teaching and research. To a large degree, also, they were right in believing that the objectives and functioning of universities are genuinely resistant to crude criteria of loss and gain, and that the whole nature of the enterprise may receive a kiss of death if subjected to rigid economic analysis or bureaucratic interference. People who had spent their working lives in universities were rightly sensitive to their unique virtues and felt, rather than understood analytically, that in the best cases they were sophisticated and mature living organisms; to interfere with them drastically in the interests of 'justice', 'efficiency' or 'economic pay-off'—especially if innovation were dictated from outside—might destroy their whole character and even their success in material terms. No such radical change has occurred and (although I have spoken critically of the complacency and ignorance of the social sciences displayed by many responsible for directing and administering British universities), I am profoundly glad that it has not.

Let me attempt to summarize the changes I have described so far before considering their implications. These seem to have fallen into four distinguishable, though related, categories—first a partial emergence from the ivory tower and an increased recognition that universities and colleges, although in some senses apart from society, interact with it and bear some responsibility to it, especially in a willingness to expand when demand expands; second, a greater preparedness to meet students half-way, instead of demanding unreservedly that they accommodate to the rules (often arbitrary) of the institution; third, a slow breaking down of barriers between different kinds of institution (and this is the least evident of many kinds of change, perhaps listed more from hope than realism); finally, and very markedly, an enormous change in attitude to the social sciences and especially to empirical studies of higher education by psychological and sociological techniques.

It sometimes surprises educationists of other nationalities to discover how far research into education in England has been generally unrespectable until very recently—though one must not say 'in Britain'. Attitudes in Scotland have been very different, and it would make an interesting and useful sociological research to investigate the reasons for this difference. I have tried to analyse some of the main factors in a contribution to a book called *University Perspectives* (edited by Jevons, Swanton and Knapp, 1970). For example, the Scottish Council for Research in Education was formed some 20 years before the National Foundation for Educational Research in England, which has existed only since the Second World War. This was one turning-point, but one that produced very little change in the field of tertiary education—since its financial support came from the Local Education Authorities and its terms of reference confined it almost exclusively to the study of education in primary and secondary schools.

The great breakthrough in the study of tertiary education occurred between 1963 and 1965 with the publication of the Robbins Committee Report, the establishment of the Social Science Research Council and the provision by the University Grants Committee (for the first time) of substantial research funds for investigation of university teaching methods. Some of the outcomes have been surveyed and summarized in a book (edited by Ernest Rudd and myself, 1972).

What do these amount to in terms of human resources? Only a small beginning, but an important one. Universities, Polytechnics and Colleges have tentatively begun to design or modify their procedures in the light of research findings. The unreliability of essay-type examinations, the existence of new kinds of ability tests, the study of cliques and sub-cultures in student residences, all these have actually helped to shape policy. The changes made have not been very drastic—nor should they have been. At the present stage of the art, educational research is valuable chiefly for raising questions and suggesting plausible hypotheses rather than for providing permanent answers.

It will not be possible to review comprehensively the whole area of research into higher education, which has burgeoned so rapidly in the last decade. A convenient classification of such research (see Venables and Venables, 1972) is in terms of input, process and output. Input studies are concerned with selection, choice of university or college, attitudes on entry and so forth; process variables with socialization, change, etc. inside the university; output variables with degree standards, vocational choice, graduate unemployment and so forth.

More time will be devoted to input and process variables than to output, if only because least work has been done on the output. Even the study of graduate students has an extremely sparse literature as compared with that of undergraduates, and follow-up studies of graduates for a decade or more are equally rare. Most work has been done on selection procedures, and the relating of pre-university or pre-college qualifications to performance in the university or college. It cannot be claimed, though, that the degree of prediction obtained is ever very impressive.

The problem is a particularly severe one in the U.K. because of the high selection ratio and the relatively small proportion of the age-group that enters whole-time education beyond secondary school. At the time of the Robbins Committee report in 1963, 4% of the age-group entered universities and about 7% all kinds of tertiary education institutions combined. Apart from its general recommendations for expansion, that committee made two specific recommendations about selection procedure.

For some 20 years the main instrument of selection for higher education has been the Advanced level of the General Certificate of Education, taken two years after the 'ordinary' level. The universities normally only demand two passes at Advanced level, but in fact require (for popular subjects) three passes at a very high grade (far above a mere pass). This excessive dependence on 'A' level results has long been criticized on several grounds.

The 'A' level examination does not always correlate highly with university performance, whether intermediate or final (correlations of around +0·2 are quite typical); the university requirements enforce an undue specialization in the upper forms of schools; pupils from Scottish schools (where less severe specialization occurs) are thereby handicapped and often unable to obtain places in English universities—except for a few very selective Scottish schools that adopt the English system; the examination is conducted by a number of different boards, whose standards are not demonstrably equivalent—or if they are equivalent, it is more by luck than judgement . . . and so on.

Usually the only other evidence a University Selector has to go on is an open-ended report from the candidate's headmaster. Drever (a member of the Robbins Committee) satirized these reports by suggesting that typically they would contain something like 'he shows considerable promise as a slow left-hand bowler and is a great comfort to his widowed mother'.

Ten years ago therefore, the Robbins Committee made two recommendations —that a British Scholastic Aptitude Test should be developed (on the lines of the College Entrance Examination Board objective tests in the U.S.A.); and that a standardized form should be developed for headmasters' and headmistresses' reports, so that they could be more readily compared and interpreted.

These two developments have been plodding along—certainly not at any breakneck speed. The Committee of Vice-Chancellors and Principals set up a research and development committee with the unmemorable title of Inquiry into Supplementary Predictive Information for University Entrance—rapidly abbreviated to I.S.P.I.U.A.

An English S.A.T. has been constructed—in several successive forms and tried out over four or five years on large samples of sixth-formers and first-year undergraduates. On first, face-value impressions, the results so far published have been rather disappointing. These apply only to correlations between S.A.T. administered during the last year at school and first-year university performance. The correlations are low, lower than the corresponding ones for 'A' level and it also looks as though the S.A.T. scores are unlikely to add greatly to predictable variance in a multiple regression equation. (But see Christie and Mills (1973) for favourable evidence.) However it is much too early to say at this stage that the exercise has not been worthwhile. During the next few months correlations between the new S.A.T. and final degree performance will be published, and it is possible that its predictive value may be less in the very short-term but greater in the long term than 'A' level grade—just as in the old 11+ the intelligence tests' relative predictive power increased steadily over time. Furthermore the paper by Christie and Mills (op. cit.) of the University of Manchester pointing out (*a*) that in spite of the low linear correlations, cut-off analyses suggest that the new S.A.T. has been underrated and (*b*) that in any case its main value may be as a calibrating and fully standardized instrument that exercises no backwash on the sixth-form curriculum.

It will be necessary to consider process and output studies together, both much more briefly than in some other sections. Most recent research here has been in two main areas—that of student wastage or drop-out and that of university and college teaching methods. There is reason to believe that the two topics are not entirely unrelated. As with all this kind of applied research into higher education, the variables are so complex and the study so new that striking *general* findings of broad validity are hard to come by. In particular the incidence of student drop-out and the pattern of causative factors appears largely peculiar to individual institutions, and in addition tends to fluctuate quite sharply in response to external events. Nevertheless, valuable work has been done in half a dozen or more British universities which in some cases has enabled the setting-up of an effective 'early warning system' and the provision of more extensive and acceptable counselling services.

Similarly, the study of teaching methods has produced no sudden revolution, but has resulted in the increasing provision of courses for new lecturers (usually voluntary), some of which give them the opportunity of seeing themselves in action on video-tape. Some such courses also include sessions on such topics as voice production or how to conduct seminars and individual tutorials. In a word, it is now much less commonly assumed that someone who has a Ph.D. in some subject but has never taught it in his life is necessarily capable of going straight into a lecture theatre and communicating his knowledge effectively and interestingly.

The development of a taxonomy of selection (especially in the sphere of higher education) is much needed but is an enormously difficult problem. My suggestions derive from some preliminary thoughts about the topic. Even 'towards a taxonomy of selection' would be an over-ambitious sub-heading. None the less, it may be of some use to propound some first thoughts, since the topic is so neglected.

First a word about kinds of taxonomy developed in the social sciences. In the case where all variables are quantifiable, there is a well-developed and intuitively satisfying model exemplified in the technique of factor analysis. This was mainly developed by psychologists, who until fairly recently were the only people to use it, though in the last few years the situation has changed a great deal and its use has become not uncommon in subjects as diverse as sociology and dietetics.

Without going into technicalities, the most obvious feature of factor analysis is that it is a *dimensional* approach; it operates on variables that are quantitative, at least implicitly, and in its classic form it reduces these to a smaller set of artificial variables that are orthogonal, i.e., statistically independent. These factors or dimensions of classification are at right angles to one another and generate a Euclidean space. Consider for a moment the situation in which people are given a battery of psychological tests to answer that will assign them scores on three statistically independent dimensions—general intelligence, extraversion and neuroticism. Each original test or each person can then be represented as a point in this kind of three-dimensional space; people who are similar in terms of all three dimensions will form close clusters, and more generally the overall similarity between individuals can be directly assessed by the Euclidean distance between them. My example incorporated only three orthogonal dimensions, because we can then easily imagine this space; we can make a physical model of it, take a ruler and measure the distance between individuals and so on. With more than three dimensions we can't do this and have to switch from geometry to algebra, but of course this is no reason why we should not classify in four, five or any number of dimensions.

The second kind of model is usually called a facet model, and is illustrated in Figure 1.

Figure 1. Guilford's scheme of ability factors

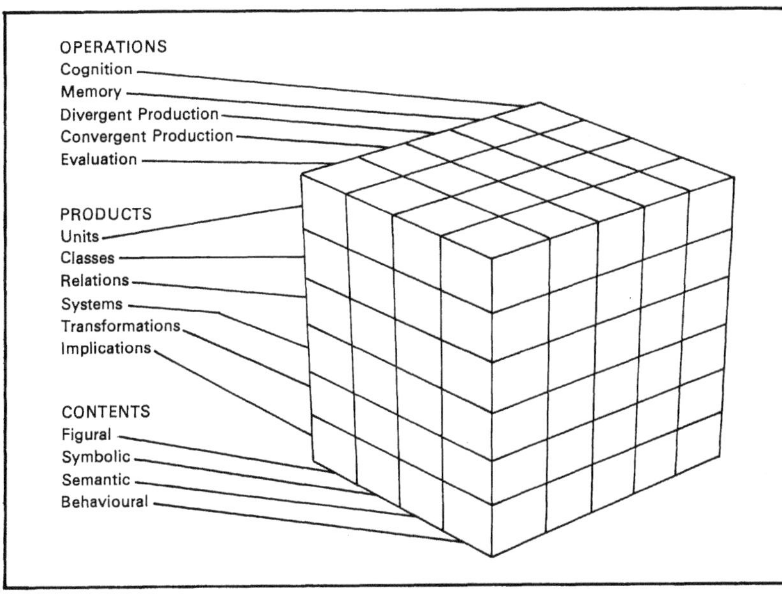

It can readily be seen that although the various sub-facets or categories of classification are arranged in three dimensions—hence the cube in the diagram—the model is not dimensional in the same sense as my earlier example. In this new conceptualization the divisions along each dimension are qualitative, not quantitative. On one of the illustrated dimensions, for example, it allows for a test to be classified as measuring either convergent production or divergent production, but not for it being a measure of both in varying degrees, as would the fully dimensional model. Note however that this constraint only applies if there are more than two sub-facets within the facet or dimension. It is generally familiar in elementary statistics that a dichotomous variable may be treated as either qualitative or quantitative. One final technical point about these alternative models is that they do not readily mix. If some of the principles of classification are quantitative (dimensions) and others qualitative (facets) the model becomes hard to conceptualize and even harder to investigate empirically.

Partly for this reason my first crude attempt at a taxonomy consists of four dichotomous contrasts; they are interpretable either as dimensions or facets.

Further thinking and development may lean in one or other direction, or possibly necessitate a mixed model. The four contrasts are:

(1) Criterion-referenced versus norm-referenced (cf. Ward, 1970).
(2) Actual versus potential.
(3) Ability versus non-cognitive qualities.
(4) One-shot versus sequential.

The distinction between criterion-referenced and norm-referenced procedures is an important one, and visible in both selection and assessment. Entry to most American and French universities depends upon reaching a certain specified academic standard—graduation from High School or the acquisition of a Baccalauréat. British universities also apply a minimum standard in terms of G.C.E. 'A' levels, but attainment of it by no means ensures acceptance, especially in popular subjects. In some cases, less than one in ten qualified applicants will be accepted by a particular university department. The same distinction is equally crucial in examinations, though it is usually difficult to determine which principle is operating. Boards of examiners may either attempt to carry in their heads an ideal standard from year to year, or they may reckon that one year's candidates are very much like another's and award a relatively constant number of passes (or of firsts, seconds, etc.). Either procedure is open to criticism, and some kind of compromise between the two principles is probably most common in practice.

The second contrast is almost self-explanatory. In some selection situations, the emphasis is mainly on what the candidate has so far achieved; in others future potentialities are the main consideration. One would suppose, because of the limited time-span of individual human development that the later in life the selection takes place and the older the candidates the more necessary it becomes to consider achievement *vis-à-vis* potential. Higher education lies somewhere midway on this continuum, between selection for secondary school and promotion to management.

The distinction between selection primarily in terms of ability and primarily in terms of personality or motivation is again conceptually clear enough, although very complex in actual practice. It is more natural to treat this as a system of facets than as a single dimension, since each of the main categories readily can be (and has been) broken down into subclasses. In practice, as in our last case, selection is not usually *exclusively* for intellect or for personality, though there are situations that approach these extremes.

The last contrast, between once-for-all assessment and a sequential series of hurdles, is clearly more like a dimension and admits of any number of gradations. In the context of higher education, one extreme is represented by continuous assessment, the other by the system prevalent, in the past at least at Oxford and Cambridge, in which it was often possible to obtain, say, a first-class honours degree by two or three months' super-intensive work at the end of a four-year course.

These suggestions form little more than a first thinking-aloud about the most plausible categories in which to classify methods of selection and assessment. Perhaps too an over-elaborate and formal set of dimensions would serve no very useful purpose; the social sciences have sometimes produced examples of 'taxonomy gone mad'. But an explicit formulation, however provisional and simplified may have this value—that each of the four contrasts represent a policy decision on the part of the selecting or assessing body and one that is often made almost by accident rather than considered intent. Nothing but good can come if selecting and examining boards formulate more explicitly the main criteria by which they are intending to operate.

References

BUTCHER, H.J. and RUDD, E., 1972, (Eds.), *Contemporary Problems in Higher Education* (London: Mc-Graw Hill).

CHRISTIE, T. and MILLS, J., 1973, *The use of a scholastic aptitude test in University Selection* (Department of Education, University of Manchester).

GLICK, P.C. and MILLER, H.P., 1956, Educational level and potential income. *American Sociol. Review*, **21**.

GUILFORD, J.P., 1967, *The Nature of Human Intelligence* (New York: McGraw-Hill).

KNAPP, J., SWANTON, N. and JEVONS, F.R., 1970 (Eds.), *University Perspectives* (Manchester: Manchester University Press).

PACE, C.R. and STERN, C.C., 1958, *A criteria study of college environment* (Syracuse University Research Institute).

PARNELL, R.W., 1951, Mortality and prolonged illness among Oxford undergraduates. *Lancet*, p. 731.

ROBBINS COMMITTEE, 1963, *Report on Higher Education* (London: H.M.S.O.).

VENABLES, E. and VENABLES, P., 1972, The study of higher education in Britain. Ch. 2 in Butcher and Rudd (see above).

WARD, J., 1970, On the concept of criterion-referenced measurement. *British Journal of Educational Psychology*, **40**, 314–323.

Peter Spurgeon holds a psychology degree. After initial training he did research into aspects of assessment in education at the London School of Economics. He is now a lecturer in the Applied Psychology Department, at the University of Aston in Birmingham, England.

2:2

Performance criteria in the context of teacher training

P. Spurgeon

Within the context of overall human resource utilization both the educational system and individual training programmes have vital roles to play. The educational system of any country has the broad task of developing and channelling human potential. The system's link with the world of work may in some instances be clear cut, but in other cases be somewhat tenuous. Such distinctions can often lead to a conflict of objectives, particularly in the sphere of higher education. Training programmes in contrast have a much more specific contact with the working world. Teacher training programmes have the difficult task of meeting both goals. Student teachers are still developing individuals requiring education in the widest sense but they are also moving towards a specific occupational context.

As a consequence of the Robbins Report (1963) the sphere of higher education, including teacher training, has seen a huge increase in student numbers. Clearly the teaching profession has benefited from such expansion in terms of the improved pupil-teacher ratio. A figure of 22 : 1 has recently been announced by the Department of Education as the national average pupil-teacher ratio. However, in the light of this improvement a government White Paper (1972) proposed a severe cut-back in the number of student teachers, i.e., a proposed reduction of one third of the present intake by 1980.

While the overall pupil-teacher ratio has certainly dropped it may well be that such a drastic cut-back is unwarranted at this stage. Initially it foregoes the opportunity of reducing the pupil-teacher ratio further and creating the possibility of small classes throughout state schools. It also seems to take less than adequate account of a number of other factors:

(1) The proposal to provide universal state nursery schools which will require a large force of as yet non-existent teachers.
(2) Educational priority areas still have considerable staffing shortages despite financial incentives to attract teachers.
(3) Wide discrepancies in the pupil-teacher ratio throughout different regions of the country.
(4) The very large comprehensive schools potentially create an impersonal system which may be solved by creating very small class sizes.
(5) Finally, a wastage rate in existing training colleges running between 6% and 10%. Although this is not excessive the impact of the new two year higher education diploma is unknown. It may be that many

potential teachers will leave after two years to take up alternative employment as recognition of the diploma increases.

Manpower planning considerations have typically taken a predominantly quantitative approach to such issues. There is also within teacher training a qualitative problem. Trained teachers themselves form part of the process by which human potential is developed and as such the quality of teachers produced is an important aspect. Such a view has gained in force in recent years as a result of a number of research reports. There is an increased awareness of the impact of individual teachers upon intellectual achievement and also upon a host of 'social' features—attitudes, motivations and aspirations (Kennedy and Willcutt, 1964; Yamamoto, 1963; Harvey *et al.*, 1968).

There has also been, especially within the primary sector, a drastic change in the role of the teacher. This change has occurred both from within the profession and externally. As the teacher's salary has lagged behind gains made by other occupational groups and ironically as the general level of education in the population has increased the status of the teacher has fallen. The teacher's relationship with parents is now much more open and demanding. There have also been changes in curriculum and teaching method which have altered the role of the teacher within the classroom. He is operating within a much more fluid, free environment with more open contact with pupils. Thus the teacher has a loosely defined and changing role to play placing great strain on his personal resources.

The classic response to such considerations would be to attempt to improve selection procedures in the hope of reducing wastage and raising the quality of teachers at intake. However, when we select we select for various tasks and these vary in complexity. It may well be that for less complex tasks where adequate and agreed taxonomies exist selection can make a significant contribution. Teaching, however, is an extremely complex task and selection in such circumstances becomes a less viable procedure. A great deal of work has been conducted on student teacher selection without producing results of great practical value (Halliwell, 1965).

The difficulties of selection stem largely from the problems of defining adequate criteria of teaching performance. The existing approaches to defining performance criteria may be stated briefly:

1. Expert judgement—this involves an expert (usually a college tutor, or headmaster) making an assessment of teaching performance. Although widely used the technique suffers from obvious subjectivity and considerable evidence of inconsistency (Start, 1968).

2. Pupil change—this involves any form of change in pupil ability (intellectual or social) that may be attributed to the influence of the teacher. However, the major problem lies in determining whether the teacher is the sole source of the change. A number of extraneous factors such as peer groups, parents, the media and a previous teacher may each be more important in the development identified.

3. Finally, rating scales present the most successful technique to date. These sub-divide into high and low inference type scales. Inference is concerned with the degree of interpretation allowed the observer between noting the actual behaviour and assigning a performance score. High inference scales typified by Ryans (1960) again suffer from the problem of subjectivity. The low inference

techniques such as Flanders (1966) are rigorous but limited in their capacity to encompass the entire teaching process.

It would appear that neither selection nor assessment methodology is equal to the task. However, the problems outlined remain. It may well be that the acquisition of teaching competence is too complex to be viewed as part of an input (selection)–output (assessment) continuum. The process of acquiring teaching competence is not fully understood thus making the transition from input to output an unreliable process. It may be seen more appropriately as a developmental process and one requiring constant monitoring rather than a final assessment situation.

As an initial study it was proposed that a modification of the Flanders interaction analysis system be used as a monitoring device. This modification developed by Hough (1967, Figure 1) is slightly larger and has the virtue of encompassing a greater range of teacher behaviours. Interaction analysis focuses upon verbal teaching behaviours and as a consequence certain important aspects of non-verbal communication are inadequately covered. However, the technique is relatively rigorous and does enable one to describe the behaviour of a particular student teacher at least within one defined sphere of activity. It is not proposed that the interaction analysis technique shall exist as the criterion for teaching performance, rather it should form part of the developmental monitoring.

A sample of 30 student teachers were observed on teaching practice using the modified Flanders technique. They were observed on different occasions and a matrix produced to describe their teaching pattern according to the procedure defined by Flanders. The first important hypothesis to be examined was whether it would be legitimate to join the different matrices for each subject and so have one matrix describing that individual's pattern of behaviour.

Table 1. Observational system (Hough, 1967)

TEACHER INDIRECT VERBAL INFLUENCE

1. *Affective clarification and acceptance*—acceptance, clarification and recognition of pupil's emotional states. Nonevaluative.
2. *Praise and reward*—statements with a positive value orientation directed at pupil behaviour.
3. *Cognitive and skill clarification and acceptance*—statements showing acceptance of, or clarification, of pupil ideas or performance. Nonevaluative.
4. *Teacher questions*—questions with a specific expected answer.
5. *Response to questions.*—direct answers to student questions.

TEACHER DIRECT VERBAL INFLUENCE

6. *Initiates information or opinion*—all statements regarding content or process that give information or opinion.
7. *Corrective feedback*—statements designed to indicate the inappropriateness or incorrectness of pupil behaviour. Confined to cognitive or skill areas.
8. *Requests and commands*—includes directions, requests and commands to which compliance is expected.
9. *Criticism and rejection*—statements that criticize or reject student ideas or behaviour without reference to clearly identifiable authority, i.e., definition, empirically validatable fact.

STUDENT VERBAL BEHAVIOUR

10. *Elicited responses*—conforming responses to narrow questions, commands and requests and highly predictable responses.
11. *Emitted responses*—responses to broad questions or requests.
12. *Student questions*—comments which ask for information, procedure or opinions of the teacher or another student.
13. *Silence*—all remaining components—directed practice, demonstration, confusion or silence.

The matrices were compared using the formula developed by Darwin (1959) which overcomes the inadequacies of X^2 in the comparison of matrix data.

Comparison of matrices

Likelihood Ratio Criterion (Darwin)

$$2[\underset{(K)}{\sum n_{jkl} \log_e n_{jkl}} - \underset{(L)}{\sum n_{j.l} \log_e n_{j.l}} - \underset{(M)}{\sum n_{jk.} \log_e n_{jk.}} + \underset{(N)}{\sum n_{j..} \log_e n_{j..}}]$$

(A dot in place of a suffix means that summation has been carried out over the replaced variable.)

It was found, for all subjects, to be legitimate to combine matrices into one matrix. Such a result is important in that although some variation occurs over a short time period (maximum five weeks) teachers exhibit a sufficiently similar pattern of behaviour for the different samples to be grouped.

Additional personality and attitudinal measures were gathered from the subjects and it is intended later to examine specific patterns of teacher behaviour and any possible relationship with 'social' variables. It would be useful also to examine expert judgement in conjunction with the interaction analysis data to determine whether a relationship exists between the overall teaching grade assigned and the pattern of teacher behaviours exhibited.

However, in conclusion as far as the present study is concerned it would seem a useful proposal in teacher training schemes to institute a constant monitoring programme. It is envisaged that this would incorporate a low inference rating technique such as Flanders Interaction analysis to provide reliable data and also micro-teaching facilities. Micro-teaching is essentially a form of teacher training involving the student in presenting a short lesson which is recorded on a closed circuit television system. A matrix of the student behaviour is made and this is discussed with the student when the recorded lesson is replayed, thus providing immediate feedback on the student's performance. Flanders has in fact been experimenting along similar lines in the United States of America in recent years.

In this way it is suggested a fuller understanding of the process of acquiring teaching competence would be achieved. As a student reaches a specific stage in his course he can be introduced to new teaching techniques and learn to use these in the monitored, controlled situation under the direction of his tutor. Such a procedure would also hopefully lead to a clearer definition of performance criteria used in assessing teacher effectiveness which could then be linked to additional criteria such as pupil development.

References

DARWIN, J.H., 1959, Note on the comparison of several realizations of a Markov Chain. *Biometrika*, **46**, 412–419.

EDUCATION: A Framework for Expansion. Cmnd. 5174 HMSO 1972.

FLANDERS, N.A., 1966, *Interaction analysis in the classroom* (University of Michigan, School of Education).

HALLIWELL, K., 1965, An investigation into the validity of methods of student selection for teacher training in a training college. *Ph.D., University of Sheffield.*

HARVEY, O.J., PRATHER, M.S., WHITE, B.J. and HOFFMEISTER, J.K., 1968, Teachers' beliefs, classroom atmospheres and student behaviour. *Amer. Educ. Res. J.*, **5**, 151–166.

HOUGH, J.B. and AMIDON, E.J., 1967, Interaction Analysis: Theory, Research and Application (Addison-Wesley).

KENNEDY, W.A. and WILLCUTT, H.C., 1964, Praise and blame as incentives. *Psychol. Bull.*, **62**, 323–332.
ROBBINS COMMITTEE REPORT ON HIGHER EDUCATION, 1963, (H.M.S.O.).
RYANS, D.H., 1960, *Characteristics of teachers, their description, comparison and appraisal* (Washington D.C.), American Council of Education.
START, K.B., 1968, *Selection, Training and Professional Progress of Teachers* (University of Manchester).
YAMAMOTO, K., 1963, Relationship between creative thinking abilities of teachers and achievement and adjustment of pupils. *J. Exp. Educ.*, **32**, 3–25.

Professor Daniëls holds the chair of Organizational Psychology at the Department of Industrial Engineering, University of Technology, Eindhoven (The Netherlands). He started his career as an industrial psychologist with K.L.M. Airways. Afterwards he was Head of Research, later Director of a private consultant institute. He teaches part-time at the Royal Netherlands Military Academy.

Dr. M.A.J. Van de Sandt holds sociology degrees of the University of Nymegen (The Netherlands). For some years he did personnel research in a large industrial firm. Now he teaches social psychology at the Royal Netherlands Military Academy (Breda) and is head of the Educational Research Department of that institute.

2:3

Military training and academic studies at a military academy

M. J. M. Daniëls and M. A. J. Van de Sandt

Introduction

Although since its foundation in 1828 the Royal Netherlands Military Academy has experienced a number of changes, probably none has so deeply affected both the structure of the education and the organization of the institute, as the reform in the early sixties.

Before that the education at the Academy was regarded as higher vocational training, offering a mainly technical and practical preparation for the officer's profession. The main objective of the re-organization was to give the Academy a firm scientific basis. For the technical Arms and Services this meant an upgrading of the technical education. Further, social and economic sciences were added to the curriculum, providing the foundation for the training in military leadership and management for the traditionally non-technical Arms and Services. Thus the Academy became more like a branch of higher education (Van Doorn, 1965). Breadth and depth of the subjects are still primarily determined by the supposed needs of the armed forces, i.e., by the demands to be made on the future officer of Army and Air Force. However, an analysis of the functions which ought to lead to a definition of these demands, has never been undertaken.

The re-organization of the education led to a plurality of objectives. Besides 'offering military professional knowledge and skills' a new objective appeared: 'giving a basic academic knowledge and fostering academic attitudes'.* This plurality of objectives is also reflected in the present organizational structure of the Academy. Organizationally academic studies and military training are completely separated. Academic education is given in five departments: military science and general education, which are compulsory for all cadets; a technical, a social and a financial department, providing specialized studies for

* From the *Study Guide of the Royal Netherlands Military Academy* (1972–73), pp. 9–11.

cadets of different Arms and Services.* With the exception of the department of military science each of these departments has been placed under the direction of civilians, while the teachers are mostly civilians too.† Military training takes place in the so-called cadets' battalion, naturally under military command and by military instructors. For the greater part it is also separated from the academic studies as to time and place.‡

The accentuation of the academic aspects of the officer's education and the rather sharp separation of military training and academic studies caused a number of educational and organizational problems, as was shown by a survey-investigation carried out in 1970.

In this investigation three populations at the Academy: cadets, officers and civilian teachers, were asked the following questions:

(1) Which of the two main elements of the officer's education in their opinion should be the most important in principle: military training or academic studies.

(2) Whether they thought that in fact too little, too much or just the right amount of attention was given to either of these two elements.

(3) Questions mentioned under (1) and (2) were also asked with regard to 20 sub-elements, into which 'military training' and 'academic studies' were subdivided.

(4) The opinions of the three populations were asked about the relevance of the academic studies to the cadet's future professional duties.§

(5) The cadets also took a study motivation test.¶

Now we shall briefly mention some results of the investigation. On that basis a number of problems can then be formulated.

I. Results of the investigation

(*a*) *The structure of the education*

As Table 1 shows, over 50% of the cadets think the military training the most important element of the education, against only 34% who think the academic

* In the department of military science lectures are given on strategy, military history, tactics, logistics and military law. In the department of general education the subjects are political science, international affairs, history and modern languages. The department of technical sciences has a five-year training-course for cadets of a technical Service as well as a four-year training course for Infantry-, Cavalry- and Artillery-cadets and for Air Force cadets of the Flying and the General Services (dependent on preliminary education). The department of social sciences is meant for cadets of a supporting Service (Army Service Corps, Transport) as well as for Infantry-, Cavalry- and Artillery-cadets and for Air Force cadets of the Flying and the General Services (dependent on preliminary education). It is a four-year course. The department of military finance has a course for cadets of the Finance Corps only. It takes five years.

† The ratio between the number of civilian teachers and the total number of teachers is 9 : 10 in the department of general education, 29: 36 in the department of technical sciences, 14 : 19 in the department of social sciences, 7: 9 in the department of military finance.

‡ The military training starts with a basic training during the first four months after arrival, to be followed by the first term of the academic studies in January of the first year. At the end of each of the first three years the general military training is resumed for a period of two months. It comprises among other things endurance marches, fieldcraft, combat-training with the commandos, practical leadership training and—at the end of the second year—a posting with a unit of the Arm or Service chosen. The entire last year of the education is devoted to the training in the special techniques of the cadet's Arm or Service, which generally takes place entirely outside the Academy.

§ The opinions on the relevance of the academic studies were measured by means of a Likert-type scale, consisting of 10 items.

¶ The study motivation of the cadets was measured by a scale of 42 items, derived from Crombag (1968). For the study motivation of cadets more fully, see Van de Sandt (1972).

studies the most important.* When asked on which elements of the education they wanted to lay special emphasis, a large majority appeared to want to have the military aspect more accentuated, against less than half wishing to accentuate the academic studies more. So in the opinion of a large number of cadets the military training does not get the right amount of attention in view of its primary importance.

Table 1. Opinions on the structure of the education

Population	*Elements of the education*	*Most important element of the education*	*Desired emphasis*			
			More (score 3)	*Equal (score 2)*	*Less (score 1)*	*Mean score*
Cadets (N=438)	Military training	54%	62%	21%	17%	2·47
	Academic studies	34%	48%	24%	28%	2·17
Officers (N=71)	Military training	73%	79%	13%	8%	2·73
	Academic studies	24%	27%	36%	37%	1·90
Civilian teachers (N=55)	Military training	66%	44%	45%	11%	2·42
	Academic studies	31%	76%	15%	9%	2·74

They asked especially for more Arms or Service training, more or longer postings with a unit and more practical military exercises.

From these data—corroborated by a replication of the investigation in 1972 (see Appendix)—one may conclude that there is considerable discrepancy between the wishes of the cadets and the reality of the education as seen by them. The conviction that academic studies are indispensable for a future officer—a conviction underlying the re-organization in the sixties—is apparently not shared by all cadets. The practical military element, on the other hand, is in the opinion of many cadets too much neglected.

Probably these wishes reflect the expectations the cadets had when entering the Academy. In that case the education is for them a source of frustration.

The officers, on the whole, think military training even more important than the cadets do. Also to an even higher degree than the cadets the officers think the military element should be stressed more, while in their opinion the academic studies should receive rather less attention.

Finally, the civilian teachers hold quite different views. It is true that a majority of them also designate the military training as the most important element, but only a minority think it necessary to put more emphasis on the military training.

Though, on the other hand, only a minority of the civilian teachers think the academic studies the most important aspect, yet a large majority of them believe that at present insufficient attention is paid to it.

(b) *Two types of cadets and officers*

Further analysis demonstrated that—among cadets as well as among officers—the data presented above are not only mutually connected, but are also related with other data, which corroborate the different opinions (Mans and Van de Sandt, 1971). The cadets who think the military training most important, wish

* The remaining 12% designated other elements of the education as the most important ones, such as physical training or Cadets' Fraternity life.

to lay much more emphasis on that element and on the whole they find the attention actually given to the academic studies satisfactory (Table 2, column 3).

Posting with a unit and Arms or Service training are in their opinion the most important sub-elements of the education (column 4). The greater part of them think the academic studies not very relevant to their future profession (column 5) and—not surprisingly—they show a relatively low study motivation (column 6).

Table 2. Two types of cadets and officers

Population	*Most important element of the education (sub-populations)*	*Desired emphasis on Military training (mean score on scale 1–3)*	*Desired emphasis on Academic studies (mean score on scale 1–3)*	*Most important sub-element of the education*	*Relevance of academic studies (mean score on scale 1–7)*	*Study motivation (mean score on scale 1–6)*	*Types*
(1)	(2)	(3)		(4)	(5)	(6)	(7)
Cadets ($N=438$)	Military training ($N=238$)	2·78	1·93	Posting with a unit and Arms or Service training	3·71	3·56	Military orientation ('hero')
	Academic studies ($N=151$)	2·05	2·62	Studies in specialized department	4·15	3·91	Academic orientation ('manager')
Officers ($N=71$)	Military training ($N=52$)	2·87	1·67	Arms or Service training	4·02	—	Military orientation ('hero')
	Academic studies ($N=17$)	2·35	2·59	Studies in specialized department	4·59	—	Academic orientation ('manager')
Civilian teachers ($N=55$)	Military training ($N=34$) Academic studies ($N=16$)	2·42	2·74	Studies in specialized department	4·82	—	Academic orientation

The cadets who think the academic studies the most important (Table 2, second row), want more attention to be given to that element and consider the military training sufficiently accentuated. The specialized studies in their own department are in their opinion the most important sub-element.

More frequently they have a favourable opinion of the relevance of the studies and, on an average, they show a higher study motivation.

Similar interrelations could be demonstrated among the officers.

On the basis of these interrelations we came to a description of *two types* of cadets and officers: those with a *military orientation* and those with an *academic orientation*. In these types are reflected two different views of the education of the career officer. One view puts the emphasis on the practical military aspects; academic studies are thought to be less relevant to the future professional practice of the cadets (with the exception of typically military science).

The other view stresses the academic studies, especially those in the specialized department of study, which are regarded really relevant to the officer's profession. From other data we were able to infer that the academic type is more military oriented than the military type is academically oriented.

Among the civilian teachers such a difference in orientation could not be demonstrated. Their opinions correspond—as might be expected—to a high degree with those of the academically oriented cadets and officers.

It is tempting to connect the two views of the officer's education with the two conceptions of the officer's profession, described by Janowitz (1961) as the 'heroic leader' and the 'military manager' respectively (Cf. Van Doorn, 1969 and Kourvetaris, 1971).

Not accidentally, we found the military-type cadet—corresponding with the hero-type officer—most frequently among the cadets of the tactical Arms (Infantry, Cavalry, Artillery), irrespective of their year or department of study, for they are destined for command functions with the troops.*

The academic type is most frequent among the cadets of the Finance Corps, again in all years of study. Among the cadets of the technical Arms and Services, the two types are represented in about the same degree (Table 3).

Table 3. Distribution of types of cadets over Arms and Services, years of study and departments of study

Types of cadets	*Arms and Services*	*Years of study*	*Department of study*
Military orientation	Tactical Arms	all	Social sciences/ Technical sciences
	Logistic Services	1st	Social sciences
	Operational Services AF	1st	Social sciences
Academic orientation	Finance Corps	all	Military finance
	Logistic Services	2nd–4th	Social sciences
	Operational Services AF	2nd–4th	Social sciences/ Technical sciences
Both orientations	Technical Arms and Services	all	Technical sciences

For the officers, belonging to one or the other type proves to a high degree to be related to the element of education in which they find their occupation. Officers who are engaged in military training, are clearly more militarily oriented; those who occupy themselves with the academic studies, have a stronger academic orientation.

(c) *Compatibility of military and academic objectives*

Only among officers and civilian teachers we investigated the opinions about the compatibility, in fact and in principle, of the two main dimensions of the education at the Academy: the military dimension and the academic dimension.

On the whole they hold a rather negative view of this compatibility (Table 4, column 2). It is true, the objections concern the actual co-ordination of the two aspects rather than their fundamental compatibility.† Especially the greater part of the civilian teachers think in principle the demands of academic studies to be very well compatible with those of a military training (column 3).

* A similar result was obtained by Lovell (1964) among the cadets of West Point.

† Measured by means of a Likert-type scale, consisting of five items. Four of these items concern the actual co-ordination, one the fundamental compatibility of the two dimensions. For this last item the results have been reproduced separately in column 3 of Table 4.

Table 4. Opinions on the relations between military and academic dimension

Population	*Coexistence of military and academic dimension (mean score on scale 1–7)*	*Compatibility of military and academic dimension (mean score on scale 1–7)*	*Role performance of (mean score on scale 1–7)*		*Taking account of (mean score on scale 1–7)*	
			Officers	*Civilian teachers*	*The academic studies by Officers*	*The military training by Civilian teachers*
(1)	(2)	(3)	(4)		(5)	
Officers (N=71)	3·73	4·82	4·43	3·95	4·73	3·28
Civilian teachers (N=55)	3·84	5·57	3·72	4·52	3·72	4·63

The difficulties in the relations between the military and the academic dimensions also appear in the way officers and civilian teachers think about their own and each other's role performance, especially with regard to mutual communication and co-ordination.* Nearly half of both officers and civilian teachers are apparently dissatisfied with the role performance of the other group. This dissatisfaction concerns in the main the mutual exchange of information and the willingness to take account of each other's part in the education. It is striking that they are clearly more satisfied with their own role performance than with that of the other group. When asked about the role of the officers, the opinions of the officers are more favourable than those of the civilian teachers. When, on the other hand, asked about the role of the civilian teachers, the opinions of the civilian teachers are more positive than those of the officers (column 4).

Officers and civilian teachers hold different opinions about the degree in which they take account of each other's part in the education. Most officers think the civilian teachers show too little consideration for the demands of the military training, while most civilian teachers think themselves to do so sufficiently. On the other hand, most civilian teachers think the officers too little concerned with the demands of the academic studies, while most officers think themselves to do so sufficiently (column 5).

II. The problems specified

The results of the investigation described so far, enable us to come to a formulation of a number of educational and organizational problems with which the Academy is confronted:

(1) Among the different groups concerned with the education widely divergent opinions exist regarding the desirable *contents of the career officer's education.* Most cadets and officers would like the military aspects to be given greater emphasis. On the other hand, a smaller part of the cadets and of the officers, as well as most civilian teachers would like to accentuate the academic studies. The importance of an

* Investigated with the aid of a Likert-type scale, consisting of six items, among other things concerning the willingness to inform each other about each other's part in the education, to co-ordinate these parts or at least to take them into account, to be open to each other's ideas, wishes and complaints.

academic preparation for the officer's profession is apparently not recognized by all cadets and officers to the same degree as meant by the planners of the programme.

(2) A crucial problem concerns the *relevance of the academic studies* to the future professional duties of the cadets. We saw that many cadets think the academic studies to be not very relevant. In this respect, however, the opinion of the academically oriented cadets is much more favourable than that of the militarily oriented cadets. Almost the same can be said about the officers. So the strong emphasis many cadets and officers would like to lay on the military aspects, turns out to go together with the conviction that the academic studies correspond insufficiently with the demands of their professional practice.

(3) The opinions the cadets have regarding the relevance of the academic studies prove to be correlated with their *study motivation*: the less favourable the cadets' opinions regarding the relevance, the lower their study motivation.

(4) Although most officers and civilian teachers think the demands of an academic and a military education compatible in principle, they criticize the actual *co-ordination of the two dimensions*, although from different angles. Many officers think the academic studies correspond insufficiently with the military training. Many civilian teachers consider the applying of non-academic (i.e., military) criteria besides academic ones an impediment to the functioning of the Academy as an institute of higher education.

(5) Both officers and civilian teachers are fairly dissatisfied with the *role performance* of the other group, especially with regard to communication and co-ordination. Many officers think the civilian teachers don't inform themselves sufficiently about the demands of the officer's profession and don't take them sufficiently into account.

Conversely, many civilian teachers think they are insufficiently informed about the objectives of the military training, and in their opinion the officers are insufficiently aware of the demands of the academic studies.

Many of the problems mentioned can be seen as interferences between two sub-systems within the Academy: a military and an academic one.

Each of the two sub-systems has its own environment from which they derive their values and norms: the armed forces and the institutes of higher education. These norms often don't run parallel, could in some cases even be conflicting, e.g., when academic freedom interferes with the restraints of the military organization. The fact that military training and academic studies form completely separated organizational hierarchies, only meeting at the very top, makes a solution of social interferences between the two sub-systems the more difficult.

III. Implications for educational policy

The complex of problems and their interrelations provide a number of clues for some practical implications:

(1) To further the study motivation of the cadets it will be necessary to improve the *relevance of the academic studies* to the future professional practice of the cadets. But it will also be necessary to make the cadets more *aware* of the relevance of academic aspects to the whole of their education and to their future profession. This concerns in particular the cadets of the tactical Arms, who are characterized by a rather negative opinion about the relevance of the study and a relatively low study motivation.

It is doubtful whether the image they have of the officer's profession is still in accordance with reality. It rather seems that the modern commanding officer, too, is developing into a 'military manager', for whom academic qualities, as well as 'heroic' ones, are indispensable.

(2) The relevance of the academic studies would greatly benefit from a better *co-ordination between military training and academic studies*. The development of military skills and the confrontation with military practice on the one side and the academic approach of relevant problems on the other should support each other. Recently therefore, the designing of a new educational model has been undertaken, in which academic studies and military training will be integrated to a high degree. The tension between theory and practice, between studies and training, can only be reduced if the two are conceived in one military-academic approach, aiming at the application of academic knowledge in practical military situations.

(3) The designing of such an educational model requires *the objectives of the education* to be made explicit. These objectives should be conceived as norms indicating what ought to be the results of the educational system. They should be formulated in terms of observable behaviour, for only then it is possible to judge at the end of the road to what extent the objectives have been reached, i.e., to what extent the behavioural changes aimed at have appeared. A research-project aiming at an adequate analysis of the objectives of the officer's education is in preparation.

In this project both the nature and the relative importance of the different—rather heterogeneous—objectives and sub-objectives will be considered.

An advantage not to be underestimated is that—unlike the future occupations of university students—the tasks of our graduates are known in detail. When changes occur, the education could be adapted if necessary.

Since our graduates are employed in the same organization, it is also easy to keep track of their achievements, so that an immediate feedback to the education is, in principle, possible (Daniels, 1965).

(4) The realization of an integrated educational model makes some *organizational adaptations* necessary. The interferences between military training and academic studies could probably be reduced considerably by improving the communication between the battalion and the academic departments. Military instructors and civilian teachers ought to inform each other thoroughly about the objectives and methods of each other's part in the education. Priority rules ought to

be set up for the cases in which the demands of the military training and of the academic studies may conflict (for instance in the case of decisions concerning the promotion of cadets to the next year of study).

Lastly, it would be desirable to create within the organizational structure of the Academy horizontal connections between the military and the academic segment.

Appendix

Some results of the replication of the investigation in 1972

For the replication of the investigation in 1972 a somewhat different questionnaire was used. The cadets were now asked to indicate, by means of a number of points, first, what weight each element should carry, and after that, what importance was given to it in the actual curriculum.

As Table A shows, the proportion of cadets that thought military training most important, was about equal to the proportion that thought academic studies most important.

Probably the dissimilarity to the results of 1970 can partly be explained by the fact that in 1972 the cadets could also designate the two elements as equally important, a possibility made use of by 10% of the cadets. Further it appears that the proportion of cadets thinking that the military training should be the most important aspect, is much larger than the proportion of them who think that this is shown by the actual curriculum. On the other hand, the proportion of cadets thinking that the first place in the curriculum has in fact been attributed to the academic studies, is much larger than the proportion of them who think that this should be so.

Table A. Cadet preferences

Most important element of the education	*Ideal curriculum (% of cadets)*	*Actual curriculum (% of cadets)*
Military training	34	4
Academic studies	38	75
Equal weight for both elements	10	5
Other elements (e.g., physical training, Cadet's Fraternity)	18	16

When we consider per cadet the difference between 'ideal curriculum' and 'actual curriculum', it appears that nearly three quarters of them attach greater importance to military training than is given to it in the actual curriculum, so they wish to lay more emphasis on military training. At the same time two-thirds of the cadets attach less importance to academic studies than is given to them in the actual curriculum, so they wish to lay less emphasis on them (Table B).

These results corroborate the conclusion of the 1970 investigation, viz., that there is considerable discrepancy between the wishes of the cadets and the reality of the education as they see it.

Table B. Ideal v. Actual

Elements of the education	*Desired emphasis (% of cadets) (Difference between ideal and actual curriculum)*		
	More (pos. difference)	*Equal (no difference)*	*Less (neg. difference)*
Military training	73	13	14
Academic studies	22	12	67

References

CROMBAG, H.F.M., 1968, *Studiemotivatie en Studieattitude* (Groningen:Wolters-Noordhoff).

DANIËLS, M.J.M., 1965, *Tussen Droom en Daad* (Between Dream and Reality), pp. 5–9 (Breda: Royal Military Academy).

JANOWITZ, M., 1961, *The Professional Soldier*, pp. 21 ff. (Glencoe: The Free Press).

KOURVETARIS, G.A., 1971, The Greek Army Officer Corps: its professionalism and political interventionism. In: Janowitz, M., and Van Doorn, J. (Eds.), *On Military Intervention*, pp. 153–201 (Rotterdam: Rotterdam University Press).

LOVELL, J., 1964, The professional socialization of the West Point cadet. In: Janowitz, M. (Ed.), *The New Military*, pp. 119–157 (New York: Russell Sage Foundation).

MANS, J.H. and VAN DE SANDT, M.A.J., 1971, A military academy in transition: a survey investigation. In: Van Gils, M.R. (Ed.), *The Perceived Role of the Military*, pp. 49–70 (Rotterdam: Rotterdam University Press).

VAN DE SANDT, M.A.J., 1972, Study attitude and study motivation of cadets at a military academy. In: Piret, R. (Ed.), *Proceedings of the XVIIth International Congress of Applied Psychology*, Vol. 1, pp. 273–278 (Brussels: Editest).

VAN DOORN, J.A.A., 1965, The Officer Corps: a fusion of profession and organization. *Archives Européennes de Sociologie*, **VI**, pp. 262–282.

VAN DOORN, J.A.A., 1969, The military profession in transition. In: Wilson, N.A.B. (Ed.), *Manpower Research*, pp. 451–459 (London: English Universities Press).

Professor Singleton holds physics and psychology degrees. After skills research at Cambridge, he worked on ergonomics and training problems in the shoe industry. Subsequently, he taught ergonomics and is now Head of the Applied Psychology Department at the University of Aston in Birmingham, England.

2:4

The role of the computer in vocational guidance

W. T. Singleton*

Introduction

The occupational situation in western countries has changed radically during this century. The system which contributed to and reflected a highly stable society involved a class structure and strong family traditions. Occupational choice depended primarily on the occupation of the father, secondarily on the occupation of other older members of the family and thirdly on other jobs regarded as confirming the individual's identity as a member of the class he was born into. This system led to an even distribution of abilities across all jobs and a minimization of competition between individuals. The development of a technologically based society resulted in the apparent need for some filtering of abilities to concentrate high ability individuals in particular kinds of jobs. There then developed a corresponding ethic that individuals of greater abilities were entitled to more extensive education, training, responsibilities and rewards.

The two world wars increased flexibility by disturbing the whole structure of national man power. They provided individuals on a large scale with an opportunity to rethink their occupational choice and to take appropriate action. There has been no such opportunity for 30 years now and during this period we have maintained in England an educational system based on selection at 11 and 18. The extent of filtering at these ages has depended more on available resources than on any consistent objectives or standards. The change in national occupational structure continues with some jobs reducing in either importance or availability while others correspondingly increase. The result is a gradual realization of the importance of vocational and occupational guidance. The young men and women leaving the educational system are well aware of the importance of guidance. So are their parents who would like to help but are not equipped to do so. Teachers are too busy and anyway have inadequate knowledge and training for this purpose. There is an almost desperate need for good professional services of this kind. An attempt to meet the need is made by the Local Government through the Youth Employment Services and by National Government through the Employment Exchanges and Occupational Guidance Units. The difficulty is the very high cost of providing effective and comprehensive services. This cost stems from the level of skill required of guidance

* Much of this paper is an extract from a paper commissioned by the Department of Employment, U.K., and presented in a more complete form in Singleton (1973). The views expressed are, of course, those of the author and are not necessarily those of the Department of Employment.

officers which can only be obtained by long training and experience and must there-after be adequately remunerated, the time required per client (a matter of hours) and the necessary backup services of tests, details of occupations and so on. These information services need to be constantly updated.

Such a guidance service can, in principle, be made more effective by reducing the time required to acquire guidance skills, by making it possible for less gifted individuals to perform the service adequately, by reducing the time required per client and by improving the structure and flow of information about the client and the available occupations. All these would be facilitated if we could clarify the content of the guidance task. That is if we could identify the necessary steps in the process, the information required at each step and the most appropriate structure of that information. This analytical process is identified in training technology as Task Analysis or Skills Analysis (Miller, 1962, 1967).

Task analysis of the guidance process

A task description consists essentially of a detailing of the outputs of a system, together with the corresponding detail of the information required in order to generate the specified outputs. In the case of guidance the outputs at a particular time are mostly to do with a particular individual, the client. The client requires some clarification of his long term goals in the occupational context, in other words ideas about his career. He may also need to make a more short term decision about the job or jobs he would like to pursue. Since a system of this kind must currently be designed on rather vague principles arrived at from previous experience rather than on scientific principles. The system should be designed to be self-adaptive. That is, it should be capable of being modified on the basis of further experience and thus another output is required—an assessment of how successfully it is performing as a system (Figure 1).

Figure 1. Task description

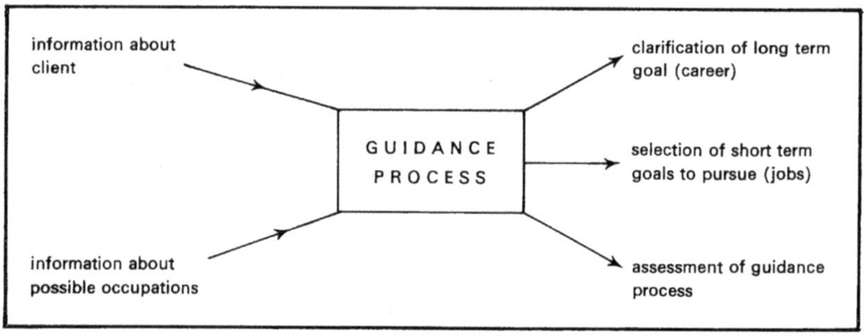

There are at least two individuals involved in the system, one client and one counsellor. The function of the counsellor is to receive information from the client and to integrate this with other information about occupations so as to present the client with a more structured picture on the basis of which he can make his own decisions (Figure 2).

This is not to suggest that the role of the counsellor is entirely passive. On the contrary he must play an active creative part in:

Figure 2. People-based functional diagram

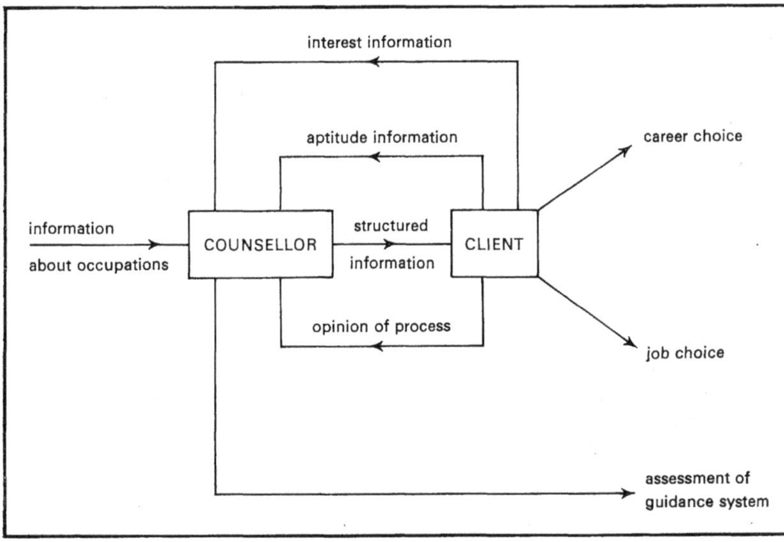

(*a*) ensuring that the client has presented all the relevant information about himself which he already possesses perhaps unknowingly
(*b*) using tests and other techniques to generate new information about the client
(*c*) conducting an intelligent search and selection amongst all potentially available occupations
(*d*) perhaps indicating his own opinion about the relative suitability of a number of selected occupations.

Nevertheless as a matter of principle he will leave the final decision to the client.

The client participates in this process in order to gain new information about himself and about occupations and to receive an experienced, unbiased, unemotional presentation of the total situation as the counsellor sees it.

The counsellor is also involved in training other counsellors, facilities to do this also need to be built into the system which is now client/computer/counsellor/trainee counsellor.

Having structured the problem so far by the use of a technique borrowed from the training specialists we now need to consider the more precise separation and allocation of functions within the system. For this purpose we borrow a technique from ergonomics known as the 'allocation of function between man and machine' (Singleton, 1974).

The role of the computer

The widespread use of computers both as data stores and as aids in human decision-making has provided generalizations which are applicable in the guidance situation.

Inevitably the computer reinforces the trend which is there already, to rely on numerical data and to take these data out of context. This in turn leads to the acquisition of data on the basis of ease of measurement rather than relevance and when finally decisions are to be made there will be an over-weighting of factors which have been thus quantified. For example, a well-designed personnel appraisal form contains details of when and under what circumstances it was completed and who completed it. This is the context which is often lost when the information is computerized. The information about the subject will usually be of two kinds, ratings of various dimensions along scales (e.g., general competence on a scale from 0–4 with 0 meaning quite unsuitable to 4 meaning supremely good at the job), together with verbal details in which the assessor may comment on the suitability of the dimension, the confidence he attaches to his own judgement, qualification of the total rating on the grounds that the rating applied to some aspects but not others, e.g., in terms of competence the subject may be good at the interpersonal relationship aspects of his job but poor at the administrative aspects. When the information is computerized the temptation will be to enter for that subject only the dimension and the rating and to discard all the verbal comments. When a decision has to be made about that subject, perhaps years later by a promotion board, the computer print-out will reveal nothing except a set of ratings which will certainly be inadequate and may also be quite misleading. The problem here is that an existing procedure has simply been mechanized. The remedy is to avoid this method of introducing computers. It is essential to re-appraise the situation and review the procedure before introducing computerization (Rosove, 1967).

Even then the computer often gains an unfair advantage. When the decision has to be made about whether to invest in a computer system or to justify an investment decision already made, it is common practice to compare the new revised and improved system including the computer with the old system which was probably out of date anyway. Comparing the best of one kind with the worst of another is not a fair or effective process. It is often salutary to compare the potential performance of a computerized system with what could be achieved by making a similar investment in re-analysing, redesigning, retraining and so on for a manual system.

These difficulties can be reduced by attempting a direct comparison of these two basic ways of doing things, that is by employing people or by employing hardware. This is best done not for the complete task but for the separate functions within tasks. This is the process known in design circles as 'allocation of function' between man and machine. Starting with the general properties of men and machines it is agreed that machines are superior in speed of work, in the generation and application of power, in consistency and in the abilities to do several things at a time, i.e., 'multichannel activity'. Men on the other hand are superior in versatility of their locomotor and manipulative abilities, in the sensitivity and range of their input devices (eyes and ears) and in their ability to deal with unpredicted or unpredictable situations. Men also provide the creativity in a system, that is, they adapt and improve systems either as the environment changes or simply to improve the system performance on the basis of experience. There are an intermediate range of functions where relative abilities have to be agreed in more detail. Considering memory, machines are better for short term storage and for literal reproduction, human memories are better for principles and strategies and in terms of cross-referencing facilities. On computation machines are fast and accurate but poor at error correction, men are the opposite. In reasoning machines are better for deduction and men for induction. This situation is summarized in Figure 3.

Figure 3. Allocation of function between man and machine

MACHINE ADVANTAGES		MAN ADVANTAGES
CLEAR	PARTIAL	CLEAR
Speed of operation Generation and application of power Consistency Multi-channel activity	MEMORY Short-term / Principles and Literal / Strategies COMPUTATION Fast / Slow Accurate / Error prone Poor at error correction / Good at error correction REASONING Deductive / Inductive	Versatility of locomotion and manipulation. Sensitivity and range of input systems. Coping with unpredicted and unpredictable. Creativity

Converging on the more specific issue of machines as aids in data processing, i.e., computers, the general situation remains as described above. The computer is fast, accurate and good at literal storage, the man is good at error detection, at versatility in access to stored materials and at detection of patterns. The machine is free from emotional responses, laziness, fatigue and dishonesty. The man is good at making decisions which involve a complex weighting of many factors, he is easy to re-programme and he has a high tolerance of ambiguity, vagueness and uncertainty (Figure 4). In terms of creativity he has

Figure 4. Allocation of function between man and computer

MACHINE ADVANTAGES	MAN ADVANTAGES
Speed Accuracy Storage of data	Versatility of data access Error detection Storage of principles Decision making involving weighting of many factors. Easy to re-programme Provides design creativity
free from: Emotional responses Laziness Fatigue Dishonesty	high tolerance of: Ambiguity Vagueness Uncertainty

the ability, while performing in a system, to assess its effectiveness in relation to known objectives and he will modify the objectives or the procedures to improve the service provided by the system. If he is reasonably motivated he will do this even though it is not part of his accepted responsibility. Men never simply 'do as they are told' and although this may sometimes be a liability it is more often their greatest asset.

Converging again, on to the particular case of the guidance situation we have at least two 'men' involved, a client and a counsellor together with a computer. In principle it is possible to eliminate the counsellor but in view of the need for versatility and the need to deal with the unpredictable, he is obviously going to be required at least as a backup service. His role is also essential as a continuous observer and improver of the system performance. We do not know very much about the guidance process, with or without computers and it is imperative that there should be intelligent observers within the system assessing its utility and thinking of methods of improving it. On the other hand the potentiality for non-emotional interaction would suggest that the client should be in direct contact with the computer which itself is clearly best suited for the storage of data and for any deductive processes which can be identified in relation to vocations and occupations. The position so far arrived at is summarized in Figure 5.

Figure 5. Preliminary functional allocation for guidance systems

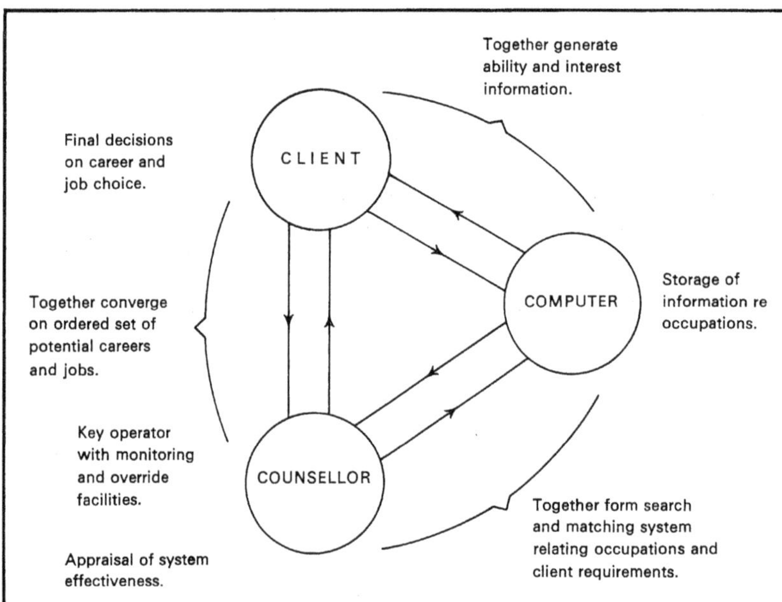

Apart from a comparison of properties the allocation of functions between man and machine depends on their relative cost and on the provision of integrated and graded tasks for operators (in this case—counsellors). There is no realistic and systematic way of approaching the cost problem. The difficulty is that 'Human asset accounting' is in its infancy (I.P.M., 1972). We are not yet able to quantify the cost of successful and unsuccessful guidance. Thus, at present, decisions about the acceptable case for guidance systems remain political rather than economic. Clearly, however, there is scope for research here perhaps by the introduction and modification of 'cost-benefit analysis' to the guidance situation.

The concept of graded and integrated tasks implies that in large systems at least, the tasks allocated to man should be of varying difficulty and responsibility to provide scope for individual differences of ability, experience and seniority. Nevertheless, each of these tasks must form an integrated whole so that the man is not a filler-in-of-gaps in the process carried out mainly by a computer. On the contrary the task of the computer is a filler-in-of-gaps in a process essentially carried out by the counsellor.

Taxonomic problems

The information flow within the triangle shown in Figure 5 depends on the provision of adequate ways of describing jobs and people. A description implies that the individual person or job is set within a context of all persons and all jobs. Both these contexts are enormous, there are in Britain about 25 million workers and if one wishes to be pedantic it can be said that they are all different and that they each have a job which is different from all other jobs. To operate within an information system of this kind the first essential is well defined classification schemes which provide some orderly structure.

This is a common problem in all biological sciences. A large variety of species have to be classified. The classification system will inevitably have a number of dimensions and the problem is to choose the minimum number of dimensions which will adequately describe all the species considered and also to select the dimensions with some sensitivity to the underlying natural origins and causes of the observable variety. This is the problem of devising a taxonomy. Any such taxonomy will inevitably result in some oversimplification and loss of detail. The art of designing such a scheme depends on achieving the right compromise between being parsimonious but precise, flexible but definitive. This applies to all three problems; the classification of jobs, the classification of people and the matching methods.

Parsimony is not a problem for the computer but it is for both the client and the counsellor. They need to be able to comprehend that part of the total job/person context in which they are operating for the benefit of the particular client. The degree of precision required is difficult to specify. Without some precision the whole system is useless, one may as well assign people to jobs randomly yet too much precision would not only be prohibitively expensive and probably unattainable but it is not even necessary. Individuals are adaptable, they are moderately successful as judges of their own abilities and interests in the future. This is the beginning of flexibility but there are other aspects. The job can be modified to suit the man by work design and ergonomics, the man's abilities can be modified to suit the job by further training. There is a complex relationship between interests and expectancy. Both may be modified by race, nationality, class, family and area as well as education (Lancashire, 1971). In other words, most people are reasonable and realistic. Their expectancies, interests and abilities are more or less in line with what they want to do, what they can do and what they consider they would be interested in doing.

Interests and preferences in fact need to be accepted with caution not only for the above reasons but also because they may be based on false premises. School leavers and others of limited knowledge of particular occupations may state an interest in and preference for certain occupations based on a total misconception of the jobs within that occupation.

The definitive nature of the scheme is bound to be limited. People and jobs are not such that comprehensive but exclusive categories are possible. The best we can hope for is overlapping sets. To put it another way, the dimensions will never be orthogonal. This implies that the complete categorization cannot be left to the computer, human judgements on the part of the counsellor or the client or both will be required to place an individual along and within the chosen dimensions.

The expectancy problem arises in relation to jobs as well as people. For example employers or other job designers will often state minimum educational qualifications for particular jobs. This choice is inevitably subjective and arbitrary and is often based not only on the job requirements but also on the state of the relevant labour market. For example a secretary in India is usually male and a university graduate but a job designer for essentially the same job in Europe will probably specify that candidates should be female and non-graduates. Again this kind of uncertainty and flexibility can be coped with by people but not by computers operating independently.

It is clear that specifying people and jobs is not going to be easy. The obvious way to start on the problem is to consider what occupational psychologists have achieved so far.

Classification of people

It is worth noting that we are not attempting to classify people generally, merely in relation to work and even more particularly in relation to vocational guidance.

The operational problem is that one individual, the counsellor is faced with another individual, the client who he has never met before. The counsellor must establish mutual confidence, find out what is relevant to their joint operation and convey his findings to the client all as expeditiously, precisely and effectively as possible and with a minimum of skill required from the counsellor and a minimum of insight from the client. Here we can return to more orthodox approaches to guidance. In order to make a start we can temporarily set aside computer aspects and consider classical problems of how to interview efficiently. This problem has been studied and developed mainly by experience but with some research support from occupational psychology (Shouksmith, 1968).

The established approach is to use the 'seven-point plan' (Rodger, 1952) (Figure 6). This was an enormous step forward in the development of the interview method for guidance and selection. It has been used very widely. So much so, in fact, that it is now very difficult to change for the same reason that it is impossible to envisage changing a typewriter keyboard layout. It solves the operational problem of structuring the interview and does so at just about the right level in providing the interviewer with enough key-points without restricting too much his method or order of acquiring information. There is no significance in the order of the points and no implication of relative importance —this depends on the context in which it is used. Rather less desirably there is no indication of relative reliability of data and of different qualities of data—to take two extremes the answer to the questions about his education are of quite different reliability and subjectivity to questions about 'appearance and bearing'. This may not be of great consequence for a human assessor but it does mean that the system must not be directly computerized. Rodger attempts, somewhat apologetically, to supply a theoretical structure for the seven points by suggesting that occupational success depends on a primary split of external influences

Figure 6. The Seven Point Plan

1. PHYSICAL MAKE-UP

Has he any defects of health or physique that may be of occupational importance? How agreeable are his appearance, his bearing and his speech.

2. ATTAINMENTS

What type of education has he had? How well has he done educationally? What occupational training and experience has he had already? How well has he done occupationally?

3. GENERAL INTELLIGENCE

How much general intelligence can he display? How much intelligence does he ordinarily display?

4. SPECIAL APTITUDES

Has he any marked mechanical aptitude? manual dexterity? facility in the use of words? or figures? talent for drawing? or music?

5. INTERESTS

To what extent are his interests intellectual? practical-constructional? physically-active? social? artistic?

6. DISPOSITION

How acceptable does he make himself to other people? Does he influence others? Is he steady and dependable? Is he self-reliant?

7. CIRCUMSTANCES

What are his domestic circumstances? What do the other members of the family do for a living? Are there any special openings available for him?

(circumstances) and internal influences. The internal ones can be separated into the mainly physical and the mainly psychological and these latter in turn can be split two ways: cognitive and non-cognitive, natural and acquired. These result in the seven points in the way shown in Figure 7.

Nevertheless the seven-point plan is what Miller (1967) calls a descriptive non-rigorous taxonomy in contrast to the ideal of an explanatory rigorous

Figure 7. Occupational success related to the seven-point plan shown in Figure 6

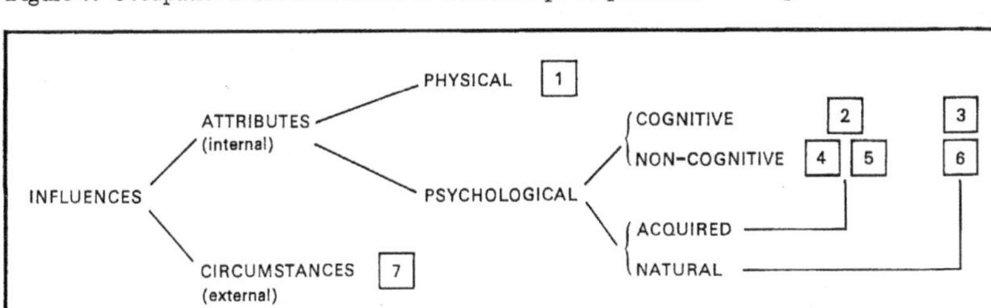

taxonomy. An explanatory taxonomy is almost a theory in that the classes imply some fundamental concepts about the system under study, e.g. as in the periodic table, rigorous means that the classes are mutually exclusive. The seven-point plan achieves neither of these standards. For face to face interview perhaps it does not matter that the twin problems of what we need to know and how we find it out tend to get inextricably mixed. When we introduce the computer, however, we must separate the problem of identifying the required information from the problem of acquiring the information. To put it in more operational terms, we need to separate the structure of the required information from the structure of the interview since we now propose to 'interview' by using conversational interaction between a computer and a client.

One approach to the question of what information is needed about a person in order to orientate him towards an appropriate job or occupation is to examine real situations where guidance, systematic or otherwise, has been successful and unsuccessful. That is, to compare the characteristics of people who have left a job for reasons other than promotion and were therefore presumably unsuccessful with others who have proved good at the job. It ought then to be possible to identify the critical characteristics or job decision factors which seem to determine success or failure at the job. Some work of this kind has been initiated (Lawrence, 1972). An alternative approach would be to attempt to correlate satisfaction and satisfactoriness in certain jobs with specifically psychological factors as measured by a variety of personality tests. If a relationship could be found between satisfaction and satisfactoriness in particular occupations and particular profiles of these factors then progress would have been made. Such a research project requires greater investment than the previous one and has not yet been initiated on any large scale in the U.K.

In studying the interaction between client and computer the required effort is development rather than research. An interrogation programme could be written and tried out on a great variety of clients and compared with results obtained from client counsellor interviews. This should lead to a progressive refinement of the interrogation system. Some attempt to do this has been made in America, e.g., Sanghary *et al.* (1966).

Classification of occupations

A penetrating and comprehensive review of the situation in this field has recently been carried out by Morgan (1972). He points out that occupational classification systems, by analogy with measuring scales, can be divided into four kinds: nominal, descriptive, relational and explanatory. Many systems have no more than nominal status as instruments of measurement although the more recent ones attempt to be descriptive and even relational. Almost all systems have been constructed on an intuitive basis. That is by thinking about the number of dimensions needed to establish classification. Some attempts have been made to use correlational techniques, e.g., Fleishman (1967), and there have been attempts, notably by McCormick and his associates at Purdue to identify more fundamental job dimensions using questionnaire techniques, e.g., McCormick *et al.* (1967).

The most comprehensive American scheme is that developed by the Department of Labor and known as D.O.T. (*Dictionary of Occupational Titles*) (1965). This is in two volumes, the first contains verbal descriptions of all jobs listed in alphabetical order. The second is more interesting from our point of view in that occupations are classified in terms of what is done and also in terms of worker requirements. What is done is classified in terms of the industry and the type of work. Worker requirements are categorized by training time, required aptitudes, temperament and physical capacity. Minimum levels of the attributes for average performance are given. These are mainly intuitively based although attempts are being made to obtain appropriate scores for as many jobs as possible on the General Aptitude Test Battery (G.A.T.B.) (1967). Working conditions are also described. Thus some attempt has been made to relate the general classification system to the needs of those concerned with selection, guidance and training.

The nearest British equivalent of this scheme is C.O.D.O.T. (1972) (Classification of Occupations and Dictionary of Occupational Titles). In terms of broad categories the two are compared in Figure 8. The C.O.D.O.T. numbering system attempts some rough grouping by level of skill, qualifications and functions but it is not precise in any of these respects.

Within the U.K. there are two other large scale projects to devise classification systems. One by the Department of Trade and Industry (D.T.I.) which attempts to distinguish purpose, function, level, skill and skill level and one by the Institute of Manpower Studies (I.M.S. S.O.C.) which has four basic criteria; kind of work, level of skill, level and job knowledge.

There is also an international system developed by the I.L.O. I.S.C.O. (International Standard Classification of Occupations) (Figure 8). This is not so comprehensive as the national schemes which is not surprising since it was deliberately designed to give guidance to national governments wishing to develop or review their own schemes. It is also intended as a means of identifying specific national occupations of international interest.

All these systems have been developed basically for statistical purposes. D.O.T. and C.O.D.O.T. are based on vast numbers of job descriptions obtained by observation and interview of people engaged in the occupations. For example the Department of Employment carried out about 20,000 job studies in order to arrive at their 3,500 occupations.

Relating people and work

Given that we have some data about an individual obtained by interview and by measurement of capacities—physical and intellectual and that we know something about jobs through some kind of dictionary of occupations we have established the two end points which are to be related by the guidance process.

Establishing the relationship requires that we start from each of the end points and move towards the other one. In the case of the individual we have to try to place him or her within a broader class or classes which are closer to the requirements of occupations. That is, we have to say what kind of person he or she is in terms which relate to occupations both for abilities and achievements and for aspirations and interests. Starting from the complete repertoire of occupations we have to reduce it to a comprehensible feasible set which the client can consider and, if possible, we have also to provide him or her with criteria for selecting within this set (Figure 9).

Classifications of people in relation to work

The nearest academic approach to this is through the various personality tests known as value, interest or preference measures. Each designer of such a test has made his own classification of the categories which he regards as correlating

Figure 8. American and British Occupational Classifications

D.O.T. (U.S.A.)	*9 one-digit divisions*	*84 two-digit divisions*	*603 three-digit divisions*	*21,741 occupations*
e.g.	2 Clerical and Sales	25 Sales and Services	258 Salesmen in printing and advertising	258·358 Advertising Sales Representatives and Solicitors (print and pub.)
	7 Bench Work	70 Fabrication, assembly and repair of metal products	701 Fabrication, assembly and repair of tools and related products	701·381 Saw Filer Tool Grinder
C.O.D.O.T. (U.K.)	*18 major groups*	*73 minor groups*	*381 unit groups*	*3,000 occupations*
e.g.	VII Selling Occupations	37 Sales Representatives	372 Sales Representatives (wholesale goods)	372·10 Sales Representatives (food, non alcoholic drinks)
	XIV Processing making and repairing	71 Metal Processing forming and treating	719 Metal Processing forming and treating not elsewhere classified	719·86 Rolling Mill labourer
I.S.C.O. (International)	*11 major groups*	*73 minor groups*	*201 unit groups*	*1,345 occupations*
e.g.	3 Sales Workers	3– 3 Salesmen, Shop assistants and related workers	3– 31 Salesmen and Shop assistants	3– 31·20 Salesmen (wholesale)
	7/8 Craftsmen, production–process workers and labourers not elsewhere classified	7– 3 Furnacemen, Rollers, Drawers, Moulders and related heat treaters	7– 33 Rolling mill operators (metal)	7– 33·50 Cold Rolling mill operator (metal)

Figure 9. Relating people and jobs

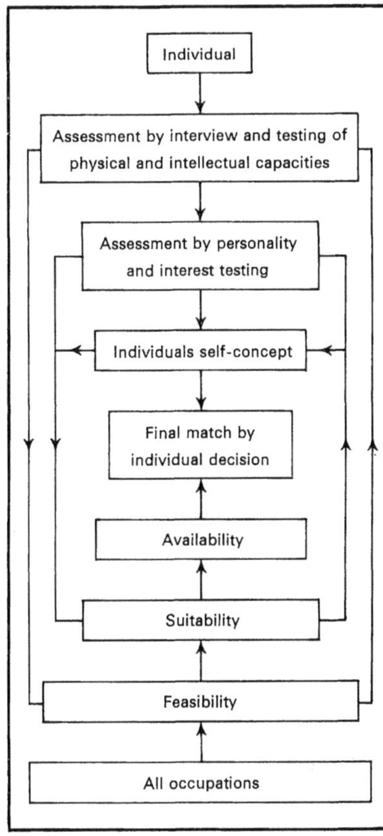

with his test measures. Sometimes this is done, as for occupational classification, by trying to think of the relevant categories first and then designing appropriate questionnaires, sometimes the questions have been rather loosely framed initially and categories have been identified by statistical techniques such as factor analysis. In neither case is there any safeguard that the categories identified form a comprehensive picture of the individual. It would therefore seem appropriate to examine all the taxonomies already developed and to try to integrate them into a comprehensive but reasonably parsimonious list. Their reappraisal and integration is another research and development project which would be timely and relevant to the general problem. One example of such a taxonomy is that used in the Kuder Preference Record (Kuder, 1956) and shown in Figure 10.

Availability of occupations

The final focusing on appropriate jobs is based on more dynamic criteria about particular jobs in that particular country or region or town. That is, factors such as:

Current shortages and surpluses.
Availability of training.

Conditions and rewards.
Possibilities of developments.
Prospects in terms of advancement.
Particular duties.
Particular companies with vacancies.

The computer support of a counsellor is particularly appropriate in this role since the computerized data is relatively easy to update continuously. Even so it is not a substitute for the awareness of the national and local position both currently and in terms of trends which is the particular forte of the skilled counsellor.

This is a relatively unexplored area and research is required to determine more precisely the 'allocation of function' between counsellor and computer and the associated problem of procedures for updating the computerized information.

Figure 10. The Kuder Preference Record

The Kuder Preference Record (Vocational)

1. Outdoor
2. Mechanical
3. Computational
4. Scientific
5. Persuasive
6. Artistic
7. Literary
8. Musical
9. Social Service
10. Clerical

The Kuder Preference Record (Personal)

1. Being active in groups
2. Familiar and stable situations
3. Working with ideas
4. Avoiding conflict
5. Directing others

Discussion

The possibility of introducing the computer into the guidance process has, to date, had mainly beneficial effects. Just as the introduction of teaching machines stimulated extensive research and thinking into the whole problem of teacher/learner communication so also will the computer stimulate more rigorous investigation of the counsellor/client relationship.

This is a potential danger in that if computers are introduced into guidance systems by superficial programming methods a lot of money will be spent and a great deal of damage could be done to the reputation of guidance and also to the general concept of computer aided decision-making. This is the standard dilemma of the applied psychologist. If he proceeds too slowly the problem will be taken out of his hands by others who perhaps do not have the same awareness of the variety and complexity of variables to be considered. The introduction of a computer always seems to have enormous momentum of its own. If on the other hand, he proceeds too quickly he is bound to make a lot of mistakes because of the range of expertise needed and the relative weakness of some of the relevant support subjects.

The guidance system is a nice example of the way in which human resource utilization problems cut across the traditional boundaries of disciplines. This paper has attempted to demonstrate that the investigator in this field needs to draw on the task analysis technique from training, the allocation of function technique from ergonomics, the broad technology of computer based information systems, the interview know-how of the occupational psychologist and the information about people in education and at work scattered between educationists, employers, applied psychologists, careers counsellors, man-power planners, demographers and others.

Computers can only work with numbers, numbers imply categories and categories must be based on sensitive taxonomies. Progress in this field depends on the basic taxonomies of jobs (what individuals do) of tasks (what has to be done) and of people (how we describe and distinguish individuals in the context of work).

References

C.O.D.O.T. (1972) Classification of Occupations and Dictionary of Occupational Titles (3 vols.). Department of Employment (London: H.M.S.O.).

D.O.T., 1965, Dictionary of Occupational Titles (2 vols.) *U.S. Dept. of Labor* (Washington: Government Printing Office).

FLEISHMAN, E.A., 1967, Performance assessment based on an empirically devised task taxonomy. *Human Factors*, **9**, 349–366.

G.A.T.B., 1967, General Aptitude Test Battery (4 vols.) *U.S. Dept. of Labor.*

I.P.M., 1967, *Human Asset Accounting* (London: Inst. of Personnel Management).

I.S.C.O., 1958, *International Standard Classification of Occupations* (Geneva: International Labour Office).

KUDER, G.F., 1956, *Kuder preference record—occupational* (Chicago: Science Research Association).

LANCASHIRE, R., 1971, Occupational Choice Theory. In: Warr, P.B. (Ed.), *Psychology at Work* (Harmondsworth: Penguin).

LAWRENCE, D., 1972, A revised proposal for a two year 'interview project'. *Applied Psychology Department, University of Aston.* Unpublished paper.

McCORMICK, E.J., CUNNINGHAM, J.W. and GORDON, G.C., 1967, Job dimensions based on Factorial Analysis of worker orientated job variables. *Personnel Psychology*, **20**, 417–430.

MILLER, R.B., 1962, Task description and analysis. In: Gagné, R.M. (Ed.), *Psychological Principles in System Development* (New York: Holt, Rinehart and Winston).

MILLER, R.B., 1967, Task Taxonomy: Science or Technology. In: Singleton, W.T., Easterby, R. and Whitfield, D. (Eds.), *Human Operator in Complex Systems* (London: Taylor & Francis).

MORGAN, T., 1972, Occupational Description and Classification. Air Transport and Travel Industry Training Board. *RRD19.*

RODGER, A., 1952, The Seven Point Plan. *Paper No. 1, National Institute of Industrial Psychology.*

ROSOVE, P.E., 1967, *Developing Computer based information systems* (New York: Wiley).

SANGHARY, J.W., FREISEN, D. and HURST, R., 1966, Auto Coun.: a computer based automated counselling simulation system. *Personnel and Guidance Journal*, **45**, 1, 6–15.

SHOUKSMITH, G., 1968, *Assessment through interview* (Oxford: Pergamon).

SINGLETON, W.T., 1973, Occupational classification and vocational guidance. *AP Report 46, Applied Psychology Dept., University of Aston in Birmingham.*

SINGLETON, W.T., 1974, *Man-machine systems* (Harmondsworth: Penguin).

M.C. Killcross holds a psychology degree and a post-graduate education qualification. After working in educational/occupational guidance and selection as a lecturer in the Applied Psychology Unit, University of Edinburgh, he moved to the Ministry of Education, Zambia, where for three years he was head of the Psychological Service. Since 1971 he has been Principal Psychologist in the Manpower Studies Section of the Army Personnel Research Establishment, c/o R.A.E., Farnborough, Hants, U.K., and concerned with research in psychological measurement.

Mr. Cassie graduated in Psychology just before the war. After a brief spell in industry he served in the Royal Air Force. Since 1945 he has been a Psychologist in Government Service and is now Head of Psychology at the Army Personnel Research Establishment.

2:5

The potential use of tailored testing for allocation to army employments

M. C. Killcross and A. Cassie

Introduction

Although one speaks of the Army as a collective unit, it does in fact embody a large range of occupations, skills and specializations. At the recruit selection stage the problems are of two main types: is the applicant suitable for the Army employment of his choice or—more difficult to answer—in which employment can the man's skills most effectively be developed and used, equally for himself and for the Army. With something like 100 different trades available it presents a sizeable problem in vocational allocation, particularly for the entrant who is not committed to a particular trade. In U.K. all Army recruits, outside Scotland, now go through a single central selection process where the main instruments in both the selection and the vocational allocation procedures are the interview and a conventional battery of paper-and-pencil cognitive tests. It is recognized that the tests and the battery represent something of a compromise between what is appropriate to aid the decision process and what is practicable for large group testing in a limited time. Each individual recruit presents an individual allocation problem for which the general purpose test battery is seldom the most effective instrument. Ideally each recruit should have his own test battery, constructed specifically to give the optimum measure for his particular abilities. Using conventional testing techniques this would be quite impossible unless each entrant were treated individually. However, tailored testing (T.T.)—the idea of measuring aptitude or attainment by a sequence of test items determined in turn individually and optimally for each person from a large item pool—presents a means of moving towards this ideal which may be feasible in a high volume centre.

The basis of T.T. is the existence of some built-in capacity for the adjustment of a testing procedure to the individual testee. Each person receives a test-treatment tailored to some extent to suit him: two other names given to this kind of adjustable procedure are individualized testing and adaptive testing. There are some parallels between T.T. and programmed teaching procedures.

One obvious variable in the possible approaches to T.T. is the degree of adjustment that the approaches allow. To take as an example a fairly sophisticated degree of tailoring, this would usually mean that some kind of testing terminal linked to a computer must be used. This testing terminal may be a TV screen and keyboard, for example; one test question from an available question stock is displayed on the screen and the testee keys in his answer. Which test question to display next is decided at the time on the basis of what is already known about the testee and especially on the basis of how he has done on the questions so far presented to him. Such a matching of test items to the individual testee on the basis of accumulating information is programmed into and carried out by the linked computer. Such a high degree of flexibility in putting a tailored test together demands, among other things a large available stock of questions—tried and tested questions of known characteristics. This item pool or item bank may take the form of a structured network which may be as shown in Figure 1. This shows the first five stages of a pyramid-shaped branching item network. All testees start with the same *start* question on the left and move through the network towards the right taking upward or downward courses depending on whether their answers to questions are right or wrong.

After the five stages shown, six levels of differentiation or scores may be noted—as given at the right of Figure 1. Many testees could work simultaneously at individual terminals and go their individual ways through the item network.

Figure 1. A branching item network

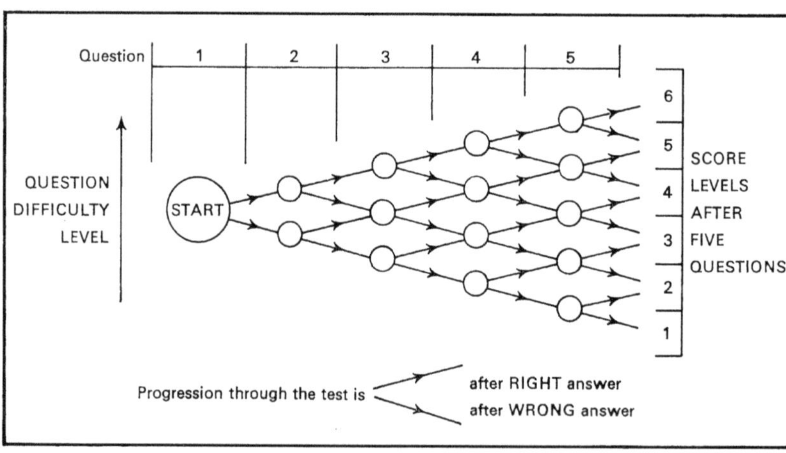

In contrast to this high degree of flexibility, if we look at the simpler, less adjustable, end of the T.T. spectrum, there are approaches like two-stage testing. Here all testees take the same initial test which is used as a routing device to direct individual testees to one or a number of second stage tests which vary in some systematic way. Most commonly second-stage cognitive tests would vary in difficulty level—but for, say, assessing occupational interests the second-stage tests could concentrate on more narrowly defined occupational areas. Such two-stage testing requires little if any advanced technology and its component tests can be constructed by only slight adaptation of conventional test constructional techniques.

So much then is by way of introduction to T.T. In its more flexible manifestations it is best regarded as a new testing method: in some ways it is a hybrid form with clear ancestry in both group-testing (from which it takes standardization of presentation but not uniformity of content) and in individual-testing (from which it develops individualization of content but not individual administration): however, it is not only a favourable hybrid but also a mutant with some novel characteristics, two of the more significant of these may be the ready variability of test length and the ready availability of item response times.

The virtues that have been claimed for T.T. all stem from its increased time-on-target which results in both a direct mechanical improvement in reliability and arguably in an indirect improvement in motivation, this following the increased appropriateness of the material presented. A number of studies have shown increased validity as compared with conventional pencil-and-paper tests, or equivalent validity within shorter testing times: some studies have also shown superior sensitivity of T.T. to the distribution of the characteristics being tested. It is, however, a mistake to try to evaluate T.T. solely in terms of comparisons with conventional tests; in some situations conventional tests are, in their own terms, superior to T.T., but T.T. also has attributes not available in conventional testing and which are lost in any comparison—and I shall be saying more about both these points later.

The reason why the Army now sees T.T. as worth investigating are

(1) Firstly as it now operates a centralized recruit selection and allocation system it does possess a high-volume centre which would or could justify the technological infra-structure necessary for the more flexible forms of T.T.

(2) Secondly T.T. does potentially offer the possibility of expanding the range of cognitive skills assessable by testing without expanding the testing time. This is possible not only because of probable time saving in individual test areas but also through the widening of the concept of tailored testing from the individual test to the test battery. In the same way that an individual test can be tailored to suit a testee by selective drawing from an item pool covering one area, so can the battery taken by an individual testee be tailored to suit him by selective drawing from a test pool covering a variety of cognitive areas —In a simple example instead of all testees taking a standard battery of five tests they might all take two tests in common areas and then a further three selected from an available pool covering 10 cognitive areas. The proper basis for adjusting the test battery to match the individual brings me to the third reason for believing T.T. to be a beneficial research area.

(3) Thirdly, by integrating the test measurement procedures with the decision processes of a selection/allocation system it is believed that T.T.—'tailored' now conceived in a general systems sense—can direct

the information gathering (and perhaps also the information disseminating) processes of both testing and interviewing so as to collect information of enhanced quality in relation to the specific decisions appropriate to the individual testee. Tailoring is thus regarded as extending to the occupational preferences of the individual recruit, to the qualifications for the available Army employments and to decisions on his acceptability for specific jobs. Figure 2 illustrates a simple integrated testing/decision process.

Figure 2. A test decision procedure

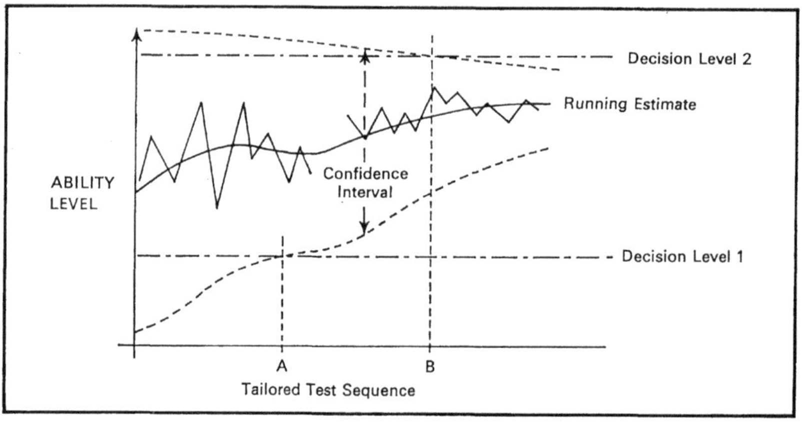

The solid curve plots the running estimate for a testee of the characteristic being measured. Initially when based on only a few items the estimate is error prone and has a very wide confidence band. As testing proceeds the running estimate settles down and the confidence band narrows. Decision Levels 1 and 2 represent qualifying levels for two possible employments. At point A in the testing sequence along the horizontal axis the lower confidence limit goes above Decision Level 1, the testee is thus acceptable for this job and testing could stop here if this were the only option. Later in the sequence at point B the upper confidence limit falls below Decision Level 2 and testing then stops with the testee acceptable for employment 1 but not for employment 2. Less able applicants would establish their unsuitability sooner as would more able applicants their suitability. Testing continues for as long as necessary and no longer. Figure 3 shows the average number of items necessary in a T.T. approach to match the Operating Characteristic curve (for the decision Ability Level, θ, less than 0) of a conventional test of 60 items—both approaches drawing on identical items. Note that as pre-tailored items are used the gains are entirely from the ability of T.T. to stop earlier, i.e., from decision tailoring not from item tailoring.

The form of T.T. to be investigated in A.P.R.E.'s current research plan uses an item pool and visual display units (V.D.U.'s) linked to a computer. It is not, however, planned to employ an item pool structured into a branching network

Figure 3. The average number of tailored test items needed to obtain a corresponding operating characteristic curve to a 60-item peaked test (after Green, 1970)

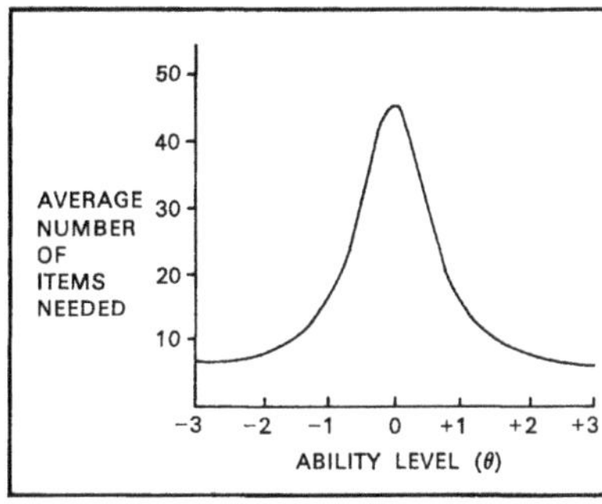

such as that described earlier. The item pool will rather take the form of a catalogued stock or item library; from this library the item most closely approximating a specification generated for the next item required will be drawn. There will be no pre-specified network of routes, simply classified items and rules of procedure. The research will concentrate both on the technical psychometric aspects of this form of T.T. and on the nature and effect of such V.D.U. interaction on a testee. The psychometric factors of research interest centre on the rules of procedure and the characteristics of the item library. The general ideas are those of zeroing in on an applicant's ability and of stopping testing once criteria for specified decisions are met. Topics of interest are the difficulty levels of successive items, the detailed formulation of item selection and testing termination rules and the interactions between these requirements and the characteristics of ideal and real item libraries. These topics have been

Figure 4. Comparisons of measurement efficiency (after Lord, 1970)

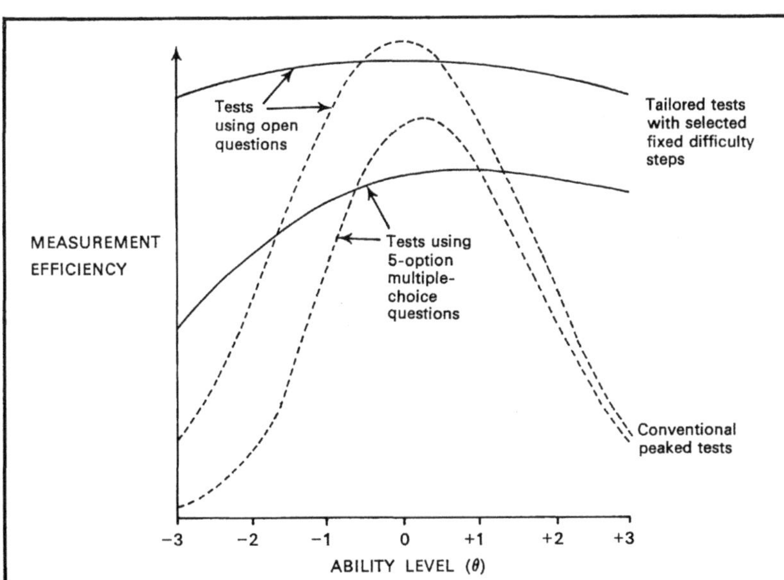

explored to varying extents already by several workers. Figure 4 illustrates the kind of results that have come from a series of theoretical studies. Here the measurement efficiency of branched-item-network-tailored-tests (the solid curves) are compared with conventional peaked tests of the same length (the dotted curves) both with and without chance success—that is for tests with multiple-choice questions and with open questions. The horizontal axis plots ability level, and the peaked tests consist of items of equal difficulty optimum for Ability Level $\theta = 0$.

The peaked tests are most measurement-efficient around the average level of ability and relatively poor outside this middle range, while the T.T. have a much flatter curve generally superior except about the average (where, of course, most people are). The with-chance success curves are lower illustrating a degradation of measurement efficiency resulting from the possibility of guessing correctly; however, the assumption made here is of random guessing which probably over-estimates the loss. Especially for T.T. random guessing may be rare. Note that it is measurement efficiency that is being compared here not selection or allocation utility; there is item tailoring here but no decision tailoring. The T.T.'s diagrammed in Figure 4 used a fixed step change in level of difficulty between successive items; certain shrinking step size procedures have been investigated and offer marginal gains on the curves displayed here, but their item networks need to be much larger.

Looking now at the man/machine factors pertinent to the testee/V.D.U. interaction, testee motivation will be of major interest. One possibility that has been raised is that of the effect on motivation of immediate feedback of item performance or alternatively for multiple-choice questions of allowing testees to continue answering until correct.

The references give a number of entry points to the literature: Lord 1974 and Weiss and Betz, 1973 are helpful reviews.

References

ATKINSON, R.C., KRANTZ, D.H., LUCE, R.D. and SUPPES, P. (Eds.), 1974, Contemporary Developments in Mathematical Psychology (San Francisco, Calif.: Freeman, 1974 in press).

GREEN, B.F., 1970, Comments on Tailored Testing. In: Holtzman (Ed.), pp. 184–197, below.

HOLTZMAN, W.H. (Ed.), 1970, *Computer-Assisted Instruction, Testing and Guidance* (New York: Harper and Row).

LINN, R.L., ROCK, D.A. and CLEARY, T.A., 1972, Sequential testing for dichotomous decisions. *Educational and Psychological Measurement*, **32**, 85–95.

LORD, F.M., 1970, Some test theory for tailored testing. In: Holtzman (Ed.), pp. 139–183, above.

LORD, F.M., 1971, A theoretical study of two-stage testing. *Psychometrika*, **36**, 227–242.

LORD, F.M., 1974, Individual testing and item characteristic curve theory. In Atkinson, Krantz, Luce and Suppes (Eds.), above.

WEISS, D.J. and BETZ, N.E., 1973, Ability measurement: Conventional or adaptive? Department of Psychology, University of Minnesota. Psychometric Methods Program Research Report 73–1.

Dr. Hasan Tan is professor of psychology and the chairman of the Department of Social Sciences, Middle East Technical University, Ankara. He received his undergraduate and post-graduate education in Ohio State Univ., and Univ. of Maryland, U.S.A. He specializes in psychological counselling and is currently concerned with interests and interest measurement.

2:6

Newspaper Headings Test: a measure of interests as means in educational and vocational planning

H. Tan

Introduction

The interest pattern of an individual may be considered one of the main dimensions in his educational and vocational planning. Interests may be defined as an individual's relatively stable tendency to seek out or avoid certain types of activities. Functionally they represent 'the strength of one's desire or tendency to attend to an activity, person or object for a considerable length of time, even in the face of difficulty, because satisfaction is experienced in concentrating upon the activity, person or object. Interest connotes absorption of attention because of the satisfaction experienced' (Germane and Germane, 1941, p. 164). Strong (1943, p. 6) takes it as a liking or disliking reaction. The individual likes, or dislikes, or may be indifferent to something. When he is aware of his disposition to that object, event or person, then, an interest is present.

An interest is not an independent entity, but is better viewed as an important part of an individual's personality structure (Roe, 1956, p. 83).

Such a tendency or psychological entity in the individual affects the kinds of work that he will engage in, or the type of activities in life that he will enjoy. Thus, it has been a concern of psychologists to measure interests as a predictor of the individual's chance of future success in a given area of vocational or educational activity. Although small, there exists some positive relationship between interests, and job performance (Strong, 1943, pp. 13, 386–500) occupational choice (Strong, 1955; Barnett, 1951) and job satisfaction (Perry, 1955). The relationship between interests and ability is rather more complex. Certainly for an interest to be durable the individual should have a minimum ability to understand, and deal with the thing or situation satisfactorily. While interests do not compensate for lack of ability in job performance a combination of a reasonable amount of ability and interest, may be a good predictor of an individual's future success in a certain occupation (Lipsett and Wilson, 1954). Success and achievement in an activity certainly nourish interests. It is not possible to have a strong and durable interest in an activity if no success exists. Thus, such an important psychological entity as interests needs to be measured in an attempt to guide educational and vocational development.

Various approaches in the measurement of interests

There are several unique approaches in measuring interests. The main approaches may be summarized as follows:

		COMMENT
1. Initial checklist approach (recreation, reading, occupations)	Pressey & Pressey, 1933 Lehman & Witty, 1927	Unsystematic, but developing a new area.
2. Checklist of occupations	Cleeton, 1943	Susceptible to social desirability, stereotyped response and faking.
3. Strong Vocational Interest Blank (Empirical approach: Interests of selected occupational groups)	Strong, 1943	Comprehensive. Weakness involved illusion that interests were part of job success, not necessarily the case.
4. Kuder Preference Record (Factor analytic approach: identified interest areas)	Kuder, 1957	Forced-choice minimized faking, but relationship between vocation and measured interest not established.
5. Projective techniques: (Pictures, incomplete sentence test, book titles)	Geist, 1964 Dole, 1960 Van Krevelen, 1962	Useful for less verbal subjects. Familiar problems of projective data.
6. Academic Interest Measures (Focus on school interests, avoids over emphasis on adult interest patterns)	Halpern, 1966	Still in developmental stage.

A new type of approach is the Newspaper Headings Test which is the main concern of this paper.

Newspaper Headings Test (NHT)

Description of the test

The Newspaper Headings Test (NHT) was recently developed by the present author in 1966 in an attempt to provide an instrument for those concerned with vocational counselling. The test was standardized in 1972 (Tan, 1972).

The test employs newspaper headings as items. It has twelve interest areas: Science, Technical, Arts, Literature, Medicine, Education, Business, Administration, Law-Politics, Agriculture, Entertainment, and Open Air pursuits. These areas were identified through examination of the literature and existing interest measures.

The basic assumption in the preparation of the Newspaper Headings Test was that a newspaper reader, in general, would rather be selective in reading news in terms of his interests, especially if he has a limited time available.

There are 20 items for each of the 12 scales on the test. The pool of newspaper headings as items were selected from the leading Turkish newspapers. The following criteria were used in their selection:

(1) An item should have an interest value pertinent only to one of the 12 areas under consideration. Any items that included interest elements for more than one area were either discarded or reworded so as to focus only on one area.
(2) Items should represent stable, long-term interest areas. Thus, the headings that were concerned with the heated discussions of the time were not selected.
(3) Strong emotional or cultural values should be avoided.

The items selected by this procedure were also evaluated and assigned to one of the twelve interest scales by a group of judges. Finally 240 items were selected, 20 for each scale.

The items themselves were arranged in groups of four, representing the interest areas. Care was taken to equalize the competition between the areas as far as possible.

The test employs forced-choice techniques somewhat like the Kuder Preference Record. Subjects were asked to read each of the groups of four items and indicate the item representing his most and least preferred area of reading.

It will be clear from the preceding description that the NHT is using a single reference situation, a hypothetical newspaper reading situation, instead of checking the names of occupations or judging different activity situations. It is assumed that 'an unchanging reference situation' will establish a relatively stable 'set' in the subject answering the test.

Standardization of the test

The NHT has been standardized on 3,640 students from four universities and seven higher professional schools in Ankara and Istanbul, providing a sound national sample. There were 52 groups, 31 of which were freshman classes (covering 65% of the subjects) and 21 senior years (35% of the subjects). The groups were selected to reflect the nature of the scales on the test. That is, some specific groups were included in the sample for each scale such as Science Faculty groups for Science Scale, Fine Arts College for Arts Scale, School of Medicine for Medicine Scale, etc. Senior groups were included in the study in order to be able to follow up the development of the interest patterns in specific occupational and educational groups. Thirty-five per cent of the sample were female. The age of the sample ranged from 17 to 36 with a mean age of 19·8 for the freshmen groups and 22·2 for the senior groups.

The data collected were examined for:

(1) The ability of the scales to differentiate certain educational and professional groups.
(2) Degree of independence of the scales.
(3) Item analysis for each scale.
(4) Validity and reliability of the scales.
(5) Identification of the group patterns.

The sensitivity of the scales to identify the interests of the groups which were specifically included in the sample for given scales were checked through mean scores on the scales. The groups which had M's above 0·5 SD are shown in Table 1. It will be clear from the Table that the scales were found remarkably sensitive to the interests of the specific groups. For example, science groups had higher means on the Science Scale, medicine groups on the Medicine Scale, etc. Another important point was that the means of the relative groups on each scale increased in the senior years as compared to the corresponding freshman year.

The test also clearly distinguished groups of students making their initial subject preference decision. Thus it was concluded that the scales were sensitive to the interest patterns of different groups. The independence of the scales was examined with Pearson Product Moment correlations. Most of the intercorrelations in each group (52 groups in total) were either negative or zero. Table 2 presents the number of groups in which a correlation of 0·25 or above occurred between each of the scales.

Table 1. The Groups Above the 0·5 SD on Each Scale

Scales	*Freshman class*	*M and*	*SD*	*Senior class*	*M and*	*SD*
Science	U.A. Science	11·27	0·80	M.E. Science	12·43	1·51
	T.C. Science	11·03	0·73	U.A. Science	11·59	1·25
	M.E. Science	10·66	0·64	U.I. Science	10·77	1·00
	U.I. Science	10·35	0·56	U.A. Medicine	9·59	0·63
Technical	M.E. City Plan.	8·74	1·12	M.E. Eng.	9·41	1·23
	M.E. Science	8·00	0·87	I.T.U. Eng.	9·22	1·17
	M.E. Eng.	7·96	0·86	Maritime Coll.	7·64	0·99
	M.E. Arch.	7·61	0·74	M.E. City Plan.	7·58	0·97
	Army College	7·34	0·65			
	Maritime Col.	7·12	0·57			
Arts	Fine Arts	12·32	2·05	Fine Arts	11·80	2·08
	Conservatory	11·30	1·77	M.E. Arch.	7·23	0·86
	T.C. Music	8·63	1·06	M.E. City Plan.	7·08	0·82
	M.E. Arch.	7·61	0·78	U.I. Philology	6·24	0·59
				U.I. Pedagogy	6·12	0·56
				(Conservatory and Teachers College groups have no senior years).		
Literature	U.I. Philology	7·74	1·10	U.I. Philology	10·83	1·66
	Conservatory	7·73	1·10			
	U.I. Pedagogy	6·41	0·66			
Medicine	U.A. Medicine	11·73	1·66	U.A. Medicine	14·01	2·32
	T.C. Science	9·06	0·74			
	U.A. Science	8·64	0·61			
Education	T.C. Educ.	12·62	1·94	U.I. Pedagogy	11·88	1·43
	T.C. Music	9·65	0·96	U.A. Educ.	11·82	1·42
	T.C. Science	9·15	0·80	(Teachers' College groups have no senior classes.)		
	T.C. Language	8·86	0·70			
	U.I. Pedagogy	8·70	0·65			
	U.A. Educ.	8·41	0·56			
Business	U.I. Econom.	4·75	0·94	U.I. Econ.	7·24	1·39
	M.E. Admin.	4·56	0·85	M.E. Adm.	6·95	1·27
	Maritime Col.	4·10	0·64	U.I. Journal	6·00	0·93
				U.A. Pol. Sc.	5·49	0·74
Administration	U.A. Pol. Sc.	6·90	1·61	U.A. Pol. Sc.	9·03	1·89
	M.E. Adm.	5·83	0·79	U.A. Educ.	7·66	1·42
	U.I. Law	5·32	0·62	U.A. Law	7·16	1·25
				M.E. Adm.	7·13	1·24
				U.I. Law	6·91	1·16
Law-Politics	U.A. Pol. Sc.	7·71	0·90	U.A. Law	10·87	1·87
	M.E. Adm.	7·63	0·87	U.A. Pol. Sc.	9·46	1·44
	U.A. Law	7·41	0·81	U.I. Law	8·79	1·23
	U.I. Law	6·93	0·66			
Agriculture	U.A. Agric.	9·23	1·92	U.A. Agric.	11·69	2·76
	U.I. Forestry	6·00	0·82	U.I. Forest	7·01	1·18
Entertainment	T.C. Phys. Ed.	6·35	0·74	Fine Arts	8·90	1·59
	Fine Arts (Decoration)	5·69	0·52	U.I. Philol.	5·66	0·51
Open Air	T.C. Phy. Ed.	10·65	2·78	(No senior years.)		
	U.I. Journal.	5·65	0·81			
	Navy Col.	4·89	0·52			

Table 2. The Number of Groups in which the Size of Intercorrelation are 0·25 or Above

	II *Tech.*	III *Arts.*	IV *Lit.*	V *Med.*	VI *Ed.*	VII *Bus.*	VIII *Adm.*	IX *Law*	X *Agric.*	XI *Enter.*	XII *Open Air*
Science I	**27**	1	—	**27**	—	—	—	1	1	11	1
Tech. II		—	1	7	—	8	1	1	**25**	—	4
Arts III			**33**	1	2	—	—	—	—	10	3
Liter. IV				—	6	—	5	6	1	4	3
Med. V					1	2	—	1	6	2	—
Ed. VI						1	15	5	3	—	—
Bus. VII							11	3	6	3	5
Adm. VIII								**41**	2	—	—
Law IX									2	—	—
Agric. X										—	2
Enter. XI											**40**

On the whole, however, from the nature and size of the intercorrelations, it is suggested that the scales are measuring different types of interests and that these are in the main independent. The items on each scale were analysed with the point biserial correlation method for the internal consistency. It was found that the items worked well for their scales.

The validity of the scales were studied in the following ways:

(1) Did the scales differentiate the specific interest areas of selected relevant groups?
(2) Was there an increase in the scores of freshmen and seniors on the relevant scales?
(3) Were the means of the students who selected a specific field of study as their first preference higher than their groups in general?
(4) Were the ranges of responses on the scales large enough to ensure the sensitivity of the items to attract the subjects?

Table 3. Means of the Freshman and Senior Groups on the Scales

Scale and Groups	*Freshman*	*Senior*
SCIENCE SCALE		
U.I. Science	10·35	10·77
U.A. Science	11·27	11·59
M.E. Science	10·66	12·43
TECHNICAL		
M.E. Engineering	7·96	9·41
I.T. Engineering	—	9·22
Maritime Col.	7·13	7·64
ARTS		
Fine Arts Col. (Painting)	14·00	11·80
Fine Arts Col. (Decoration)	11·35	11·80
U.I. Philology	5·28	6·24
LITERATURE		
U.I. Philology	7·74	10·83
MEDICINE		
U.A. Medicine	11·73	14·01
EDUCATION		
U.I. Pedagogy	8·76	11·88
U.A. Education	8·41	11·82

Table 3. Means of the Freshman and Senior Groups on the Scales—*Contd.*

Scale and Groups	*Freshman*	*Senior*
BUSINESS-SALE		
U.I. Economics	4·75	7·24
M.E. Admin.	4·56	6·95
U.A. Political Sc.	3·24	5·49
ADMINISTRATION		
U.A. Political Sc.	6·91	9·02
U.A. Law	4·83	7·16
U.I. Law	5·32	6·91
M.E. Admin.	5·83	7·13
LAW-POLITICS		
U.I. Law	5·32	8·79
U.A. Law	7·41	10·87
U.A. Polit. Science	7·71	9·46
AGRICULTURE		
U.I. Forestry	6·00	7·02
U.A. Agriculture	9·23	11·69
ENTERTAINMENT		
U.I. Philology	4·56	5·66
U.A. Medicine	3·77	4·71
T.C. Phys. Ed.	6·35	—
Fine Arts (Decoration)	5·69	8·90
OPEN AIR		
T.C. Physical Ed.	10·65	—
(No other specific groups for this scale).		

The results suggested that the scales were satisfactory with respect to each of the points.

The reliability coefficients and median score for each group is presented in Table 4. The data show that the scales are reliable enough.

Table 4. The Range of Reliability Coefficients of the Scales and their Medians

Scale	*Range*	*Median*
Science	0·13–0·84	0·65
Technical	0·15–0·70	0·58
Arts	0·36–0·79	0·60
Literature	0·22–0·78	0·65
Medicine	0·08–0·79	0·59
Education	0·04–0·67	0·54
Business	0·17–0·71	0·52
Administration	0·27–0·81	0·66
Law-Politics	0·35–0·85	0·70
Agriculture	0·36–0·73	0·63
Entertainments	0·16–0·80	0·67
Open Air	−0·49–0·77	0·60

In summary it was found that the Newspaper Heading Test, as a new approach to interest measurement as well as the first interest test in Turkish culture, was a sensitive, valid and reliable measure suitable for use in educational and vocational counselling work.

Two studies carried out since standardization suggest that the test will prove a useful and effective instrument in measuring and identifying the interests of senior high school and university students.

References

BARNETT, L.W., 1951, An occupational aptitude pattern for engineers. *Educ. Psych. Measur.*, **11**, 52–66.

DOLE, A., 1960, *Vocational Sentence Completion Blank.* Experimental ed., 1950–60 (University of Hawaii Bookstore).

GEIST, H., 1964, The GPII: General Form: Male. *Psycho. Abstracts*, **38**, 451.

GERMANE, C.E. and GERMANE, E., 1941, *Personnel Work in High School* (New York: Silver Burdett).

HALPERN, G., 1966, *Development of an Interest Test: Academic interest measures* (Princeton, N.J.: Educational Testing Service) RM-13.

KUDER, F.E., 1957, *Kuder Preference Record.* Research Handbook (2nd ed.) (Chicago: S.R.A.).

LEHMAN, G.C. and WITTY, P., 1927, *Psychology of Play Activities* (New York: Barness).

LIPPSET, L. and WILSON, J.W., 1954, Do suitable interests and mental ability lead to job satisfaction? *Educ. Psych. Measur.*, **14**, 373–380.

PERRY, D.K., 1955, Validities of three interest keys for U.S. Navy yeoman. *J. Appl. Psych.*, **39**, 134–138.

PRESSEY, S.L. and PRESSEY, L., 1933, Development of interest-attitude test. *J. Appl. Psych.*, **17**, 1–16.

ROE, A., 1956, *Psychology of Occupations* (New York: Wiley).

STRONG, E.K., 1943, *Vocational Interests of Men and Women* (4th printing) (Stanford, Calif.: Stanford University Press).

STRONG, E.K., 1955, *Vocational Interests 18 years after College* (Minneapolis: University of Minnesota Press).

TAN, H., 1972, *Gazete Haberleri Testi: Gelistirilmesi ve Standardizasyonu* (Ankara: Turkiye Bilimsel ve Teknik Arastirma Kurumu).

VAN KREVELEN, J. 1961, Introducing the Book Catalogue Test. *Psy. Abstracts*, **36**, 112.

Dr. Keith Duncan is at present a Senior Lecturer in Psychology at the University of Hull. After graduating from London University, he worked as an applied psychologist for the Ministry of Defence, mainly on problems of equipment design and training. His current teaching responsibilities and research interests are in training, problem solving skills and long term retention.

2:7

An analytical technique for industrial training

K. D. Duncan

Introduction

Describing human performance

Consider how the performance of an industrial task may be described. The investigator, e.g., a training officer, will implicitly or explicitly select a level of description which appears to be appropriate. Sometimes this may be a rather gross account of performance. For instance, describing the duties of a hall porter might entail no more detail than the statements that he must, for example, call taxis, take up and bring down luggage, arrange for early calls, provision of newspapers and tea or coffee in bedrooms. Similarly, the preparation of a simple dish may be adequately stated for training purposes at the recipe level, but in *cordon bleu* cooking, many of the steps in preparing the dish may require extensive redescription of the various sub-routines involved, for example, use of a *bain-marie*—but not if the new recruit has been apprenticed to an Escoffier! In the pharmaceuticals industry the task of 'analgesic compounding' consists of operations such as weighing ingredients, tumble-mixing the ingredients and granulation. (The familiar aspirin tablet is one of many produced in this way.) Taking just one of these operations, weighing ingredients, one could and, for training purposes, probably should redescribe it, in terms of the selection of a container, use of the weighing machine, selection of a scoop and one could even specify the approximate number of scoops of the various ingredients which would be necessary. In fact, this would not be simple because the ingredients powders change considerably in density. One could go further and specify hand movements such as pick up scoop, place in bin, transport to container drum, and so forth, although probably few training officers would go this far. They would recognize that few, if any, novices need detailed explanations of how to handle a scoop. So the level of description which is appropriate depends on the task and on the trainee who has to learn to perform it.

Experimental psychology endorses the view that skilled performance may be observed at many levels of detail. Specifically, the acquisition of skill seems to consist of changes from smaller to larger units of performance. Classical studies of morse telegraphists and typists traced the progress of these skills from operating with single letters, to syllables, to words and eventually to phrases (Bryan and Harter, 1899; Book, 1908). Anyone who has learned to speak a foreign language will recall the progression from halting strings of words, to phrases and sentences. He will, if he listens to a skilled simultaneous translator, be amazed at the lag between the original speech and the translation. This expertise deals in units of three or four sentences, even short paragraphs.

Welford's (1968) review of the experimental evidence defines the acquisition of skill as dealing with incoming data and outgoing actions in larger units; as the recognition of sequences of events and the establishing of performance routines. Annett and Kay (1956) have persuasively argued that skill involves perceiving the redundancy in series of events which enables larger performance sequences to be organized. Miller, Galanter and Pribram (1960) proposed that a higher unit may drive one or more lower units, whilst testing for a mismatch between an actual and a model state of affairs. Depending on the mismatch there may be more or less *activity* by the lower units and, since the lower units are also model-matching devices, there may be more or less *variety* of observed behaviour until the controlling mismatch is removed. Variation of performance with a constant outcome, in other words, flexibility or adaptability, is a characteristic, some would say the characteristic, of skilled performance. So Miller, Galanter and Pribram's suggestion of how lower units are organized into higher units is an appealing one.

Everyday observations, laboratory studies, theories of skilled performance, all suggest that, if task analysis is to be a serious practical enterprise, it must deal with the level of description problem.

An adequate method must also recognize the associated problem of how smaller units of performance are organized into larger and characteristically cohesive, purposive units of performance. In short, it should be no surprise if the classical molar-molecular controversy in psychology proved difficult to escape in the applied field. That skilled performance may be described at several levels of detail is recognized by a number of writers on task analysis (King, 1964; Folley, 1964; Smith, 1964; Mager and Beach, 1967). Some specify how many levels of description are to be employed. Thus Smith (1964) proposes four levels of description, namely jobs, e.g., motor mechanic, duties e.g., tuning the motor, tasks e.g., adjusting the carburettor, removing, cleaning, adjusting or replacing spark plugs, and elements, e.g., turning a screwdriver adjustment anticlockwise. Mager and Beach (1967) distinguish three levels of description which they name vocations, e.g., painter, X-ray technician, landscape gardener, tasks, e.g., preparing a surface, mixing paint and steps in performing a task e.g., selecting appropriate paint, removing old finish. Again, Seymour (1966) is very explicit. One must choose a single level of analysis, 'To prevent confusion a uniform level of breakdown must be maintained.' He cites three levels from which one can be chosen for most purposes (Crossman, 1956; Seymour, 1954 and 1959).

The T.W.I. (Training Within Industry) Job Breakdown, perhaps the most widely used method in Britain, ignores the problem by leaving the level of description to the discretion of the analyst. The T.W.I. scheme assumes that supervisors can be trained to collect adequate data for industrial training by listing in a table the operations in a task and in a separate column commenting on any relevant difficulties which they encounter or anticipate that a novice will have to overcome.

If, then, the problem is recognized, there is no general agreement as to the terms for designating different levels of description, nor as to the number to be employed, although a fixed number is generally assumed. The several levels of description which have been proposed are at best exemplified rather than defined.

Between the most general statements of performance and the language of physiology or anatomy there are in principle an indefinite number of levels of description which will clearly be difficult to limit or specify. It will be argued that this should not be attempted but rather that a method of analysis is needed which is flexible, which varies the level of description in the same task and which does so on some systematic basis.

Progressive redescription

Recognizing that skilled performance can be described at many levels and that the problem is what to record, at what level of description and in what degree of detail, then tasks should be analysed by progressive redescription. Analysis begins with the most general statement of the task, and determines what subordinate operations are entailed, the operations they entail and so on. The first stages of the analysis of a continuous process control task are illustrated in Figure 1. This task is chosen as an illustration because its various subordinate operations comprise a range of skilled performance which includes tracking, procedure following, discrimination, concept attainment and problem-solving. Other tasks which have been analysed in this way present less variety of components, e.g., electrical maintenance of transfer lines, controlling a steel radiator production line, the operation of office printing machines and the legal procedures of 'conveyancing' when houses are bought and sold—a high grade clerical skill.

Information recorded is minimized by ceasing analysis whenever the probability of inadequate performance, **p**, or the costs, **c**, to the system of inadequate performance are together unacceptable. Alternatively, analysis ceases when the training required for adequate performance is clear.

Although Figure 1 only illustrates the first stages of analysis of this task, further description has already ceased in the case of four subordinate operations. These have been underlined. It is assumed that the trainee operator is probably able to push buttons (operation 139), make a telephone call (operation 169) and learn with acceptable errors to keep the log in his first week in the control room, i.e., **p** is appreciable but **c** is negligible (operation 8). Fourthly, the training for acceptable performance is clear in the case of operation 160, obtaining a sample at R2 Condenser Drain Valve. The trainee must learn sufficient plant geography to find R2 condenser and then to discriminate the drain valve from others in the immediate vicinity. This sort of training is a major requirement for this task, which involves some 130 manually operated valves on open plant. Thus the degree of detail reached, at the point where analysis is broken off, can vary considerably in the same task.

Whether or not the rules for analysis presented here are defensible, they are explicit and exclude collection of data *ad lib*. Data collection is not analysis. By incorporating **p** into the rule for analysis, it is recognized that the population of students or trainees is always to a degree 'sophisticated'. The practical problem is to decide which sub-routines they can already perform and which not. Cost, **c**, as used in the analysis rule, is broadly defined in terms of anything which the system values. It includes costs not only in the sense of financial losses accruing from wastage of material or damage to tools and equipment, but also considered are consequences of performance which might contribute to illness hazards, or which constitute a threat to safety in the workplace, or

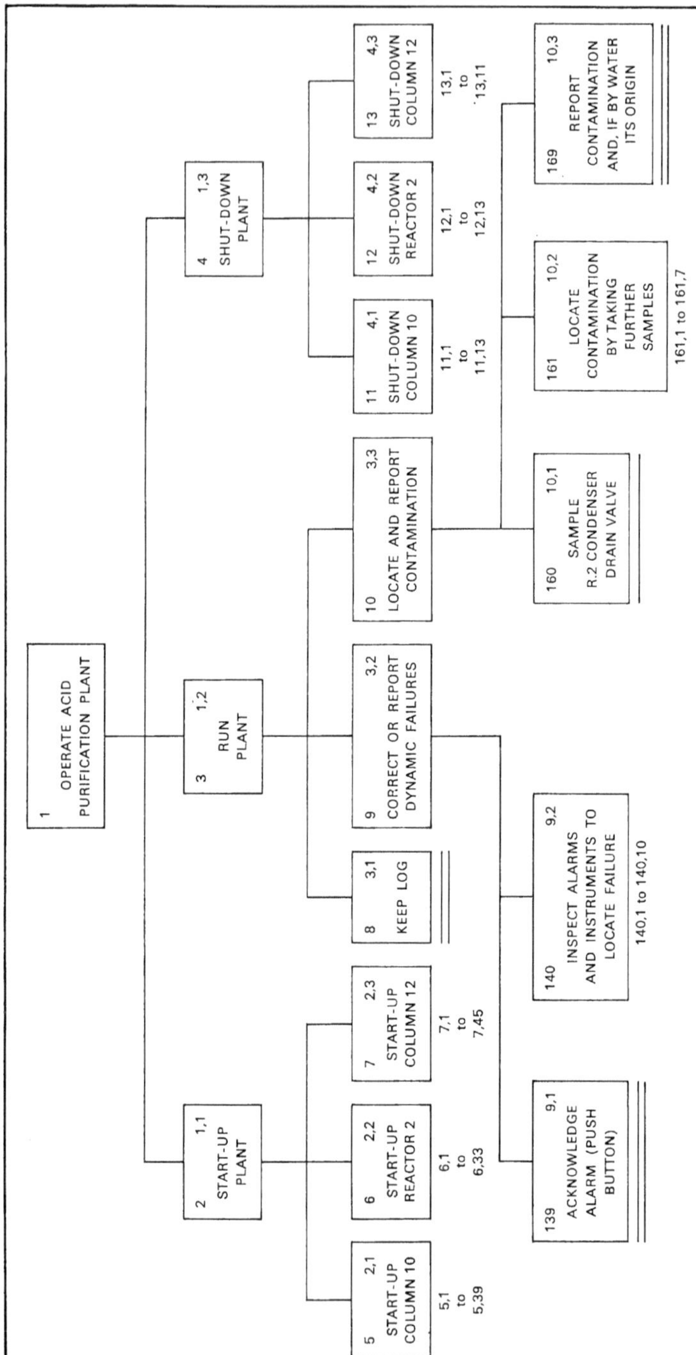

Figure 1. Main operations in the acid purification task. Under a box is either a set of numbers indicating subordinated operations (thus operation 5, start-up Column 10, has 39 sub-operations) or underlining to indicate that analysis has ceased. Double underlining is used to indicate that probability of inadequate performance and attendant costs are acceptable, single underlining to indicate that training required for adequate performance is clear

Figure 2. Box diagram indicating hierarchy of all operations recorded in the acid purification process control task

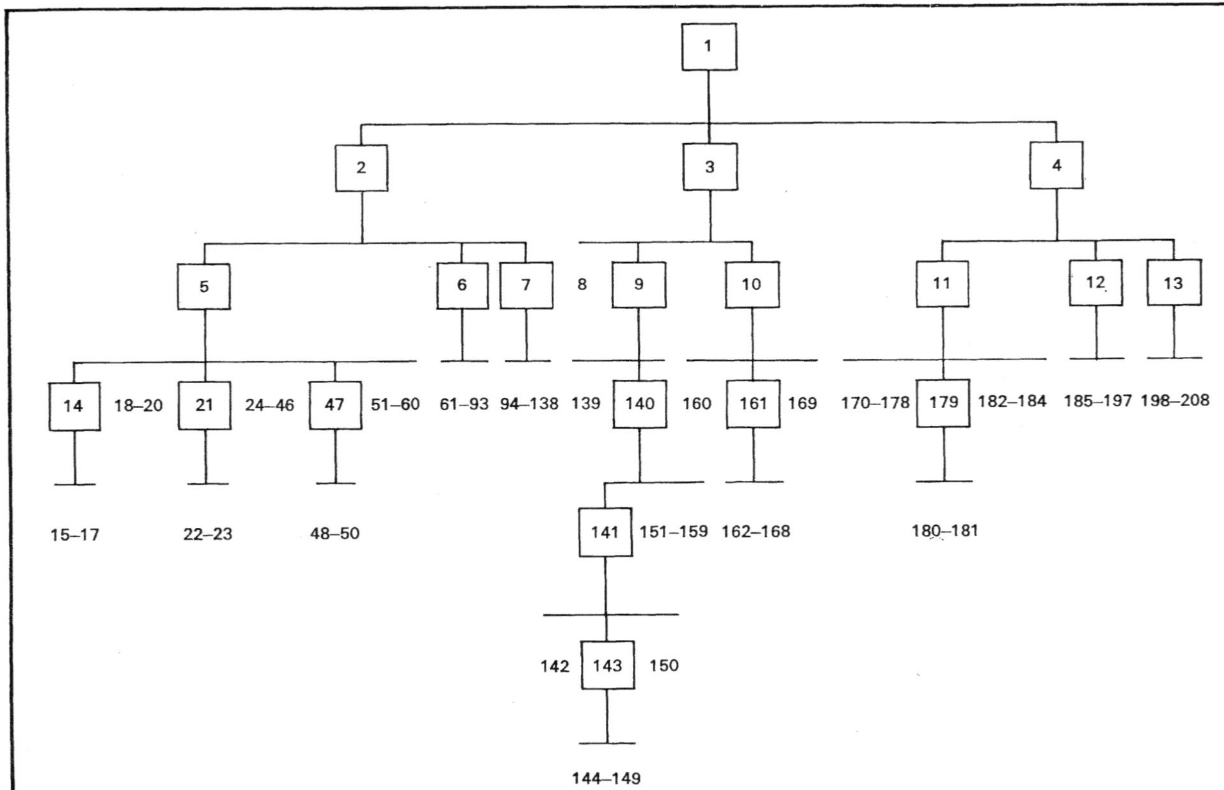

which affect the demands made on other people elsewhere in the plant. Training in safe practices and training of emergency procedures is not therefore the subject of a separate analysis. Such training should be an integral part of the whole training scheme and not something which is grafted on as an afterthought.

Figure 1 shows only the first stages of analysis. Other representative extracts are discussed later and are illustrated in Figures 3 and 4. The complete hierarchy of operations in this task is shown in Figure 2. The task presents a variety of training problems but, before discussing these, a distinction will be made between *operations* and *plans*.

Operations and plans

To redescribe an operation in terms of its subordinate operations implies a plan. Performance of the task requires that subordinate operations are appropriately sèlected and ordered in sequences. A plan is operationally defined in terms of the manner in which subordinate operations are selected and sequenced. A familiar plan is the invariant sequence or procedure. Thus 'starting up column 10' (operation 5 in Figures 1 and 2) involves not only 39 subordinate operations but also a plan namely, that these are carried out in a fixed sequence. Representative subordinate operations of this procedure are shown in Figure 3.

Figure 3. Representative subordinate operations in a start-up procedure

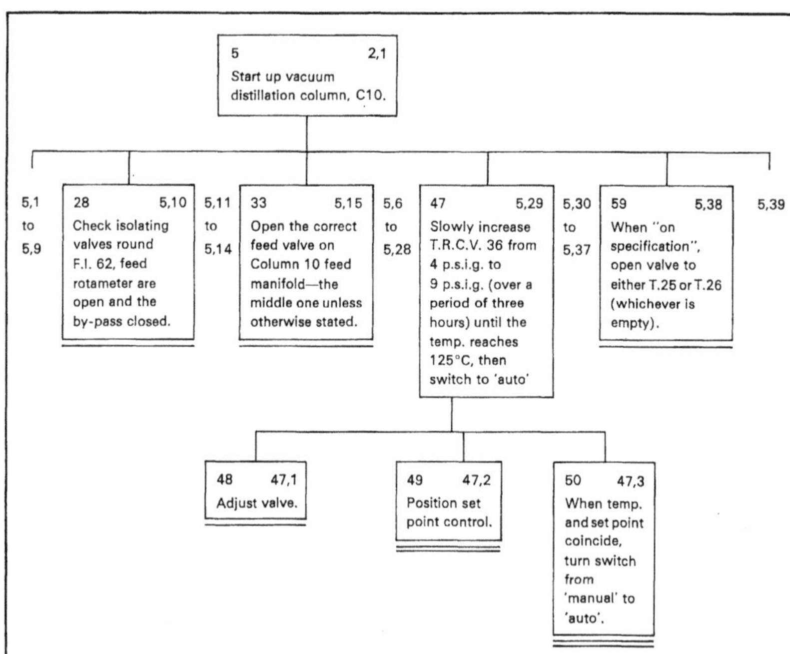

Locating contamination (operation 161 in Figures 1 and 2) involves seven subordinate operations, which may be carried out to obtain samples of the product at different points on the plant, and a plan which selects and sequences

them. However, this plan will select a varying set of sampling operations and will vary the sequence in which they are carried out in order to locate the source of contamination. Thus if an operation obtains a contaminated sample the next operation would be one which samples further upstream; if the sample obtained were 'clean', one of the operations sampling downstream would follow. An efficient plan would clearly minimize the number of subordinate sampling operations to isolate sources of contaminant. Representative sampling operations can be seen in Figure 4.

Figure 4. Representative subordinate operations in locating contaminant

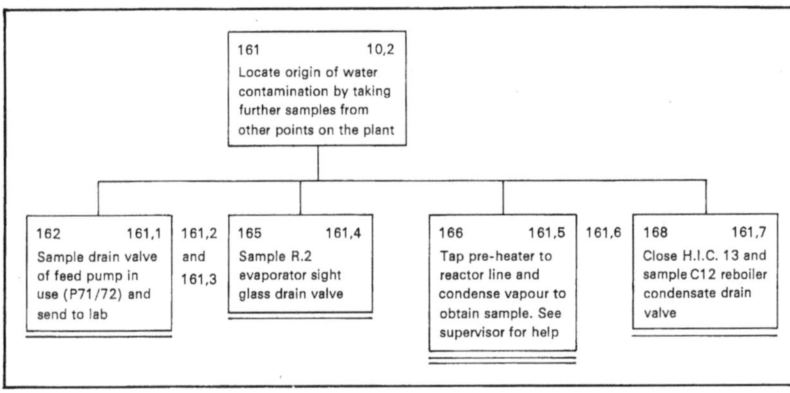

Operations—console instrument locations

As one example of an operation consider the problem of identifying controls and indicators. The operator must discriminate between 50 controls and indicators on an instrument console in the control room. One of these instruments is the temperature recorder-controller, T.R.C. 36 with its steam remote controller, set point control and automatic or manual switch (operations 48, 49 and 50 in Figure 3). These control room instruments are labelled, but it is essential for two reasons that the operator has mastered instrument locations and does not need to rely on scanning the labels to find one of them. On the one hand, when plant failures occur, he will have very limited time for diagnosis and should not have to waste any of this time searching for an indicator. On the other hand, he must be able to perform extremely quick sequences of console operations in the event of an emergency shut-down of a unit of plant such as a distillation column or a reactor. The costs of inadequate performance, to recall the analysis decision rule, are unacceptable.

Swift location of console instruments seems to be an instance of what, in some taxonomies (Gagné, 1965b; Gilbert, 1962) is called multiple discrimination. The basic requirement for this category of learning is to make the cues distinctive, so emphasis of the position cues was attempted by having trainees practise labelling outline drawings of the instrument console. It was also decided to try to apply a principle, which has been recommended for this kind of learning, namely, grouping potentially confusable cues. This was done by having trainees practise the locations and functions of all flow instruments together, and likewise by grouping practice of all temperature, pressure and level instruments. A comparison study found that practice in labelling outline drawings did indeed enhance learning of instrument locations, but that this application of the grouping principle had no significant effect (Duncan, 1969).

Plans—procedures

In considering training of the operations in this task, the analyst is on fairly familiar ground. This is not the case for some of the plans. The point has already been made that several of the plans, those for starting-up and shutting-down the three principal units of this plant, are the familiar *fixed* sequences or procedures. These plans do not ordinarily present difficult training problems, compared with plans which *vary* the selection and sequence of subordinate operations. Indeed the familiar procedural plan only presents a problem when, as in this task, it is a lengthy sequence. Since fixed sequences of as many as 45 subordinate operations were involved, it was decided to construct job aids for start-up and shut-down procedures. The nature of the task is thereby changed, intrinsic task information has been drastically augmented. Information which the trainee might otherwise have to memorize has, as it were, been placed into an external store and a much more realistic training objective of correctly retrieving information from the store has been substituted. Or, at least, mastery of the procedural guides for start-up and shut-down of plant is the short term objective. In the long term it is intended that the trainee should master these long procedures without being dependent on procedural guides. To this end, the subordinate operations which were seen by experienced operators to go together, were grouped under a relatively small number of headings, e.g., 'start feed', 'heat the still', 'start reflux'.

Plans for fault location

Sheer length of sequence aside, fixed sequence plans will present few difficulties. Rather it is variability in the selection and sequencing of subordinate operations which makes learning a task difficult and which characterizes many sorts of skilled performance. Indeed, one reason for operationally defining the plan in terms of selection and sequencing of subordinate operations is to give the task analyst some practical purchase on a widely recognized feature of skill, namely, that performance can vary considerably whilst the end or the goal remains constant. Variation is of the essence in the difficult fault finding plans. One fault location plan has already been briefly described. Periodically the operator sends samples of the pure product for laboratory quality control analysis. A common adverse laboratory report is of water contamination and an experienced operator must determine its origin by taking further samples of product at different points on his plant. He must decide in the light of successive laboratory reports an appropriate sequence of sampling operations with always the same end in view, to minimize sampling costs. As can be seen in Figure 4, the cost of sampling operations can vary considerably in terms of convenience, e.g., a sample might sometimes be quickly and conveniently obtained from a drain valve in liquid form. On the other hand, it may be necessary to take a sample at a point in the plant where the product is under vacuum in gaseous form, in which case it will be costly in terms of time, inconvenience or even hazard.

Initially, to enable the trainee to perform this plan, two regimes were considered. Under one regime, the trainee was simply given a decision tree and practised using it in an exercise in which the instructor provided him with simulated laboratory reports for given faults. The faults occurred in random order and with frequencies corresponding to their specified probabilities. In the second training regime, the trainee had a flow diagram showing the differing fault probabilities and sampling costs and was simply instructed to minimize the latter. In other words he had to try to work out an efficient plan of his own. Using two groups of the company's apprentices as subjects, the two regimes were compared in terms of excess sampling costs, that is in terms of the sampling costs entailed in locating the faults by the most efficient strategy. During initial practice the group who used the decision tree, not surprisingly, had average excess sampling costs of zero and a variance of zero, whereas the group which had to work out a search plan on their own had excess samplings costs of 31%.

However, the company were not only interested in differences in regimes, but also in different criteria, namely retention and transfer. Deprived of the decision tree, the first group performed worse on both of these criteria. On the retention criterion this group now had excess sampling costs of 47% whereas the group that had had to work out a search plan on their own had a significantly smaller average excess sampling costs of 26%. The two groups did not differ significantly on the transfer criterion, i.e., a search task of the same form but with differing probabilities and costs of sampling distributed differently, but again the difference favoured the group whose members had been left to work out their own search plan during initial practice (Duncan, 1969).

The possibility of training only a limited number of apprentices in each of the two conditions on any one occasion raised the question of the contribution of different delays between training and testing to the retention and transfer effects. There was no significant decline in transfer as a function of training to testing interval and performance on the transfer task was superior to that of an untrained control group. On the other hand, in the retention data, there *was* significant evidence of forgetting but only in the group whose initial practice was with the decision tree.

A subsequent experiment, in which transfer of this search skill remained stable over six months, provided further evidence that search strategy is well remembered and a specific search plan is more easily forgotten (Duncan, 1971).

In practice, a decision must be made whether or not to trade retention and generality of learning of search strategy for the excellent performance which is immediately obtained when the subject is simply provided with a decision tree, or whether to adopt some expedient which attempts to achieve both. A similar decision is required for the plan which selects one of ten subordinate operations when the control room alarms are set off by a plant failure, for example failure of a pump, or an empty feed tank, or failure of a steam supply. Such decisions can only be made in terms of the objectives of the personnel sub-system and not by the task analyst who should rather draw attention to training options and their consequences.

Training design

Task analysis is necessarily complemented by pilot training schemes. Its nature is hypothesis generating, to be complemented by appropriate hypothesis testing. But in one respect the analysis departs from completely neutral task description—it assumes that skilled performance is hierarchically organized. In this one respect therefore it prescribes training, it is prescriptive with regard to training sequences. This is not to say that analysis will specify a unique training sequence. In the acid purification control task, the order in which fault diagnosis, fault location, start-up and shut-down procedures are trained is not specified, but, for each of these operations, the analysis does specify antecedent mastery of plant valve discrimination and control console instrument location. In other words the task hierarchy constrains the sequence of training. Practice of a given operation should not begin before its subordinate operations have been learned.

In the process control task training course it was decided that practice in procedures should precede practice in fault location and fault diagnosis. So when these last operations were practised, the trainee had already learned, indeed to some degree overlearned, the necessary subordinate operations on the plant and in the control room. Therefore at this stage, the trainee could more easily concentrate on the difficult fault location and fault diagnostic plans, but this sequencing decision was an intuitive one, it is not prescribed by the analysis.

Mager's (1961) research into the sequences preferred by the trainee raises two points in connection with the method of analysis described here. Firstly, when the task hierarchy allows for more than one possible sequence at a particular stage in the programme, then one would do well to consider the sequence preferred by the trainee, since to do so apparently has powerful motivating effects. Also to be considered carefully, since this analysis generates learning sequences which progress from lower to higher order operations, is Mager's subjects' evident desire to see 'the big picture' at the beginning of training. This observation and the tendency of many training officers to start a training course with some kind of 'technical story' (Shriver *et al.*, 1964), leads one to suspect that the student's interest is probably aroused in the early stages of training by a description of the structure of what he has to learn. It has been suggested that representations of the task such as those in Figures 1, 3 and 4 might help to serve this purpose, but the suggestion has thus far not been tested. It does, however, seem reasonable in view of the claims which have been made for the effectiveness of 'advance organizers' (Ausubel, 1968). It is interesting, if highly speculative, to link this argument with the requirement of programming languages like ALGOL for declarative statements at the beginning of the programme, i.e., the declaration of terms, which are not primitives in the language concerned.

A shortcoming of this and other methods of analysis, which must be acknowledged, is that it tends to address the problem of training individuals, when increasingly the problem of how to train teams is being encountered in industry, not least in continuous process control tasks such as those found in petrochemical industries. It is known from studies of radar crews that the performance data of individual members does not reveal the extent to which they co-ordinate their activities (Alexander *et al.*, 1962). Perhaps no single individual has the information which is necessary to learn to improve the co-ordination of his activities with those of his colleagues. In this case, the training problem is not different in principle from the individual training problems which have been discussed. The intrinsic task information is inadequate and must be augmented if the team is to learn to co-ordinate its activities. Or the problem may be that what behaviour on the part of individuals constitutes effective co-ordination with other members is either not clear or not agreed. A study of the effects of discussions between crew members suggests that this may be the case (Jensen *et al.*, 1961).

Can it therefore be assumed in analysis and training design that the information necessary for individual learning and performance should be examined in the same way regardless of whether it comes from other people or from inanimate sources? Is it necessary to distinguish between performance of the individual alone and performance of the individual in the presence of others? An influential paper by the social psychologist Robert Zajonc (1965) suggests that such a distinction must be made. Reviewing the conflicting findings from studies of the effects on individual performance of the presence of others, Zajonc points out that decrements were found when the subject's task required substantial learning, whereas increments attributable to the presence of others were found when the task required well established performance or little or no learning. Whatever the mechanism may be for this neat reconciliation of the findings of social facilitation experiments, the psychologist seriously interested in training should consider that, other things equal, trainees in the early stages of learning a task will probably work best alone, but that their performance may even be enhanced, if they work in the presence of others, as their scores approach an asymptote.

Training design, properly considered, raises questions which are not just training questions, questions which are best answered by other disciplines or in consultation with other disciplines such as social psychology. The analysis of the acid purification control task tried to show that there will often be more than one way of securing adequate performance, sometimes more than one training solution to a problem and some solutions which are not training solutions at all. Task analysis must recognize not only training problems but problems of equipment design, problems of personnel selection, placement and development and problems of education.

Communication with other professions

Equipment design

The engineering of the hardware in any system necessarily sets limits on personnel strategies in selection and training. Two features of the acid purification plant will serve to illustrate this point. Instrumentation and associated alarm systems may either provide a large number of signals of specific failures, for example 'the feed pump to the evaporator has stopped', or a much smaller number of signals, typically that a parameter, for example, a flow or a liquid level, is out of tolerance. The former instrumentation philosophy is, from the engineering point of view, expensive but it removes, or drastically reduces, training costs whereas the latter instrumentation philosophy is relatively inexpensive from an engineering point of view but does present the difficult training problem of fault diagnostic skill. A rational solution would probably trade-off the costs of equipment design and of training in this situation. The trade-off might also take account of personnel selection and placement strategies, which recruited more or less intelligent operators for this task.

In the same way it would be rational to consider trade-offs of this kind in the case of operating plant valves. Durable labelling in an open acid purification plant is costly. For this process alone there are 130 such valves. However, 90 of them are easily identified given mastery of four or five functional *categories*, (such as 'isolating' and 'by-pass' valves) i.e., for these, training is not so time-consuming and retention may be better. It is the remaining 40 valves which will be costly in terms of training and expensive mistakes due to forgetting, since there are no rules to support identification and each must be separately learned. The point in this trade-off is that the psychologist would distinguish where engineers or accountants might not, between the cost of labelling all the hand operated valves on the plant and the 30% or so which present disproportionately high training costs.

From human factors work on both sides of the Atlantic there is a growing understanding of how psychologists and design engineers may collaborate. The collaboration achieved so far may be modest but, at least in British industry, is probably under-utilized.

Personnel selection, placement and development

Recruitment for the acid purification control task and others of comparable difficulty varies. The preferred policy is to promote operators of less complex plant or 'pump and line men', men who already have relevant experience, in short a population who are already capable of many of the subordinate operations in the task. Specifically, such men will be able to distinguish between, for example, isolating and by-pass valves, or be familiar with instrument nomenclature and therefore will more rapidly master the location of instruments on the control room console. On occasions, men who are new to the company or indeed sometimes new to the process control industries, are appointed to perform this task. Invariably, the new operator from whatever background, is confronted for the first time with an automatically controlled process.

These processes are perceived by operators and management alike as extremely demanding. Conscientiousness and intelligence are seen as important in preventing shut-down and locating product contamination. There is talk of boredom, particularly on night shifts, which is perhaps to be expected when intelligence has been a criterion in appointment to the job. It is also recognized that boredom can impair performance and that the most able are not necessarily the most diligent.

The contradictory requirements of this task, and other personnel factors, present rather general problems in the way in which they interact with training design, or the use of jobs aids such as decision trees. Arguments favouring the use of decision trees were that performance supported by them should be less dependent on intelligence and that relaxation of the intelligence criterion would permit more freedom to appoint operators on other grounds such as conscientiousness. It was generally appreciated that employing intelligent men to do very little for long periods of time, but to perform intellectually difficult operations on rare occasions, was an unhappy situation. Given that fault location might have to be time-shared with emergency actions on another system, then one could add the further argument that, under these conditions, performance supported by decision trees should be less vulnerable to disruption. However the dangers of trading retention and possibly transfer for efficient performance were also seen. The loss of transferable skill is, in the event, the more serious, since, as subsequent experiments showed, it is fairly stable over long periods of time.

Whenever an industrial task has a problem solving component, like the fault diagnostic and fault location operations in the acid purification control task, it may be possible to use decision trees to support performance which, at least on short-term criteria, may be indistinguishable from that of a very skilled man. In the short-term at least, the same behaviour can have very different bases. It will generally be very much easier to *programme performance* to meet immediate short-term criteria than to *programme learning* of the general principles which apparently support enduring problem solving skills. Which of these courses of action is taken or whether some intermediate strategy is adopted, may be decided in the light of many personnel factors which will now be briefly discussed. All, however, hinge on the objectives of some system and in practice on the rationality of its management. Unfortunately, decision trees and other algorithmic techniques have been described in terms which are hardly conducive to rational evaluation. At one extreme they have been described as devices for reducing man to an automaton and on the other hand have been somewhat sensationally defended as intelligence amplifiers.

In practice, one basis for choosing whether or not to use decision trees is the nature of the trainee population. Less able groups may be expected to follow the procedures specified by a decision tree with more success than they would have from interpreting general principles. Indeed, less able trainees may be enabled to perform problem solving tasks of which they would otherwise be incapable. On the other hand, for more able populations, extensive use of decision trees with little explanation might make a task intrinsically boring and would largely exclude any gains from the transfer of learning over different tasks involving the same principles. It would also fail to exploit transfer from previous learning to the current task. If mobility of operators from plant to plant within a factory, or within a company, is an objective of a personnel system, then training generalizable skill would clearly be preferred wherever possible.

The stability of the population to be trained will also be important. High labour turnover will tend to make the use of decision trees more economic since mastery of general principles will usually entail longer periods of instruction or more sophisticated instructional techniques. A danger to be considered, however, is that in situations of high labour turnover, the use of decision trees, and consequent boredom among the more able operators, may in fact augment, or be a principal cause of the labour turnover problem.

Education

The acid purification control task and the increasing number of tasks like it in industry raise problems which invite collaboration with education, or at least problems which *prima facie* fall within the province of education. Intellectual skills are increasingly a feature of the industrial scene. *What* principles taught in *what* way will support or facilitate carrying out the fault location and diagnostic plans which control of the acid purification process requires? It seems clear that at some stage the trainee must practice identification of failures consistent with a set of symptoms and must also practice locating the origin of water contamination from a series of laboratory reports. The problem is how to introduce him to the consequences of pumps stopping, of steam or cooling water supplies failing and of heat exchangers leaking steam or coolant into the product. A minimal technical story was tried but with only modest success.

It is possible that teaching more general principles which are relevant and which extend beyond the restricted context of this particular plant, might well support mastery of these difficult fault location and diagnostic plans. But this mastery would be the training research psychologist's main or sole decision rule as to what principles to teach. It might not be the educator's decision rule, which would most likely be syllabus oriented, that is to say, the set of principles selected for teaching would be coherent and representative of some body of knowledge. An unfortunate feature of the dialogue between education and training has been a tendency either not to recognize that different decision rules are applied, or simply to assert that one set of rules is 'correct'. In consequence, neither the objectives of education nor training may be realized. The study by Williams and Whitmore (1959) which tested both maintenance men's knowledge of electronics theory and their ability at fault finding in field equipment, showed that learning of the latter had hardly begun on leaving the school and only increased with length of service in the field. From a strictly training point of view, little had been achieved which was immediately useful and the sooner practice in operational situations began the better. From an educational point of view, the outcome is less than satisfactory, for although scores on tests of theory were initially high, they declined rather drastically with increasing periods of service in field units.

These are specific instances of a more general lack of accord between two professions which, in principle, would collaborate to their mutual benefit. The disagreement is well illustrated in the differing attitudes to the objectives of instruction. The 'taxonomy of education objectives' (Bloom, 1956) is largely concerned to codify the extent and variety of existing objectives in education. Existing objectives in education are regarded as given and the major concern seems to be to indicate in what ways they differ and in what ways tests may be devised to see if these different objectives have been attained. Indeed, major uses of the taxonomy have been classifying test questions (Stanley and Bolton, 1957) and in this way checking the validity of test content (Cox, 1965). This contrasts sharply with the attitude of psychologists working in industrial and military training, who regard any instructional objectives as open to strict questioning in terms of eventual contribution to some system's objectives.

The milieu of education is one thing, that of training quite another. Training must meet stated objectives because the military or industrial systems which it serves must meet stated objectives and must meet them more or less efficiently. However, education is arguably serving the aims and aspirations of a social system, a system with ill-defined objectives. Consequently the conscientious teacher is confronted very frequently with ill-defined objectives, such as fostering an appreciation of music and painting, or encouraging a critical attitude which seeks out premises, identifies questionable ones and questions them. Now it might be possible to 'unpack' such complex objectives as these into operational definitions and to devise effective instructional techniques, but the psychologist will do well to recognize that this is a more difficult exercise than he is accustomed by his discipline to undertake. It should, nevertheless, be undertaken by someone.

Discriminating between functionally different categories of valves on process plant may seem a minor problem compared with the higher order concepts which have to be mastered in schools and universities. Indeed, by confining his activities to learning tasks, which in the current state of the art, he can demonstrably influence or control. the psychologist necessarily lays himself open to accusations of indulging in trivia. Nevertheless, the gap between what can be achieved by applied psychology and what must be attempted in educational practice is narrowing. A good example is in this very field of concept attainment, specifically in the recent work of Bourne (1970) on the acquisition of combination rules in concept learning. Particularly impressive is Bourne's experimental demonstration of higher order learning, of swift recognition that the rule has changed and rapid identification of the new rule. This is indeed a skill to be conjured with. Of course, intellectual skills of this higher order of abstraction have long been known to exist and have long been the business of education. However, this elegant experiment provides psychologists with *one* way in which they can talk about higher mental processes without the familiar unpleasant feeling of not really knowing what is being talked about.

Task analysis—assumptions

Levels of description

The method of task analysis just described makes a number of assumptions which must now be examined. The problem of levels of description is a natural starting point.

No attempt is made to define levels of description, nor to specify a list of performance elements. A workable list of performance elements would be one way of achieving a rigorous method of analysis—as Gilbreth saw. But in the current state of psychology such an approach to the problems of training does not seem to be realizable or even foreseeable.

In the absence of such a list, task analysis may achieve some rigour, first of all by proceeding from general to detailed statements and by observing an explicit rule as to when analysis must cease. The rule which is proposed, based on the probability of inadequate performance, **p**, and the cost, **c**, to the system of inadequate performance, besides being explicit, is hopefully exhaustive of the major considerations in any personnel problem, namely the existing capabilities and disposition of people and the many different outcomes of their behaviour, which may be more or less costly to the objectives of the organization in which they exist. The formal definition of **p** recognizes that its value is determined and may be changed, not only by industrial training, but by other areas of expertise such as human engineering and equipment design, personnel selection and placement, personnel development policies, occupational guidance, education and manpower studies. The definition of **c**, on the other hand, recognizes that personnel problems can only be defined and solutions can only have meaning in terms of the *values* of some system.

The decision to redescribe an operation should, strictly speaking, depend on the product of **p** and **c**. The mundane operation of filling a bucket would not ordinarily require much redescription, nor would filling a vessel with water if the feed-line is remotely controlled with considerable time lag for, although this would make the value of **p** rather higher, the value of **c** would be zero or near zero unless the system is suffering from a chronic water shortage. On the other hand, filling a beaker with a radio-active isotope might well be redescribed in some detail because, although the probability of inadequate performance, **p**, is not very high, the consequences or costs of inadequate performance, **c**, would probably be unacceptable. All this is not to say that the analyst must always obtain accurate measures of **p** and **c**. Depending on how important or critical the training scheme is, **p** and **c** might be based on more or less extensive data collection, but for the most part, it is envisaged that **p** and **c** will be estimated subjectively. The point at issue is not accuracy of measurement, rather that the multiplicative relationship is recognized—if either **p** or **c** is zero, then the product is zero and no further redescription is required.

The point must be made that some rule specifying what information to include and what to exclude from the analysis of a task should be explicit if the analysis is to be viable in practice. This is a criticism of other methods of task analysis. Sometimes an arbitrary level of description is implicitly assumed to be appropriate which, if it is too fine, fails to reveal higher order operations and how the task is organized, or if it is too gross, fails to describe perceptual acuity and motor co-ordination when these are crucial for performance of the task. Sometimes the philosophy of analysis seems to be to record everything, on the assumption that the information required for training or anything else must be somewhere in the record. This leads to the generation of masses of paper and other records and the risk that analysis will be abandoned. It also means that the training officer gets a mass of information from which he must somehow extract the useful details for a training course and introduces another time consuming stage into training design.

Having adopted a method of task analysis by progressive redescription, it seemed essential for practical purposes to attempt an operational definition of the relationship between superordinate and subordinate terms. A distinction is therefore made between operations and plans. The redescription of an operation includes (1) a set of subordinate operations, and (2) a plan which is any selection and sequencing of subordinate operations which completes the superordinate operation, i.e., which achieves its goal.

Use of 'operation'

An operation is an action statement indicating how the action is completed or achieved. Since no psychological elements are assumed, an operation is a statement in natural language. It is an instruction to do something, which is intelligible to a competent operator, which is as plain and non-technical as possible, but which is not necessarily without some peculiar expressions if these are current usage. For instance, such terms as 'crack the valve' or 'kettle level' or other shop-floor jargon and dialect may be part of the statement of an operation. Indeed such expressions are often a convenient shorthand for what would otherwise be complex and tortuous statements.

If an operation is not redescribed, more formally, if it is a primitive, the analyst has decided that the trainee, or a trainee population, can perform this operation with acceptable probability of success, or that by various expedients, acceptable probability of success can be assured. It is useful to distinguish between two sorts of difficulty which may have to be overcome to achieve acceptable performance: difficulty in performing the action, or difficulty in processing the signals entailed by the operation. Thus, on the one hand, performing some of the operations in the acid purification control task entailed distinguishing different indicators in the control room and manually operated valves on the open plant. On the other hand, an operation was described, in which the rate at which a steam control valve was opened, constituted the difficulty. Difficulty in performing an operation is not necessarily overcome by training, but might be resolved, for example, by changes in equipment design, specifically by enhancing displays, or by changing display-control relationships.

Stating operations in the form of natural language instructions, keeping the analyst's notes about the nature of difficulties and possible training, etc. quite separate, has the advantage that procedural guides and operating instructions can be rather directly extracted from the analysis and used as they stand. In the task analysis just described, the long procedural guides for starting-up and shutting-down units of plant could be extracted with a pair of scissors.

Use of 'plan'

If an operation cannot be treated as a primitive, i.e., if it is redescribed, then a plan must be stated. A plan is any selection and sequencing of subordinate operations which completes the superordinate operation or achieves its goal. It should be added that sequencing includes timing of subordinate operations. Mastery of the timing, or of the time-sharing involved in a task, can, of course, constitute a major difficulty.

A plan may be stated more or less precisely. The fixed sequence or procedure is a common and very precise plan. Sometimes plans for variant selection and sequences of operations can be precisely stated. An example in the acid purification control task is the plan which specifies that, at fixed intervals, the operator always performs one operation, sending a sample to the laboratory and then, depending on the laboratory report, he either does nothing, or reports a contaminant, or, when the contaminant is water, both reports and begins the operation of locating it. If it is possible to state a plan in the form of a precise rule, specifying the set of permissible sub-routines, then obviously this should be done. However, plans cannot always be stated with such precision. The plan for fault diagnosis requires the selection of a subordinate operation which will either correctly report a plant failure or remedy it. Just how this is to be done is, at this stage not clear, nor is it clear how the plan shall be executed for locating the source of water contaminant, which simply states that costs of sampling should be minimized. But that these difficulties exist is necessarily made clear, because the method of analysis insists that when operations are redescribed a plan must be stated.

Plans may also be more or less efficient. When the operations of a skilled man are redescribed, the plans may not necessarily be consistent, rational, optimal or even explicit. But they should always be stated. It will sometimes be possible, before considering the difficulties in mastering the plan, to re-state it more precisely, or substitute a more efficient plan on logical grounds. The latter will sometimes be the case when a plan has been derived from observing an experienced worker. But the experienced worker's performance is only one source of data for the task analyst and the standard of his performance is not necessarily the objective of a training scheme. The location of water contaminant in the acid purification plant is a case in point. This task exemplifies an insidious feature of a lot of searching activity. There are many possible sampling sequences, varying considerably in efficiency, but which will all find the fault. If the operator confuses his 'success' in finding the fault with successful strategy, then he may superstitiously cling to whatever strategy he adopts—especially since it always works. Simply practising may have this effect whenever intrinsic task information does not indicate improvements. Practice is not instruction. The general principle that intrinsic task information may have to be augmented, if performance is to improve, applies no less to plans—indeed, in the case of plans, it may present special difficulties.

Is it not possible that the reason why some social skills are so illusive, so subtle, is that whilst we recognize them when they occur, that is to say we recognize successful outcomes when we see them, we tend to observe the operations, which are probably not difficult and therefore not very informative? What we do not perceive is the nature of the plan which varies the operations in such a way as to guarantee the outcome. Such plans are likely to be very complex, in the sense that mastery of effective selection and sequencing rules is not easily achieved. But, as in Fiedler's 'contingency model', it is the selection and sequencing of operations in the social skill we call leadership which is of the essence and which ensures that the outcome, the leader's manifest influence, remains constant (Fiedler, 1968).

Hierarchical analysis

This specification of how operations and plans should be stated is an attempt at a logically consistent set of rules for describing the performance of a task. Statements of operations and plans are *not* statements about psychological processes. These statements may have to be made in language which has psychological connotations, but such connotations are incidental and best regarded as hypothetical. Statements of operations and plans must be regarded as psychologically 'celibate' for practical purposes, since, as has been demonstrated here and by other applied psychologists, the same performance may be supported by quite different psychological processes. Furthermore the psychological processes which support some performance may be very obscure. Any method of task analysis which required human performance to be described by categorical statements about psychological processes would be unworkable, for it would assume that a complete, and theoretically consistent psychology exists.

However, although seeking to avoid statements of operations and plans in psychological terms, the method of progressive redescription is based on the view that behaviour is hierarchically organized. In particular, it assumes a model of man like that put forward by Miller, Galanter and Pribram, although some psychologists might consider it an unwarranted liberty to borrow the word 'plan' and give it a special definition for task analysis. However, it does attempt, at the outset, to represent the flexible, adaptive, character of skilled performance, the facility to achieve constant outcomes in a variety of ways.

This is one reason for a form of analysis based on the assumption that behaviour is hierarchically organized, much as a computer is controlled by executive or control programmes with their sub-routines. Another reason for the formal representation of task data in this way, for wandering from what Miller (1962) called 'task description' is that a complete and psychologically neutral account in terms of stimuli and responses does not seem feasible. Even if the effective stimuli for skilled responses in industrial situations can be specified, this involves *ad hoc* assumptions about what is a functional unit of behaviour, assumptions which become more numerous and arbitrary as tasks and the systems they are helping to control become increasingly complex, as new technologies develop and methods of production change.

Finally, when proposals are made for training, or any other measures to improve performance of either operations or plans, then, like others, this method of analysis appeals to psychology. But these proposals are hypothetical. For example, the development of defensible categories of learning and performance is a difficult, but potentially fruitful enterprise. However, category—specific training methods, whatever their origin, are probably best regarded as hypothetical. Task analysis is a *hypothesis generating* activity. It is the business of training design to evaluate the various training proposals empirically, ideally in pilot training schemes, or other experimental training studies. Training design is a *hypothesis testing* activity.

Conclusion

Besides addressing the topic of analytic techniques in training, this paper has attempted to identify points of contact, however few, with other disciplines, to recognize gaps which have to be bridged and explicitly to acknowledge disagreements in principle. Following task analysis, it will often be the case that there is more than one, or perhaps several, solutions to the sponsor's problem. Besides training, the solutions may involve, equipment design or selection, placement and personnel development schemes, or education. Better communication between disciplines is important, because the implications of solutions to personnel problems, which are chosen in practice, are not all seriously considered by the sponsor. Or if the implications are not ignored, the sponsor's stated objectives may be short-term and only optimize a system which is part of larger and largely unexplored systems. One frequently suspects that optimization within the larger context is rarely considered by anyone. The larger context may be an industry, a nation or a whole way of life.

The method of task analysis which has been described deliberately formalizes the study of a task in its context. It would be arrogant to assume and indeed it is not assumed that other analysts ignore system context. Rather, the method of analysis has been devised so that it cannot be performed at all without continually considering two major system constraints, namely the performance capabilities of a population and the objectives of the system in terms of which inadequate performance is costly. One of the reasons for this insistence on continuous reference to system constraints is to acknowledge that technologies and professions, in an important sense, *serve* a system. It is the system's values which determine a particular implementation of expertise—in training just as in any technology. For the application of task analysis, it does not matter whether the system's objectives are far-sighted and philanthropic, or short-sighted and misanthropic. It is only necessary that they are clear.

References

ALEXANDER, L.T., KEPNER, C.H. and TREGOE, B.B., 1962, The effectiveness of knowledge of results in a military system training program. *Journal of Applied Psychology*, **46**, 202–211.

ANNETT, J. and KAY, H., 1956, Skilled Performance. *Occupational Psychology*, **30**, 112–117.

AUSUBEL, D.P., 1968, *Education Psychology* (New York: Holt, Rinehart and Winston).

BLOOM, B.S. (Ed.), 1956, *Taxonomy of Educational Objectives* (New York: Longmans).

BOOK, W.F., 1908, *The Psychology of Skill*. University of Montana Studies in Psychology, Vol. 1. Republished 1925 (New York: Gregg).

BOURNE, L.E., 1970, Development of Conceptual Rules. *Psychological Review*, **77**, 546–556.

BRYAN, W.L. and HARTER, N., 1899, Studies on the telegraphic language. The acquisition of a hierarchy of habits. *Psychological Review*, **6**, 345–375.

COX, R.C., 1965, Item selection techniques and evaluation of instructional objectives. *Journal of Educational Measurement*, **2**, 181–187.

CROSSMAN, E.R.F.W., 1956, Perceptual activity in manual work. *Research*, **9**, 42–49.

DUNCAN, K.D., 1969, Task analysis evaluated. *La Recherche en Enseignment Programmé: Tendances Actuelles* (Paris: Dunod).

DUNCAN, K.D., 1971, Long-Term Retention and Transfer of an Industrial Search Skill. *British Journal of Psychology*, **62**, 439–448.

FIEDLER, F.E., 1965, The Contingency Model: A Theory of Leadership Effectiveness. In: Proshansky, H. and Seidenberg, B. (Eds.), *Basic Studies in Social Psychology* (New York: Holt, Rinehart and Winston).

FOLLEY, J.D., 1964, Development of an improved method of task analysis and beginnings of a theory of training. *NAVTRADEVCEN 1218–1*, U.S. Naval Training Device Center, New York.

GAGNÉ, R.M., 1965a, The analysis of instructional objectives for the design of instruction. In: Glaser, R. (Ed.), *Teaching Machines and Programmed Learning*, Vol. II. N.E.A. Washington.

GAGNÉ, R.M., 1965b, *The Conditions of Learning* (New York: Holt, Rinehart and Winston).

GILBERT, T.F., 1962, Mathematics: the technology of education. *Journal of Mathetics*, **1**, 7–73 and **2**, 7–56.

GLASER, R., 1968, *Proceedings of UNESCO Seminar on Programmed Instruction*, Varna, Bulgaria.

JENSEN, B.T., TILTON, J.R. and ANDERSON, D.N., 1961, Differential effects of knowledge of results and discussion. *Ergonomics*, **4**, 183–188.

KING, S.D.M., 1964, *Training Within the Organization* (London: Tavistock).

MAGER, R.F., 1961, On the sequencing of instruction content. In: Davies, I.K. and Hartley, J. (Eds.), 1972, *Contributions to an Educational Technology* (London: Butterworths).

MAGER, R.F. and BEACH, K.M., 1967, *Developing Vocational Instruction* (California: Fearon Press).

MILLER, R.B., 1962, Task description and analysis. In: Gagné, R.M., (Ed.), *Psychological Principles in System Development* (New York: Holt, Rinehart and Winston).

MILLER, G.A., GALANTER, E. and PRIBRAM, K.H., 1960, *Plans and the Structure of Behavior* (New York: Henry Holt & Co.).

SEYMOUR, W.D., 1954, *Industrial Training for Manual Operations* (London: Pitman).

SEYMOUR, W.D., 1959, *Operator Training in Industry* (London: Institute of Personnel Management).

SEYMOUR, W.D., 1966, *Industrial Skills* (London: Pitman).

SHRIVER, E.L., FINK, C.D. and TREXLER, R.C., 1964, FORECAST systems analysis and training methods for electronics maintenance training. *Research Report 13* (Alexandria, Virginia: Human Resources Research Office).

SMITH, R.G., 1964, *The Development of Training Objectives* (Alexandria, Virginia: Human Resources Research Office).

STANLEY, J.C. and BOLTON, D., 1957, Book review section. *Educational Psychology Measurement*, **17**, 631–634.

WELFORD, A.T., 1968, *Fundamentals of Skill* (London: Methuen).

WILLIAMS, W.L. and WHITMORE, P.G., 1959, The development and use of a performance test as a basis for comparing technicians with and without field experience and the Nike Ajax I.F.C. Maintenance Technician. *Technical Report 52* (Alexandria, Virginia: Human Resources Research Office).

ZAJONC, R.B., 1965, Social Facilitation. *Science*, **149**, 269–274.

Mr. Shepherd holds a psychology degree. He was engaged in research into teaching electronics concepts and then taught psychology in a technical college. He is currently employed at the University of Hull, England, on research into fault-finding training in the Chemical Industry.

2:8

A classification scheme for decision-making tasks in the chemical industry

A. Shepherd

Introduction

Classification schemes or task taxonomies are useful tools for designing training. Their value is that tasks may be assigned to categories such that members of a specific category may each benefit from similar training conditions. Some task taxonomies attempt to classify the *behavioural* structure of tasks. For example, Gagné (1965) suggests that useful categories might be signal learning, stimulus response learning, chaining, etc., while Miller (1967) prefers information processing language such as scanning, identification of relevant cues, interpretation of cues, etc. These two are representative of rather a large number of behavioural classification schemes. An alternative to this approach is to classify the *operational* structure of tasks. This would involve stating the problem that a system poses an operator and his objectives in solving that problem.

A behavioural scheme might be useful when a trainer is approaching a type of task for the first time, since it will provide him with a set of hypotheses with which to devise training methods. But on a subsequent occasion when he encounters a task which makes similar demands on the operator, he can resort to the basic approach that he employed previously, if it proved successful. This suggests that a different type of scheme to classify tasks would be more useful to trainers who find that while the jobs that they are to train differ considerably, they often contain similar components. Nearly all chemical plant operators, for instance, must be able to identify and operate valves, they are nearly all engaged in one or another type of fault-finding and they must all be capable of undertaking necessary safety procedures.

Furthermore, the similarity of these tasks is not just peculiar to one training officer but similar problems exist throughout the whole industry and in many allied industries. There are considerable advantages, therefore, if these common types of task are identified and useful recommendations for analysis and training made available for each of these. A taxonomy of *operations* is preferred for this type of scheme for several reasons. Firstly, in many cases it is not clear what the operator's ideal behaviour should be. Always to accept experienced worker standards is unwise. This is certainly so in fault finding tasks. The fact that operators can eventually find faults is no indication that they can do so in an efficient, desirable or safe manner. On the other hand, the objectives of the operator's behaviour and the problem set him by the industrial system that he is operating can usually be stated quite categorically. It makes more sense for the trainer to identify the type of task that he must train and *then* review the various suggestions concerning assistance that can be given to the operator in meeting these objectives. For instance, displays might be improved, better procedures might be developed, or perhaps efficient job aids could be used. By specifying tasks in operational terms, all of this information can be communicated to a training officer or other members of works management, allowing them to decide which solution suits them best for economic, safety or any other reasons.

A second advantage of classifying tasks in operational terms is related to the fact that training information must usually be communicated across disciplines. Trainers on the one hand are often recruited from within their particular industry whereas training researchers usually have a background in psychology or allied sciences. It is, therefore, unwise for the latter to communicate task or training information attached to psychological labels. This would require trainers reliably to classify tasks according to behavioural concepts with which they are not familiar. It is doubtful whether even psychologists do this very efficiently. If, however, the researcher can discriminate between types of tasks on grounds which suit his purposes for research and furthermore, can describe these different types with suitable exemplification in a way that an industry based trainer can readily accept, then the communication problem will have been solved.

A third reason concerns the activities of the researcher. It can often be advantageous to an industry if the researcher's brief does not constrain him to investigate only *one* means by which an operator might execute a task. If tasks are described in operational terms then the researcher is in a better position to keep an open mind about the type of solution, whether it depends on selection, training, ergonomics or a modification of procedures. The case frequently arises where industrial or military sponsors decide that a particular behavioural objective for training is desirable and request that a research team investigate suitable training methods. The classic case is the assumption that knowledge of the theory of a system is a necessary pre-requisite to its fault-finding, for example, in electronics systems, biological systems and almost certainly with chemical plant.

This paper is concerned with the development of a classification scheme in operational terms, for decision making tasks which are encountered by plant operators in the Chemical Industry. By decision making tasks is meant those tasks where the operator must decide which of several courses of action he should adopt, given the conditions of his plant at that particular time—for example, the selection of suitable remedial action when a failure occurs.

These tasks are common throughout this industry and, furthermore, present considerable training difficulties. The problems arise not from the particular operations that must be performed in order to complete the task, as these are often quite simple, but rather from the manner in which these operations must be selected and sequenced in order to execute the task efficiently. In other words, the difficult nature of these tasks arises from the fact that the operator needs *complex plans* to organize what are often very *simple operations*. This argument has been developed by Dr. Duncan in his paper.

The scope of the classification scheme

The scheme has been restricted to the activities of chemical plant *operators*. However, it would have been in principle possible to include activities of several other classes of personnel within the industry, such as management, instrument technicians and fitters, all of whom are engaged in complex decision making of some kind. But this research project, like others, must be completed within a limited period of time. By considering only the activities of operators, detailed study of the particular types of task in the scheme is possible. This allows research proposals to be more clearly formulated and enables training recommendations to be made by modifying findings from research which has investigated tasks of a similar structure. One obvious example where this last point has been used to advantage, is in applying some of the literature from electronics fault finding to the training of 'searching' tasks that are encountered in the chemical industry. It is fair to say that no matter how well a scheme classifies a set of tasks, it is of little value if no training recommendations can be made for each of the classes.

The chemical industry

Before the scheme is described, it will be necessary briefly to outline the role of chemical plant operators and to describe one or two features of the industry which are relevant to the present discussion.

In general, the operator's job is to ensure efficient day-to-day running of his plant. This will involve starting-up and shutting-down of the process where necessary, and maintaining efficient running, which involves routine tasks such as log keeping and collecting samples and non-routine tasks which are usually connected with the location of any faults which occur during running. The actual task of rectifying the faults is usually referred to instrument mechanics or fitters, and the more unusual types of fault location problems are usually dealt with at plant management level. On most plants, instruments which measure and control process parameters are displayed centrally in a control room and it is here that operators spend much of their time. For some tasks though, they are obliged to go out onto the plant where they must have a knowledge of plant geography in order to locate specific pumps or drain valves.

Processes in the chemical industry can roughly be divided into batch and continuous processes. In batch processes, the various feed-stocks to the process are measured and are used to make a specified quantity of product. One consequence of such processes is that the whole batch is subject to the same operation at the same time. For example, the whole batch will, at any one time, be subjected to either reaction, or to separation of some kind. Since samples are usually taken at each stage then the location of any failure is easily done.

On the other hand, continuous processes are designed to maintain continuous production from a continuous feed. Two features of these systems are relevant to the present discussion. Firstly, material flows continuously through all the operations in the plant and secondly, equipment is designed such that all of the process parameters at different points in the system, usually temperatures, pressures, levels and flow rates, are kept constant over time. If there is a failure at some point in the plant, then these values will not be maintained and symptoms will be referred to different parts of the plant.

Most of the types of task that will be described in the classification scheme were encountered in continuous processes. The few instances of tasks in the scheme that are encountered in batch processes are either very straightforward involving a one-to-one relationship between symptom and failure, or involve self-contained continuous operations. A typical example of this last case is where a specific quantity of product is being made but, in order to control the heat given off in reaction, the feedstocks are mixed gradually over a period of time. This means that one or both of the feeds are pumped into the reactor at a rate that is sufficiently slow to permit adequate cooling of the reactor. The control that is exercised over flow rate gives this operation the characteristics of a continuous process.

The classification scheme

The scheme proposes two major categories of decision making tasks and organizes the specific categories within these. These two categories distinguish between two principal objectives that an operator may have in his execution of the task. The first, and probably the most common, is *fault-finding* which has already been briefly mentioned. In these tasks, the operator is given an indication of some disturbance to the system in his charge and must discover, as quickly as possible, the failure that is disturbing it. Speed stress arises for at least three reasons. Some situations demand a rapid solution for safety reasons, some situations demand a rapid solution because the symptoms will develop to an extent where no discrimination between failures can readily be made and, finally, a rapid solution is sought because product to the correct specification cannot be made at all, whilst the disturbance persists and this is expensive.

In some plants, however, it is possible to maintain production after a failure has occurred by taking some kind of compensating action to eliminate the disturbance caused by the failure. These tasks have been called *compensation.* They usually result in less efficient production than normal running, but this is preferred to shutting down the plant altogether, which is a very costly process. A fault-finding task is usually associated with compensation.

The complete classification scheme is as follows:

Fault Finding	*Compensation*
(*a*) Static diagnosis from a panel	(*f*) Balancing production and consumption in an integrated plant
(*b*) Dynamic diagnosis from a panel	(*g*) Trimming continuous running
(*c*) Searching in an unstructured system	(*h*) Fault elimination
(*d*) Searching in a structured system	
(*e*) Grouping units for testing	

Each of these classes will be explained and, where it is felt necessary, an instance of a task from the industry will be given. However, it will be impossible to describe training hypotheses for each of these classes within the scope of this paper. The two categories of which most is known, are described elsewhere. These are *Static diagnosis from a panel* (Shepherd, 1973a) and *Searching in a structured system* (Shepherd, 1973b).

(*a*) *Static diagnosis from a panel*

When the operator is required to make a diagnosis in the static situation, his attention is drawn by an auditory alarm to a flashing alarm on the control panel which indicates the first symptom that has occurred. He will cancel the auditory alarm and proceed with his diagnosis by referring to the indications given by the instruments, including any further alarms, on the panel. The operator will have to refer to several symptoms before the correct failure can be distinguished from other possibilities, since there exists considerable overlap of the symptom patterns for different failures. The task is clearly similar to instances of diagnosis encountered in other fields, for example, electronics and medicine. Where the task as encountered in chemical plant does differ, is in the stress under which diagnosis takes place. There is a real need to locate a failure in a very short time which, in the electronics or medical situation, may be desirable but is rarely crucial.

(b) Dynamic diagnosis from a panel

The other principal diagnostic activity in the control room is *dynamic* diagnosis. In static diagnosis, the operator is able to make his diagnosis by reference to the indications given by the instruments. In dynamic diagnosis, however, a decision can only be made by reference to the *order* in which alarms occur. The task is complicated by the fact that sometimes the operator will not be on hand to see which alarms occur first. It seems important that some modification should be made to panels to enable the order of alarms to be preserved. Beyond this, little is known about the execution or training of this type of task from the research literature in either pure or applied psychology.

Contamination problems

When the presence of contamination in unacceptable concentration is detected in the final product, it is the operator's job to initiate a search for its source.

Three types of problem where the operator must locate the source of contaminant in a system have been identified. Each of them involves several units, any one of which could have been the source of the contamination. They differ in the manner in which the units are interrelated.

(c) Searching in an unstructured system

If product from several unconnected units flows into a common channel and if contaminant is detected in this common channel, then the operator must decide which of the units is causing this. Since there is no structure in the system, the operator can only locate the failure by examining each unit in turn. Each unit may have a different probability of failure and may require a different amount of work to test whether or not it is at fault. While several situations of this structure are encountered in the industry, only rarely do they prove to be a problem for the personnel concerned.

One instance, however, which may represent a common problem, was encountered which seemed to be presenting some difficulty to training staff. In this case, three plants were contributing to a common smoke stack. The three plants, although independent, are operated by one operator from three different panels in his control room. When smoke appears on the stack, he can only decide which plant is at fault by making a diagnosis of each panel in turn. If the probabilities of the failure occurring in each of the three plants remain constant, then there is little trouble in supplying the operator with a fixed sequence with which to examine each panel by trading off the probability of failure of each plant with the average time to make a diagnosis of the associated panels, i.e., the 'cost' of making the test. The logic of selecting units for testing on the basis of probability and cost is quite straightforward. The unit to be tested first is the one which maximizes the ratio of probability to cost. A *fixed* order of testing can thus be specified. Unfortunately though, it is more likely in these situations that the probability of failure can and should be frequently revised by an operator according to his knowledge of the state of equipment on the plant. In such an event, an operator might be trained to effectively trade-off his subjective probability of failure with the cost of testing, before he embarks on a diagnosis.

There has been considerable attention to this type of problem in the literature, for example, Detambel and Stolurow (1957) have shown that in these tasks, the probability variable weighs more heavily than the cost variable in the operator's evaluation of priorities. They interpreted 'cost' in terms of the amount of work that the subject had to perform in making each test. Their units consisted of a set of panels screwed to a base board. On the base board hidden by each panel was printed the letters 'O.K.'. If the unit was at fault, these letters were covered by sticky tape. The cost of testing each unit was varied by using a different number of screws to fix a panel to its base. Therefore the subject had to remove a different number of screws to see whether each unit was 'O.K.'. Detambel and Stolurow evaluate *physical* work, whereas in many instances in the chemical industry, physical work is not involved. Now in the example given concerning the smoke stack, the operator may modify his strategy according to how *difficult* the diagnosis from each panel is, but it cannot be assumed that the same relationship exists between 'searching' and *mental work* as is shown to exist by Detambel and Stolurow between 'searching' and *physical work.*

Of equal importance though is that a concept of cost which is subjective to the operator and is concerned with his effort in seaching may be at odds with the concept of cost that *management* would desire that he uses. The point has been made that one of the values of rapid diagnosis is to avoid 'down-time' of plant. Cost in management terms, therefore, will be in terms of the likelihood of incurring down-time. Even if operators were trained to take account of management costs, it is unlikely that this performance would be preserved on the job since the effort he makes in diagnosis will continue to be present and obvious while the 'costs' of management will not. This problem will be avoided if the operator's performance is rigidly programmed by using a job aid.

(*d*) *Searching in a structured system*

A more common set of problems is *searching in a structured system.* A structured system is one where units are arranged so that a material or a signal can flow through the units in a fixed sequence. This is common to all continuous process chemical plant which consists of a series of vessels, each performing a different operation on the material, connected in sequence by pipework. In many of these vessels, material is either being heated up or cooled down. This heat exchange is affected by cladding the vessels in pipes through which a hotter or cooler fluid is passed. The fluid is often water or pressurized steam. If a leak occurs between the cladding and the vessel, then water will enter into the main system and this will be detected in the final product from a routine sample.

The operator must locate this source of contaminant by taking samples from different points on the plant with the knowledge that if the sample he collected is contaminated, then the source must be upstream, that is, somewhere nearer the start of the process, whereas if the sample is pure, then the source of contamination must be downstream from the sample point. Strategies for searching in structured systems are well known, especially in connection with electronics fault finding (Dale, 1958). Problems of search in chemical plant are among the most difficult that can be encountered in structured systems. Both the costs of making tests and the probabilities of units failing can vary and no solution exists for *generating* optimal decision trees. This can be done iteratively, but this is time-consuming, and may not be worth the effort. An attempt has been made elsewhere by this writer (Shepherd, 1973b) to adapt many of these search rules to a form which is appropriate to searching in the Chemical Industry.

(*e*) *Grouping units for testing*

The third task involving contamination has been given the label of *grouping units for testing*. This task involves a system of units which are unconnected, yet contribute product to a common output. As such, it is similar to the case of *unstructured search*. However, while the case of unstructured search demands that the operator select one unit for testing, 'grouping' permits the operator to test as many as he likes at one time. For example, if the system contains twenty units, one of which is at fault, the operator can test any number of these units simultaneously to see whether the faulty unit is among them. Furthermore, the task differs from *structured search* where, although units can be tested in groups, the only combinations permitted are those defined by the structure of the system, i.e., only units *upstream* from a sample point may be tested together. In 'grouping' where no structure exists, any combination is permissible.

This type of structure is exemplified by a piece of equipment called the Niagara Filter which is schematically represented in Figure 1. The liquid to be filtered is pumped into the pressure vessel where it passes through one of several filter leaves into a common manifold through which the clarified liquor leaves the vessel. Since the manifold is common to all of the leaves, then a faulty

Figure 1. The Niagara Filter. The material to be filtered is pumped into the pressure vessel. It passes through the filter leaves and into a common manifold then leaves the vessel. If the filtration is unsuccessful this is indicated by cloudiness in the sight glass

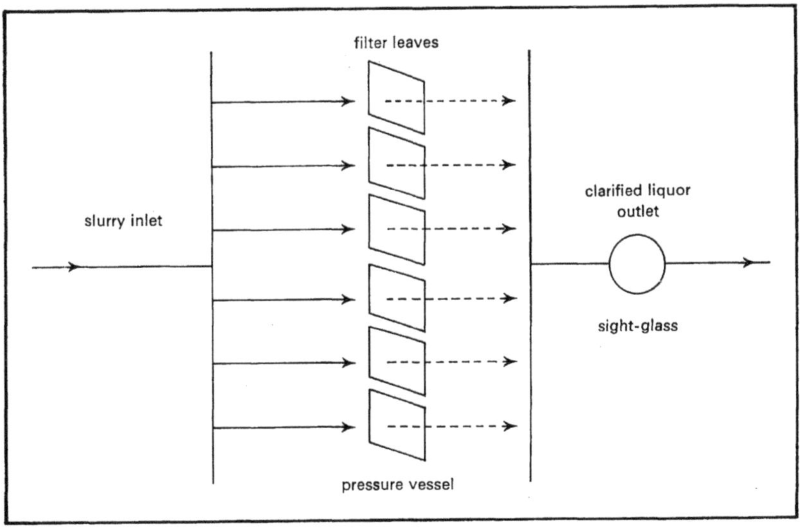

leaf cannot be directly identified if the sight glass on the outlet from the filter proves to be cloudy. The operator can conduct his search by replacing as many leaves as he wishes with bungs and then attempting the filtration again. In this way, he can reduce the set of possible failures as he wishes, the best strategy being a process of successively dichotomizing the possible array of failures.

It must be stated that this description of fault-finding a Niagara Filter has been deliberately over-simplified. There are some failures of the filter external to the vessel but these can be determined directly without any resource to complex reasoning. It is also common to be able to determine some of the leaf failures by visual inspection. The 'grouping' problem arises when these other, more readily diagnosed failures, have been eliminated. The question of 'grouping units' will be returned to later in connection with the *fault elimination* task, again with reference to the Niagara Filter.

(*f*) *Balancing production and consumption in an integrated plant*

The *balancing* task is encountered where an operator must balance the rate of production of some resource with its rate of consumption. The problem is made complex by the fact that there are usually several factors which contribute to production and several factors determining consumption. In its structure, it must be very similar to many managerial tasks.

A common instance of the task is matching the production of power at a works with its use by the different plants on that works. The problem here is in distributing the power that is available to the different plants in the most economical manner possible.

A more complex instance was encountered on a large integrated plant, where gas was produced from several units and was piped directly to several different users. This system is schematically illustrated in Figure 2.

Among the factors affecting production which the operator must consider

Figure 2. Integrated production and consumption. Gas is produced in units A, B and C and is then piped to the liquification plant and the two user plants. The emergency absorption plant is not normally used but acts as a safety valve to absorb excess gas in the system if, for example, one of the user plants has to shut down suddenly

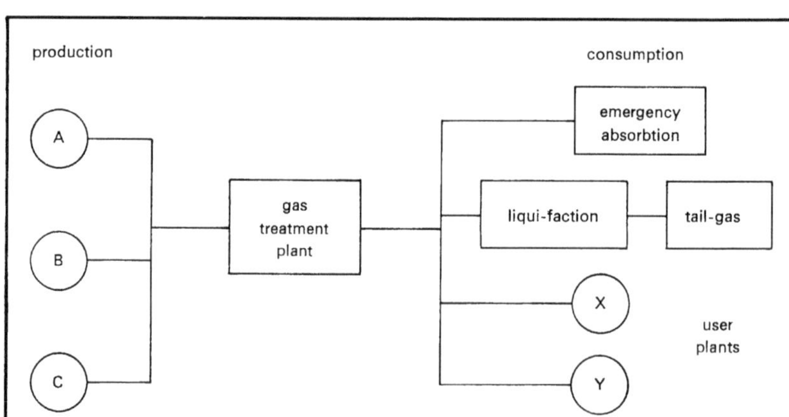

are the availability of power required to produce gas; the availability of equipment to use the power provided; whether the gas that is produced can be adequately treated and whether he can use or store the gas. On the consumption side, a shut-down or partial shut-down by any of the users may require the operator to cut back on production of gas. If all of the users are available but production of gas is limited, then the operator's task is to distribute the gas between the users in the most economical manner, usually dictated by current customer demands. But these problems only scratch at the surface of the complexity facing the operator.

The objective in analysing this task is to discover rules which can be easily stated and learned by a trainer.

The first apparent difficulty facing the operator is the vast amount of varied indications he will receive that there is an unbalance of the system. One of several hundred specific instances will occur for which he must have a plan to restore balance to the system. Fortunately, there are only a few different courses of action that he may take and each specific instance can be classified into a group whose members will all require the same course of action to restore balance. Instances can be assigned to groups, according to whether they are, for example, concerned with the *production* or *consumption* of gas, *increases* or *decreases* in either of these and whether the operator receives *warning* that any of these events will occur or whether he is given an *alarm* for immediate action. For example, if the operator is told in advance that there will be a shut-down of part of the work's power station for scheduled maintenance, he can treat this in the same way as he would treat a planned reduction of power due to an increase in the tariff of electricity from the National Grid.

Analysis has so far revealed 24 general kinds of instances and it may be possible to reduce this number still further when the courses of action that operators use are scrutinized. Situations may also occur in combinations of two or even more events. It seems unlikely that this addition increases the number of different courses of action the operator must take, but instead, he may employ rules to assign priority to one course of action rather than another. These rules remain to be investigated.

A further implication for training is that the operator needs only to perform 15 *operations* to execute the 24 courses of action. Each course of action consists of some of these operations. One operation is 'obtain load distribution' which will inform the operator of the existing load assigned to each production unit. Another is 'check availability of standby equipment' which will tell him the extent to which he may use the 'treatment plant'. The management of this plant sees no difficulty in training these 15 operations. The difficulty of the task arises from selecting the appropriate course of action to rebalance the system given a specific disturbance and *planning* each course of action by selecting and sequencing from the set of operations.

(*g*) *Trimming*

It has been suggested on numerous plants that a feature of the good operator is that he consistently monitors his panel, even though an alarm has not indicated a specific source of trouble. In this way he may notice some relatively minor disturbance to some of his instruments and may be able to return the plant to more efficient running conditions. This task of *trimming continuous running* has been classified as one of *compensation* for the reason that the operator is not primarily concerned with what is causing the disturbance, but is simply taking action to overcome that disturbance. In a lot of cases though, there will be a real fault developing which he must deal with. It may be that the fault will develop to such a degree that an alarm will trip and he will be in the more urgent business of diagnosis. On the other hand, if he is sufficiently skilled, he may be able to identify a fault before it gets too critical and switch to standby equipment so as to revert to efficient running of the plant.

(*h*) *Fault elimination*

It may be the case that fault *elimination* can be encountered with any of the systems described in connection with the fault-finding tasks. In most of these systems a fault can only be eliminated if it is first discovered and then its correction will be a straightforward procedure like switching in a standby pump. One system, however, provides the opportunity to eliminate a fault, even though the source of failure is not detected. This is the system described in (*e*) which permits grouping units for testing. Again, the equipment in which this was encountered was the Niagara Filter.

When these filters are used in *batch* production then any holdup in the filtering operation will usually mean that the material must be delayed in the reactor until the filtration can be concluded. This will cause delays in the reaction of the next batch and this will be costly. If the operator's objective is to filter a batch in the shortest possible time, rather than simply to find the fault, then it can be shown that he can minimize the overall time for filtration by taking steps to *eliminate* the fault, rather than *find* it. While a filtration can proceed with less leaves than the maximum, it will do so in a proportionally greater time. On the other hand, the more leaves that are removed from the filter, the more likely it is that the leaf at fault is among them. Ideally, the operator would trade-off these two factors and so determine the optimal number to remove for a particular batch. The expected time for the filtration will depend, to some extent, on how long it takes to clean off leaves after each failure. Since cleaning time varies with the characteristics of the material being filtered, the optimal number of leaves to be removed will vary depending on the material being filtered.

The procedures suggested here illustrate that operators must be certain about their objectives in performing a task and that management must make these objectives clear. Among the operating criteria of this industry are efficiency and safety. Efficiency is served in batch production by completing a batch as quickly as possible. Which, in the example given, is best achieved by eliminating any failure rather than seeking it.

General operational classification schemes

The fact that the proposed scheme attempts to classify only a restricted range of tasks might be seen as a distinct disadvantage. It is acknowledged that statements which can be generalized beyond specific industries and organizations are potentially most useful. However, one is forced to question the accuracy of these general schemes. It is doubtful that one research team can have sufficient experience of the range of industrial processes or situations that would be required to establish a truly representative classification scheme whether it is based on a behavioural or an operational structure of tasks.

While the present scheme has attempted to classify one type of task performed by a specific grade of personnel in a specific industry, it is possible with sufficient efforts in other contexts, in industry and elsewhere, that a more general scheme will emerge. By reconciling different schemes in different situations, it may emerge that classes of operations are common across industries. This will require a definition of class membership to be stated in terms which are not specific to a particular industry, yet which retain the logical and psychological distinctions that are necessary to warrant the selection of different approaches to training. This has been attempted in the present scheme, even though for the purposes of training officers, each class can also be exemplified with terms used in the Chemical Industry. From the general statement describing each class, in the present scheme, it is clear that there exist problems that will be encountered in other industries. The obvious example is the similarity between the duties of a chemical plant operator and the duties of an electronics maintenance technician. Another is the problem of 'balancing production and consumption in an integrated plant' which presents features of tasks that might elsewhere be conducted at managerial level.

Application of the scheme

The proposed scheme is not intended as a tool for analysing tasks but rather as a tool for *retrieving* training information once an analysis has been completed. Unfortunately it is impossible to assert that *any* technique of analysis which identifies constituent operations of a task may be used. Some forms of task analysis specify a *fixed* level of description of tasks and, in several cases, this will be different to that used in the classification scheme. The scheme is usefully employed in conjunction with the analytic technique described by Duncan (1972) which has the advantage of *not* specifying a fixed level of description. According to this technique the analyst will describe a task in terms of its constituent operations and a plan which specifies when these operations should be performed. If no obvious training recommendations can be made for any of these operations then they are further redescribed until hypotheses for training are forthcoming. This ensures that at some stage an operation will be identified which is described at the same level as the classes of operations in the proposed scheme.

An example of this general procedure is illustrated in Table 1 which is part of a task analysis described by Duncan. Two of the operations he identifies are types of decision making tasks which are represented in the present classification scheme. Operation 140 is an instance of 'static diagnosis from a panel' whilst operation 161 is an instance of 'searching in a structured system'. Duncan offers some hypotheses for training these operations in his table but these need to be empirically tested.

Concluding remarks

The classification scheme integrates the activities of the training officer and the researcher. A scheme where members of each category all require similar training assists the training officer in developing his specific training programme. It is the job of the training researcher to develop and evaluate methods of training for each of these categories.

Table 1. Examples of entries in the Task Analysis Table (from Duncan, 1972)

No.	*Description of Operation and Training Notes*	*I or F*	*A*	*Redescribed*
50 / 47,3	When temperature and set point coincide, turn switch from 'manual' to 'auto'.			=
	* * * * *			
60 / 5,39	Open *manifold valve to T.25/26* and shut *valve to T.23.* **I** See 33.	X	—	—
	* * * * *			
78 / 6,18	Set up a pressure of 1 p.s.i.g. on the gauge after the block valve. Then check that there is a purge through the system by putting a hand over the outlet vent. **F** Must find way through plant to outlet vent. Once pointed out, vent is easily identified.	X	—	—
	* * * * *			
140 / 9,2	Inspect alarm panels and console instruments to locate failure. To allow sufficient time to take action in the case of preventable plant shut-down, a diagnosis must be made in the control room within three minutes. **I F** A prerequisite for training is highly practised location of every console instrument to avoid wasting time searching for instruments at the expense of diagnosis. **R** Diagnosis, i.e. selection of *one* of the ten sub-operations, is a major training requirement. Simulation inevitable since opportunities for practice—if acceptable to management—would be infrequent. Three possibilities are: 1. Rote learn associations between sets of indications and faults —a difficulty will be overlapping indications (see attached symptom list). 2. 'Technical story' plus practice in identifying failure consistent with a set of symptoms. A prerequisite: learn conventions for designating the function of an instrument, e.g. LIC (level indicator-controller). 3. Construct decision trees specifying a branching sequence of the minimum instrument readings to reach a diagnosis.	X	X	141, 151 to 159
141 / 140,1	Restore Column 10 feed (*P.71/72*). **I** See 78. **R** First try restarting pump-in-use (it may have been switched off). If pump-in-use fails to start, change over to stand-by as quickly as possible. Then report need for repairs (*both* pumps may fail to start).	X	X	142, 143, 150
142 / 141,1	Try start switch of pump in use.			=
143 / 141,2	Change over to stand-by pump. **R** Memorizing the fixed sequence 143,1 to 143,6 is vital (acid could be pumped out of an open drain valve).	—	X	144 to 149
	* * * * *			
161 / 10,2	Locate origin of water contamination by taking further samples from other points on the plant. **R** The number and order of samples taken, i.e. sub-operations, varies. *Given* (a) a relative cost index for each of 7 sampling points *and* (b) for each of 8 plant components, estimated probability of failure (i.e. contaminating product), the operator must apply a search strategy which minimizes sampling costs. Need flow diagram showing only relevant information, i.e. (a) and (b). Simulation inevitable (see 140)—in this case instructor might provide 'lab. reports' for a random series of 'faults' (occurring with a frequency proportional to their probabilities). Should trainee 1. be told efficient strategy, e.g. decision tree prescribing branching sequence or samples? or 2. attempt unaided to minimize his sampling costs?	—	X	162 to 168
	* * * * *			
165 / 161,4	Sample *R2 evaporator sight glass drain valve.* **I** See 33.	X	—	—

References

DALE, H.C.A., 1958, Fault-finding in electronic equipment. *Ergonomics*, **1**, 356–385.
DETAMBEL, M.H. and STOLUROW, L.M., 1957, Probability and work as determiners of multichoice behaviour. *Journal of Experimental Psychology*, **53**, 73–81.
DUNCAN, K.D., 1972, Strategies for analysis of the task. *Strategies for Programmed Instruction*, edited by J. Hartley (London: Butterworths).
GAGNÉ, R.M., 1965, *The Conditions of Learning* (New York: Holt, Rinehart and Winston).
MILLER, R.B., 1967, Task Taxonomy: Science or Technology? *Ergonomics*, **10**, 167–176.
SHEPHERD, A., 1973a, Training in diagnosis in Chemical Plant. In preparation.
SHEPHERD, A., 1973b, Locating contaminant in Chemical Plant. In preparation.

Dr. Bainbridge holds degrees in psychology and industrial engineering. She first worked at I.A.M. Farnborough on human factors in air-traffic control, then with Professors E.R.F.W. Crossman and R.J. Beishon on manual process control, particularly in the steel industry. She is now lecturer in Psychology at the University of Reading, England, and studying skills and complex cognitive processes.

2:9

The representation of working storage and its use in the organization of behaviour

Lisanne Bainbridge

1. Introduction

This paper discusses the use of working storage and its place in the organization of cognitive behaviour, and introduces a technique for describing these explicitly.

These issues arose during a study of verbal reports (protocols) from subjects doing a process control task. In such a task the operator (subject) controls a (manufacturing) process: he maintains it in a steady-state by continuously checking for errors and making corrective actions if necessary. The data below come from a task of regulating the overall use of electric power by five steel-making furnaces. Each of these furnaces goes through a sequence of stages in the steel-making process, and each of these stages requires a different amount of power. The subjects controlled a digital simulation of this process, and were asked to 'think aloud' while doing the task. These verbal reports were recorded. These reports showed that the controller alternated between checking for a control error and other types of behaviour. When the process was in an unacceptable state the controller chose which furnace to change the power supply to, and the size of the change. When the process was under control he monitored the present and predicted the future stages of all the furnaces. He also assessed whether any future changes in furnace operation would lead to an unacceptable control state, and if so what the correction should be. The complete analysis is presented in Bainbridge (1972), a summary in Bainbridge (in press).

This was not a problem-solving task, as the controller worked within predefined aims, strategies and priorities. The task did not develop from a starting point to a solution, the same behaviour was required repeatedly to maintain a constant situation. The subject was interacting with and controlling a dynamic environment. Two aspects in particular of the verbal protocol behaviour were difficult to model, its flexibility and its parsimony. Behaviour with the same general aim varied in detail or method on different occasions; for example the size of control action to make might be chosen by numerical calculation (digital) or by judgement (analogue). There were no unnecessary repetitions of previous behaviour; for example, when a control error was developing the controller would choose an action, when a later check of the control state showed that the error was fully developed he made this action without repeating the decisions. The verbal protocols were analysed by the usual method of attempting to develop programmes which would produce the same sequence of behaviour as in the protocols. It was found that both the flexibility and parsimony of behaviour could be modelled by making the use of working storage in these programmes explicit, using the technique described below.

This technique was originally developed to account for particular data. Now it has been developed however it may be useful for describing cognitive behaviour in other tasks, particularly for specifying working storage requirements. We can also look at the general properties of the technique. The description of the power control task which was made using this technique has several features which may have general implications for the nature and organization of cognitive behaviour.

Section 2 introduces the method for explicitly including working storage in descriptions of information processing routines, and discusses when to use stored data, the choice between alternative methods of obtaining the same data, and the relations between routines. Section 3 describes the determinants of the sequence in which routines are used, the place of different types of working storage in different levels of cognitive organization, and the nature of context effects. Section 4 questions the nature of the limits to working storage capacity, and Section 5 discusses the relation of working storage to longer-term learning.

2. Storage and routines

When studying information processing in cognitive tasks one wants to know what operations are carried out and how these are executed, including the use of working storage. The technique used to describe the information processing must make these explicit.

An example of the simplest traditional method for describing processing routines is given in Figure 1a. This type of description implies a rigid blind mechanism. The sequence of operations is always the same when the routine is used. The aim of the routine, the data required (in this example the overall power usage after an event) is not named until the end of the routine, at the operation by which it is found (unless the routine has been developed as a sub-routine or procedure). This technique is inadequate for the present purpose.

2.1. *Explicit working storage*

The descriptive technique used in the power control study is illustrated in Figure 1b. The routine is centred round the data item required, which is named at its 'head'. This data item is represented in three parts; the item's name, a location or 'box' for storing its present value, and a link to the routine(s) by which this value can be found. This routine is itself specified in terms of the data items required. These items are also represented in three parts, their values are found by routines, and so on. The way in which operations or routines at one level are actually implemented by operations of a similar nature but at a lower level is therefore made explicit.

Distinguishing the data item from the routine gives the classic independence of a routine from the point at which it is used, the separation of instrument from purpose. This is useful for several reasons. The same sequence of operations may be used for several purposes, for obtaining similar data items in different parts of the task: see for example the use of the 'choice of furnace to alter' routine (Figure 4b) in Figures 3 and 4a. Less space will be needed to store cognitive routines if such a sequence of operations is stored once in a way which can be

Figure 1. Routine to calculate overall power usage after change of furnace stage
(*a*) Described using traditional method
(*b*) 'Box' description of same routine. Many operations which were implicit in (*a*) have been made explicit here
(*c*) Box symbol in a conditional statement

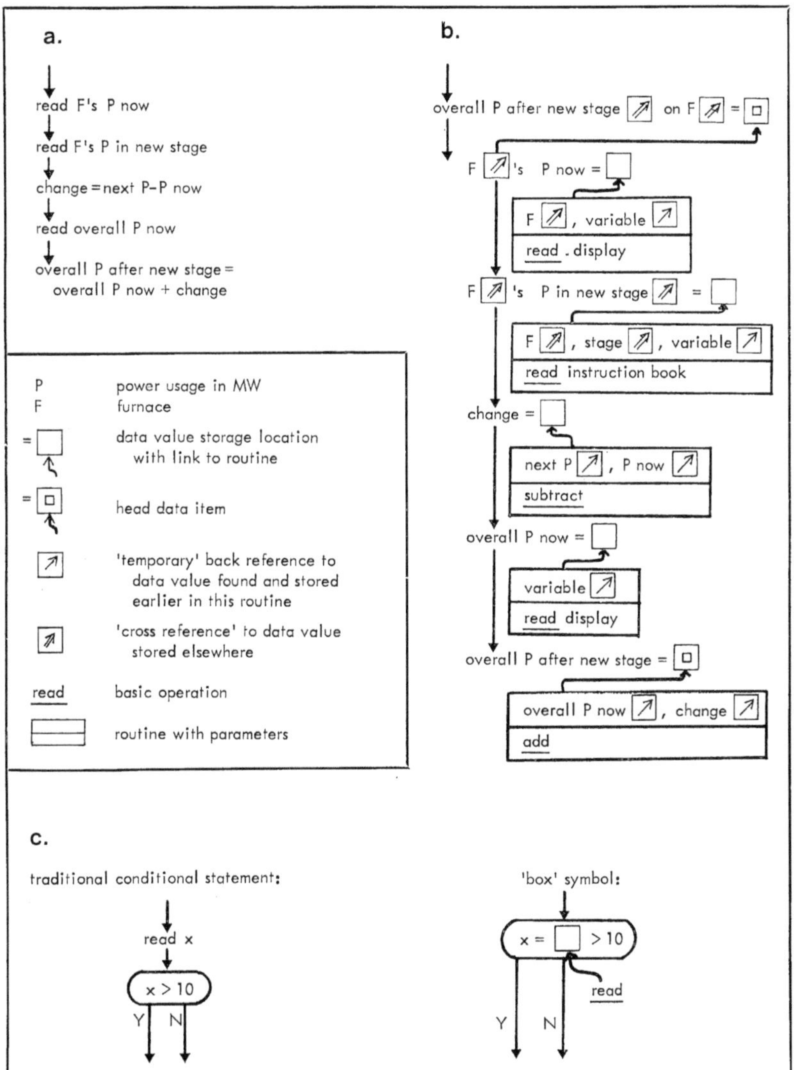

referred to from several points, rather than permanently reproducing it in full in each context where it is needed. If purpose and routine are independent this allows one routine to be called on from several data value storage points; conversely, one of these points could call on several alternative methods for finding the same value. This could provide a mechanism for the flexibility found in the protocol behaviour (see Section 2.2.2.).

The boxes in the diagram make the use of working storage explicit. If a data value has been found and stored earlier in the behaviour, then there is no need to repeat the routine to find this value when it is needed again. An arrow in a box in the diagram shows this back reference to a previous value, and so implies a data storage requirement (see Sections 3.2.1 and 4).

The first time a data item is needed there will be no value in the box, so all the routines will be carried out and the values stored. The next time this item is needed one could recap the stored result without repeating the routines. This provides a mechanism for parsimonious behaviour without unnecessary repetition, but such a simple mechanism raises several problems. In any realistic behaviour the decision to compute data must depend not only on the presence or absence of a stored value but also on its reliability and relevance (see Sections 2.2.1 and 3.2.1.). The continuity of working storage however does provide a mechanism for context effects and the way in which these determine the sequence of behaviour (see Section 3.2.2). In the remainder of this section the different functions of the three parts of the data item will be discussed more fully.

2.1.1. *Data names*—As mentioned above, routines are specified in terms of the data items required. This gives a goal- or data-oriented description, as the aim of a routine is stated before the routine is used. This reflects behaviour in the verbal protocols, the subject often mentioned the data required before using the routine to find it, e.g., 'now, how long has it been melting?'. These are information-processing rather than feedback-control goals. One might call this feedback-control with 'lack of data' as the 'error', but this would trivialize the term feedback, as no quantitatively varying error correction is involved here.

This naming could also describe the way in which subjects (particularly the inexperienced) can know what item they need the value of, but not how to find this value. This situation could be represented by an item without an associated routine. The lack of routine could initiate a search for method, by asking questions, reading task instructions or working it out for oneself. Once a routine has been acquired it could be called on when needed.

2.1.2. *Data storage*—A 'box' in the diagrams represents the functional location at which data values are stored or referred to.

In the power control study various types of data value were stored. Numerical values could be obtained by: reading displays, written notes or the task instructions; from memorized constants; by calculation using a slide-rule or long-hand on paper; or by judgement. Names, for example reference letters, the names of process stages, or quantitative categories (above, alright, action required, etc.) could be obtained by reading displays or by information processing. Some boxes were needed simply to note whether a named item existed or condition was met, e.g., next power usage changing event compensates for present power usage error—yes or no.

Most of the these stored values were data items which were not displayed explicitly to the controller. There was good evidence that some of the displayed values were also stored however and that the controller acted on these stored values, e.g., the subjects sometimes acted according to past rather than present values of the process. Presumably these values were stored because this allows quicker access, or because the stored data was organized in a more useful way than the displays, e.g., the present furnace stages were displayed in alphabetic order, the behaviour of experienced controllers showed that they remembered them in lists of furnaces in the same stage.

Each location stores one value. A series of 'boxes' is used for a list of values. Past, present and predicted future values of the same item are stored in separate boxes. This is appropriate as a different routine is used to find the value in each case. A box containing an arrow acts as a 'token' for data stored elsewhere. The number of items which must be available for reference at any one time can be counted from the diagrams drawn for the power control task, and imply the amount of working storage which is necessary for this behaviour at a particular time (see Section 4).

The word 'box' has been used with quotation marks because it is not intended to imply a particular mechanism for working storage. It has been used as a symbol in the diagram because it is easily identified, and it can be used for noting data values when working through the routines by hand simulation. If working storage has a box-type mechanism some representation of the data value would be transferred to and 'put in' this location. In an alternative mechanism a pointer at this functional storage location would refer to some data value representation which was stored elsewhere. A copy of this representation would be transferred only when its value was actually needed in computation (see Section 5).

2.1.3. *Routines*—The data name and storage location refer to a routine for finding the required value. Each routine must contain at least one operation which finds this value (symbolized in the diagrams by a double-lined box). Two types of routine were needed to describe behaviour in the power control task. In one the data value was found in the final operation of the routine. In the other type the routine progressively refined the data value by considering more dimensions of the situation, so the routine included a succession of operations which gave a data value, each of increasing accuracy.

Each routine is implemented by routines themselves consisting of three-part items, and so on. Routines also contain other types of component. The routines in the power control task sometimes contained alternative behaviours which were appropriate in different circumstances, and conditional statements were needed to describe the decision between these alternatives (see Section 3.1). The routines did not go to an infinite depth of routines implementing routines, they eventually referred to 'basic operations', indicating by underlining in Figure 1b. These might be mental actions, i.e., basic cognitive processes or information processing 'primitives', or they might be physical actions, interactions with the external world. Some of these physical interactions (e.g., reading, asking questions, using a slide-rule) gave data for use in cognitive processes, so affected the state of the internal world. Other physical actions affected the state of the external world (e.g., by making a control action). These basic operations are integrated into meaningful sequences of activity via the three-part data items, but conversely routines only become operational via these basic operations, in a sense they are otherwise only tokens or symbols.

2.2. *Deciding to use a routine*

Several decisions must be made at the point at which the data requirements of one routine lead to the use of another routine. The subject must decide whether to repeat a routine even if a value is already stored. When alternative methods are available he must decide which to use. Decisions at this point could lead to a wide range of different behaviour sequences from the same substrate of available routines.

Any breakdown in these decisions could lead to the sort of errors in working storage usage which tend to occur under stress or fatigue (e.g., Davis (1948), Welford, Brown and Gabb (1950)). In these circumstances subjects tend to forget sections of behaviour altogether, or to repeat data-finding behaviour unnecessarily, or to act on out-dated information. The point at which the subject decides whether to use a routine could be the locus for these errors.

2.2.1. *Deciding to repeat a routine*—The subject should decide to repeat a routine if the stored data value is either untrustworthy or irrelevant. For example a stored value may have decayed or have been disturbed (if the limit to working storage capacity is such that the stored values are continually changing), so that the value is no longer a true record of what was originally stored. The external world may have changed dynamically with time, so the stored value no longer represents the actual state of affairs. Finally, if the routine was last used for a different purpose its stored values will be irrelevant.

To be able to decide whether to recompute, the subject must have data about these dimensions of the stored values, and a mechanism for assessing the data. The subject must be able to assess the reliability of a data value as a true record, perhaps from its 'noisiness'. He must also be able to assess the likelihood that a particular dimension of the external world has changed. One could suggest many methods of making this assessment for particular data items in the power control task (it is interesting that many of these methods would require some knowledge of when the last sample was made), but this would be speculation. Behavioural data should indicate the actual processes involved. There is some evidence on the repetition of routines in the power control task, but the data analysed on this so far is rather limited and only simple inferences can be made. When the control error was unacceptable the controller usually repeated all the routines. It is important to be correct in this situation. When control error was acceptable the controller monitored the present and future stages of all the furnaces. He repeated this survey twice, and then started to chat in general, keeping an eye on the process for any change. This might suggest that two repetitions were sufficient for retention of the data values. Unfortunately the idiosyncracies of the particular situations in which this behaviour occurred meant that later behaviour did not need to make use of these data values so did not show whether or not the values were remembered.

Stored data values are irrelevant if a routine was previously used for a different purpose. It will be easier to understand the wider implications of data and discussion on this after some more points have been made (see Section 3.2.1).

2.2.2. *Choosing between alternative routines*—Many data items may call on the same routine and one data item may refer to several alternative routines. This suggests that the item-routine link is a complex one.

In the power control task there were two different types of alternative method for finding a data value. One routine might refine the data value it found, by progressively considering more dimensions of the situation. In this type it was necessary to decide how far to go in adding refinements within one basic method.

Figure 2. Suggested nature of link between data item and alternative routines for finding its value

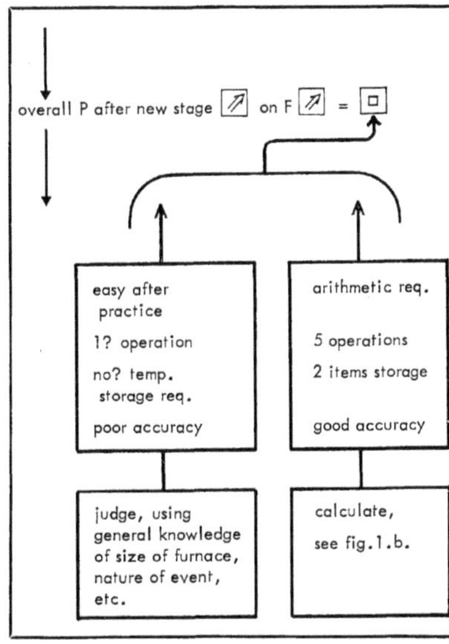

In the more usual case there were different methods of finding the same value, as in Figure 2, so it was necessary to decide between them. Both these types of choice between alternatives could lead to a speed-accuracy trade-off in performance, as the less time allowed the less accurate the method used.

Data from the power control task suggest that the factors used in deciding between alternative methods may be the difficulty of the methods, the time they take, and the amount of working storage they need. The controller found the value of the control error by judgement instead of making long complex calculations (data in Bainbridge (1971)). He alternated between action choice routines and checking the control error, when error was unacceptable. When the control error was more unacceptable the interval between control error samples was shorter, implying that shorter routines were used. This suggests that the urgency of the situation influenced the duration of the routine used. The 'choice of furnace for action' routine in Figures 3 and 4 illustrates the type of data which might be obtained on the effects of working capacity requirements. This routine was used at two different 'depths', alone (direct from Figure 3), and via the 'future assessment' routine (Figure 4a, which is called by Figure 3). If there is a limit to working storage capacity then there might be less capacity available for use by a routine when it is called via another routine, so the routine might be simpler in form. The behaviour shows that this choice of action routine was simpler when used in choosing a future action. Unfortunately this particular example does not provide good evidence about working storage capacity as possible alternative actions are fewer in the future than in the present, so the routine for choosing a future action can be simpler. We are only beginning to understand how to find evidence on this type of question.

The data suggest that the above factors influence the nature of the routine used. This suggests that the following are required by a data item, to provide a link to the routines. There must be a list of the alternative routines (with pointers to where they can be found). Data on the costs and values of using each routine must be available, at least relative measures of the difficulty of the cognitive processes involved, the time and working storage needed, and the value (e.g., the accuracy obtained) of using it. There must also be a decision mechanism which can assess the currently permissible levels of these costs and values, and use them as criteria in choosing between the routines.

2.3. *Levels in the organization of routines*

It is traditional to describe the organization of behaviour in terms of the branching levels of a goal-oriented hierarchy (cf., Bryan and Harter (1899), Miller, Galanter and Pribram (1960), Newell and Simon (1961)). In practice however it is often difficult to define what constitutes a 'level', or to identify the level of a particular piece of behaviour. The present technique describes behaviour as a goal-oriented branching structure. The organization here is not hierarchical however, and the reason for this demonstrates both why it is difficult to identify the levels in any real behaviour and also the general inadequacy of a hierarchy as a description of behaviour.

The key to these limitations lies in the lack of unique links between goals (data items) and the routines for implementing them. These links may be unique because of limits to the logical or physical possibilities in a particular task, or because a subject has not learned that some routine has more general application, but this is not necessarily so. The result is that it is not possible to draw a unique or 'tree' type of description for the branching in task organization.

Each data item calls on routines which consist of data items, and so on. This apparently defines level of organization. It does not define a constant value of level for any particular routine however. If items are free to call on any routine then a particular routine may be called on by any of these levels, so that its own level can only be defined in relation to a particular context, not in general. (See the 'choice of furnace for action' routine in Figures 3 and 4.) It is also at least logically possible for one routine to lead to another and so on until it leads back to itself. In such a freely interconnecting network one item may at a particular time be the 'top' item from which others lead. If other data items can also be the focus of organization however, then the level of a particular routine will not be constant but will depend on its relation to the top item at any particular time. Thus levels cannot be identified within the static structure of task organization, but a functional hierarchy may appear when this structure is used dynamically to do a particular task.

Complete freedom of interconnection between routines does not appear in real behaviour. This freedom will be limited by the possible meaningful relations in the task. Also any limit to working storage capacity may restrict the number of routines which can lead on from one another at a particular time. In the power control task a 'top' and 'bottom' to the interrelations between the routines were defined by the sequencings 'above' the routines, which determine the order in which the routines are used (see next Section), and the basic operations 'below'. Within these limitations one can suggest however that routines are related in a network or heterarchy of interconnections, rather than in a hierarchical tree.

3. Conditional determinants and behaviour sequencing

In the power control task the verbal protocol could be divided into sections which were described by about a dozen routines. These routines found the values of a dozen main data items. These were identified as main or 'top' data items

Figure 3. Simplified description of sequencing when control error was unacceptable. In this and later figures, routines may be described verbally or using brief implicit notation, for simplicity

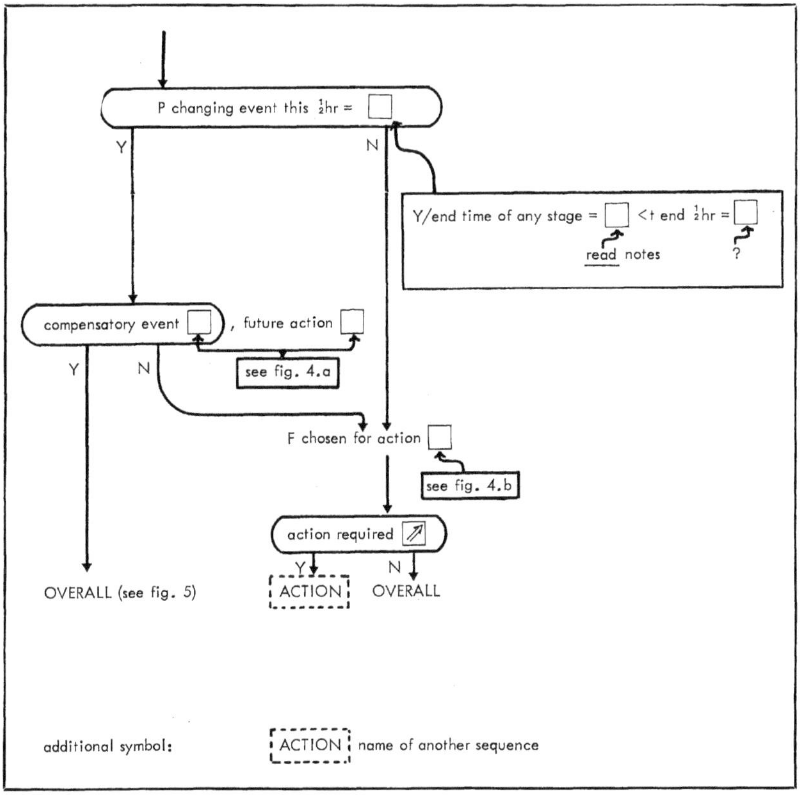

as they were not necessarily named within another routine when they occurred, finding their value could be the overall aim in a section of the protocol. Examples of these items are the furnace to alter, the size of the control error, the size of action to make, or the effect of a future event.

Once these basic units of the behaviour had been distinguished the variables determining the sequence in which they occurred could be identified. These determinant variables, and their effects on the sequence of behaviour, were then described by flow diagrams which consisted chiefly of conditional statements, but also contained data items and physical actions. The conditional statements described the decisions between alternative behaviours. These 'sequencing' diagrams were not sub-ordinate to some head data-item, to finding the value of a single variable. Any single overall name for a sequencing would have to be the name of a type of activity, not the name of a data item. About five different sequencing diagrams were developed, which determined the routines to use when the control error was acceptable, unacceptable, etc. Figure 3 is a simplified version of the sequencing when control error was unacceptable.

In all, there are three distinct types of 'branching' in the description of behaviour used here. There is one type of branching in the way that one

Figure 4. Routines used by sequencing in Figure 3

(*a*) Assessing effect of future event

(*b*) Choice of furnace for power supply change. This is used in both Figure 3 and Figure 4a

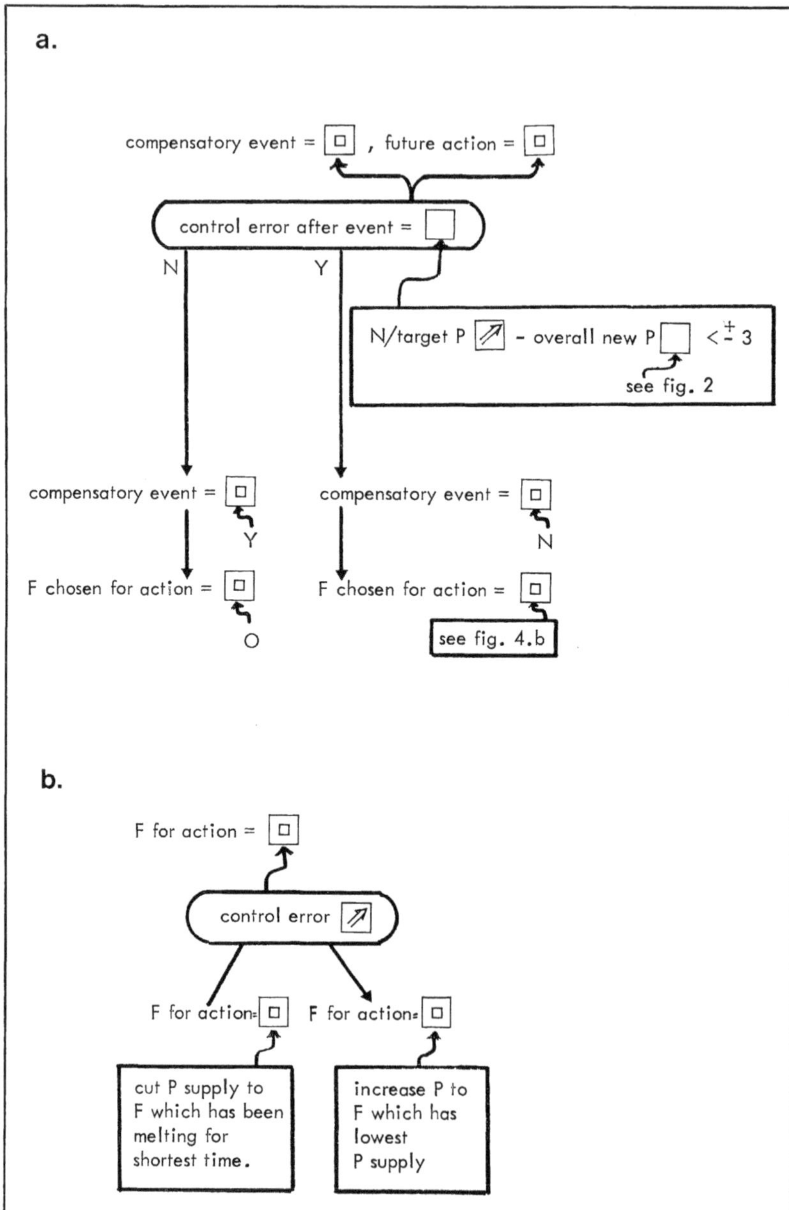

routine is implemented by others. Branching exists where there are alternative methods for finding one data item. The choice between alternative behaviours which are appropriate in different circumstances is a third type.

3.1. *Conditional statements*

The choice between alternative behaviours is determined by comparing a variable value with a criterion, e.g., if control error is greater than ± 3 units the controller acts, otherwise he monitors. This choice is usually described in a programme by using a conditional statement containing the variable and criterion. In the power control task conditional statements appear in the routines and more particularly in the sequencings.

We can consider whether it would be useful to describe the variables in these conditional statements in the same three-part way as used above, distinguishing between name, storage location and link to routine. At points in the power control protocols where alternative behaviours were available the data showed that different methods might be used to find the value of the variable determining which behaviour occurred. Also, if a value of this variable was already available the routine to find it was not repeated, very often the appropriate behaviour followed immediately without explicit mention of the determinant, as if the behaviour followed a pre-set switch. These findings suggest that the same methods should be used, for the same reasons. An example of this type of conditional statement is given in Figure 1c. The data storage location is incorporated within the decision test, to imply a mechanism which switches to the next appropriate behaviour when the data value is available.

This mechanism can be extended to describe cases where the behaviour sequence is determined by multiple conditions. There are two ways of representing the effect of multiple conditions, these methods are equivalent in outcome but not in mechanism. One method uses a branching tree of (not necessarily binary) conditional statements. The other uses table-look-up; all the determinant variable values are used simultaneously to define a cell in the table, the behaviour to do next is named in this cell. We can consider which of these methods would best describe the cognitive behaviour, given the evidence from the power control task. Branching conditionals imply that the determinants have their effect via a sequence of one-dimensional decisions. In the power control task, when all the determinant data values required were available the determinant variables were not mentioned and the appropriate behaviour appeared rapidly; this would support a table-look-up mechanism. However, if the determinant values were not available then routines to find them must be executed in sequence. A special mechanism for this would have to be added to the table-look-up method. These data-finding operations are inherent in the conditionals method, while if the data values are available then each condition can act as a switch. A sequence of conditionals could behave like a vector of switches, and so give an immediate effect. It might appear difficult to describe interactions between determinants by using branching conditionals. There is no evidence on this in the power task, but if interactions are dealt with by interaction in cognitive processing then this could be incorporated.

3.2. *Functionally distinct levels of organization*

The sequencings and the routines used to describe the power control behaviour differed in that the sequencings were not sub-ordinate to some head data item,

Figure 5. Overall determinants of sequencing, on basis of control error

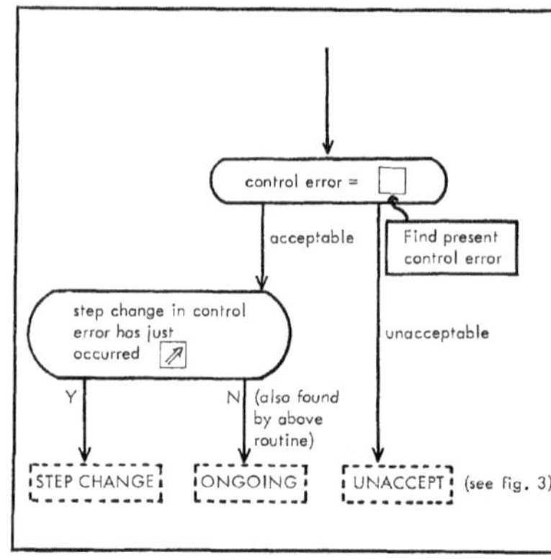

sequencings determined the overall use of the routines, and all operating instructions were within the routines. This suggests that we can identify sequences and routines as two structurally and functionally distinct types of organization. Sequencing is a level of organization 'above' the routines, as the sequencings determine how the routines are used. In the power control behaviour, sequencings could follow on from sequencings, in a way which showed that the relations within the sequencings level of organization could also be best described as a network rather than a tree.

The nature of the link between the sequencings and the routines is particularly interesting. The set of main data items and the set of sequencing determinants in the power control task were identified independently using different methods. Importantly, it appears that the main data items and the sequencing determinants are very similar (see table in Bainbridge (in press)). We can therefore suggest that the main data items are the items which occur in the sequencings, particularly within the conditional statements. The 'top' of the routines level of organization (the main data names, storage locations and pointers to main routines) is within the sequences level of organization.

Two further levels of organization could be identified in the power control task, making four levels in all. The basic operations formed a distinct level 'below' the routines. The order in which the sequencings occurred was determined by a higher 'overall' level of determinant variables, particularly by the size of the control error, as described in Figure 5. In the power control task it was at this level that the controller judged the adequacy of control and selected the appropriate general type of behaviour, at this level the behaviour interacted with the feedback control task in the external world.

3.2.1. *Level of organization and working storage*—As the names and storage locations of the main data items are actually within the sequencings, the use of working storage might differ with level of organization, and evidence from the power control task does suggest this.

Two types of working storage were needed in the diagrams developed to describe this task. 'Temporary' storage was required for any data values found in a routine which were used again later in the same routine. A single arrow in a box indicates back reference to such a value. Longer term 'cross referenced' storage was needed for data values which were found during one routine and made use of during another (shown by a double lined arrow). Inspection of the diagrams for the power control task gives evidence about the incidence of these two types of storage. This is only weak data about storage, as it is extracted from descriptions of the behaviour, not from the behaviour itself.

All the temporary storage occurred within the routines, and so within the routines level of organization. (In fact this is necessarily so, as sequencings do not contain instructions for computations, etc.) Each temporary item needed to be stored for a few seconds at most. The next items required temporarily might be completely different in nature, e.g., times then furnace names, etc.

Most cross-references in the diagrams were from within the sequencings level, either in conditional statements or as parameters of routines finding the main data items. All the main data items were cross-referenced or made use of at some other point in the cognitive behaviour. Importantly, all the cross-referenced data items were in the sequencings. This suggests that all this longer term working storage was within this sequencings level of organization.

Although this relation between level of organization and durability of storage is an empirical finding, it is actually a necessary characteristic of any information processing organization in which routines are independent of the purpose for which they are used. In such cases, data values found in one use of a routine are not necessarily relevant the next time the routine is used. Any data values relevant to a particular purpose must be stored separately from the routine to avoid loss or confusion. The question of how to judge whether stored data values are irrelevant so a routine must be repeated was raised in Section 2.2.1. This discussion suggests that all data values below the main items are recomputed, so that decisions about relevance do not arise. This also implies that though the main data values will be remembered the data used in finding them will not be. It would be interesting to know whether these findings are also true of other cognitive tasks. The power control task was cyclic in nature, and some data values remained the same over a period of time. The same effect might not be found in sequential tasks, such as maintenance diagnosis or problem solving.

Stronger evidence about the longer term storage of main data items should be obtained directly from the behavioural data. We require evidence that main routines are not repeated unless the stored value is unreliable or has changed, and evidence that these values are cross-referenced instead of recomputed when the data is needed elsewhere. The protocol data was analysed for such evidence by charting the protocol behaviour when each main routine should have occurred, and noting the incidence of repetitions. Unfortunately the nature of the data makes it difficult to obtain firm evidence for storage. In verbal report data, if a particular operation is not mentioned but its consequences appear, this is not evidence that the consequences depend on storage rather than executing the operation, as the operation may have been done but not mentioned. This difficulty is somewhat reduced in the present data, as there was evidence that this protocol reported a random sample of the operations carried out, so one might infer at least that if an operation never appears in a given context, it is never done. Against this, it is unlikely that a routine will never be repeated, as the stored data may be unreliable or unrepresentative, so that such evidence is unlikely. Really strong evidence for storage is only obtained when the subject acts on a past rather than present value of an item. Despite these difficulties there was reasonably good support at least for retention of the results from decisions about the size of the control actions, and for the subject keeping his place within the general survey of all furnace states.

No comments can be made here about any use of working storage in the basic operations level, as these operations are not verbalized. At the 'overall' level the main data item was the size of the control error. This was frequently recomputed of course, as it could change rapidly. There was strong evidence however that its value was retained between computations. It was an important determinant referred to by many conditional statements in the sequencings (see e.g., Figure 3 and 4). It was also a major criterion in the decisions which select which routine to use, according to the urgency of the situation (see Section 2.2.2).

3.2.2. *Context effects and prediction of the environment*—The decisions which determine the sequence of behaviour refer to the values of the main data items. These item values can be identified as both the 'context' in which the task is done, and the controller's 'mental picture' of the present state of the process. In this task, the storage of these values in the sequencing level of organization provides the location and mechanism for these concepts and their effect on behaviour. As these data values are obtained by working through the data-finding routines, so this general orientation to the task takes time to develop.

Some of the main routines made predictions, such as what the next power changing event will be, when it will occur, what its effect on control error will be, and what action will be needed when it occurs. As data items these predictions did not differ in type from the results of other routines, they could also affect the sequence of behaviour. For instance, there was no need to make an action to reduce control error if an imminent furnace stage change would change power usage by the required amount, see Figures 3 and 4. Thus predictions were also part of the context or mental picture of the environment, and the importance of this was that external events were anticipated.

In the power control task the controllers' ability to make and use predictions developed with experience. Inexperienced controllers (university students) at first used feedback control, changes in the process were unexpected and dealt with after they occurred. More experienced controllers (steel workers) predicted and anticipated these changes. This was a form of feed-forward control, which allows much greater control over the environment.

3.3. *Practical uses of this technique*

A technique which describes information processing tasks in a way which makes the use of routines and working storage explicit can have many uses. This technique might be used in experimental studies of working storage, to specify a priori the amount of working storage required in a given task at a particular time. This could give a measure of the relative difficulty of using working storage in different tasks. It could also provide a normative basis for developing tasks of different levels of difficulty.

A task description in this form might also provide a job-aid for human factors and training scheme designers. It could help the human factors designer to identify the items which are used together so should be placed together on a console. It also indicates variables which are not directly monitored from the process but could usefully be computed and displayed. The power control task data suggests a warning about this however. In order to make rapid decisions the controller needs an up-to-date mental picture of the state of the environment. This does contain data values which are explicitly displayed, and it takes time to develop. This may account for the way in which industrial process controllers take time to 'get the feel of the system' when they come on shift. It also suggests that if rapid manual-take-over of control is required when there is a breakdown in automatic control, then the controller must have been actively involved in the ongoing events and decisions of the process, even though this is not technically necessary, so that his mental picture of the process is fully developed and up-to-date and can be used immediately for appropriate control decisions.

This technique might also provide reminders about various aspects of training scheme design. It indicates which routines and basic operations must be learned, and their interrelations. It should make explicit any alternative methods available, and the costs and values of using them; some of these methods may need to be encouraged or discouraged in training. It also shows what working storage is required, particularly the items found in one part of the task which are used in another. The data from the power control task suggest that inexperienced subjects take some time to appreciate the possibilities for cross-referencing data, if left to pick them up for themselves. It is necessary to point out however that this technique should probably only be used as a basis for training of routine tasks. It does not necessarily describe the task operations in such a way that the controller knows how they can be re-combined to deal with new situations.

4. Working storage capacity

The discussion so far has concentrated on the location and use of working storage in information processing. Any complete account of this storage must also discuss its capacity, and the nature of capacity limits. Inferences about the storage capacity required in the power control task can be made from the diagrams describing the behaviour.

The items which must have been stored during the power control task were the items referred to by the boxes containing arrows. The number of items which must be stored at one time varied dynamically throughout the behaviour, as some items were no longer needed and others became necessary. It is therefore most useful to count the maximum number of items which may be required simultaneously. The controller made written notes of some data values, particularly of arbitrary values such as event times, so storage of these was not necessary. A count of storage requirements which does not allow for this may be misleading. (Newell and Simon (1972) have initiated an interesting discussion on the effect of this 'external memory' on task strategy.)

In the power control task a maximum of four 'temporary' items might be required simultaneously by a routine. The majority of the sequencings used a maximum of three 'cross-referenced' items, but the sequence which surveyed the present and future states of the furnaces involved up to 19 such items. As the temporary and cross-referenced items were required at the same time these figures imply that a capacity for storing seven to 23 items was necessary to do this task. Experimental data on short-term storage indicates a capacity of about seven static items (e.g., Miller, 1956) or two to three running items (Yntema and Meuser 1960, Bisseret 1971). The capacity requirements of the power control task were apparently larger than this, so raise several questions. Either the working storage capacity can be larger than indicated by the above experiments, or less working storage was used in the power control task than is suggested by counts from the diagrams. There might have been restrictions to the use of working storage which have not been identified in the present study. For example only sub-sets of the cross-referenced items might actually be available at a particular time.

Several points suggest that storage capacity may be larger than is indicated by the above experiments. The apparent capacity may be a function of the technique used for measuring it, in the same way that the apparent amount of material retained in long-term memory depends on whether this is measured by recall or recognition. The above experiments were all strong tests of memory, as they used recall. Also this was recall of arbitrary items. Different results might be obtained by using meaningful material in a patterned context. The possible variable values in the power control task came from a limited set. For example there were only eight different furnace stages; the different sequences in which these could occur were very constrained, variations in the sequence depended on the size of the furnace and the type of steel being made. Once such constraints are known, at any one time the rest of the task will give many recognition cues to the value of a particular item. The classic experiment on recoding quoted by Miller, op. cit. apparently showed that the effect of patterned organization on the amount remembered is such that capacity is still limited by the number of items. The untrained subject remembered a certain number of binary items; after training on more complex codes the subject could remember the same number of items or 'chunks', each of which had a higher information content. Although the notion of a chunk is useful in thinking about the organization or patterning of material, it is difficult in practice to find single names to represent each complex organization or chunk, except where there is a 1:1 mapping between different entropy codes as in Miller's experiment. It may be that the important aspect of that experiment is the demonstration that learned patterns of organization allow a subject to handle a larger quantity of material, and that the fact that the subject remembered the same number of items after learning in this experiment is a bit of a red-herring.

Obviously a great deal of further evidence is needed to investigate and resolve these questions. The actual behavioural data, rather than the diagrams, which have been analysed so far for the power control task contain too few examples to give more than anecdotal evidence. Some types of protocol behaviour would show that data values are not available from storage. For example, if the controller worked through all the routines after changing from one sequencing to another, this would imply that no relevant cross-referenced data was available. If routines were simpler in form when used deeper in behaviour this would imply a capacity limit (see Section 2.2.2). Conversely, the behaviour would indicate that stored data was available if the controller could go through a sequencing without repeating the routines. One section of the observed behaviour indicates the possibility of a large capacity: the controller alternated, apparently independently, between considering a power increasing action to correct a present low power usage, and considering a future power decreasing action to correct the effect of a future furnace change when power usage will be too high. Storage would also be indicated if the controller's behaviour was appropriate to a past rather than present state of the process.

The discussion so far has been concerned with the use of working storage within a task. Storage is also necessary for the controller to be able to do other types of observed behaviour: to return to his place in the task after an interruption; to do more than one task at a time (storage is needed both in scheduling attention between the tasks and in keeping track of one while doing the other(s)); and to note that new data accounts for some unexplained past event. These uses of working storage are not necessarily made explicit by the present technique.

Evidence from the power control task has questioned the limits to working storage capacity. This descriptive technique might give some clues to the nature of the capacity limit. Whatever the mechanism of storage it must be very flexible to allow for the rapid changes in temporarily stored items. Using pointers would be a simple way of implementing this flexibility. Temporary items might not be retained simply because they were not referred to again. Cross-referenced items might be rehearsed by the process of reference. The above discussion on the possible effects of meaningful context suggests that capacity may also depend on much more complex mechanisms, such as pattern recognition, which are by no means accounted for in the present technique. The next section will discuss this further, and will raise other points which show that any simple notion of working storage is inadequate.

5. Working storage and learning

The word 'storage' has been used throughout this paper, rather than the word 'memory'. Traditionally 'memory' involves the ability to reproduce past events, a function which is not accounted for by the mechanism described here. 'Storage' refers to data values which describe the present and future states of the environment and which are required temporarily while doing a task. These values originate from samples of the external world, for inexperienced subjects at least. Although these stored values reflect the variety in the environment and decisions about it they can still provide the basis for learning.

Learning the values of constants is a simple case. Repeated sampling of a constant valued data item will give the same result each time, so the pointer from the storage location to the data value representation can become permanent. The dynamic character of short-term storage can change to the static structural nature of long-term storage simply because the stability of storage reflects the stability of the environment.

When a data item has alternative possible values the case is more complex. For instance in the power control task there are five different furnaces, and eight different furnace stages. The controller can soon learn this set of alternatives, in a simple case. One can suggest that the storage location then has access to this set of alternatives, and it is only necessary to identify which one is relevant at a particular time. This could have various effects on the efficiency of performance. In choice reaction-time experiments, practice reduces the amount of time required to handle a given number of alternatives (Mowbray and Rhoades (1959)). A reduction in handling time per item would have implications for rehearsal models of storage capacity limits. In this type of theory capacity is limited by the number of items which can be rehearsed in a given time. If each item comes to require less time then more items could be rehearsed within the time limit, so capacity should increase with practice. The reduction in time presumably reflects a change in the difficulty of handling the data values.

This might occur for instance because the set of pattern recognition devices required have been identified, or developed and refined.

For some data items there is a large number of alternative values, and these are not peculiar to the particular task. For example 'time' (e.g., 14.56) uses numbers, which are also used for other purposes. In a simple pointer-to-representation mechanism for storing time values, all possible times would have to be represented. This is obviously uneconomical. Of course representations of all the digits are required, but for longer numbers it would be more parsimonious to have an extra mechanism which specifies the sequence of digits to store at a particular time. Laboratory studies of memory have invariably used these non-task-specific and infinite-set types of item, which may require special mechanisms to handle.

For many data items the possible values are not discrete alternatives but vary along a continuum. Examples in the power control task are the level of power usage and the size of the control error. Different samples of these data items can give infinitely graded different values, but at least these values can only vary within the dynamic limits of the process (environment). Each new sample must therefore both fit in with and contribute to the controller's knowledge of the possible states of the process. With increasing knowledge of the process dynamics the controller can make more accurate predictions (judgements) about the effects of actions or events on future states.

This type of dynamic knowledge might be represented and accessed either by an input/output table, or by a general template or pattern of the dynamic changes. An input/output table, using the mechanisms available in the present technique, could be entered by using multiple-output conditionals. These could not reasonably distinguish between all the values on a continuum, so would have to be restricted to distinguishing a limited number of categories of value. This mechanism therefore implies that absolute judgement or category scaling would be used to measure values on the continuum. There is good evidence that this is so in process control (cp., Cooke, 1965; Bainbridge, 1971). A general template of the possible dynamic changes could be used by a routine to generate the relevant state in particular circumstances. Such a routine could be included with the other routines used in doing the task.

The flow diagrams or programmes for the power control task represent the controller's knowledge of appropriate information processing operations. This can be distinguished from his knowledge of the static and dynamic characteristics of the furnace process. The latter knowledge could be identified as the controller's 'mental model' of the external world. The values in this knowledge could be the data value representations referred to by the pointers from the storage locations in the processing programmes. The working storage data values, or 'mental picture', would be the sub-set of these possible values which actually exist at a particular time. The pointers from the storage locations to these values would be the links between the programmes and the mental model.

It may be however, that the distinction between programme and data is not so clear as this implies. This distinction may be an artefact of the technique used to describe cognitive activity here. A minimum number of routines and sequencings were developed to account for the consistent repeated sections of power control behaviour. There are still similarities however between what have been described as distinct routines and between them and sections of protocol which do not match any of these routines. This might imply that the controller has a general structure of knowledge about the process and the operations which it and he can carry out, from which sequences of behaviour can be generated for particular purposes. The consistently repeated sequences of behaviour which have been identified as routines might appear because the same circumstances recur and the response to them becomes overlearned. Whatever form this structure of task knowledge takes it must allow its possessor to overview the static structure and dynamic functioning of the external world, to describe as well as to perform his task operations, and to comment on and revise his performance and strategy. It must also incorporate working storage as a basis for learning about both data and operations.

Acknowledgements

Collection of the data described in this paper was supported by the British Iron and Steel Research Association.

The author would like to thank Dr. D.A. Allport, Dr. M. Coltheart and Professor W.T. Singleton for their useful comments on an earlier draft of this paper.

A. Bisseret has pointed out that while the air traffic controller remembers about three attributes of an aircraft he remembers these values for 9–10 aircraft, his measures are therefore similar to the capacity reported here.

References

BAINBRIDGE, L., 1971, The influence of display type on decision making. I.E.E. Conference Publication No. 80, *Displays.*

BAINBRIDGE, L., 1972, An analysis of a verbal protocol from a process control task. Unpublished Ph.D. Thesis, University of Bristol.

BAINBRIDGE, L., Analysis of verbal protocols from a process control task. In: Edwards and Lees (Eds.), *The Human Operator in Process Control.* (In press.)

BISSERET, A., 1971, Memoire operationnelle et structure du travail. *Bulletin de Psychologie,* 1970–1971, **24,** 280–294. English summary in *Ergonomics,* 1971, **14,** 565–570.

BRYAN, W.L., and HARTER, N., 1899, Studies in the telegraphic language. The acquisition of a hierarchy of habits. *Psychological Review,* **6,** 345–375.

COOKE, J.E., 1965, Human decisions in the control of a slow response system. Unpublished D.Phil. Thesis, University of Oxford.

DAVIS, D.R., 1948, *Pilot Error.* Air Ministry Publication A.P. 2139A., H.M.S.O.

MILLER, G.A., 1956, The magical number seven, plus or minus two: some limits on our capacity for processing information. *Psychological Review,* **63,** 81–97.

MILLER, G.A., GALANTER, E. and PRIBRAM, K.H., 1960, *Plans and the structure of Behaviour* (New York: Henry Holt & Co.).

MOWBRAY, G.H., and RHOADES, M.U., 1959, On the reduction of choice-reaction times with practice. *Quarterly Journal of Experimental Psychology,* **11,** 16–23.

NEWELL, A., and SIMON, J.A., 1963, G.P.S., a program that simulates human thought. In: Billing (Ed.), *Lernende Automaten,* Oldenbourg, 1961. Reprinted in Feigenabum & Feldman (Eds.), *Computers and Thought,* McGraw-Hill.

NEWELL, A., and SIMON, H.A., 1972, *Human Problem Solving* (Prentice-Hall).

WELFORD, A.T., BROWN, R.A. and GABB, J.E., 1950, Two experiments on fatigue as affecting skilled performance in civilian aircrew. *British Journal of Psychology,* **40,** 195–211.

YNTEMA, D.B., and MEUSER, G.E., 1960, Remembering the present states of a number of variables. *Journal of Experimental Psychology,* **60,** 18–22.

Professor Rohmert holds electrical engineering degrees. After engineering work at A.E.G. in industry, he worked on ergonomics and muscle physiology problems at the Max-Planck-Institut für Arbeitsphysiologie in Dortmund. He taught Arbeitsphysiologie at the University of Technology of Aachen and now is head of the Institut für Arbeitswissenschaft at the University of Technology of Darmstadt, Germany.

2:10

Analytical problems of work design

W. Rohmert

Introduction

Ergonomics is concerned with the study of men at their work from many aspects: the individual, engineering and technology, economics and society. The main interest is in the relationship between output of work and human input. Ergonomic formations of question involve also the conditions of human labour and its evaluation, these are regarded as just as important as the output of work. This defines Ergonomics as distinct from the mainly technologically or economically orientated disciplines on the one hand and the mainly man-orientated human or social sciences on the other hand. In ergonomics, techniques and methods from different disciplines have to be combined and new ones have to be developed. Work design problems cannot be solved by using techniques concerned only with the analysis of what a man is doing at work, work system interrelations must also be considered. While accepting this it may be worthwhile to summarize some of the techniques, which are available for appraising what a man is doing at work without going into corresponding detail in the field of system's design.

Job descriptions and analysis may be made from two different points of view. The more inductively orientated procedure involves considering occupations (e.g., International Standard Classification of Occupation, 1969) or jobs (e.g., Work Performed Manual, U.S. Department of Labour, 1959) sometimes using algorithmic descriptions (e.g., Krivohlavy, 1966). More deductively orientated procedures on the other hand start not with job analysis but with the development of models from which categories can be deduced, for example in a very simple concept of human work with a hierarchical functional structure; 'job' 'task' 'operation' and 'element' (Beishon, 1967; R.E.F.A., 1971). There are other taxonomies mainly from psychology and human engineering starting with basic human functions for the perception-, identification-, decision- and effector-mechanisms (Baker, 1970; Christensen and Mills, 1967; Keenan, 1967; Kendrick, 1969; Miller, 1967; Welford, 1965). Specific models mainly based on the concept of control can be used as elements for job description (Beishon, 1967; Birmingham and Taylor, 1961). It may be useful to utilize elements from both inductive as well as deductive procedures for job analysis.

Analysing man's task in a work system

Man's task must be clearly defined in the context of the particular work system. Two different points of view may be possible: looking at the role which man plays in the whole system, that is, his share in the task completion, or looking at the demands of the job and the effects on man.

In any work system the most important areas or partial functions are effecting, controlling and monitoring. By the function of effecting the actual changes in the work object will be made. The process will be controlled (or guided) by information processing. Monitoring serves to maintain the functional capacity of the system, that is the internal checking and clearing of impediments. The functions of effecting, controlling and monitoring may be realized by either man or technical equipment. Figure 1 demonstrates steps of technical design logically derived from different possible kinds of work system. The term 'manual' performance means all direct human actions and also non-manual actions such as speaking. By the identification of the steps of technical design the interaction of the human operator with technical equipment is characterized revealing distinguishable types of human performance.

Figure 1. Work system with human and technical functions

WORK SYSTEM	PARTIAL FUNCTIONS OPERATED BY MAN		
'manual' performance	effecting	controlling	monitoring
mechanized performance	effecting	controlling	monitoring
automatic performance	effecting	controlling	monitoring
	PARTIAL FUNCTIONS REALIZED BY TECHNICAL EQUIPMENT		

Job demands are not influenced only by the technical advancement of the work system. Four different design areas are important (Figure 2). Objective demands on man result from the aim of the work system and its design in a four-step process. Technological design selects the type of technique and fixes the basis for production capacity and general working conditions. Technical design is related to the utilization of technical equipment based on applied technology. The result of this design is the functional work partition between man and machine (see Figure 1). By separating man from work process, man is dependent upon the influences of technological and technical design. Ergonomics design covers all influences of adaptation of work to the man, in particular to his abilities and capacities. The main objectives of ergonomics design are work fulfilment by man and the working conditions for the man. By organizational design is meant the job partition between man and man. Problems of specialization and job enlargement have to be solved as well as problems of dependence

Figure 2. Job demands for man in a work system by different design areas

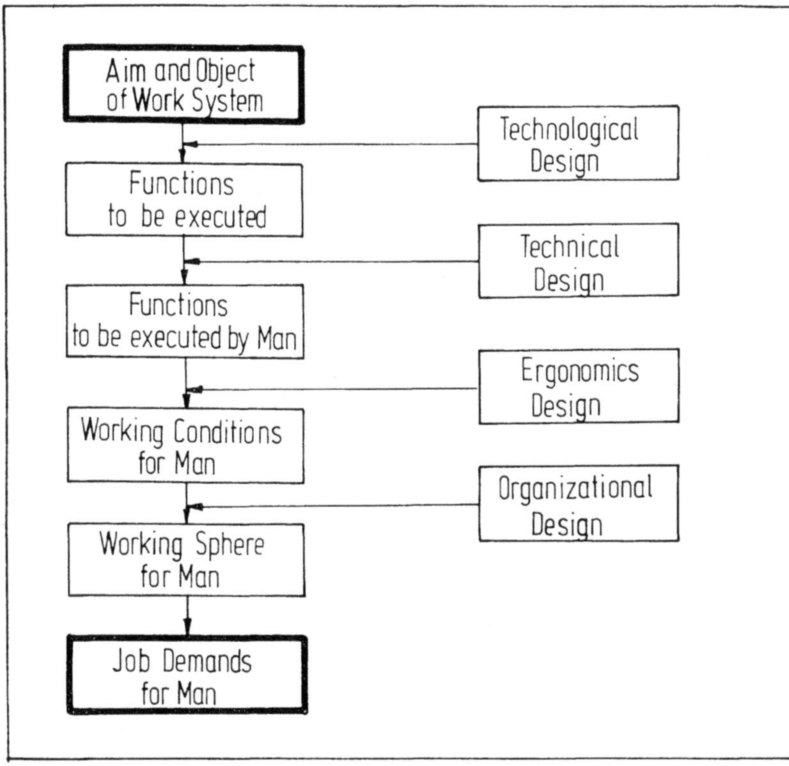

of the different tasks from each other or from other factors, problems of working time and rest pauses, the daily position of work and rest and problems of shift work.

Job demands for man can be described in terms of a concept of final determination or in terms of a concept of causal determination (see Figure 3). Job demands can be described in terms of skills and stress. Skills are what man must know to perform his task. Stress is concerned with the way demands are made on these skills by the job. When related to the subject (worker) job demands will be described in terms of aptitude and strain. How far stress leads to strain in man depends on his individual working capacity. The skills required can be achieved by an individual worker through education and experience. Additional flexibility is provided by selection of workers. The special abilities of an individual in the context of the job demands form the worker's aptitude. They are the basis for the effects of job demands on the strain of the worker. It may be that the momentary individual working capacity is dropped by fatigue which means, that any evaluation of job demands on man must be related to general human capacities and to the individual aptitude of the worker. The aptitude of man related to the given job demands must be sufficient to provide the positive fulfilment of the work as well as the negative resistance to stress.

Figure 3. Description and assessment of jobs

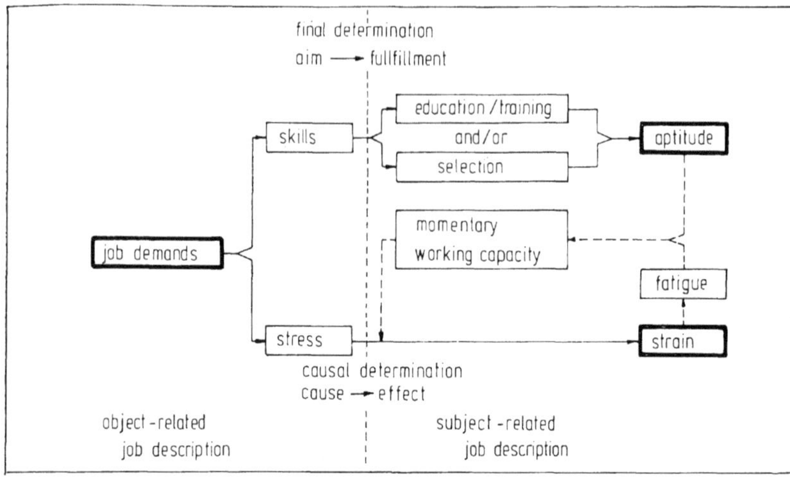

Figure 3 emphasizes that analysis of job demands may lead to work design in the sense of fitting work to man and also fitting man to work. With this in mind we must consider the origins of job demands in functions and their attributes (see Figure 4). Every job is composed of different tasks the smallest unit of which is a function which cannot be subdivided because it has a special purpose. This purpose can be achieved only by an elementary dynamic process of the work system, aimed at changing a work object or information from input to the desired output. A function consists of the component's energy for the change itself and information for controlling the process in different situations depending on the particular purpose. The factors of these components and therefore also of the function are type, intensity and duration. These are the most general and the most important factors for describing the job demands with respect to man's abilities and reactions to stress. The job demands which determine skills and stress are made up of the execution of the job or task and the general and specific working conditions. These conditions (e.g., work place and physical or social environment) vary the job demands mainly as additional stress which can be attributed to a more or less good work design.

There are many analytical methods available to describe skills and aptitude, stress and strain. The application of these methods to man-at-work problems must take account of the fact, that any work man is doing could or should be his life's work. Therefore application of results from analytical studies to any concrete work design has to consider and to satisfy a four-level hierarchy

(1) level of practicability
(2) level of tolerability
(3) level of imputation
(4) level of satisfaction.

The interest of ergonomics application in evaluating and designing man-at-work systems is mainly limited at present to levels 1 and 2. Ergonomic standards

Figure 4. Components and factors of job demands

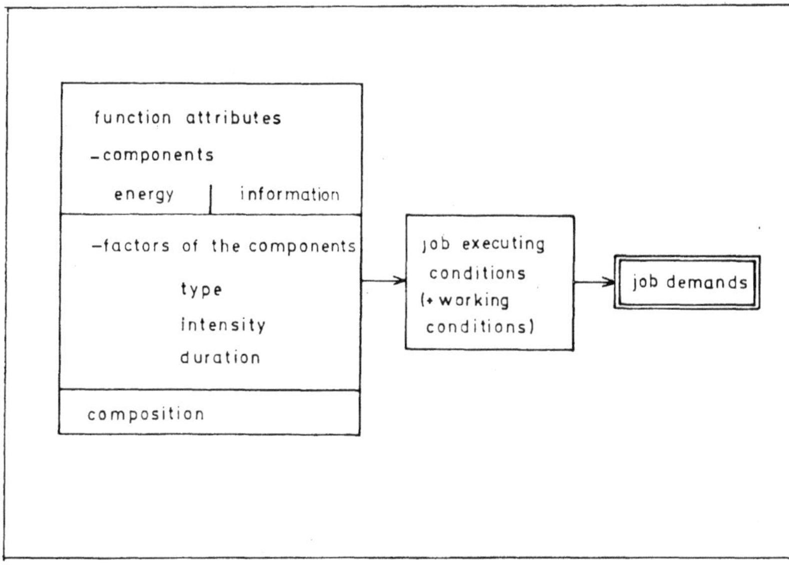

of work design consider maximum (instantaneous) human capacities and tolerable endurance limits. These limits are based on strain measurement by using Ergonomics procedures based on physiological, psychological or biochemical methods. (Classical work study techniques will also be applied.)

As an example of both Ergonomics and Work Study applications current research in Air Traffic Control Tasks can be considered (Figures 5 and 6). In A.T.C.-research our purpose is to give advice to designing A.T.C.-tasks, equipment and organization in order to make A.T.C. safe, orderly and expeditious and also to study operator strain in order to ensure controller's health and well-being. This example of A.T.C.-research illustrates the necessity of extending research also to the level of work design standards of imputation and individual job satisfaction. We should be interested also in covering the acceptability of work design standards for established institutions—for example the acceptance of those standards by Employer's Federations and Unions. Last but not least suitable standards with regard to individual job satisfaction are necessary. There is a real lack in suitable techniques or devices, which are available for setting standards in these areas.

Engineering interest in work design

Technical development and work design efforts by engineers can be classified in relation to man as follows:

Amplifying man's capacities.
Supplementing man's attributes and capabilities.
Removal of man's work load.
Replacement of man's working inset.

Figure 5. Experimental arrangement in ergonomics field research

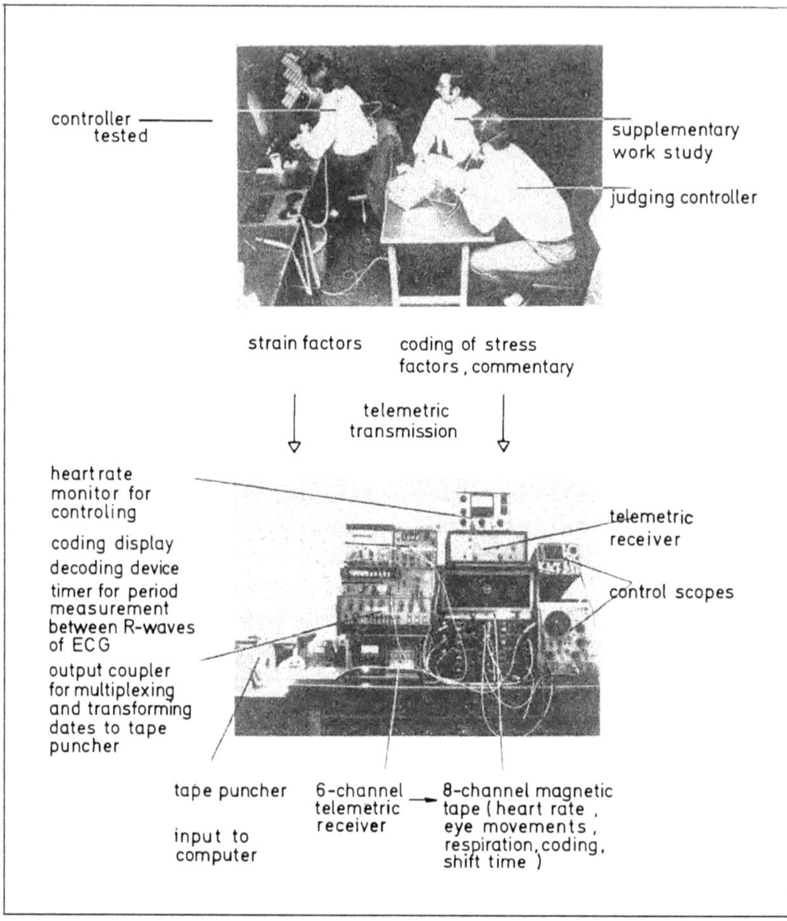

Man-related reasons for any work design are manifold, Figure 7 offers a summary without any claim to completeness. The examples given for augmentation of engineering efforts in work design are not identical with the man-related aims of work design. To illustrate this an extensive aim-hierarchy of work design will be discussed in detail.

Task-analysis related to man's strain

One of the most important factors in evaluating work design is the strain on man. Identifying strain to defined tolerability levels is therefore a main point of interest in evaluating any work design as well as in designing itself. This is one reason for analysing strain in more detail.

From the study of jobs on real professional work places one may deduce specific work contents or types of tasks out of the infinity of possible human tasks. Figure 8 shows an order of tasks which are distinctly different by different

Figure 6. Studies for assessment of work load in air traffic control tasks

Studies for Assessment of Work Load in Air Traffic Control Tasks

Study	Object of Investigation	Method
Workplace	dimensions of work place devices of work and information used body position demanded environmental conditions (noise, illumination, vibration, climate)	description drawing photographic documentation physical measurement
Process	chronological, spatial and information-technical flow of defined work content	description graphic representation use of standard analysis charts film analysis tape records telemetric coding
Motion	sequence of hand (and body) movements of the controller	use of standard analysis charts use of predetermined motion time systems film analysis
Time	chronological flow and/or time of work elements of the controller	stop-watch method work sampling automatic registration continuous film records sampling film records
Information Content Analysis	aircraft - and/or controller - related operators and logical operations	algorithmic description flow diagram (LJAPUNOW-language) graph representation (GERT) radio-telecommunication-transcriptions study of flight control strip photographic radar recordings (each 90 seconds time of exposure)
Stress	amount and flow of stress	rating of difficulty of controller's work coding of incoming flight control strips coding of aircrafts under control time budget studies experimental shift work study of attitudes of the controllers towards work and working environment
Strain	amount and flow of strain	heart rate measurement long-electrocardiography respiration measurement electromyography electroencephalography electrooculography catacholamine secretion in controllers

strain of human organs using specialized human abilities. Strain is explained as the sum of all different effects of stress in man interacting with different individual characteristics. The heaviness of strain depends on the heaviness of stress as well as on the individual characteristic:

$$\text{Strain} = f_1 \text{ (Stress, Individual capacities)}$$

Stress is defined as the sum of all factors influencing man at work, which are perceived or sensed mainly through the receptor system or which put demands on the effector system. In analysing real tasks one has to consider, that all

Figure 7. Reasons for work design

FACTOR	REASONS FOR IMPLEMENTATION
technological	material, endangering man's health
technical	exceeding man's capabilities, possibilities for mechanization and automation
economical	cost, quality of work, increase of efficiency
labour-economical	lack of manpower, high cost of education and training
organizational	position and duration of working time, job partition
physiological anatomical- biomechanical	limits of capacity, optimal development of capacity, body dimensions, energy requirements
industrial-medical	endangering man's health
industrial-hygienic and safety-technical	dangerous work, safety laws, health regulations
psychological	motivation, leadership and interpersonal behaviour
sociological	group behaviour, job dissatisfaction

measures appear as time dependent values corresponding to alternating work contents. Therefore one has to distinguish between a work-content-related dimension of stress and a time-related dimension (Rohmert, 1962);

$$\text{Stress} = f_2 \text{ (Intensity of work, Duration of work)}$$

In Figure 8 work content is defined as generally as possible but as specifically as necessary. The differences between the distinguished specific work contents, based on strain, have lead to specific ergonomics terms. The summary in Figure 8 allows a ranking of most tasks found in practical working situations. For mixed tasks the job demands must be generalized to deduce the specific work content. However, one has to consider that different amounts of physical or non-physical work are related to the content of work as well as to its variation. In most industrial situations work content varies during the shift. Also the type of strain and the stressors often change in time. This variation of work must be considered in addition to physical and social environmental stressor, if a definable task is classified in Figure 8.

In this context strain is evaluated on the level of tolerability. Figure 9 indicates that each evaluation of work design is also necessary at the highest level of individual job satisfaction.

Figure 8. Basic types of working tasks

type of work	specific work content	mainly strain of organs and capabilities	Ergonomics term	examples
mainly physical	producing forces	muscles (in case heart and circulation)	muscular work	handling loads
	coordination of motory and sensory functions	muscles + sense - organs	senso-motoric work	assembling, crane operating
mainly non-physical	converting information into reaction	sense - organs + muscles	mainly non-muscular work	controlling
	transformation from input- to output-information	sense - organs + mental abilities		programming, air traffic controlling, book-keeping, translating
	producing information	mental abilities	mental work (in the narrow sense of the word)	dictation, designing, problem solving

Figure 9. Aspects and evaluation—criteria of work design

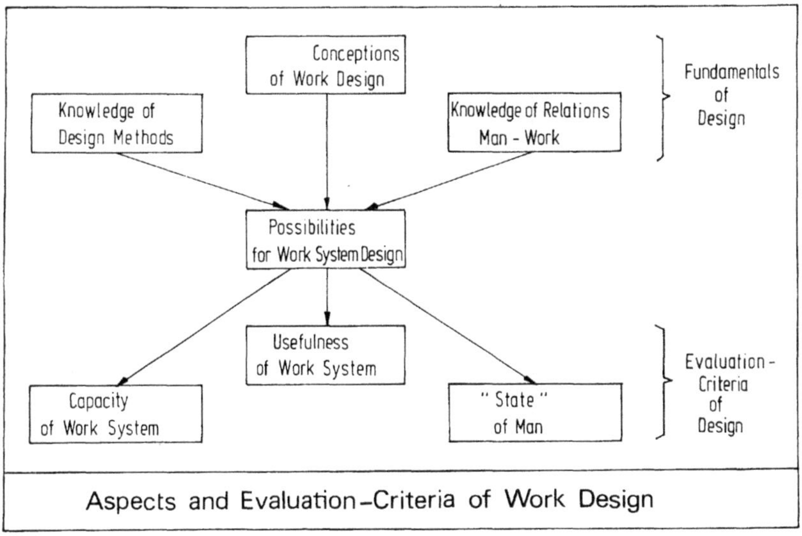

References

BAKER, J.D., 1970, Quantitative modeling of human performance in information systems. *Ergonomics*, **13**, 645–664.

BEISHON, R.J., 1967, Problems of task description in process control. In: Singleton, W.T. *et al.* (Eds.), *The Human Operator in Complex Systems*, pp. 77–86 (London: Taylor & Francis).

BIRMINGHAM, H.P. and TAYLOR, F.V., 1961, A design philosophy for man-machine control systems. In: Sinaiko, H.W. (Ed.), *Selected Papers on Human Factors in the Design and Use of Control Systems*, pp. 67–87 (New York: Dover Publications).

CHRISTENSEN, J.M., and MILLS, R.G., 1967, What does the operator do in complex systems. *Human Factors*, **9**, 329–340.

INTERNATIONAL STANDARD CLASSIFICATION OF OCCUPATIONS, 1969, Ed. (Geneva: National Labor Office).

KEENAN, J.J., 1967, Interactionist models of the varieties of human performance in complex work systems. *Annals of Reliability and Maintainability*, **6**, 76–85.

KENDRICK, P., 1969, Analytical training of operators in the process industry. *International Symposium on Man Machine Systems*, Vol. 1 (Birmingham).

KIRCHNER, J.-H. and ROHMERT, W., 1973, Problemanalyse zur Erarbeitung eines arbeitswissenschaftlichen Instrumentariums für Tätigkeitsanalysen. In: *Arbeitswissenschaftliche Studien zur Berufsbildungsforschung.* Ansätze zu einer interdisziplinären Forschungsstrategie. Ed. Präsident des Bundesinstituts für Berufsbildungsforschung, Berlin, pp. 7–48 (Hanover: Gebrüder Jänecke Verlag).

KŘIVOHLAVÝ, J., 1966, Möglichkeiten der Anwendung von algorithmischen Analysen. In: Ingenieurpsychologie und Volkswirtschaft. Hrsg. von F. Klix u. a., pp. 175–182 (Berlin: VEB Deutscher Verlag der Wissenschaften).

MILLER, R.B., 1967, Task taxonomy: science or technology? In: Singleton, W.T. *et al.* (Eds.), *The Human Operator in Complex Systems*, pp. 67–76 (London: Taylor & Francis).

R.E.F.A., 1971, *Methodenlehre des Arbeitsstudiums, Teil 1, Grundlagen* (Munich: C. Hanser).

ROHMERT, W., 1962, *Untersuchungen über Muskelermüdung und Arbeitsgestaltung* (Berlin: Beuth-Vertrieb).

ROHMERT, W., 1973, Bycho-physische Belastung und Beanspruchung von Fligletsen (Berlin: Beuth-Vertrieb).

WELFORD, A.T., 1965, Performance, biological mechanism and age: a theoretical sketch. In: Welford, A.T. and Birren, J.E. (Eds.), *Behavior, Ageing and the Nervous System*, pp. 3–20 (Springfield Ill.: C.C. Thomas).

WORK PERFORMED MANUAL, 1959, (Washington: U.S. Department of Labor).

Dr. Caille has worked extensively on issues involving psycho-physiological interaction. He is currently working in a French military establishment on problems of vigilance and 'man-machine' interaction.
Didier Kessler served in the French Navy, working on recruitment and selection problems and studied the decision-making process involved in submarine detection. He is presently a M.B.A. student at the Stanford University Graduate School of Business Administration.

2:11

A taxonomic review of the place of the operator within a man machine system

E. J. Caille and D. Kessler

Introduction

While performing a vigilance task, the operator bears a considerable mental work load. Over many years, Caille has demonstrated that the mental load, as measured through the E.E.G. process, is related to variations of vigilance which develops through three periods: hypovigilance phase, optimal vigilance phase and hypervigilance phase. By refining the E.E.G. signal treatment, Caille *et al.* (1971) have described the covariations of α rhythms (sensoriperceptive activity, especially visual, of the C.N.S.) and β rhythms (integrative or aperceptive and cognitive activity of the C.N.S.) with the variations of other signals (electro-cardiography, respiratory rhythm, electro-oculography, electromyography) and to other psychophysiological criteria from the field of psychomotor capacity during the three vigilance phases. Furthermore, Caille has also improved his treatment of the covariations of the E.E.G. signal spectrum using post analogue-digital conversion, involving the three Hjorth (1970) parameters; activity, mobility, and complexity. These can be considered as predictors of the mental activity of the operator when piloting a complex system or working out an elaborate task. This approach, leads to the setting up of an auto-regulated vigilance loop, and to the introduction of a safe investigating method. It also takes into consideration other factors which are relevant: cultural level, understanding level, general personality factors and possibly anxiety state. In this way it is possible to obtain information needed to define the adaptation of the operator to the task with which he has to deal.

The adaptation can be considered taxonomically:

From the operator to the system, in order to promote, in relation to the system:

(1) Information synthesis (gathering, coding, referencing).
(2) Data processing (interpretation).
(3) A continuous information flow.

From the system to the operator, with reference to the system, in order to work out:

(1) The layout of the devices.
(2) The aggregate system itself within a general system.

From the system to the operator, in connection with the operator, in order to consider:

(1) The system corresponding to the operator's abilities: physical, intellectual, cultural, psychomotor and psychological.

(2) The integration of the system by the operator in terms of the objectives
=military objectives
=tactical and operational objectives
=strategic objectives.

From the operator to the system, in relation to the operator, in order to carry out:

(1) The operator's judgement concerning the data from the system.

(2) The operator's judgement of cost or value in the context of the operational situation.

It is of interest to consider the distinction, Singleton (1972), between 'job description' and 'task description', the first term pointing to the description of the work phases, while the second touches upon the way in which the task is to be done. It seems essential to use both analyses to obtain the work pattern as adapted to the operator's informational and decisional capacity in relation to the objectives of the system.

In order to improve the man-machine relationship, the adaptive ability of the operator on the particular task determines the adjustment required. Taxonomic analysis suggests auto-adaptation of the operator in relation to the variable data-processing within the system provided that the operator has been trained to analyse his task, and afterwards, his performance.

Offensive or defensive military systems are constituted as semi-automatized "biodynamical huge sets" and their efficiency relies on the quality of the "operator-machine" dynamic interaction in precise environment conditions. Few studies have been concerned with this last parameter, although the obvious importance of stressors (noise, vibration, thermal charge, electro-magnetic effects and so forth) is well documented.

1. General methodology for a long-range efficiency check

A new 'man-machine' system must be designed in relation to the financial resources and by successive levels. The taxonomic analysis of the preceding system provides a constructive starting point highlighting deficiencies to be avoided. The exercise suggests that the system must be understood by each of those involved in order to generate a better performing and more reliable system.

For instance, for the human operator, the 'performance' aspect is only a behaviourist approach to the criteria of human efficiency within the 'man-machine-environment' loop. Such a specific direction is too restricted for the physician who cannot accept the criterion of immediate performance without taking into account the long-term effects on mental health and the psycho-somatic troubles of personnel.

An improvement in the 'man-machine-environment', in any case, must not focus attention only on technological parameters; every psychologist knows that a laboratory experiment places the 'subject' in competition (even unconsciously) and that such an operator will reach performance levels via vigilance thresholds (at least during short-duration tasks) which he could not attain in an operational situation which is monotonous and non-motivating.

Therefore, it is necessary to test the behavioural criteria (psychometric performances, psychomotor reactions, attention, memory) by appropriate biological predictors to detect the origin or the mechanisms of the fatigue or stress of the operator.

The co-variations of the biochemical changes (indicators of the hormonal action, of the cellular exchanges), of the electrobiological signals (indicators of the activation level of the circulatory and nervous system), of the individual performance and of the thymial modulations during the nycthemeral period predict the adaptation to the system. Most of the research in the field of 'man-machine' relations has been by non-physician specialists and this implies a global scotomization of the biochemical, electrobiological and character predictors in evaluating human fatigue: actually, the operator is most often considered as a transducer for which only the inputs and the outputs are surveyed in a Watsonian view which satisfies the engineers. The 'transfer functions' of the human operator are only simple patterning schemes without any heuristic value since their linearity does not coincide with the human capacities of changing learning phases and fluctuations of motivation. The human operator is a non-linear system, only the piloted object is linear.

Surely, so complex a mechanism requires interdisciplinary groups: biochemistry, neurophysiology, clinical psychology and information processing. Man is not 'simple' and we should not study him by selecting only the easiest behavioural aspects. We should also investigate the long-term effects of his ordered tasks. No armed system or military data synthetic processing system should be serially built without long term studies on a personnel sample really involved in tasks and without consulting the mental health and psychosomatic medical services that are able to weigh the long-term effects of such systems.

2. The adaptation criteria of the human operator

The adaptation of volunteers who have been carefully classified in terms of their cultural, intellectual and personality characteristics and motivation were studied in experiments lasting for about 20 days. The following parameters were measured:

(*a*) Biochemical effects: repeated dosages (three times by nycthemeral period) from blood (radiocompetition cortisolemy) and from urine (5-HIA elimination, kaliury . . .).

(*b*) Physiological effects: nycthemeral variations of blood pressure, of temperature, peak expiration flow.

(*c*) Electrophysiological effects:
Heart rate periodicity and arhythmia.
Central nervous system activation level, through the statistical analysis of the E.E.G. signal; time series analysis (voltage related to time from on-scalp E.E.G. channels) according to different algorithms; Hjorth's method (E.E.G. signal activity, mobility, complexity).
Fast Fourier Transform through the Cooley-Tuker algorithm.

Hyper- and hypovigilance phases periodicity.
Quality of the sleep, periodicity of the activated sleep and of the slow sleep (short waves).

(*d*) Effects on behaviour: as precisely and objectively as possible mental capacity is measured by:
Abstract conceptual understanding (G-factor psychometric test).
Mental computation, binary coding test.
Short-term memory: verbal numeric series.
Attention: double-barring task (auditory and visual).
Vigilance: radar detection with symbolic display.
Recognition of significant 'gestalten', with cross-balanced weight, amongst unsignificant symbols (NTDS system simulation).
Storage of the danger-mark within aleatory time intervals.
Study of the detection rate.
Study of the latencies (histogram of the times).

(*e*) Psychomotor capacity measured by:
Simple or complex reaction time.
Ambidexterity and psychomotor co-ordination.
Electronic aiming test or limited shooting test.
Accuracy in data-registering on computer evaluation of short periods (tempo).
Mood evaluation (thymia) and adaptation to the group, various tracking tests, including a vigilance test which detects the synchronization periods of the own parieto-occipital rhythm of the operator (auto-regulation of the proper power density of the E.E.G. signal rhythm, with re-activation of the synchronizations which make the vigilance slowing down obvious).

We shall enlarge upon this last subject which seems to be of great interest in detection systems and weapon systems.

3. Regulations of the perceptual and decision capacity and of the psychomotor performance of the operator

The forecasting methods and the reliability patterns of the operator performance can represent useful cues but because of the non-linearities linked with motivation and tiredness, we suggest that it is more objective to draw from the operator himself the proof of his capacity to treat and to decode the information and to carry out an efficient operating strategy.

Figure 1 summarizes the covariations of the electrophysiological characteristics (E.E.G., E.C.G., E.O.C. particularly) and those of the global vigilance level during long-term tasks (Quality of the sensorial filtering, latency and variability of the psychomotor reactivity, general characteristics of the behaviour according to the nervous tension which expresses the central nervous system activation level.)

It is simple and unobtrusive to the operator to collect his spontaneous potentials from the scalp bi-front and bi-occipital areas (light helmet with variable depth silver electrodes). Those potentials are amplified (20 to 100 V) and they are analysed in analogue (a 48 dB cut-off filtering) or digital (after a conversion at 100 Hz) form. They enable us to compute an activity rate incorporating

Figure 1. Peformance criteria

C.E.R.P.A. Toulon 1973 *Efficiency as a function of vigilance level* *Stages*	*Hyper vigilance*	*Optimal level*	*Hypovigilance*
I. ELECTROPHYSIOLOGICAL CRITERIA			
(1) E.E.G.—general aspect	Desynchronized	normal	synchronized
dominant frequency (in c/s)	$\beta 2$ (18–30)	$\beta 1$ (15–29)	
mobility and complexity (M and C)	eventual θ rhythms M> C>	small α	slower and higher α M< C<
amplitude (in μV)	10–20	20–40	50–70
activity $(\sigma A)^2$ in μV^2	A<		A>
power spectral density			
$\bar{\epsilon}$ in $\mu V^2/S$	$\bar{\epsilon}$<	average	$\bar{\epsilon}$>
Coherence (0–1)	coherence>	average	coherence<
(2) E.C.G. (frequency rhythm)	slight tachycardia sinusal arrhythmia decreases	normal	bradycardia sinusal arrhythmia increases
(3) R.R. (Respiratory rhythm)	Quick small amplitude	regular	Low, more regular
(4) E.O.G. (amplitude rhythm)	increases accelerated	normal	decreases generally accelerated
(5) E.M.G. (amplitude)	lesser	normal	larger
II. PSYCHOPHYSIOLOGICAL CRITERIA			
Sensorial afferencies	filtered	optimal regulation	defective filtering
Perceptive area	focalized	well adjusted	'lapses'
consequences in detection	'false alarms'	possibility of anticipation and subception.	free associations; omissions
psychomotricity			
mean reaction time (m)	shorter	normal	longer variability
standard deviation (σ)	increases		increases instability
III. PSYCHOLOGICAL CHARACTERISTICS OF OPERATOR	Tension irritability	optimal alertness attentiveness	relaxed wandering attention

(*a*) Synchronization rate of the α rest rhythms (9 to 11 c/s) which reliably translates the central nervous system activation level (Hjorth's parameters 'mobility' and 'complexity')

(*b*) Activation rate of the cognitive rhythms (18 to 34 c/s) from the front cortex.

The capacity of the human operator to treat information is weak if the α rhythm rate is high and the signal of a high amplitude (the display is quickly adjustable to the specific characteristics of the operator); the frontal rhythms are rare and of low amplitude. On the other hand, if the observer has been saturated with information, and is in a state of hypervigilance, the collected signals are of low amplitude and of variable frequencies (at about 10 HZ, at about 13 Hz and heightened between 18 and 24 Hz).

From the compared activity rates of the right frontal and occipital areas (for the right-hand operators) the amount of information to be presented to the human operator for efficient treatment can be estimated. In some cases, it will be necessary to foresee two complementary work-posts: two complementary data presentation systems will be better than a wrong human decision based on the utilization of only one visual display.

4. Display being studied

A psychologically and electrophysiologically monitored operator (15% of subjects generate too weak potential E.E.G. signal) faces a task which involves dealing with a computerized register of digital data. This data is placed on the visual display of the computer.

Equipped with four frontal and occipital electrodes, which permit the collection and statistical analysis of the E.E.G. signal, the operator auto-regulates the complexity of his task by 10-second integration periods, for each 10-second period, the computer (HP 2100 A) yields the energy of the two E.E.G. signals (power density obtained through Hjorth's activity). A comparator of frontal and occipital energy results in more or less complex visual presentation. The 'man-machine' retroaction display works in cybernetics according to the ability of the two operators—on-line—and since it avoids long-term fatigue the continuous efficiency of the system is maintained.

In this way the efforts of the electrophysiologists and engineers converge on improving the 'man-machine' relations in military data processing systems.

References

CAILLE, E.J., BOCK, G., BERNARDINI, A., TITLI, A. and BERTAILS, A., 1971, Necessity of an exhaustive criteriology in complex vigilance tasks study. Digital computer analysis of operational and psychophysiological parameters *Deutsche Gesellschaft fur Ortung und Navigation Ev. Dusseldorf*, **12**, 23.

HJORTH, Bo., 1970, EEG Analysis based on time domain properties. *EEG and Clinical Neurophysiology*, **29**, 306–310.

SINGLETON, W.T., 1972, Total activity analysis: a different approach to work study. *Le Travail Humain*, **35**, **2**, 241–250.

Dr. Bates holds sociology degrees. She has worked in psychiatric hospitals, in health education research, in administrative research and is now Lecturer in Behavioural Science in the School of Health Administration, University of New South Wales, Australia.

Mr. Moore has a degree in commerce. He has held various civil service posts, in research and in administration. He is now an Inspector, New South Wales Public Service Board, Australia.

2:12

Job stress in Australian organizations

Erica M. Bates and B. N. Moore

Introduction

It is a fact of life that most organizational jobs entail a certain amount of stress, and of course, a certain amount of stress is needed to keep us awake. But generally the problem we face today is that of excessive stress and excessive pressure in the working environment. A study by the University of Michigan has shown that only one out of every six people in the United States work force is prepared to say that he is free from tension caused by job stress (Kahn *et al.*, 1964). The same study suggested that the higher levels of job stress were likely to occur in the following areas of activity:

(1) *Supervision:* where the job occupant is responsible for the work of others
(2) *liaison:* people who are working across organizational boundaries
(3) *innovation:* those who are 'thinkers' working to produce new solutions to non-routine problems.

Many individuals report that their jobs force them to be 'in the middle', between two or more sets of conflicting demands, or expectations. Any job involving supervision or liaison, especially at lower levels, tends to force the person in the job into such a position. For instance, Beynon (1973) has recorded how the foreman in a motor vehicle plant is expected to behave with due concern for production and discipline, but his subordinates expect him to behave in ways quite inconsistent with management policy.

An individual in a liaison job (and this includes the sales representative) is often physically remote from, and has little communication with, people in his own organization, which weakens his ability to identify himself wholeheartedly with his organization's particular set of values. At the same time he is in constant contact with customers, or people in other organizations, and inevitably begins to appreciate their points of view. If there is a conflict between the things people in his own organization expect him to believe in, and the things his external contacts expect him to believe in, then the individual working across organizational boundaries may experience the discomfort of being a marginal man.

In a job where a certain amount of innovation is involved, the individual is less likely to feel 'in the middle'. He is more likely to feel that he is nowhere in particular. The ambiguity which arises from not having firm expectations, or a fixed set of job procedures, can be distressing for some people.

A study by Kahn and Quin (1968) indicated specific jobs where stress was most likely to be severe. These included:

Newly created jobs.
Jobs in an expanding organization,
Jobs in an organization where the environment was rapidly changing,
Jobs of an 'assistant to . . .' nature.

In all of these jobs there is a degree of conflict and ambiguity. A changing environment renders previous expectations obsolete, and produces ambiguity. Filling a newly created job often involves trespassing on what had previously been somebody else's preserve, and so producing conflict. In addition, there is often a lack of resources to carry out the responsibilities of the job, as it is progressively defined by the occupant and those around him. This is a special sort of conflict, often described as role overload. Resources which can be provided by the organization (money, equipment, authority) do not always arrive when needed. Also, the personal resources of people in new or developing jobs are not always adequate to the tasks they are called upon to perform. Thus, the major sources of stress are:

(1) Not knowing quite what the job entails or how to do it (role ambiguity),
(2) Being a marginal person between two groups (role conflict), and
(3) An excessive amount of work (role overload).

Objectives

The original theoretical objective of this research was the comparison of stress levels recorded in the United States with stress levels in similar work situations in Australia. However, the practical objective of the authors was to solve some problems in their own organizations—a most relevant factor in all behavioural science research, even if it is seldom reported.

The School of Health Administration (S.H.A.), in the University of New South Wales, was one of the two organizations whose purposes were thus being served. The objectives of the S.H.A. are not easily defined. In a general way, it identifies with the university aim of pushing back the frontiers of knowledge. However, it also has a special interest in the well being and effective functioning of professional people employed in the health services. If its research activities lead to the identification and elimination of deficiencies in the training of these professionals, or deficiencies in their social or physical environment, then practical, as well as theoretical objectives are achieved.

The hospital staff selected for this study were therefore drawn from professions which were already known to be subject to considerable stress. Always in the background was the desire to initiate changes which would reduce this stress.

The second organization concerned in this study was the New South Wales Public Service Board (P.S.B.). The P.S.B. is responsible by law for 'ensuring the continuance of a proper standard of efficiency and economy' in a number of state government departments. To this end it controls the recruitment, promotion and training of staff; it creates or abolishes jobs and it decides on classification, pay and responsibilities for some 60,000 public servants.

The P.S.B. is therefore concerned with the existence of areas where there is job stress, because in such cases there may be a valid reason for increasing the number of jobs, re-defining responsibilities, or investing in a training programme. The public servants selected for this study were not a random sample of the Public Service work force. Many were selected from areas where re-organizations were taking place, or were being planned. Always in the background was the need to make an immediate administrative decision.

Taxonomy

Stress can be thought about in a number of ways, but we have restricted ourselves to two of these—stress as a major cause of illness, and stress as a system of inputs and outputs.

(1) *Stress as a major cause of illness*

There is considerable research evidence that stress is a major cause of illness. A major change in a person's life is inevitably stressful, even if the person eventually adapts and even if the change is later seen as an improvement. There is, for example, considerable evidence that the greater the change in a person's life in the course of a year, the more serious and frequent will be his illnesses in the following year. Toffler (1970) in his work on 'Future Shock' has quoted many of the research results which support this conclusion. If the stress extends over a long period of time, as when a person is working in a job which is continually stressful, even though some adaptation is always made, the chances of developing some illness are very high.

Durkheim (1933) divided societies into two types: the mechanical and the organic. In the former, the individual's total personality is involved in his role performance, as it is in a small community. As society becomes more industrialized, with a more complex division of labour, each individual assumes a number of separate roles, each of which requires for its performance only a segment of his personality.

A man's domestic problems, for example, are not supposed to interfere with his efficiency at work.

Some jobs, however, even in complex societies, do require the involvement of the individual's emotions, as well as his intellect. It was hypothesized that such jobs are inevitably stressful, though the stress involved may be reduced by manipulation of the work environment. As examples of people in such jobs, we took resident medical officers and nurses in a number of hospitals. Administrative and clerical officers in a number of government departments were selected as examples of people in jobs in which, theoretically at least, they need only be intellectually involved. Hospital administrators, who work in the same organizations as resident medical officers and nurses, but who perform similar duties to the administrative and clerical officers in government departments, were taken as a comparison group, on the hypothesis that, not being directly involved with patients, they would be able to segment their roles.

(2) *Stress as a system of inputs and outputs*

This approach provides a useful frame of reference for classifying the causes of stress. The person in a job is seen as the focus of a system, with an output (job *performance*) and two types of input (*expectations* regarding job performance, and *resources* available to achieve this performance). Inputs may be further classified as set out in Figure 1, below.

Figure 1. Job inputs

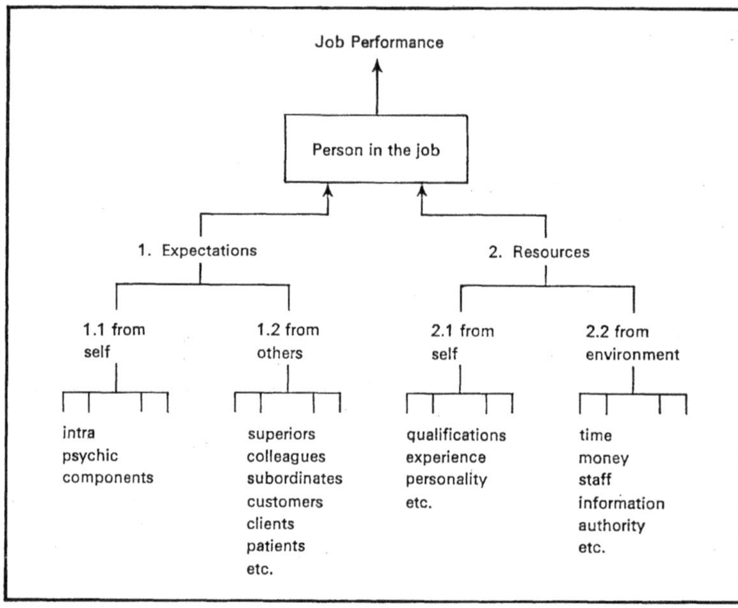

Causes of stress

One cause of stress in any type of job is *role ambiguity*, a situation where the person in the job cannot clearly perceive expectations of others (1.2). The following statement would be an example of such a situation.

> 'We see patients, we take histories, etc., but they have been seen before. We don't admit patients, we don't take part in discussion of treatment. It's all been done before and there are 10 or 20 students doing it too. We have plenty of patient contact but it's superficial—we go on rounds, we take histories, but we're not part of a team—we're a bit of a nuisance.'
>
> (resident medical officer)

A second cause of stress is *role conflict*, where the expectations of others are contradictory (e.g., 1.2 v 1.2), where the expectations of others are in conflict with the expectations of the person in the job (e.g., 1.2 v 1.1), or even where there is intra psychic conflict (e.g., 1.1 v 1.1). Role conflict is indicated by this statement:

> 'A married resident has a responsibility both to the patients and to his wife. This is often hard to sort out in the early years. Priorities of work are

Figure 2. Stress questionnaire (Kahn *et al.*, 1964)

Respondents were given the following instructions:

'Every job has its own peculiar set of problems. Please indicate how *frequently* you feel bothered by each of the following cases.

1. Feeling that you have too little authority to carry out the responsibilities assigned to you.
2. Being unclear on just what the scope and responsibilities of your job are.
3. Thinking that you'll not be able to satisfy the conflicting demands of various people over you.
4. Feeling, in your own heart, that you may not be qualified to handle this sort of a job.
5. Other people thinking you are not fully qualified to handle this sort of a job.
6. Not knowing what your superior thinks of you, or how he evaluates your performance.
7. The fact that you can't get information needed to carry out responsibilities assigned to you.
8. Having to decide things that affect the lives of individuals, people that you know.
9. Feeling that too heavy a work load has been imposed upon you.
10. Not having sufficient time or resources to do all the things you feel should be done.
11. Feeling unable to influence departmental decisions and actions that affect you.
12. Not knowing just what the people you work with expect of you.
13. Thinking that the *amount* of work you have to do may interfere with how *well* it gets done.
14. Feeling that you have to do things on the job that are against your better judgement.
15. Feeling that your job tends to interfere with your family life.
16. Feeling that you have too much authority and responsibility delegated to you.
17. Feeling that you'll not be able to satisfy all the demands of clients (or patients, or students) and members of the public.'

The following response categories were provided:

Never (score 1)
Rarely (score 2)
Sometimes (score 3)
Rather often (score 4)
Nearly all the time (score 5)

The respondent's score was obtained by calculating his mean score on all items.

hard to sort out for anyone. For the married resident it is doubly hard. This creates pressures . . .' (medical superintendent)

Thirdly, there is *role overload*, a situation where resources are insufficient to meet expectations (2 < 1). This produces statements such as:

'The workload here is heavy. Bloody heavy. I need an additional Grade 1 Clerk. They are always unloading work from Head Office—delegation of authority they call it—but they never unload excess Head Office staff to help us handle these things.' (Technical College registrar)

Method of measurement

A simple questionnaire for measuring stress, developed by Kahn and his associates, was re-worded in minor respects (see Figure 2). The questionnaire was distributed to 783 members of hospital staff, in over 20 different hospitals, and to 102 public servants in 17 different departments.

In addition, interviews of varying length and format were carried out with 100 of the hospital staff and 32 of the public servants.

Results

Completed questionnaires were received from 178 resident medical officers (48% response), 225 nurses (100% response), 91 hospital administrators (64% response) and 100 administrative and clerical officers in government departments (98% response).

The higher response rate for nurses and public servants was due to the fact that questionnaires were administered to 'captive' groups. The nurses were in training groups, and each public servant could usually be located in ordinary office hours at a particular desk if follow-up action were required. Resident medical officers, on the other hand, worked in shifts, and were often difficult for researchers to locate. Hospital administrators were at conferences and moved around in different study groups.

American and Australian scores on the stress questionnaire are set out in Figures 3 and 4 below.

Figure 3. Mean tension: as measured by scores on stress questionnaire American wage and salary earners (Kahn *et al.*, 1964)

Occupational Group	*Mean*	*Standard Deviation*	*Number in Sample*
Professional, technical	2·0	Not reported	52
Managerial	1·8	,,	37
Clerical, sales	1·8	,,	60
Craftsmen, foremen	1·7	,,	86
Operatives	1·5	,,	81
Unskilled, service	1·5	,,	49

F test of overall differences among means is significant at $P < 0{\cdot}001$.

Discussion of results

Australians in the past have believed that they live in a free and easy society—a society where job stress is considerably lower than in other countries.

This belief is not supported by the results. The data in Figures 3 and 4 show

Figure 4. Mean tension: as measured by scores on stress questionnaire. Australian wage and salary earners

Occupational Group	*Mean*	*Standard Deviation*	*Number in Sample*
Hospital staff:			
resident medical officers	2·9	1·09	178
nurses	2·9	1·08	225
hospital administrators	2·5	1·05	91
Public servants:			
administrative and clerical officers	2·4	0·70	100

T test of differences between means of resident medical officers/nurses and public servants is significant at $P < 0{\cdot}001$.
T test of differences between means of resident medical officers/nurses and hospital administrators is significant at $P < 0{\cdot}05$.
There is no significant difference between means of hospital administrators and public servants.

that stress levels are quite high in our Australian samples. It is reasonably valid to compare the scores of Australian administrative and clerical officers (mean 2·4) and the scores of American managerial and clerical groups (mean 1·8). There is perhaps a slight bias in the selection of our Australian sample, because many jobs were chosen from public service departments where some reorganization was taking place or was being planned. On the other hand, the general environment of administrative and clerical officers in the public service is normally assumed to be free from extreme levels of stress.

It could also be said that international comparisons of this nature are fraught with difficulty, because one is never sure of the extent to which national differences affect the ways in which people respond to apparently similar items in a questionnaire. It is less difficult to compare different occupations within the same country. Consider, for example, the job stress scores for Australian resident medical officers and nurses (Figure 4). As an example of what we have earlier described as 'mechanical' work, we would have expected higher scores than hospital administrators or public servants in 'organic' work. The results support this expectation. Stress levels for both resident medical officers and nurses (mean 2·9) exceeded stress levels recorded for hospital administrators (mean 2·5) and public servants (mean 2·4).

The performance of the medical and nursing task is essentially threatening to the role occupant. He cannot help thinking to himself 'there but for the grace of God, go I', and even worse, 'this may still happen to me at any time'. Hence stress, anxiety, fear or tension is inevitably present when doctor and nurse confront the sick person, and such tension-reducing mechanisms as laughter and refusal to become involved, are part of the medical and nursing lore.

The administrative task, on the other hand, is not invested with such primitive emotion. Of course, the organizational environment teems with conflict, intrigue and complexity, but the administrator is not threatened daily by the presence of pain, disease and death.

Using the results

Within the S.H.A., this type of action-oriented research begins to produce effects before the results are even written up. Knowledge of the levels of stress being measured has produced in lecturers a sense of satisfaction that their own intuitive beliefs have been confirmed, and has given some individuals the confidence to press for changes in the training of doctors and nurses.

Interview notes have yielded important clues as to the causes of role conflict. Factors intrinsic to the work of a doctor or nurse were mentioned by respondents, but these are already well known and represent a rediscovery of the obvious. However the importance placed on extrinsic factors by nearly all the doctors interviewed has been quite surprising. In order to check the impressions of resident medical officers against those of their superiors, a number of medical superintendents were interviewed. Here are the comments of one superintendent:

> 'One of the things that bothers residents most, I believe, are the simple comforts—decent food when they come off, hot food; they complain about the water being cold, the towels and linen unchanged. I've insisted we get decent beds, food, carpets, etc., and I try to feed information up to them. I've heard that some hospitals don't spend as much time looking after their residents. Usually, where there's an uprising at these hospitals, it started out from something quite harmless.'

The interesting feature of these complaints is the apparent ease with which they could have been avoided by hospital administrators. As lecturers in the S.H.A. are personally involved with the training of hospital administrators, one might expect that the lessons to be gained from this research will be preached with increasing force in the future.

Within the P.S.B., action research of this nature produces long term effects on the attitudes of senior administrators which are difficult to assess. Short term effects, though, are easier to identify. Decisions affecting small segments of the public service have to be made every day, and on the basis of whatever information is to hand. If research results are available, then they too will be used, as the following two examples show.

(1) *Salary administration*

In one department there were problems with the payment of salaries and wages. One salaries clerk described his work in the following terms:

> 'Always there are new salary agreements and arbitration awards to put through, and they have to be done yesterday. Everybody wants to be paid his increase straight away. Lots of things have to take second place, like for instance when people resign or retire from the place, sometimes it is more than a month before they are paid. This makes them very irate. There is a continual pressure to get things done by the deadline. Many, of course, miss out. Like for instance the overtime which has to be done in off-pay week and if we can't get the calculations through in time, well they just miss out. The other day I have the Plumbers' Union on the phone complaining like hell about some of their members that missed out. But this can't be helped. It is the result of continual pressure.'

Could this situation have been blamed on poor staff selection or a lack of training? Or was the salaries section really understaffed?

In order to resolve this question, accounting staff throughout the department were interviewed and given stress questionnaires to complete. In accounting jobs not concerned with salaries work, stress scores were low. In jobs partly concerned with salaries, stress scores were moderate; whereas in jobs wholly concerned with salaries, stress scores were high. Result: a decision to increase the number of salaries clerks.

(2) *Regional administration*
A department claimed that its nine regional administrators were working under severe pressure, and needed more resources. The jobs held by these administrators were concerned with supervision, liaison and innovation, and hence in theory (Kahn, 1964) were very vulnerable to stress. When interviewed, two regional administrators explained their work this way:

> 'Basically I'm a facilitator. I facilitate the work of regional staff, but without breathing down their necks. I'm an "in-between" man, helping communications between the field and Head Office. I have a representative role—a sort of "front" man for the department—particularly for its regionally decentralized activities. I am supposed to speak with some authority on behalf of the department.'
>
> 'I am a "link man". The link between Head Office and field staff, between staff in different disciplines, and between the department and the local community . . .'

The regional administrators completed the stress questionnaires, and although higher than average scores were expected, they did not materialize. Scores were moderate (mean 1·8). An examination of scores on particular items in the questionnaire, and an analysis of interview notes, showed that role conflict and role overload was almost non-existent. There was, however, some role ambiguity. Results: no increase in regional staff. The question of clarifying the role of a regional administrator was given some prominence at the next regional officers' training conference.

Summary

An action-oriented research project on job stress was undertaken in some Australian hospitals and in government departments. Stress levels were measured, and doctors, nurses and administrators were interviewed to see whether modification of the organizational environment was needed in high stress jobs. Results showed that stress levels were high in a number of work situations, and modifications were made to the environment. Stress levels will be measured again at a later stage, to see whether these modifications have been effective in reducing job stress.

References

BEYNON, H., 1973, *Working for Ford* (London: Penguin).
DURKHEIM, E., 1933, *The Division of Labour in Society* (N.Y.: Macmillan).
KAHN, R.L., WOLFE, D.M., QUIN, R.P. and SNOECK, J.D., 1964, *Organisational Stress: Studies in Role Conflict and Ambiguity* (N.Y.: Wiley).
KAHN, R.L. and QUIN, R.P., 1968, *Role Stress: a framework for analysis* (University of Michigan, unpublished manuscript).
MECHANIC, D., 1968, *Medical Sociology: a Selective View* (N.Y.: Free Press).
TOFFLER, A., 1970, *Future Shock* (London: Pan).

Peter Bowen is an industrial sociologist. He holds degrees in Sociology. His industrial employment experience is in the steel and plastics industries. He has researched into problems of individual and occupational involvement in plant work control systems in the British steel industry. Currently he is engaged with a colleague in a research programme sponsored by the Social Science Research Council concerning office employment in certain U.K. industries and industrial office employees' attachment to particular trade unions. He is now the Head of the Department of Behavioural Studies at the Polytechnic, Newcastle upon Tyne, England.

2:13

Employee involvement in systems of work control

P. Bowen

Introduction

Recently completed research in the British Iron and Steel Industry by Bowen and Shaw (1972) and Bowen, Shaw and Smith (1973) suggests that the concept of a 'control system' applied to problems of job and work regulation in industrial organizations may be preferable to the more limited concept of collective bargaining. In this approach a control system in industrial relations is defined as the process whereby participants attempt to influence the behaviour of others in the regulation of work, and whereby the resulting cross-pressures are reconciled. Collective bargaining is thus one aspect of work control, but a fully developed system of social control in industrial organizations must be inclusive of the value systems (and their derivation) of rank and file employees. These employees are not formal parties to agreements covering job and work regulation but their consent to the rules of work is crucial to their successful implementation.

The research programme, aspects of which are reported in this paper, was undertaken in the iron and steel industry and completed in 1971. This particular industry was selected because of its long history of stable labour relations at least until the early 60s (Phelps Brown, 1960 and Knowles, 1952). It offered a useful site for the exploration of systems of work control associated with stable patterns of industrial relations, including the authority and rule-making aspects of control, however these arrangements are contrived. One dimension of the wider problem of the effective utilization of human resources of concern to us was the 'openness' of the work control system to mutual influence by management and labour. Our approach was shaped in important respects by recent developments in the sociology of organizations. It is our contention, for example, that the development of theories of organization control on the one hand and theories of social and human control *within* organizations on the other have become divorced, and that the largely segregated theories of systems and social integration have inhibited consideration of the interaction of systems and social influences upon the effectiveness of social control in large organizations.

In general terms a much more adequate theory of control covering these two aspects of organizations is required. However, progress towards this goal is handicapped by conceptual problems at the boundaries between sociology and industrial relations restricting the formulation of an adequate theory of work control (Bowen, forthcoming).

If this point is accepted it seems useful to consider an approach to the problem of social integration in industrial organizations which commences:

(*a*) at the level of rank and file employees and their perceptions of what rates an appropriate level of influence over the control of work, recognizing that positive work attachment is both a function of satisfaction with the level of influence over work control as well as satisfaction with the individual task, and

(*b*) reflects the fact that the control of work is basically a jointly administered activity by representatives of the employer and representatives of the trade union, and that the quality of individual work attachment and the commitment to work is as much a function of the relationship between the trade union and its membership as between the employer and his employees.

The linkage between industrial sociology and industrial relations in this area becomes important when one asserts that certain major determinants of stable social integration in industrial organizations are likely to be:

(*a*) the existence of high mutual influence over the formulation of work rules by management and trade unions as the formal representatives of the employer and the labour force in a control system, and

(*b*) the continuing consent of rank and file employees to the acceptance of these rules. This condition is achieved and sustained where employees believe that their system of work control is capable of mutual influence by management and labour at a level acceptable to themselves and when such employees experience direct involvement in aspects of work control.

Work control in the steel industry

In our research programme in the steel industry we sought to examine some, but by no means all, of the factors which contributed to the stability of industrial relations systems in steel plants. This industry shows a stable record of industrial relations over a long period measured by the low incidence of disputes between management and trade unions including unofficial strikes. Nevertheless there is increasing evidence of incipient strain in the work control systems of various plants. Such situations permit a study of the ways in which work control systems disintegrate and become reorganized under various pressures. However, there was no attempt to equate stability of work control merely with the absence of industrial strife. It was recognized that some degree of conflict is an endemic feature of work relations in any industrial situation. In considering the stability of work control, we distinguished between patterns of management-union conflict which were a normal expression of the collective bargaining process and those which arose over some perceived inadequacy in the organization of the work control system itself.

In many respects the steel industry provided a suitable research site for the study of integration and disintegration of systems of work control. Following a long period of industrial peace it is now faced with increasing labour problems induced by international competition, problems of change involving the better utilization of the labour force and the concentration of steel making into fewer and larger plants (*British Iron & Steel Federation*, 1966; *British Steel Corporation*, 1973 and Ovenden, 1973). This was reflected in an increasing level of strike activity after 1958, moving from 1·7% of the United Kingdom total to 4·4% by 1965 (Wedderburn and Jones, 1967). Moreover, there were significant shifts in the composition of the labour force: production workers declined whilst administrative, technical and clerical workers expanded rapidly.

We selected one plant for intensive study. This plant we shall call Ironhill. The limitation of one plant case studies are fully acknowledged. There were, however, previous studies by Scott *et al.* (1956) in England and by Walker (1950) in the United States. These studies provided broad comparative material on such subjects as the organization of steelwork and the attachment of steel employees to the particular form of work organization in steel industries on both sides of the Atlantic in those years. Our main hypothesis was that a significant influence upon the stable control system in this plant would be the belief by a majority of employees in the existence of opportunities for labour involvement in work control, and that this belief would be sustained by the actual experience of involvement in work regulation by the rank and file manual and non-manual worker. A 5% sample of production, service and clerical workers was selected from the plant's labour force of some 6,000 employees. A questionnaire was administered in 1970 and an overall response rate of 82% received.

Initially information was collected about certain aspects of control. This showed that the ratio of administrative, technical and clerical staff to the total labour force in the plant was much lower than would normally have been expected in a capital intensive industry. The ratio was 18·6% at Ironhill in 1969 compared with 38% in chemicals and 23% in engineering, considerably lower than the ratio in manufacturing industry. This suggested that the work control system in steel was not solely concentrated in the hands of management and that the managerial process itself was unusually diffuse. This condition was reinforced by the organization of production work covering the majority of employees into what are called 'seniority lines'. These lines provide avenues of advancement for semi-skilled workers to acquire increasing responsibility, rewards and status with experience. One effect of this pattern was to stratify the labour force in ways inhibiting the formation of unified interest groups. In addition the control of seniority lines and the placement of employees to vacancies within them rested largely in the hands of the trade unions. Whilst management reserved the right to determine initial appointments to new seniority lines, thereafter the responsibility for subsequent nominations remained with the union. It was noted finally that the settlement of unresolved plant disputes between management and trade unions was undertaken by a neutral committee system of arbitration consisting of representatives of both sides drawn in equal numbers from plants outside the affected area and with a chairman appointed by the employer. This system of arbitration had worked with apparent success over many years and provided an interesting example of a jointly-administered work control system at the interplant level.

The low ratio of indirect labour coupled with the organization of manual work into seniority lines, together with the existence of neutral committees indicated the existence of a distinctive type of work control system. It appeared also to provide a type of individual work attachment denied to many semi-skilled workers in other British industries.

The social organization of labour in the plant was complemented by the team-work organization of workers at the level of production work itself. Most production workers were located in work teams and the discretion afforded to teams and to individuals to take certain types of decision affecting the quantity and quality of output was well developed. The individual steelworker appeared to be socially located in a well-defined work system and decision-making system. To this extent the organization of steelwork and its traditions of industrial relations were apparently conducive to employee involvement in certain aspects of the control of their work situations. But how far was this assumption accepted by employees themselves?

The results of a survey by questionnaire indicated that the majority of workers experienced a relatively high degree of job and work satisfaction. Most believed their jobs to be secure and to contain a variety of features enhancing the level of individual interest and job satisfaction. These included self-reported opportunities for choice and decision-making within the context of team work; opportunities for work without close supervision and for the adequate use of skills. Yet most rated their chances of promotion to the level of supervisor and beyond as being extremely limited and two-thirds of the sample agreed that irrespective of who owned it, steelworkers would always be relatively worse off than those who controlled the industry, and would have to fight for every improvement in their condition. Thus the same group of steelworkers who believed that their jobs were satisfying, and offered reasonable opportunities of career advancement within manual work held an equally realistic appreciation of the conditions under which 'co-operative' relationships with management in the planning of change should emerge. These conditions were grounded in their view within a management-labour relationship which included the very real possibility of conflict over the distribution of scarce resources. Such a response might well be considered compatible with those of any representative group of manual workers who happened also to reside in a cohesive and predominantly working class community. Nevertheless there had been a continuous absence of serious conflict at the plant over many years. As we have already observed, this record was by no means unusual for the industry as a whole. Indeed, Scott *et al.* whose study of the impact of technical change on industrial relations in steel had been published in 1956 concluded that,

> 'In terms of the experience of other industries, the formal structure of management-employee relationships in steel and the traditional values (upon which it is based) have persisted and proved effective in limiting conflict in the face of so many problems.'

The favourable responses of the members of the sample towards their work were coupled, therefore, with an awareness of the continuing need for collective and vigilant trade union action against employers in the process of collective bargaining. Nevertheless it appeared that the underlying conflict perspective of steelworkers was compatible with their support for a system of work control in which the mutual influence of management and labour was an important characteristic.

The concept of work control

Before documenting the attitudes of steelworkers to the work control system at Ironhill in more detail, it is worthwhile considering the concept of control itself. In order to measure the perceived and preferred patterns of influence-distribution by steelworkers—we explored the use of the control graph technique. This technique was based upon the work of Arnold Tannenbaum (1968) and his colleagues in the United States, and was being applied by Jones and Wedderburn (unpublished paper) in the United Kingdom at about the time of our own research. Tannenbaum's approach is a critique of the notion that the amount of power or influence in an organization must be inevitably fixed as claimed by the advocates of zero-sum or fixed-pie models, so that there must be a limited supply of power, prestige and reward, and their distribution a persistent and enduring problem. Instead, Tannenbaum argues that effective control requires the mutual exercise of power by all participants, and that increasing the influence of one group need not necessarily imply decreasing the influence of others. Much of his work is concerned with illustrating the conditions under which the joint influence of both leaders and followers can be increased with the expansion of the total amount of influence in a control system. It follows that one possible source of stable control in industrial organizations may be found by devising means whereby rank and file employees expand their influence over work control, but in ways which need not imply corresponding contractions in the influence of managerial groups. This would constitute a condition of high mutual influence. Lammers (1967) has suggested that granting more power to subordinates to participate in decision-making may increase the joint power of all participants in the control system in that subordinates may be more willing to implement decisions so reached.

What is being implied here, however, is not a purely democratic system of work or 'workers'' control. Whilst Tannenbaum's respondents wished to wield more influence over decisions, typically they did not wish to achieve this at the expense of other groups. Indeed Smith and Ari (1963) suggest that the accumulation of influence at any one level of an organizational hierarchy could impede performance, since it is only under conditions of high reciprocal influence that effective control can be achieved. Thus,

> 'The significant exercise of control by both members and leaders leads to a high degree of identification and involvement in the organization . . . The system of high mutual influence which this pattern of control signifies provides an opportunity for members and leaders to reconcile their interests and facilitates an atmosphere of co-operation.'

There appears to exist two separate approaches to the measurement of reciprocity. The first, adopted by industrial relations analysts, is to take the rules governing the control of work and determine who made them. Difficulties here are that it is often impossible to allocate the degree of influence to one party or another; to know, for example, whether the rule in question is the product of genuine mutual influence or merely the result of unilateral control by one party with the connivance or agreement, however reluctantly, of the other. The second approach, and one followed by Tannenbaum, is to consider how members judge the patterns of existing and desired influence over work control. This approach is distinctive in that it seeks to measure both the level of total control as well as the distribution of control on the basis of averaged judgements by members in response to questionnaire items relating to individual perceptions of the profile of control in their organizations. It is achieved by asking individuals or groups of respondents at particular levels in a work control hierarchy to estimate the amount of influence they perceive to be held by others both in the existing organizational situation and in an ideal or preferred situation. Measuring employee judgements of the distribution of influence amongst interest groups is a necessary but insufficient method of investigating the social imagery of control systems. Of equal importance is the measurement of employees' perceived involvement in the regulation of work itself. Our analysis of control, therefore, included assessing how workers defined the organization of their job, and which areas of their job experience provided opportunities for involvement in rule making. Thus the actual measurement of control used by Tannenbaum and extended in our own work was located firmly at the level of individual actors and their definitions of the amount of influence they believed themselves and others to wield.

Tannenbaum's (1968) approach to the study of organizations involved primary consideration of the process of control. A control cycle begins 'with an intent on the part of one person, followed by an influence attempt addressed to another person, who then acts in some way that fulfils the intent of the first'. Control cycles are basic units of organization structure and 'organizations are composed of large numbers of such cycles in inter-relationship'. Control processes exist in organizations, then, where individuals, groups or organizations of people can be shown to determine the behaviour of others. Perhaps the central assumption in Tannenbaum's work is that organizational performance will be enhanced where the increased level of total control is achieved by raising the mutual influence of both leaders and members in decision making. Unfortunately the examples he provides of increasing the total level of influence refer mainly to 'participative' management styles. Our contention, however, is that the existence of such styles is quite compatible with a zero-sum model of power. This in no way minimizes the importance of assessing the views of actors and *their* perceptions of the existence of mutual influence irrespective of how it is achieved. The 'power-raising' process which he defines may be achieved in certain areas of work control at the expense of contractions elsewhere. Such a situation need not imply the existence of conflict between leaders and members. Conflict would be much more likely in circumstances where members' expectations of control were moving out of line with the existing distribution of influence and as an expression of individual or group alienation from the control system itself.

Attitudes to control

We may now turn to the results of the research programme relating to manual workers' judgements of the distribution of influence within their own work control system. This analysis was confined to two areas: steelworkers' perceptions of influence distribution between different parties to work control and, secondly, the extent to which they felt their own occupation to be involved in the regulation of various work areas. In both cases manual respondents' judgement about influence distribution in the existing situation was compared with judgements about what *should* happen in an ideal situation. To measure the differences we asked respondents to consider the amount of control held by various groups—for example, divisional management, plant management, supervisors, shop stewards, etc. Their responses were averaged and weighted across a four point scale—good deal, some, very little and none—for each item. Figure 1 shows that steelworkers saw *existing* influence concen-

Figure 1. Control profile: Perceived actual and ideal distribution of influence by Ironhill manual workers

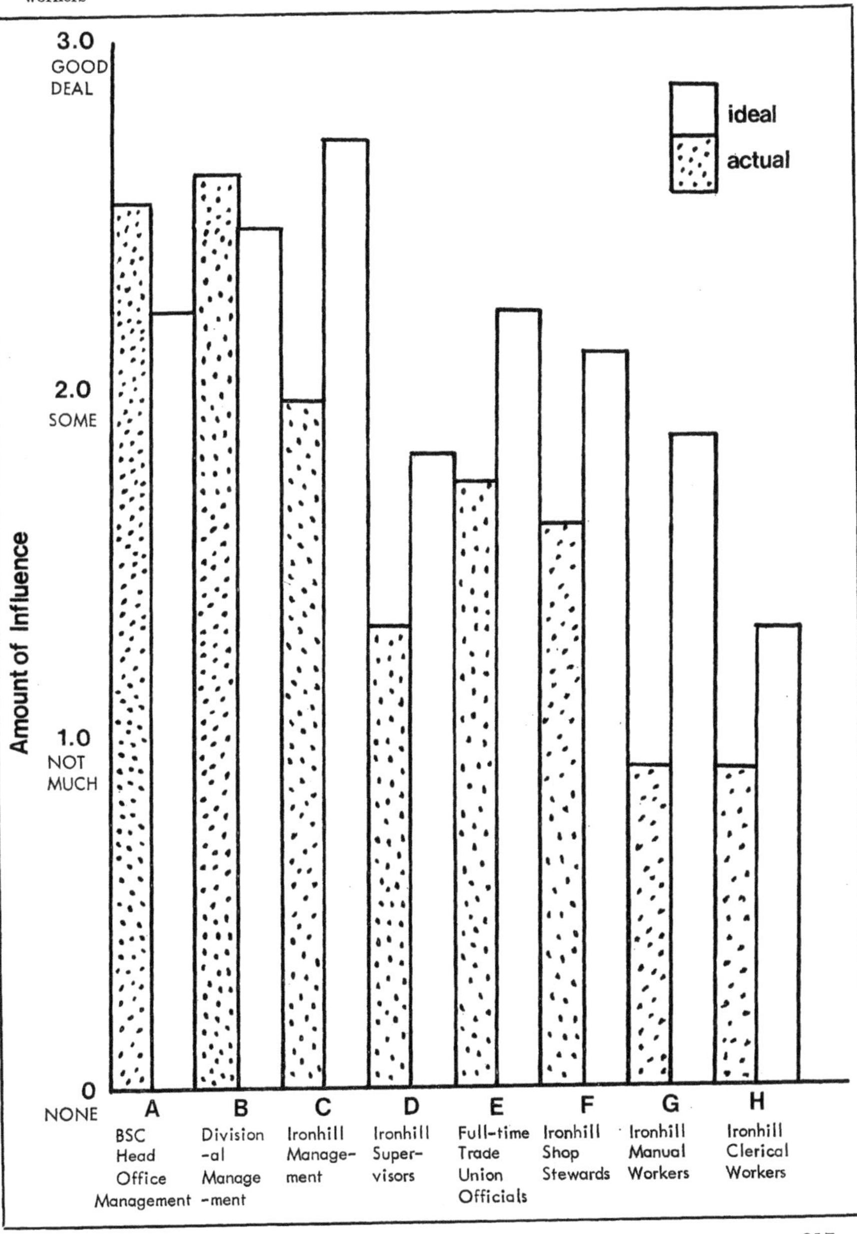

trated in the hands of management and to a much lesser extent at the level of full time trade union officers. Respondents' judgements on the *ideal* pattern of influence indicated a desire for an increase in the total amount of influence available to all groups (except British Steel Corporation national management, where a decrease was sought) but, and we hold this to be significant, whilst more influence was sought for labour this was not desired at the expense of Ironhill management. It was rather that the influence of both parties should be jointly increased. There appeared to exist a preference for a system which

Table 1. Work control categories

(A)	The pace at which members of the group have to work.
(B)	Safety matters.
(C)	Financial policy matters.
(D)	Reducing departmental costs by suggesting economies in operations.
(E)	Disciplining of employees including dismissals.
(F)	Pay rates and bonuses.
(G)	Amount of overtime available.
(H)	Fixing work standards by job evaluation and method study.
(I)	Controlling the recruitment of new employees.
(J)	The handling of redundancy problems.
(K)	Transfer of men between departments as a result of technical change.
(L)	The selection of men to positions within the seniority line.
(M)	Purchasing new machines and equipment.

would allow for greater shared control with management, rather than more unilateral control by trade unions at management's expense.

Such questions, however, reveal little about the *content* of control: those areas of work regulation in which joint control is believed to exist or would be valued. Consequently respondents were asked to indicate how much influence they believed their occupational groups had with Ironhill management in each of a number of work control categories, again both currently and in an ideal situation. The results indicated that employees saw a measure of control for themselves at the present time over most of the working areas defined (for a description of these areas see Table 1). These areas were as follows: work pace, safety, financial policy matters, economies in departmental operations, discipline, the fixing of pay rates and bonuses, overtime, fixing of work standards by work measurement, recruitment, the handling of redundancy problems, transfers of labour as a result of technical change, the selection of men to positions within the seniority line and the purchase of equipment. The control profiles for the three main occupational groups of manual workers—production and service employees, blast furnace and coke plant employees and craft maintenance workers are presented in Figure 2.

In certain areas existing control by manual workers was seen to be substantial, especially in respect of work pace, safety, fixing of pay rates and the promotion of personnel to positions within the seniority line. Only in the areas of general financial policy matters, recruitment and the purchase of equipment were low indices derived. Moreover, the highest ideal indices were obtained in areas where existing influences appeared to be already substantial, suggesting a

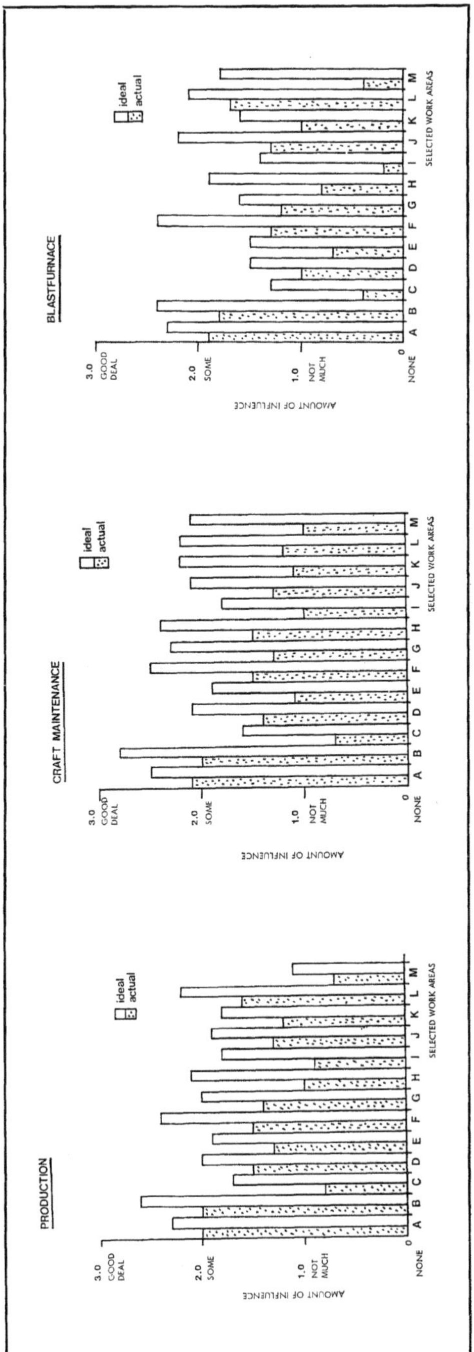

Figure 2. Control profile: Perceived actual and ideal distribution of influence over control of work areas, by occupation

fairly stable pattern of desired influence across the control categories. The greatest discrepancy between present and ideal indices existed over the fixing of work standards by such techniques as job evaluation and work study.

Occupational identity and control

The general pattern of responses presented above conceals the extent to which occupational influences tend to constrain individual judgements of control. The next step in our analysis was to explore the extent of occupational differentiation and how far this was associated with areas of strain within the control system.

Manual respondents were asked to rank the influence they believed other occupational groups possessed in their dealings with management. Four groups of high influence emerged: steel melters and steel rollers (production) and mechanical and electrical craftsmen. Three groups of low influence were defined: clerical workers, coke plant and transport workers. The possible implications of these status differentials were explored by measuring the strength of occupational attachment in the plant. Respondents were asked to indicate their attitudes to the proposition that 'there is no such person as a steelworker: only blast furnacemen, melters, rollers, welders, fitters... etc.' The results differed between occupational groups. Whereas only 37% of production and service employees agreed with the proposition, 70% of blast furnacemen and coke plant workers and 66% of craft maintenance workers agreed. These results suggested that production and service employees whose skills were highly specific to the steel industry and who formed the largest category of employees were least likely to view their attachment discretely. On the other hand, blast furnacemen and coke plant workers emerged as deviant groups amongst production workers in their high degree of occupational identification; in this respect they compared most strongly with the craft maintenance group whose sense of occupational attachment was, not surprisingly, well developed.

Further analysis demonstrated that the predisposition to oppose management was most highly concentrated amongst maintenance workers. Production and service workers constituted the largest and most cohesive group of employees whose relationship with management could be described as co-operative. Amongst production workers, blast furnacemen and coke plant staff were most likely to consider relationships with management in dichotomous terms.

Further differences existed at the level of attachment to employment. The major source of attachment to employment for both production and craft maintenance employees was either adequacy of pay for the level of skill employed or the intrinsic interest of steel work itself. For blast furnacemen, however, the sources of work attachment were negative. Over half admitted that they worked in steel because of the absence of other work opportunities. For this group the principal attachment was to the community rather than to employment. Four-fifths were highly satisfied with residence in the local community: only one-fifth claimed that they wished to leave the area for better opportunities elsewhere.

At the same time it was apparent that all three major occupational groups derived considerable satisfaction from a variety of common factors associated with the design and performance of their jobs. These concerned the opportunities of working without close supervision, as members of teams, and with the adequate use of skills. Moreover, occupational differentiation appeared to be acute in the area of promotion prospects. A marked differential appeared between the members of production departments and maintenance departments on this point. The absence of promotion prospects within manual work was a source of obvious concern to most craftsmen. Since seniority lines and team work were concentrated in direct production departments employing mainly unskilled and semi-skilled labour, the disadvantaged position of craftsmen can be regarded as a major source of discontent amongst such employees.

The responses of production and service workers (members of the Iron and Steel Trades Confederation) suggested a stronger commitment to steel work and to the existing system of work control at Ironhill. These workers were most sensitive to the potentially disruptive effects of the pursuit of independent strategies by separate occupations within the industry, and were more likely to acknowledge the intrinsic rewards of steel work. Craft workers were more emphatic in their belief that the primary allegiance of the individual employee should be to his occupation rather than to a wider group of steelworkers, and that relations with the employer were divisive. Blast furnacemen formed a deviant group of production workers in several respects. Their stronger sense of occupational attachment and attitudes towards the employer were more akin to craft workers but their attachment to steel employment was far more problematical. The source of this group's discontent appeared to be the poor rewards, especially pay, deriving from this type of work.

Further analysis of the inter-occupational perception of influence over work control and illustrated in Figure 2, showed that blast furnacemen and coke plant workers produced consistently lower weighted indices over most work areas compared with production and craft groups in both existing and ideal conditions. This implied the possibility that these employees were attached to their jobs and to the work control system by more limited aspirations and expectations.

The measurement of inter-occupational perceptions of influence provides useful comparative material on the differential attachment of employees to the control system. It may, however, be extended to the analysis of intra-occupational perceptions. In this context, a second case study conducted at Ironhill concurrently with the manual workers' survey concerned clerical workers. Its main results have been published elsewhere (Bowen and Shaw, 1972) and at this point we wish merely to refer to certain data it contained. In this case the attitudes of a one in five sample of clerical employees, stratified by age and sex, were investigated. The response rate was again high (84%) consisting of 149 completed questionnaires out of a sample frame of 177.

The results demonstrated that the orientation of employees to a work control system may be significantly influenced by the nature of their existing attachment to a trade union. After 1967 all clerical employees at Ironhill who were not then members of the major production workers' union, I.S.T.C.,* were encouraged to join in line with the policy of the British Steel Corporation. All clerks were therefore members of a predominantly manual workers' trade union when this study was conducted.

The choice of an isolated steel community for the purposes of this research permitted some assessment of how far non-manual steel clerks complied with the norms of a working class community. Since these clerks were also members

* The Iron and Steel Trades Confederation is the largest trade union in the industry with a membership of around 105,000 in 1968.

of a predominantly manual workers' union, the opportunity also existed to measure their commitment to this type of union representation, and to assess whether this had any impact on their attitudes to the work control system.

We believed that the effects of this dual exposure of the clerical employee to residence in a working class community and membership of a predominantly manual workers' union would have certain consequences: that clerical employees would identify more with working class than with middle class values, would be committed members of their trade union, that they would be job satisfied, concerned less with personal advancement than with security of employment and holding low expectations of status.

The results confirmed the commitment of these employees to the value of trade unionism, though not to the value of militant action. This was not taken to imply a rejection of militancy per se. Rather to support the view that the prevailing values of trade unionism within the steel industry had been accepted by these clerks. However, whilst accepting the utility of a trade union as the most appropriate expression of their class and occupational interest in the work control system, the sample divided on the form which union representation should take. Of those expressing an opinion, exactly one half were satisfied with their existing trade union membership. The other half would have preferred completely separate white collar type representation. It also emerged that attachment to the existing trade union varied with attitudes towards job and work. Those who enjoyed a firm attachment to I.S.T.C. were relatively satisfied with the rewards and status, albeit low status, which clerical work carried in the plant. Their perception of the gap between actual and ideal rewards from work was not sufficiently wide to create general dissatisfaction with the situation. The second group, however, distinguished by a desire for separate representation, expressed a general dissatisfaction with job and work. This dissatisfaction was induced in part by the belief that the rewards and status of clerical work in the steel industry had been allowed to deteriorate by both management and the trade union, compared with manual workers. In terms of occupational differentiation clerical employees divided into at least two groups in which perceptions of the existing situation and satisfaction with union representation varied.

A control profile was constructed measuring clerical workers' perceptions of the distribution of influence (see Figure 3). Clerical workers, like manual workers, wished for a greater degree of control for plant management at the expense of B.C.S. top management. In addition, clerks sought more control for their occupational group at about the same level as Ironhill manual workers. The analysis also indicated that the satisfied clerks (whom we called the Affiliates) rated their own occupational influence over what went on at the plant at a higher level than those who sought changes in union representation (the Non-Affiliates). Thus the Non-Affiliate clerk who sensed a serious decline in the status of his occupation and the rewards which it carried, and who was much more critical of his existing union membership, was more likely to record a lower level of existing total influence for all groups in the control system, and to rate his own level of influence as lowest of all.

The clerical workers' case study provides a useful example of the utility of control profile analysis in the identification of instabilities in work control systems induced, in this case, by strains within the clerical labour force over the appropriateness of trade union representation, and between manual and non-

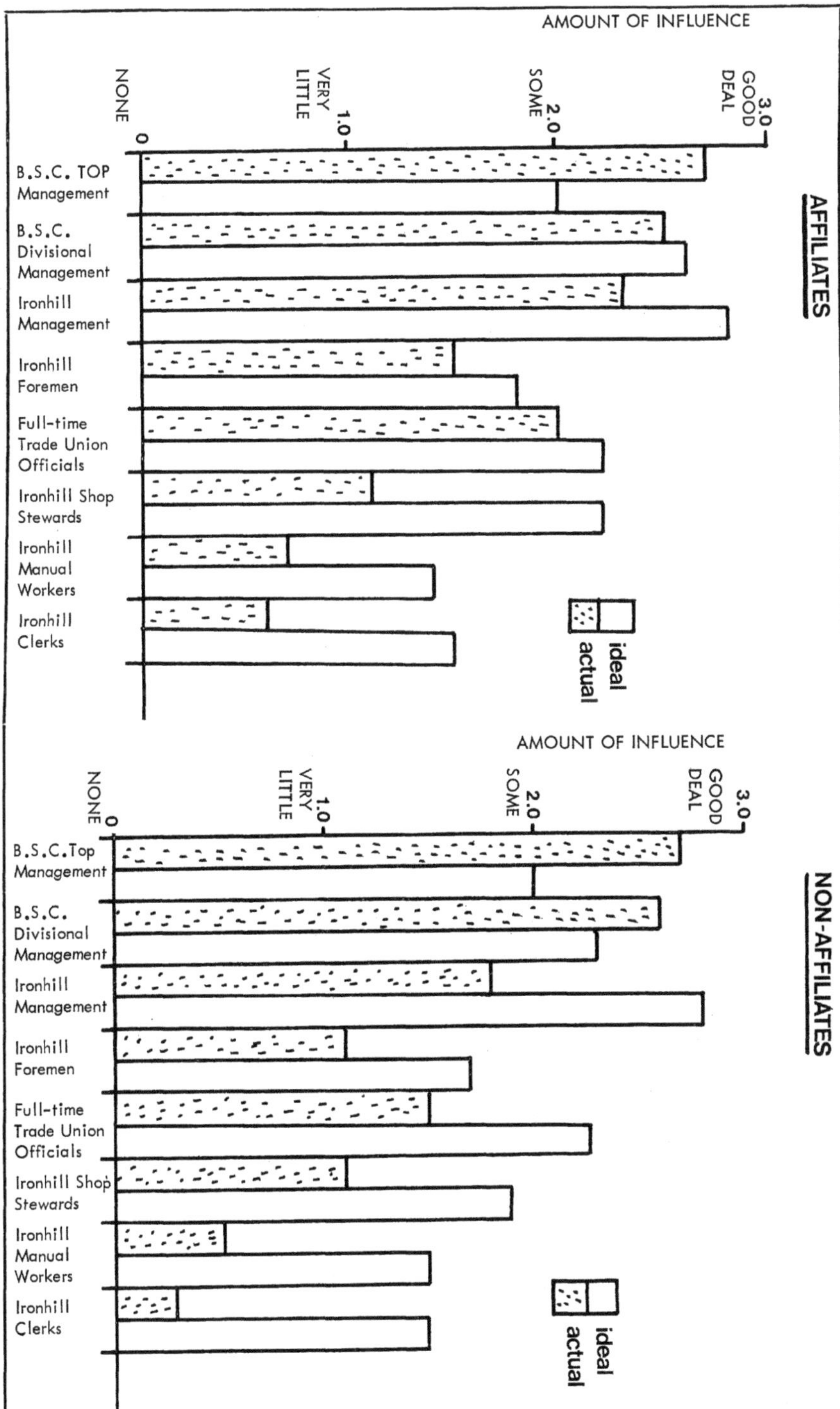

Figure 3. Control profile: Perceived actual and ideal distribution of influence by affiliates and non-affiliates

manual workers for status and rewards. It is also worth pointing out that whilst control profile analysis can indicate the areas of strain, within and across occupations, a much wider investigation of employee attachment to job and work is necessary to understand the significance of the strain.

Conclusion

The results of the research reported in this paper form part of a wider attempt to establish a model of social control in organizations and with particular reference to industrial organizations. It is our contention that such a model should include the measurement of rank and file employee assessments and expectations of personal and occupational influence in the process of control. This is based upon the assumption that the performance of such processes will be improved where employees are positively attached to a control system and experience some sense of personal or group influence in areas of work regulation which are significant to them. Stable attachment to the work control system would exist, therefore, where the development of influence was perceived by the majority of members to be moving into, rather than out of, line with their preferences. Such developments, of course, do not preclude the existence of industrial conflict, but should minimize the incidence of patterns of conflict deriving from a sense of personal alienation of work control. Incipient conflict of this type appeared to exist more clearly within the clerical work occupation at Ironhill. The condition of stable attachment to work control systems will be enhanced under conditions of high mutual influence over the control of certain valued work areas. Under these conditions reciprocity between management and labour will be maximized. The ability of labour to fully reciprocate however will be inhibited if the strategies of particular trade unions are seen by their membership to be inappropriate and unrepresentative of their occupational interests.

References

BOWEN, P., forthcoming, *Social Control in Industrial Organizations* (London: Routledge & Kegan Paul).

BOWEN, P. and SHAW, M., 1972, Patterns of white-collar unionisation in the steel industry. *Industrial Relations Journal*, **3**, 2, 8–34.

BOWEN, P. and SHAW, M., 1972, Colour collar and the unions. *New Society*, **21**, 513, July.

BOWEN, P., SHAW, M. and SMITH, R.H., 1973, 'The Steelworker and Work Control' Paper read to Industrial Sociology Group. British Sociological Association and published in the *British Journal of Industrial Relations*

KNOWLES, K.G.J.C., 1952, *Strikes—A Study of Industrial Conflict* (Oxford Blackwell).

LAMMERS, C.J., 1967, Power and participation in decision-making in formal organisations. *Amer. J. Sociol.*, **73** (2), 201–216.

OVENDEN, K., 1973, The turmoil in steel. *New Society*, 22 February, 1973.

PHELPS BROWN, E.H., 1960, *The Growth of British Industrial Relations* (London Macmillan).

SCOTT, W.H., *et al.*, 1956, *Technical Change and Industrial Relations* (Liverpool: Liverpool University Press).

SMITH, C.G. and ARI, O.N., 1963, Organisational control structure and member consensus. *Amer. J. Sociol.* **69**, (6), 628–638.

TANNENBAUM, A.S., 1968, *Control in Organisations* (New York: McGraw-Hill).

WALKER, C.R., 1950, *Steeltown* (New York: Harper & Row).

WEDDERBURN, A.A.I. and JONES, T.K., 1967, British steels' labour challenge. *Management Today*, October, 1967, 109.

WEDDERBURN, A.A.I. and JONES, T.K., Power and control in trade unions (unpublished paper).
BRITISH IRON AND STEEL FEDERATION (1966), Stage I Report of the Development Co-ordinating Committee.
BRITISH STEEL CORPORATION: *Ten Year Development Strategy*. Cmnd. 5226, February, 1973 (London: H.M.S.O.).

Mr. J.-P. Vercaemer got his licentiate's degree in psychology a few years ago. His thesis work consisted of research on psychological determinants of unemployment.

Mr. G. Van Houdt holds a degeee of licentiate in psychology. He is now head of the psychological department of the Belgian National Labour Office.

Professor P. Verhaegen holds medical and psychology degrees. After 12 years in Central Africa, devoted to research on abilities and to teaching of psychology and psychopathology at the Universities of Kinshasa and Lubumbashi, he returned to Europe. He is teaching now ergonomics and work psychology at the Catholic University at Leuven.

2:14

Some psychological factors in unemployment

J-P. Vercaemer, P. Verhaegen and G. Van Houdt

Introduction

In this paper we report a still fragmentary and largely exploratory research on psychological factors in unemployment.

The opportunity to commence this study arose when officials of our state run National Labour Office found themselves forced to conclude they were not very successful in the placement of a somewhat ill defined group of employees. These workers, mostly blue collar but also white collar people, classified here as 'unstable' employees, are in seemingly normal mental and physical health and have job qualifications, which, although frequently of a low skilled type, correspond to demands from industry. They represent a difficult challenge to the Labour Office, in the sense that, when allocated to some job, they generally lose it after a short time and become unemployed again.

They do not remain permanently unemployed, because the Labour Office is continuously seeking and finding vacancies that match the job qualifications of unemployed subjects with normal abilities. Consequently non-handicapped subjects can never become permanently unemployed. Nevertheless some lose their job at every turn and for that reason they may be called 'unstable' workers. The unemployment rate given in labour statistics, as far as it is connected with non-handicapped males is actually brought about by work instability rather than by permanent unemployment.

At the time of this study the unemployment rate oscillated in Belgium between 2% and 3% of the labour force. The absolute number of unemployed people equalled 70,000 of which 26,000 were normally able. Two-thirds of this group are females, whose unemployment has rather different characteristics which we shall not discuss here. So there remain nearly 9,600 normally able unemployed males. It is with this subgroup of unemployed man-power we are concerned here.

The very existence of this hard core group of unstable and hence most of the time unemployed employees is one of the reasons why governmental agencies became very reluctant to grant applications from industrialists wanting more immigration of foreign labour.

In this paper unstable employees are operationally defined as subjects having been employed by three different firms during the year preceding the study.

The aim of this largely exploratory study was the elucidation of possible psychological factors that differentiate unstable from stable workers in the Belgian social and economic setting. We hope it will be some contribution to the delimitation of problem areas concerning the utilization of human resources and will have some meaning for this conference, although we were not able to elaborate this study using a taxonomic frame of reference.

Method

The research consisted in a comparison of 25 matched pairs of stable and unstable employees. It was carried out in March and April 1972. Using the files of the Labour Office we took first a random sample of 25 subjects from the unemployed male population defined by the following characteristics: age between 20 and 45, affiliation with three different firms during the preceding year, absence of physical handicaps and of any history of psychiatric or psychological deviation.

For each unstable subject a control subject was chosen, living in the same city-centre or in the same suburb, having the same age, the same type of work qualification, the same level of schooling and a comparable family situation. The control subjects were also in normal physical and mental health. They were also out of work at the time they were chosen to take part in the study, because of the close down of firms in which they had been employed for at least five years.

To summarize, within each pair one subject was an unstable worker who had been affiliated with at least three different firms during the preceding year and the other subject was a stable one being out of work presumably for a short time only, after at least five years work in the same firm.

The two groups of 25 subjects were interviewed and individually invited to answer a series of questionnaires in the presence of one of use (J.-P.V.).

Hypotheses and measures

In a recent study (Tiffany *et al.*, 1970) attention is called to the fact that economic factors and factors connected with schooling and training of employees are not sufficient to explain a lot of unemployment cases. It is argued that some personality factors are also very important.

(1) One of these factors seems to be the absence of a responsible self-direction. In this connection a distinction can be made between subjects whose behaviour is determined by internal factors and others who feel more determined by external ones. Internally controlled persons are directing their behaviour by themselves, externally controlled are determined by unpredictable events in their environment.

To test the hypothesis that unstable workers are less internally controlled than stable ones, Rotter's scale of internal versus external control of reinforcements was used (Rotter, 1966).

(2) Tiffany and his co-workers (1970) found also that unstable workers have

a more negative self-concept. This was explored on our groups using a semantic differential technique (Schwartz and Tangri, 1965).

(3) The same technique was used to confirm the data from Tiffany (1970) concerning the weaker interpersonal relationships in unstable workers. We studied relationships with parents, teachers, supervisors and co-workers.

(4) Ten questions were used to study some perceived parental attitudes we wanted to explore, hypothesizing they had some importance for the development of work instability or work inhibition. We obtained this idea from a research by Musschoot (1969) who studied the significance of different aspects of child-parent relationships in the development of leader capacities. He used a non-directive interview technique to assess his subjects on different dimensions he thought important. We have preferred to submit to our subjects precisely worded questions which they had to answer on a seven point scale.

These questions concerned their parents' patient versus impatient attitude, their stressing of positive versus negative social relationships, their democratic versus autocratic behaviour, their egalitarian versus discriminating treatment of the children, their openness versus their stressing of taboos in giving information on sex, their positive versus negative attitudes towards initiative-taking by their children, their encouragement versus forbidding of independence, their acceptance versus rejection of unfair means to get results and finally father's satisfaction versus unsatisfaction with his occupational life.

(5) Each subject was asked to fill in a form detailing hour by hour the spending of his time during the work day preceding the day of the examination.

(6) Using a few simple scales each subject gave information on some perceived qualities of work, such as relations with supervisors and physical conditions at work.

(7) In the same way information was obtained on motivation by some features of work, such as money, social contacts and self-actualization.

(8) Finally Srole's anomia scale (1956) was used. The hypothesis was that unstable workers would get a higher score on this scale.

Results

The data of the two groups were compared by *t*-tests, chi-square tests or/and Wilcoxon tests. In every case a two-tailed test was used.

(1) On Rotter's internal versus external control scale there was no difference between the two groups on their total scores. Comparing then the two groups on each of the 29 scale-items separately we did not find a single item answered in a significantly different way by the two groups. On the contrary, it was striking that on nine items the choices were divided in an identical manner for the two groups and that on 10 supplementary items the differences amounted to only one unit. The groups seemed to be perfectly matched on the Rotter scale . . . And as far as this is a measure of self-direction, we must conclude that our groups do not differ in it.

(2) Our aim using semantic differentials was not the location of given concepts in a semantic space but only finding out if there were significant differences between the two groups. To ease the computations the scale intervals on the semantic differentials were considered as equal intervals and for each concept a score was computed by adding the subscores on ten scales.

For their self-concept the difference between the two groups was significant at the 5% level, the stable group having a more positive self-concept. This confirms the data from Tiffany (1970).

(3) On interpersonal relations the differences between the two groups were significant at the 1% level for the perception of the father, at the 5% level for the perception of the mother and the supervisors. The stable workers had always the more positive perception. There was no difference in the perception of colleagues and teachers.

(4) Analysing the 10 items used to study the perception of parental attitudes we found four items answered in a significantly different way ($P < 0{\cdot}01$) by the two groups. Stable workers see their parents as more patient, as less discriminating in the way they treat their children and as more democratic and they see their fathers as happier with their occupational lives. On the other items the differences if any, were also in the expected directions. On a total score the groups differed at the 1% level. Parental attitudes or perception of past parental attitudes seem to be linked to work stability. The presence of a positive father-image, stressed by many educators in different settings, is perhaps something very important here too.

(5) The analysis of time expenditure shows that many unstable subjects spend fairly well organized leisurely days. We shall elaborate on this point further in final comments.

(6) Analysing attitudes toward some features of work we found a difference significant at the 1% level on satisfaction with supervisors and with wages, the stable group being more satisfied. There were no differences on satisfaction with colleagues and with physical work conditions.

(7) Concerning motivation by different aspects of work like money and self-actualization there was no difference between the two groups.

(8) Finally there was no difference on Srole's anomia scale nor on any of its subscales.

Conclusions

The most important differences found were in the domain of the perception of parental attitudes. As already said the absence of a positive father-image is perhaps a significant factor. Negative self-concepts and negative attitudes toward supervisors were also characteristics of the unstable workers. It is of course difficult to sustain that these characteristics are determinants of work instability. That some experiences in childhood and adolescence lead to a negative self-concept seems very acceptable. That a negative self-concept makes occupational success difficult seems probable too. But on the other hand difficulties at work would probably disturb the self-concept and lead to negative attitudes towards supervisors.

While perhaps something should be done to increase the self-concept (Tiffany, 1970), the differences in perception of parental attitudes or in the attitudes toward supervisors do not suggest any practical measure for the utilization of the resources of these people.

A fourth, although less clear cut difference, not yet spoken of, might perhaps lead to some practical measures.

During the always individually performed examinations it was noted that unstable subjects were frequently very uneasy when invited to make choices on seven point scales (from -3 to $+3$) and that they decided frequently for a zero or neutral answer after having given much time and thought to it. In respect of the frequency of their zero answers the unstable subjects differ from the stable ones at the 1% significance level.

One may wonder if such choice situations are too complex for them and speculate that many work situations ask for too much discretionary choices or perhaps social skills and are consequently too difficult for many people so that they try to escape from them at every turn.

Further research must be aimed at this point, which possibly might have some practical significance.

Comments

Although we tried to confirm a few hypotheses this study was mostly an exploratory research.

In a new comparison between stable and unstable workers we shall try to split up the unstable group among people who became well adapted to their situation and people who are not. The adaptation might be assessed by an analysis of the way these people spend their much extended free time. The data on this point is not sufficiently detailed for a large proportion of our present groups. Nevertheless it was clear (and the difference was statistically significant at the 5% level) that the unstable workers had more varied and more substantial activities than the stable ones. This is understandable because the stable workers were at the time of their examination out of work for at most a few weeks. Nevertheless the impression is very strong that many of the unstable subjects are settled perhaps very happily in their unemployment: e.g., some of them became house husbands, they prepare the meals for their wife and children, bathe the children, occupy themselves with their garden and poultry, bring the children to school, drive their wives to work, etc. . . . It is understandable that it would be difficult to get such people to work again. The difference between their incomes when unemployed and when working would not be sufficiently important. It is quite possible that different psychological factors are present in people adapted to their unemployment and in people struggling to get employment. It is moreover quite possible that our unstable group was still heterogeneous on other aspects.

It is further necessary to point out that such research is largely based on self-reporting.

The matched pairs technique creates as well some problems. It is always possible to neglect some important factor in the matching process. We do not know if our subjects who were not matched on (social) intelligence (although they were on occupational and educational level) differ in this respect. In a further study this factor as well will be taken into account.

Acknowledgement

We owe much gratitude to Mr. R. Etienne, administrator-general of the 'Rijksdienst voor Arbeidsvoorziening' (National Labour Office) for making this study possible.

The ideas expressed in this paper do not necessarily reflect the opinions of the 'Rijksdienst voor Arbeidsvoorziening'.

References

MUSSCHOOT, F., 1969, Ouder-kind relaties en ontwikkeling van leiderscapaciteiten (Parent-child relationships and the development of leader capacities). *Nederlands Tijdschrift voor de Psychologie*, **24**, 638–658.

ROTTER, J.B., 1966, Generalized expectancies for internal versus external control of reinforcement. *Psychological Monographs*, **80**, No. 1.
SCHWARTZ, M. and TANGRI, S.S., 1965, A note on self-concept as insulator against delinquency. *American Sociological Review*, **30**, 922–926.
SROLE, L., 1956, Social integration and certain corollaries. *American Sociological Review*, **21**, 709–716.
TIFFANY, D.W., COWAN, J.R. and TIFFANY, P.M., 1970, *The Unemployed: A Social-psychological Portrait* (Englewood Cliffs: Prentice-Hall).

Professor Fiedler received his Ph.D. in clinical psychology at the University of Chicago, and then moved to the University of Illinois where he directed the Group Effectiveness Research Laboratory until 1969 when he moved to the University of Washington in Seattle. He has conducted research on leadership since 1951.

2:15

New strategies for leadership utilization*

F. E. Fiedler, P. M. Bons and Limda L. Hastings

Introduction

Our working life is to an amazing degree lived in groups and organizations. We are members of departments, committees, teams, crews, boards, panels, juries, task-forces; and in the armed forces, of such military units as squads, platoons, troops, batteries, staffs, companies and battalions. It can be safely said that the effectiveness of these groups is dependent, to a large degree, upon the proper utilization, recruitment, selection, placement and training of their leaders.

On the other hand, it is equally safe to conclude that our success in this regard to date has been notably underwhelming. After years of research and experience, there is today no conclusive evidence that the experienced leader performs more effectively than does the leader with relatively little experience (Fiedler, 1970). Historical examples clearly illustrate this: Alexander the Great was only 17 when he took over the Macedonian cavalry, and Joan of Arc was an inexperienced teenaged girl when she commanded the loyalist troops of France. The 19-year-old Henry of Monmouth, later Henry V of England, decisively defeated Owen Glendower, an old experienced Welsh warrior. And, the examples go on and on.

Evidence that the typical leadership training programmes in industry or in the military services increase leadership performance appear to be equally non-conclusive. Studies of post office managers, of military personnel and of police supervisors indicate that the amount of leadership training is uncorrelated with subsequent leadership performance (Fiedler, 1972; Csoka and Fiedler, 1972). It would be extremely difficult to believe, however, that experience and training have no impact on an individual's performance or behaviour. We must therefore entertain alternative hypotheses. One explanation which comes most readily to mind is simply that our previous thinking has not taken into account other important factors which might influence leadership effectiveness. If we want to make better use of our manpower resources it is essential that we not only explain some of the puzzling findings to which we have referred, but also develop better strategies for increasing the performance of leaders and their groups.

* Research reported in this paper was conducted under Contract NR177-472 N00014-67-A-0103-0012, Office of Naval Research (Fred E. Fiedler, Principal Investigator) and Contract NR177-473, N00014-67-A-0103-0013, Advanced Research Projects Agency (Fred E. Fiedler, Principal Investigator).

The present discussion is based on the Contingency Model of Leadership effectiveness (Fiedler, 1964, 1967, 1971) which not only appears to provide a more satisfactory explanation of phenomena described above but which also enables us to suggest new ways of utilizing the leadership of groups and organizations.

The contingency model

This theory holds that the effectiveness of a task group or of an organization depends upon two main factors: the leader's motivational system and the degree to which the situation gives the leader control and influence. The first of these factors distinguishes two types of leaders who have different motivational structures and, therefore, exhibit different types of behaviour in anxiety arousing and uncertain situations. Generally, one type of person under these conditions needs to relate to others and is primarily concerned with maintaining close interpersonal relations while the other is primarily concerned with group-oriented goals, i.e., accomplishing the task.

According to the model, leaders are classified on the basis of the Least Preferred Co-worker (L.P.C.) score. This L.P.C. score is obtained by first asking an individual to think of *all* persons with whom he has ever worked, and then to describe the one person in his life with whom he has been able to work least well. The description of his least preferred co-worker is made on a short bipolar eight-point scale of the semantic differential format; for example:

friendly:__:__:__:__:__:__:unfriendly
co-operative:__:__:__:__:__:__:unco-operative

High L.P.C. persons, that is, individuals who describe their least preferred co-worker in relatively positive terms, are seen as primarily relationship-motivated. Low L.P.C. persons, those who describe their least preferred co-worker in very unfavourable terms, are basically task-motivated.

The second variable, 'situational favourableness' (Fiedler, 1964, 1967, 1970; Hunt, 1967; Gibb, 1968) indicates the degree to which the situation gives the leader control and influence, the degree to which he can predict with reasonable certainty the outcome of his decisions. A situation in which decisions and actions have unpredictable outcomes tend to be stressful and anxiety arousing. Generally, situational favourableness is measured on the basis of three subscales. These are the degree to which (*a*) the leader is, or feels, accepted and supported by his members (leader-member relations),* (*b*) the task is clear cut, programmed and structured as to goals, procedures and measurable progress and success (task structure); and (*c*) the leader's position provides him with power to reward and punish, and thus to obtain compliance from his subordinates (position power).

Group situations can be categorized as being high or low on each of these three dimensions by dividing the groups at the median into those with good and poor leader-member relations and high and low task structure and position power. This leads to an eight-celled classification shown on the horizontal axis of Figure 1. The eight cells or octants are scaled from most favourable (octant I) to least favourable (octant VIII). The theory assumes that a leader will have

* A number of studies have shown that this is by far the most important single dimension (Fiedler, 1967; Fishbein, Landy and Hatch, 1969). Leader-member relations have been measured by means of members' sociometric ratings of the leader or by Leader's Group Atmosphere (G.A.) score, a ten-item semantic differential scale.

most control and influence in groups that fall into octant I; that is, in which he is accepted, has high position power and a structured task. He will have somewhat less control and influence in octant II, where he is accepted and has a structured task, but little position power; and so on to groups in octant VIII, where control and influence will be very small since the leader is not accepted by his group, has a vague, unstructured task and little position power.

Figure 1. Median correlations between leader L.P.C. scores and group performance in original and validation studies

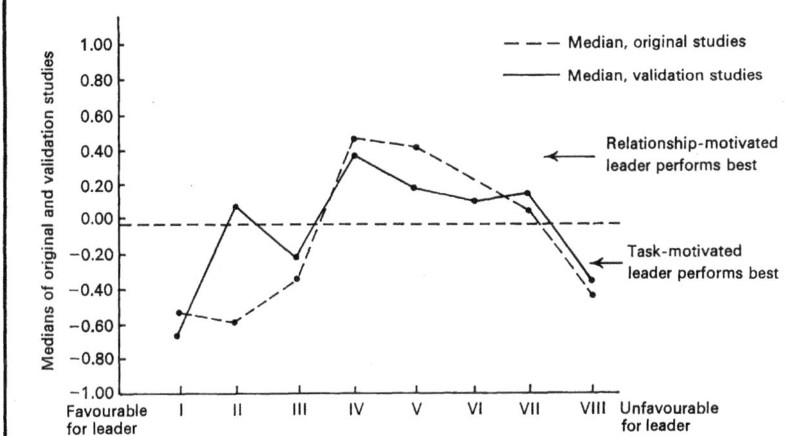

	I	II	III	IV	V	VI	VII	VIII
Leader–member relations	Good	Good	Good	Good	Poor	Poor	Poor	Poor
Task structure	Structured		Unstructured		Structured		Unstructured	
Leader position power	Strong	Weak	Strong	Weak	Strong	Weak	Strong	Weak

The research based on the Contingency Model has consistently shown that the task-motivated leaders perform best in very favourable, or in unfavourable situations while the relationship-motivated leaders tend to perform best in situations which are moderately favourable. Individuals who are in the middle of the L.P.C. scale also tend to perform around the middle on various types of tasks.

The vertical axis of Figure 1 shows the median correlation coefficients between leader L.P.C. and group performance. These correlations are based on various sets of groups studied between 1951 and 1963. A positive correlation indicates that relationship-motivated (high L.P.C.) leaders performed better; a negative relation shows that task-motivated (low L.P.C.) leaders performed better. The dashed line in Figure 1 indicates the results of the original studies, while the solid line indicates the median correlations of the validation studies conducted since 1963. The coefficients of the original and of the validation studies correlate quite highly ($\rho = 0{\cdot}75$, $p < 0{\cdot}05$) and show that the model does indeed predict group performance (Fielder, 1971). A field experiment, using

West Point cadets (Chemers and Skrzypek, 1972) almost exactly validated the predicted curve of the model.

These results show, first, that both the relationship-motivated and the task-motivated leaders perform well under some situations but not others. Second, that it is not accurate to speak of a 'good' leader or a 'poor' leader. Rather, one must think of a leader who performs well in one situation but not in another. Third, that the performance of a leader depends as much on the situation as it does on his personality.

The implication of these points needs to be stressed. We have generally assumed that we can increase leader performance by increasing the leader's control and influence. The leader who has control presumably can get his group to perform the assigned task. This is the prime reason why experienced managers frequently are chosen over those with little or no experience and why training programmes stress methods for increasing leader control and influence. For example, the leader is told how to gain member acceptance, he is told how to deal with disciplinary problems, with organizational red tape or with potential

Figure 2. The perceived change in performance of relationship- and task-motivated company managers as a function of increased experience

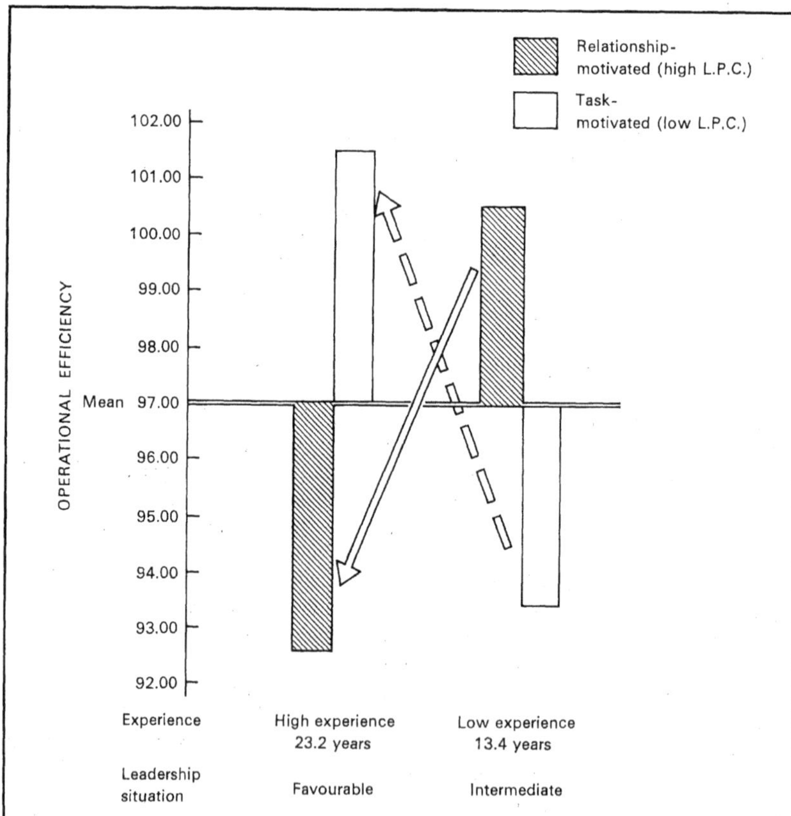

breakdown in the machinery he might supervise. Again, however, experience and training do not necessarily result in increased leadership effectiveness, as has been shown again and again in the research literature. The Contingency Model tells us why this is so: experience (and training) increases the leader's control and hence his situational favourableness, and an increase in situational favourableness will improve the performance of some leaders but it will *decrease* the performance of others; this has now been demonstrated in over eight different studies.

Data from a study of consumer co-operatives (Godfrey *et al.*, 1959) illustrate this point. The managers of these companies had high position power and a relatively structured task. Most of them were well accepted by their staff. Thus, given well-trained and experienced managers, the situation was 'normally' favourable. However, leaders who lacked experience and training found the tasks considerably less structured and their relationship, as well as their position power, somewhat weaker. Hence, for them, the situation was only moderately favourable. As the Contingency Model predicts, task-motivated leaders performed best in the very favourable situations while relationship-motivated leaders performed best in the moderately favourable situations (see Figure 2).

The effect which leadership experience and training have on performance will depend upon the type of situation within which the leader has to operate. The relationships between experience and training and the situational variables as determined by the Contingency Model are shown below:

Table 1. Effect of leader training on situational favourability and subsequent performance*

	Very favourable relations, structure and power (*Oct. I*)	*Moderately favourable relations, structure and power* (*Oct. IV*)	*Unfavourable relations, structure and power* (*Oct. VIII*)	*Extremely Unfavourable (bordering on anarchy)*
If before training leader experiences the situation as:	(probably non-existent)	×	×	×
After training the leader will probably experience the situation as:	×	×	×	(probably non-existent)
Effectiveness Prediction	Low LPC more effective than High	High LPC more effective than Low	Low LPC more effective than High	High LPC more effective than low (speculative)

* The model predicts that leadership training shifts the situational favourability (as perceived by the leader) to the next higher degree which will reverse the leader's effectiveness level.

A second study which suggested that leader experience has a differential effect on leader performance was conducted by McNamara (1968). His investigation involved principals of elementary and secondary schools in the province of Alberta, Canada. McNamara divided the principals in his study into those with more than and less than two years' experience. He further divided them into those with high and with low L.P.C. scores. McNamara then computed the average performance scores of experienced and inexperienced principals with high and with low L.P.C. scores. His findings are shown in Figure 3.

There is a reversal in performance in both the elementary and the secondary schools. In the sample of elementary school principals, the best performers were the inexperienced principals with high L.P.C. scores and the experienced principals with low L.P.C. scores. The opposite was the case in secondary schools. These data are difficult to understand unless we carefully consider the situational favourableness for experienced and inexperienced elementary secondary school principals.

The elementary schools in the McNamara sample were quite small, with an average of 13 teachers. The principal has relatively high position, he supervises

Figure 3. Average performance of relationship- and task-motivated school principals with relatively low and high levels of experience

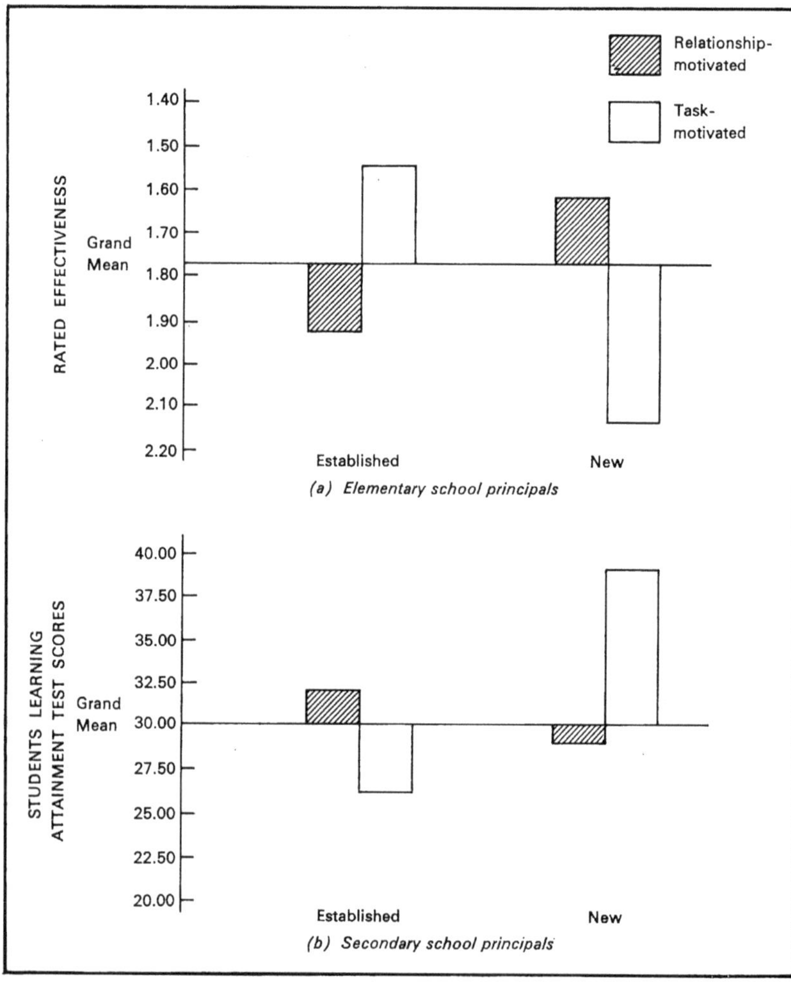

few staff members, and considering the fact that he is dealing with elementary school pupils and that the curriculum and policy decisions tend to be made at the school superintendent's level, it seems likely that the situation is highly favourable for the experienced principal. He knows his staff and he knows how the system operates (probably octant I). In these very favourable situations we would expect that the low L.P.C. leaders perform better than do high L.P.C. leaders (see left side of Figure 3*a*).

The inexperienced principal undoubtedly faces a less favourable situation. He does not yet know the ropes and he must still improvise every time a new situation arises. His relationship and position power *vis-à-vis* his staff members may also be still fairly tenuous. Hence, his situation is only moderately favourable (probably octant IV), which means that the high L.P.C. leaders should perform better than the low L.P.C. leaders, and this was again the case (see right side of Figure 3*a*). This implies, of course, that the experience obtained by high L.P.C. principals actually decreased their performance, while experience increased the performance of low L.P.C. principals.

Why was the opposite effect noted in secondary schools? These were organizations with two levels of administration, namely the school administration and the departments within the school. The schools were fairly large, having up to 40 teachers, and the principal also had to deal with teenagers who are notoriously difficult to handle. Moreover, the principal of secondary schools has a much less structured task which requires him to interact with various civic, governmental and parent organizations, and to make policy on a variety of questions which arise. Thus, although he has moderately high position power, the task tends to be unstructured, and the relations with those with whom he works are likely to be more tenuous. The experienced secondary school principal's leadership situation is, therefore, only moderately favourable (octant IV, V). Such a situation will then be unfavourable for the inexperienced principals. And, as the Contingency Model predicts, the inexperienced principals with task-motivation perform better than do the inexperienced, relationship-motivated principals. The reverse is the case for experienced high school principals. Here the relationship-motivated principals performed better than did the task-motivated principals.

Similar effects have been obtained from military units, namely, field artillery sections, training companies, mess halls and naval aviation maintenance shops (Csoka and Fiedler, 1972). In each of these units, the leaders were divided into those with relatively much or little experience, and with relatively good and poor leader-member relations. These studies showed consistently that relatively untrained inexperienced leaders performed about as well as did experienced leaders, but that the relationship-motivated leaders performed best in situations in which the leader had poor leader-member relations but relatively much experience. Task-motivated leaders performed best in favourable situations as well as in situations in which the leader had poor leader-member relations as well as relatively little leadership experience. Here again, we must assume that the additional experience in fact lowered the performance of task-motivated leaders in situations in which their relationships with group members were originally poor.

The effect of leadership experience is most clearly apparent in a recent longitudinal study by Bons and Hastings in which the same group of leaders were evaluated on performance over a period of five months. A group of 19 leaders in a U.S. Army combat battalion were rated first shortly after the unit's activation, and the second time five months later, when the troops had joined the units and had completed the initial phase of their training cycle. As can be seen in Figure 4, we again find the predicted reversal in performance effectiveness and an interaction which was highly significant ($F = 9{\cdot}136$, $p < 0{\cdot}01$), Moreover, the task-motivated (low L.P.C.) leaders tended to increase in their performance as a function of previous experience ($r = +0{\cdot}36$), while high L.P.C. leaders tended to decrease ($r = -0{\cdot}41$).

Figure 4. Change in the performance of high and low L.P.C. Leaders as a function of increased experience and more structured task assignment over five months. (P. Bons and Linda Hastings, unpublished paper)

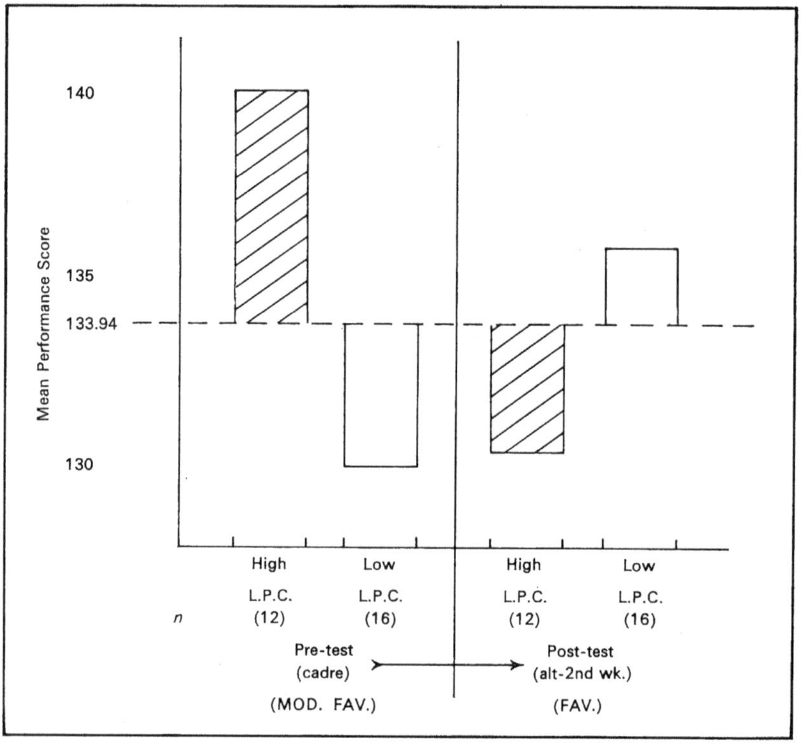

A related study investigated the effects which the diversity of previous leadership experience might have on present performance. The analysis is based on the assumption that an individual who has held a larger number of different jobs will have worked in situations which to him are less structured. Given the high position power and high task structure in an infantry unit, we would expect that diversity should favour the relationship-motivated leader while it should penalize the task-motivated leader.

An analysis of data from 41 infantry platoon sergeants partly supports this set of hypotheses. While total time in service was uncorrelated with performance for all leaders ($-0{\cdot}08$), the correlation between performance ratings and job diversity (number of different jobs per unit of time in service) correlated

$+0{\cdot}37$ ($N=18$, $p<0{\cdot}07$) for relationship-motivated leaders. The corresponding correlation for task-motivated leaders was essentially zero ($r=0{\cdot}04$, $N=23$).

On the other hand, the correlation between performance and total number of jobs (again controlling for time in service) yielded a correlation of only $+0{\cdot}01$ for relationship-motivated leaders but was $+0{\cdot}32$ ($p<0{\cdot}05$) for task-motivated leaders. This suggests that relationship-motivated leaders who were moved more rapidly from job to job performed better than did those who remained on the same job longer. Total experience on the job, and in this case, no doubt, in similar jobs, enhanced the performance of the task-motivated leader.

New strategies of utilizing groups

Let us now consider some of the implications of this theory for the more effective utilization of leaders and their groups. First and foremost, the theory contradicts the unspoken but firmly held assumption by laymen and experts alike that an increase in the leader's control and influence will result in a corresponding increase in his ability to perform well—or more specifically, in his ability to obtain better performance from his group. The underlying hypothesis of most training programmes has been that the leader who is able to control and influence his group will necessarily be more effective since he will influence his group to perform the organization's task.

This is, however, a somewhat naïve position. The successful completion of the group's task may be only one of the leader's goals, and it might, in fact, be quite peripheral in his life. Whether he is, himself, aware of it or not, the leader pursues not only the organization's agenda, but he has his own hidden agenda. He may certainly express the strong wish to succeed, but he may also have strong personal needs which may be partly incompatible with the needs of the organization. The leader may have a strong need to come to a conclusion as quickly as possible, while it may be to the organization's advantage that he discuss with others in the group, fully and in depth all the alternatives. The leader may have a strong need to be liked and accepted, while the organization would be better served by a leader who cracks the whip whether or not he is liked in order to get the job done.

The leadership situation may thus be seen as an arena in which the leader seeks to accomplish his own personal goals while attempting at the same time to satisfy the goals of the organization. It is then clear that a management intervention, be it in the form of additional experience, of training, or of increasing the leader's authority, will increase performance only if the intervention happens to result in a better match between the leader's personality, or to be exact, his motivational structure, and the degree to which the situation provides the leader with control and influence.

All this requires a new look at the leadership problem. While the graph on Figure 1 presents a static picture of leadership performance, it is equally important that we understand what happens to leadership over time. After all, organizations are not static. Leaders learn, and their leadership situations change. The basic relationship is, therefore, one in which time and the concomitant experience is an important component. The relationship of leader motivation and performance over time is shown on Figure 5. While this is almost certainly an oversimplified conception of the effect of time and experience on leadership performance, there is good reason to believe that it represents a useful working hypothesis.

Figure 5. Expected effects of timely rotation policy on the performance of high and low L.P.C. leaders

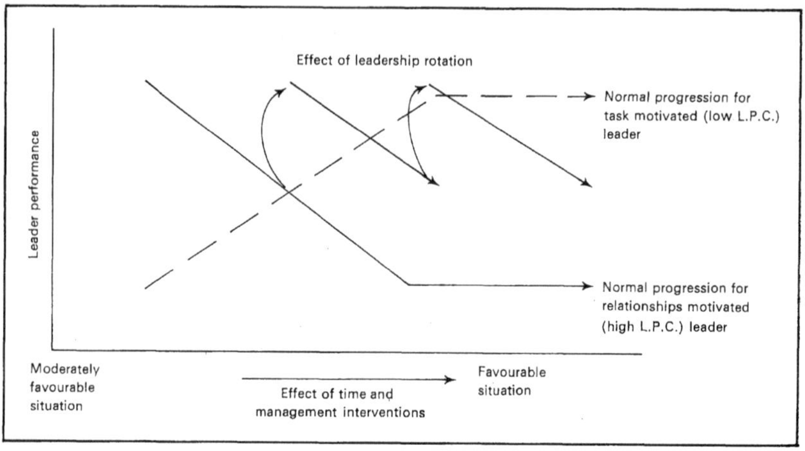

We can now superimpose on this graph the effects of leadership training, selection and rotation.

Selection. It is obvious from the graphs in Figure 5 that we must rethink our selection strategy if we wish to utilize our leadership and manpower resources more effectively. Before we select we must determine not only the motivational structure of the leader and the degree to which the situation provides the leader with control and influence, but we must also ask ourselves whether we want outstanding performance right now or whether we are willing to wait until experience and perhaps training do their work in matching leader motivation and leadership situation. In a situation which is favourable for the experienced leader (Figure 6a) we should choose a relationship-motivated leader for immediate results but a task-motivated leader for good performance later on. In a situation which is moderately favourable for the experienced leader, and therefore unfavourable for the inexperienced leader, we should choose a task-motivated leader for immediate performance, but a relationship-motivated leader for the long run.

Training. Training may be seen essentially as accelerating the effects of experience. In other words, training is essentially the experience by others presented in compressed and integrated form. Hence we should also expect that the effects will be similar to experience, which is on-the-job training. In a situation which is highly favourable for the trained and experienced leader, appropriate training of the inexperienced, relationship-motivated leader will decrease his performance more rapidly than would be the case without training, while it will increase the task-motivated leader's performance more rapidly than would otherwise be the case (Csoka and Fiedler, 1972; Fiedler, 1972).

Rotation. While there is evidence that a leader who has had a diversity of previous experience tends to perform better than someone who has not enjoyed different types of leadership experiences, it is also apparent from our data (e.g., Figure 3) that certain leaders should not be left too long on the same job. The relationship-motivated elementary principals as well as the task-motivated

Figure 6. The effects of leadership training on relationship-motivated (high L.P.C.) and task-motivated (low L.P.C.) leaders in different types of situations

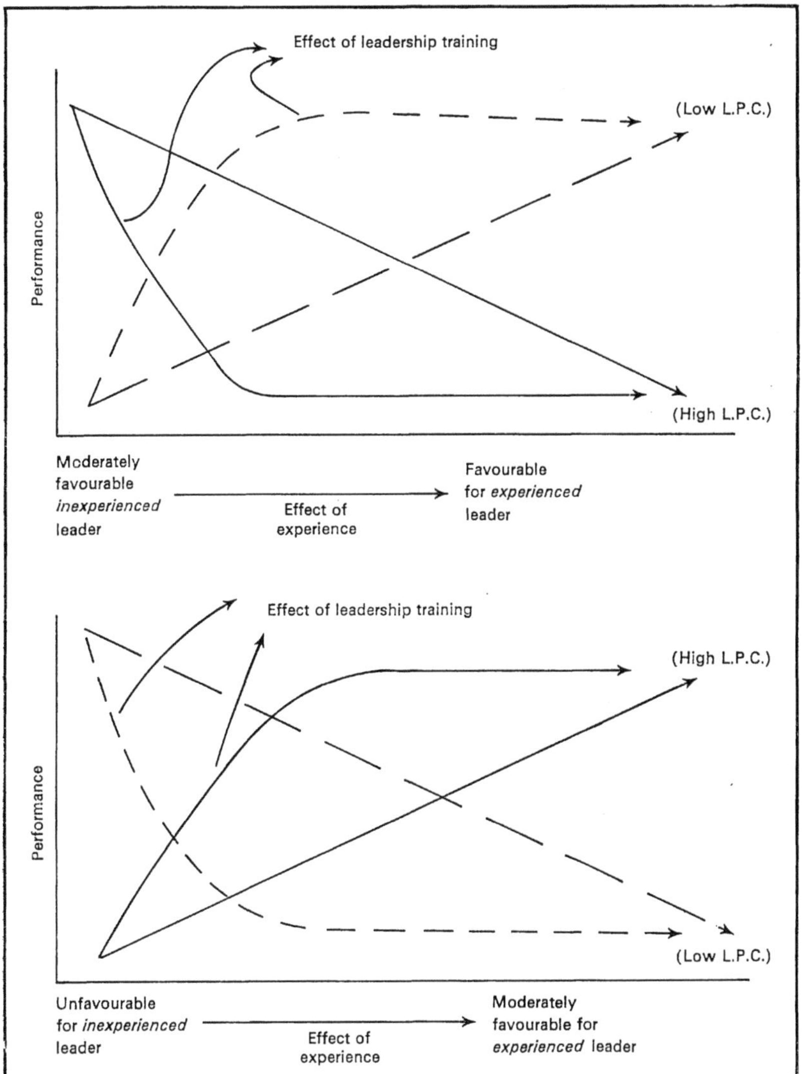

secondary school principals in the McNamara sample would probably perform more effectively if they had moved to new jobs before the third year.

Discussion

This paper has attempted a very brief and rough outline of management strategies which would result in better utilization of leaders and their groups. The limitations of space obviously preclude an extensive discussion of these strategies, or an in-depth analysis of the implications which the Contingency Model has for various other leader utilization problems. We must here limit ourselves to sketching some of the possibilities which the reconceptualization of such management interventions as selection, placement, rotation and training might have in light of the Contingency Model. Clearly all the details and facts are not yet in. However, at this time there is sufficient evidence to give us considerable confidence that we are in the right ballpark, and that the strategies which we have here suggested will provide fruitful hypotheses for the problem of leadership utilization.

References

CHEMERS, M.M. and SKRZYPEK, G.J., 1972, An experimental test of the Contingency Model of Leadership effectiveness. *Journal of Personality and Social Psychology*, **24**, 172–177.

CSOKA, L.S. and FIEDLER, F.E., 1972, The effect of military leadership training: A test of the contingency model. *Organizational Behavior and Human Performance*, **8**, 395–407.

FIEDLER, F.E., 1964, A contingency model of leadership effectiveness. In: Berkowitz, L. (Ed.), *Advances in experimental social psychology*. Vol. 1 (New York: Academic Press).

FIEDLER, F.E., 1967, *A theory of leadership effectiveness* (New York: McGraw-Hill).

FIEDLER, F.E., 1970, Leadership experience and leader performance—Another hypothesis shot to hell. *Organizational Behavior and Human Performance*, **5**, 1–14.

FIEDLER, F.E., 1971, Validation and extension of the contingency model of leadership effectiveness: A review of empirical findings. *Psychological Bulletin*, **76**, 128–148.

FIEDLER, F.E., 1972, Leadership experience and leadership training—Some new answers to an old problem. *Administration Science Quarterly*, **17**, 453–470.

FISHBEIN, M., LANDY, E. and HATCH, G., 1969, A consideration of two assumptions underlying Fiedler's contingency model for the prediction of leadership effectiveness. *American Journal of Psychology*, **82**, 457–473.

GIBB, C.A., 1968, Leadership. In: Lindzey, G. and Aronson, E. (Eds.), *The Handbook of Social Psychology*. Group Psychology and Phenomena of Interaction, Vol. 4 (Reading, Mass.: Addison-Wesley).

GODFREY, E., FIEDLER, F.E. and HALL, D.M., 1959, *Boards, management and company success* (Danville, Ill.: Interstate Press).

HUNT, J.G., 1967, Fiedler's leadership contingency model: An empirical test in three organizations. *Organizational Behavior and Human Performance*, **2**, 290–308.

McNAMARA, V.D., 1968, Leadership, staff and school effectiveness. Doctoral thesis University of Alberta, Edmonton, Alberta, Canada.

Section 3

Planning of Resources

A.R. Smith is a graduate of L.S.E. specializing in statistics. After several years in a variety of posts in the Admiralty, Ministry of Defence, Treasury and Civil Service Department he is now an Under Secretary in C.S.D. responsible as Director of Statistics for amongst other things development of Civil Service manpower planning. He has been closely associated also with the creation of the Manpower Society and the Institute of Manpower Studies; is involved in the relevant activities of the Institute of Personnel Management; and has been concerned with a number of N.A.T.O. and O.E.C.D. projects in the manpower area.

Gerald Watson is a Cambridge history graduate who has spent his career in the Civil Service. For the past four years he has been head of a division in the Civil Service Department responsible, among other things, for the evaluation and recommendation to departments in the Civil Service of methods of improving personnel management. He has been responsible, in particular, for the introduction of improved appraisal schemes, manpower planning and job enrichment studies.

3:1

Application of manpower techniques in the British Civil Service

A. R. Smith and G. W. Watson

Introduction: Corporate manpower planning

Discussion of what is meant by manpower planning in management of the British Civil Service, together with descriptions of the techniques and models in use have been published fairly widely. See for example Hopes (1973); Smith 1972). What follows in the next few paragraphs is a brief restatement of some of the points.

The mainstream of manpower planning work is concerned with increasing the chance of matching manpower availability (supply) with manpower requirements (demand), in terms of statistical aggregates, while at the same time meeting certain personnel management objectives. All civil servants are classified by occupation (group), by hierarchical level (grade), by employing department, by geographical location and so on. A general objective is to achieve matching of demand and supply for particular types of manpower (e.g., for each grade in a particular group), but not all types of manpower will require the same degree or kind of attention. For example, a grade for which rapid turn-over is an accepted fact of life (e.g., typists and clerks) will not need to be planned in terms of decisions designed to achieve supply/demand match on as long a time-scale as a grade for which it is generally accepted that fairly long civil service experience is a prerequisite. There is no standard planning horizon, and no rigid set of rules for manpower planning: each case needs to be tackled as the particular circumstances warrant, within a generalized theoretical framework.

The development of models for assessing likely situations on the manpower supply side are fairly well advanced. But the models cannot be used effectively without an accurate data-base. At present the main source of data is the Central Staff Record (C.S.R.) which provides a limited range of items of information about each of the some half-million so-called non-industrial (i.e., excluding blue-collar) employees in all Government Departments. This will be replaced in 1975 by a better and more flexible records system known as PRISM. This will consist of a ring of ten computers, each managed by a particular Government Department and dealing *inter alia* with all the pay and records of the employees of that Department and in some cases with those of a range of smaller Departments on an agency basis also. All will use standard agreed methods of classification and coding, and will feed information automatically to the central PRISM computer managed by the Civil Service Department, where novel systems for retrieval and manipulation of data have been developed. More detailed descriptions of the PRISM system and of an experimental forerunner (C.M.S.R.) which is already operational are given in Marks (1972) and Bridle and Gregersen (1971).

Statistical monitoring and analysis are being progressively refined, within the 'stock and flow' conceptual framework. The simple logic behind this is that the stock of manpower at any one point in time will have been determined partly by the stock at an earlier point in time and partly by the flows (recruitment, wastage, promotions, transfers and retirements) which have taken place over the period between the two points of time. Analysis of the stocks and changes in stocks in terms of occupational groups, grades, age-distributions and so on will be of significance for both planning and the monitoring of the state of the organization. Analysis of the flows will be of similar or even greater significance, in the sense that the flows if properly measured in statistical terms will usually reveal a pattern, and a degree of stability (rather in the sense that mortality rates are of value to the demographer or the actuary) which will be of value both for forecasting and for indicating where an attempt by management to change the stable pattern may lead to improved manpower utilization. Possibilities here, for example, are changes in retirement policy, or in the age or qualifications distributions of recruits, or attempts to identify and modify the causes of wastage amongst young staff. Sometimes the monitoring of wastage will reveal a loss of stability—a rapid rise in rates of loss for example—which will be a warning to management that action is necessary.

Forecasting is done by using a range of computerized statistical models which treat each manpower sub-system (e.g., a particular occupational group) as a dynamic system in which changes in stock are brought about by changes in flows, all of which are inter-related in the system, and in respect of which assumptions may be fed to the model in a fairly flexible way. All the flows (wherever appropriate expressed as rates) are discussed with the personnel managers, in terms of observed values and possible alternative values, and forecasting assumptions agreed with them. Some of the assumptions will be in effect that recent trends will continue; some will pre-suppose a change generated by external factors (e.g., a higher proportion of university graduates amongst the recruits); and some will pre-suppose a change in policy and will be perhaps policy-options which management is contemplating. More often than not projections are made for the express purpose of examining the longer-term consequences of a proposed change in policy, in terms of availability, promotion prospects, recruitment needs and so on—rather than for predicting as if the system were not amenable to control. We are dealing in fact with a control mechanism.

The forecasting of manpower 'demand' is no easier for Government Departments than it is for any other employer. In industry the employer is faced with uncertainty about the future state of the economy, of terms of trade, of competitor behaviour, of consumer tastes, of technology and so on. Most Government Departments have similar uncertainties, and are particularly conscious of the fact that a change of political party in power may occur at intervals of four or five years, and there may be major discontinuities in their objectives and tasks after each election. Even so, uncertainty is no excuse for not planning, or not making assumptions about future manpower demand. Decisions have to be taken from day to day on recruitment, training, movements and so on, which are essentially based on assumptions (but often unconsciously) about future needs, and it would be foolish not to base such decisions on the best possible information or most defensible sets of assumptions about future needs. There is also the point that if there is a reasonably well founded stock of information about the relationships between objectives and tasks on the one hand and manpower needs on the other it will be much easier in the light of this knowledge to adapt quickly to meet change when change becomes necessary. (It is perhaps worth stressing at this point that the planning process is not viewed by the Civil Service Department as being the preparation of some kind of detailed perfect blue-print, but rather as a repeated scanning of the 'likely' future, aimed at achieving reasonably well-informed decisions—a reasonable compromise between unforgiveable ignorance and unrealistic inflexibility.)

At present manpower 'demand' forecasting in the Civil Service is still partial, experimental and rudimentary. In so far as we are concerned with statistical assessment of demand (as opposed to establishing requirements at the individual matching level), most of the work being done falls into one of the following classes. First, there is a steady effort to improve the systematic assessment of manpower needs throughout Government Departments, using as the data-collecting framework the regular annual programme for forecasting public expenditure for the ensuing five years, with statements of manpower needs being related to statements of functions, objective, tasks and other resources. Second, in specified areas work is being done on the detailed examination of statistical relationships (using factor analysis, regression analysis and so on) between staff needs and tasks, and between tasks and the external factors which help to determine the work loads associated with these tasks. Third, similar work is being done on a broader or macro scale—for example, testing empirically-based relationships between manpower needs and public expenditure. Fourthly, something akin to a Delphi technique is being considered for use in arriving at agreed assumptions on, for example, the numbers and kinds of people needed to man the higher grades of the Civil Service in the longer-term future.

There are, then, a range of statistical techniques available for use in forecasting supply, and to a lesser extent demand, and bringing about the likelihood of matching with the minimum of undesirable consequences. We are now aiming to make these techniques readily available throughout management of the Civil Service, using a computer network with terminals and V.D.U. equipment by early 1975. But no matter how sophisticated and efficient the manpower planning techniques and facilities may be, they will be of no value if management thinking and management procedures are not geared up to use them. The

Civil Service Department has therefore devoted considerable attention to development of receptive attitudes in management.

In the early stages one-day presentations were given to all the senior staff of the Civil Service Department during which the techniques were described and demonstrated and policy implications discussed. Descriptive papers were then distributed to the Heads of Personnel of all the larger Departments, and they agreed at subsequent meetings that manpower planning should be developed as an integral part of Civil Service management. They in turn attended one-day presentations, and agreed that similar presentations should be given to their senior staff. They decided collectively that a Manpower Planning Steering Group should be set up, on which they could all be represented, to guide future work. The Steering Group in turn decided that regular one-week Senior Management Seminars on Manpower Planning should be introduced under Civil Service auspices, and this was followed very shortly afterwards by the introduction of two-week 'practitioners' courses' for middle management. Meantime the programme had been discussed with the Staff Side of the National Whitley Council (representing the Civil Service Staff Associations or Unions) and they too attended presentations and are participating in Seminars and Courses.

During the latter half of 1972 a series of presentations were given for representatives of the Staff Associations in all Government Departments. By the end of 1972 the stage had been reached at which the Staff Associations were beginning to participate in manpower planning exercises, and the availability to Staff Associations of C.S.D. facilities in the form of computerized models and statistical expertise was being considered, with the possibility in mind that they might more readily test their own policy assumptions, and examine the possible consequences of policy options they would like to discuss with managements.

It is sometimes argued that manpower planning in terms of statistical aggregates is 'inhumane' and 'treats people as no more than numbers'; and that it ignores the variability of human potential. It is noteworthy that these criticisms come usually from people who have no experience or close acquaintance with manpower planning practice, and who are accustomed to working in very small organizations where manpower planning techniques of the kind we have in mind would be inappropriate. These critics, one suspects, make the mistake of regarding the techniques based on statistical aggregates as rivals and threats to the individual matching processes. The techniques are of course not rivals to or substitutes for individual matching, but in fact provide a necessary quantitative framework within which there is a greater chance of achieving satisfactory individual matching. Ideally, the framework would ensure that there were neither too many posts nor too few against which the people would be matched. In our view it would be inhumane not to use the manpower planning techniques in any organization of size where careers matter and 'hire and fire' is not an acceptable management philosophy.

The point about variability of human potential is of course a more subtle and serious point than the criticism based on the alleged inhumanity of statistics. It is an important point, but not one which amounts to a valid criticism. The validity of the statistical manpower planning approach depends at least in part on the assumption that successive cohorts of staff which have similar objectively defined statistical characteristics (in terms of age, sex, qualifications at time of joining, selection procedures undergone, and so on) will contain similar mixes of quality, will contain reasonably similar proportions of people who will be deemed promotable in due course and so on—subject to the usual statistical theories about behaviour under the laws of chance. When using the manpower planning models the Statisticians take care to sub-divide the populations into streams which do have similar measurable statistical characteristics. Beyond this we rely upon the empirical evidence that the behaviour of statistical aggregates of people is inherently more stable and predictable than the behaviour of very small numbers or of individuals.

Constraints

So far we have tried to show how manpower planning has been developing in the British Civil Service. What has been said should, as we have mentioned earlier be considered in relation to the fuller treatment in Hopes (1973) and Smith (1972) and for this reason we do not wish to go into detail here about the problems of bringing supply and demand into balance. It may however be appropriate at this point to mention some important constraints on this, which operate in the British Civil Service more acutely than in many organizations.

The external employment market situation is a constraint on any corporate manpower plan; and at a number of points any organization depends on finding in the external market labour of the kind it wants. But in relation to the British Civil Service the free operation of this market is quite severely constrained in a number of ways. In the non-industrial Civil Service pay is determined in accordance with principles set out in the Priestley Report (Royal Commission on the Civil Service) in 1956, and procedural agreements made under the auspices of the National Whitley Council, subject of course to application of current Government incomes policy. Very broadly, the primary factor in determining pay is 'fair comparison' with rates paid for functionally comparable work outside the Civil Service; the comparisons are based on a form of job evaluation and take into account differences in other conditions of service. The facts regarded as necessary for establishing 'fair comparison' are established by the Civil Service Pay Research Unit, which is an impartial research body set up for the purpose in 1956. For each survey, in respect of a major Civil Service group, the P.R.U. investigates what it regards as a representative sample of jobs in the Civil Service, and obtains pay and related information about external jobs identified as comparable. The P.R.U. prepares a confidential factual report on which negotiations between Staff Associations and the C.S.D. are based. Most grades not covered by P.R.U. surveys have their pay determined mainly by links with other grades which are covered. These links are also subject to study, including job evaluation where appropriate, and negotiation. Application of the 'fair comparison' principle means that almost by definition rates of pay in the Civil Service must follow trends outside the Service rather than set the standards; it also means that Civil Service pay rates are those likely to be paid by a good employer outside, but are by no means at the top of the market. The system of direct comparison in some cases and the use of links in others is necessary partly for administrative simplicity but more because external analogues cannot be found for many of the functions performed within the Civil Service. This means that in some cases the connection with market forces may be tenuous. And it follows that the central theme of much theoretical economics—the dynamic relationship between demand, supply and price (or wages and salaries)—which in some socio-economic environments might have a practical place in the matching of a supply and demand for manpower, has for those of us engaged in Civil Service manpower planning only a peripheral interest. Insofar as salary levels may determine supply or demand, we have usually to regard them as a fixed constraint, rather than as a policy option.

This is perhaps the most important constraint; in addition however there is the concept, particularly in the administration group, that people enter the Civil Service as a career and thus there is a bias towards recruitment only at certain points in the structure, mainly those at which young people leave the educational system, both at the graduate and school-leaver stages. This is less marked than it used to be, especially in the lower grades; nevertheless this bias, together with pressure from the staff associations not to recruit at senior levels because it would harm the prospects of more junior staff, the importance of experience of the government machine for success in some of the more senior posts, and the comparative lack of attraction in Civil Service salaries (for the reasons set out above) to really able people who have already reached senior positions in industry, makes recruitment of mature and experienced staff to make good earlier deficiencies, or the failure accurately to forecast demand, particularly difficult. The obverse, that, again because of the concept of a career service, there is no tradition of making able people redundant except where it is quite unavoidable, also puts strong pressure on us to get our demand and supply calculations right, and provides a strong incentive to us to improve our manpower planning techniques. So much, then, for the outline of the development within the Civil Service of manpower planning techniques and applications which aim to achieve a satisfactory utilization of manpower by creating a satisfactory balance between manpower requirements and manpower supply, and the flows which determine supply, in terms of statistical aggregates. We turn now to consider how the work relates to other aspects of manpower management which come within the ambit of this Conference.

Classification

It was mentioned earlier that all civil servants are given labels which give an indication of occupation and hierarchical level (grade). There are clearly advantages in having the manpower force classified and labelled. For instance, it makes the use of the manpower planning supply models much easier than would otherwise be the case. There is a danger, however, that the existence of a system of labels will give rise to unjustified confidence in the efficiency of the classification system which lies behind it. The classification system may not adequately reflect the nature of the work to be done, or the characteristics of the people available to do the work. A labelling system may remain unchanged after years of slow, almost-unnoticed change in the nature of jobs. (A point worth pondering is that it might still be valid to use the manpower planning models with an imperfect classification if that classification were in fact the basis on which management decisions in respect of recruitment, promotion and so on were actually taken. The models are intended in the first instance to represent or aid the real-life decision-making processes, rather than to represent a non-existent ideal which management does not recognize.)

Over the course of many decades, as new techniques and functions and professions developed, the British Civil Service accumulated a massive array of occupational groups or 'classes'. By the mid-1960s, when the management of the Civil Service was being reviewed by the Fulton Committee, there were some 1,400 'classes'. The Fulton Committee pointed out that this highly-detailed classification system imposed undesirable rigidities. Over the course of time conventions had been evolved, regulations developed, and negotiations with Staff Associations carried through which created or formalized barriers to movement between classes which the Committee believed prevented efficient utilization of abilities. Following the Fulton Committee's Report (1968) a process of amalgamation of classes began. The First Report (1970) and Second Report (1971) of the Civil Service Department and the annual issues of the publication Civil Service Statistics (1970, 1971, 1972) indicate how far this process has now gone; and the Reports mention the fact-finding and job-evaluation procedures carried out before decisions were taken.

This process is clearly increasing freedom of occupational/hierarchical movement, and increasing the ability of the Civil Service to adapt to organizational and technical change. Due tribute is being paid to the much-quoted need for flexibility and adaptability. But at the same time as the creation of large groups containing people with varied experience and qualifications reduces the problems of moving people easily from one type of job to another, it creates a new problem of identifying people within these groups for recruitment or personnel management purposes; for example how in a group of this kind does one ensure that there remains an adequate supply of people with the qualifications and experience to do the different types of job and that the people in the group are at all times in the right sort of job? Thus within the newly-formed large groups there is a need for a second level of labelling to identify posts which require special skills and experience. An example of a de facto occupational specialism within the large Administration Group, which is not recognized as a distinct labelled Occupation Group, is computer work (programming and systems analysis); another type of work for which training and appropriate experience might reasonably be regarded as necessary is Personnel Management.

Ways of reconciling the need to avoid creating new barriers to movement with the need to be able to invest in (and recoup investment on) training for specialized work have yet to be evolved into systematic procedures. There are of course both efficiency and satisfaction aspects to be considered.

In the meantime a start is being made in the PRISM system towards classifying and recording skills and experience in a 'multi-axis' or multi-dimensional way which will lend itself to any set of career management procedures which may be evolved. The probability is that the old-style single-axis 'class' label will fairly rapidly lose significance, and give way to regard for several axes in both individual career planning and aggregate manpower planning.

On an experimental basis cluster analysis is now being used to examine the characteristics of jobs and people within Groups, and it seems possible that this technique will in due course be used to examine and monitor the shifting and hazy boundaries between Groups and sub-specializations.

Selection

We should now like to consider in turn a number of aspects of personnel management which are affected by, and in turn affect, our manpower planning work. First of all, selection, both at the recruitment stage and subsequently.

The Civil Service Commission has for many years been concerned with the use, development and validity-testing of methods of selecting recruits for the Civil Service. See for example Anstey (1966, 1968, 1971). This work is now carried forward by the Behavioural Sciences research staff of the C.S.D. Objectively marked tests have been developed for use in the qualifying examinations for Administration Trainees (who are intended to be a principal source of future top managers and policy-makers), as interview aids in the selection of Executive Officers, and for use in the selection of certain other grades. A start has also been made on the experimental try-out and development of written personality tests.

Plans have been put in hand for the regular systematic follow-up of new entrants to the Civil Service recruited through C.S.C. competitions so that assessments made at the time of selection can be compared with subsequent performance on the job. This will enable the validity of selection procedures as a whole and the relative contribution made by each component part to be estimated; and comparative information from different departments on how the new entrants are supervised, trained and looked after will be of value in improving career development schemes generally.

Although there is no early prospect of application, some work has been done on computer assisted selection procedures. For example Wishart (1972) has shown how Bayesian methods can be used in conjunction with readily-available computer programmes and visual display units to simulate and perhaps improve upon a personnel interview situation. Before such methods can be used in practice the psychologists will need to satisfy themselves that acceptably-valid sets of questions can be devised.

More mundane methods of providing computer assistance for selection and assignment can be made available in the form of established criteria and priorities appropriately programmed. Trials are being made of their practicability in the more promising areas, i.e., for use where large numbers of people need to be assigned amongst a number of employing organizations at more or less the same time, and when the computer can undertake that part of the work which would otherwise be done by routine clerical labour. There is no question of management being prepared to have a situation in which people's future might be thought to be 'being left to a computer'.

For the selection of people for particular posts in the course of their careers the computer has already proved itself as an aid in the higher grades of the Civil Service. The Central Management Staff Record, which was set up experimentally in 1970 (as a forerunner to PRISM) and which contains a fair amount of factual information about some 10,000 of the most senior civil servants, has proved invaluable as a quick source of information about the field of available people who might fill a particular specified vacancy (for example: Under Secretary, fluent in French, qualified economist, experience of agriculture policy work since 1965 . . .). The C.M.S.R. can report back quickly on the size of the field, and print out whatever information is needed by the people who will complete the selection process. It is doubtful whether in the absence of a computer record of this kind it would ever be possible in a very large organization like the Civil Service to be sure that every possibly suitable person had been considered.

Job appraisal and assessment of potential

By far the most important element in the selection of people for jobs is, however an accurate and reliable appraisal of their performance and potential. Improved methods of assessing the performance and potential of staff were agreed for introduction throughout the Civil Service (for all but a few hundred of the most senior staff) during 1972. They are based on a new staff report form completed annually, the major parts of which are standardized, although departments may add to it where necessary to meet any special needs. The most significant feature is that the main assessment of performance concentrates on the effectiveness with which the person reported on has carried out his tasks, and these tasks are discussed and agreed between him and his supervisor at the beginning of the reporting period. There are links here with 'management by objectives', and with the less formalized methods of target-setting or assessing of achievements which are tending to be associated with the appraisal interview, or job appraisal review (J.A.R.), which is also now a standard part of improved Civil Service personnel management.

The system of staff reporting depends on the ability of supervisors to assess their staff fairly; and its value in comparing staff with each other depends on this being done as nearly as possible to a consistent standard. Considerable emphasis was therefore placed on training staff in assessment and in the use of the new report form before its introduction. To ensure consistency in this training, and also to carry out the task using training resources as economically as possible; the C.S.D. devised a method of instruction using programmed learning techniques.

Appraisal interviews (J.A.Rs) are based on the civil servant's performance in his job in the previous year and how it should be done in the future. Here again an extensive training programme was mounted to launch J.A.Rs. A 45-minute training film was made and an explanatory booklet was produced; see Anstey, Fletcher and Walker (1971).

We are particularly concerned to calculate the effectiveness of the J.A.Rs. We are carrying out detailed research in three representative departments in an attempt to compare management and staff attitudes and, if possible, job performance before and after introduction of the scheme. Early results suggest that the J.A.Rs are being well received by staff and that the training is effective in enabling interviews to combine a generally problem-solving approach with conveying an assessment of recent performance and indicating any areas of weakness; an interim report on some aspects of one of these evaluations is contained in Fletcher (in press).

Neither assessments of performance nor of promotability or potential are at present included in computer records, and they are not at present used for aggregate manpower planning purposes. We hope, however, to find ways of incorporating information derived from staff report forms in computer records in due course in such a way that they can be used to reinforce the existing manpower planning models and in such a way that the validity of the assessments can themselves be tested against subsequent events. One method may be to hold potential information on separate discs or tapes which remain in the custody of Personnel Managers and are matched against main records inside the computer under the supervision of the Personnel Manager.

Job satisfaction studies

Manpower planning is concerned with people in jobs; with what people are going to be in what jobs in the future. Both the people and the jobs are variables, and our task is to try to achieve the best match between them—both on the macro-scale of large group supply and demand problems, and on the micro-scale of the use and development of individual talent and potential. Just as increasing concern for the environment is beginning to have an influence on decisions and policies affecting the utilization and management of physical resources, so we can expect that increasing concern for the quality of working life is likely to have an influence on decisions and policies affecting the utilization and management of human resources.

Our appraisal system has a part to play in this, but, as well as trying to get people into the right jobs we need to look at the jobs themselves to ensure that people are likely to find them satisfying. We are therefore currently sponsoring a series of 'job satisfaction' studies in the Civil Service. The aim of the studies is to investigate, by means of a number of separate experiments involving different categories of staff in different departments, the likely scope, benefits, difficulties and general implications of changing jobs in such a way as to increase the motivation and job satisfaction of the staff involved.

Each study comprises the three main steps of design, implementation and evaluation. On the basis of normal consultancy fact-finding and diagnostic procedures, brainstorming and other techniques are used to develop in close consultation with the staff concerned a set of changes designed to improve the quality of working life in terms of meaningful, interesting and responsible job content; this often produces the need for associated and consistent changes in organization, methods of working, control systems and conditions of employment. Implementation of the agreed changes is normally on an experimental pilot scale basis, with control groups where possible, leading to as comprehensive as possible monitoring of the effects of the changes, on the twin dimensions of work performance and staff attitudes.

The first step in the process of assessing staff attitudes is to find out what they think about their present situation. This is done by means of a 'reaction to work' survey where the sample members (in many cases the sample can be a full count) check a Likert-type five-point scale, i.e., 'strongly agree; mainly agree; on balance agree; mainly disagree; strongly disagree'. There is no neutral point in the scale; respondents must classify themselves as 'agreers' or 'disagreers'. The questionnaire contains statements of general impressions of the work, e.g., 'My work helps me to develop as an individual'; of various features of the work, i.e., its nature; responsibility; development; and finally, statements about the organizational support the respondent receives (or does not receive) in doing his work. All this means more than might be conveyed by the word 'job'. From the replies a bench-mark measurement is computed. After the experimental period the same procedure is used to measure again and the results are compared. The survey itself may of course indicate, along with the other methods mentioned above, possible areas for change; it can also give some indication after the count of the sort of changes which were most effective.

If it does indeed prove possible radically to alter and improve the way in which existing staff talent and potential is utilized on existing work, the implications for future manpower planning and policy development are considerable. It will not be adequate to accept the present structuring of work as a given feature of any planning model; what we will be dealing with is a dynamic system in a wider and more general sense than implied in our earlier use of the term, because the system will be responsive both to social pressures and to internally generated requirements for structural and operational change. However, this will not diminish the need to plan, or the need to make the best possible assessments of future requirements. Rather does it mean that we will approach the task of manpower planning with greater knowledge, and probably with a greater range of policy options in mind.

Wastage studies

One of the indicators which can indicate, amongst other things, the extent to which people find jobs satisfying is the rate of wastage. Knowledge of the number who leave (and the broad reasons why) are essential for manpower planning purposes; more detailed knowledge of the reasons is of considerable value to personnel managers more generally. The monitoring of wastage is partly a matter of systematically analysing the statistics of losses, and expressing them in some suitable way as proportions of numbers 'at risk'. This type of monitoring provides information for management about levels and trends, and the location of trouble-spots. When the new PRISM records system become operational there will be automatic monitoring of variations in wastage for each category of personnel between localities, departments, parts of departments and so on. Our current thinking is that the most useful form in which to present this information to management will be graphical, showing in each case on a single diagram current age-specific or service-specific rates against an agreed yardstick which may be, for example, similar rates for an earlier period, or rates which indicate some kind of satisfactory level.

The PRISM records will include limited information about whether each loss is due to retirement, ill-health, voluntary resignation or redundancy. This data will not of course permit study of the true causes of wastage, in the sense in which that term is normally used. Studies of the causes of wastage are currently being carried out amongst junior executive and clerical staff on an experimental basis in three Departments. These studies began in 1971 with pilot enquiries aimed at establishing satisfactory questionnaire and interviewing procedures. Leavers are being asked about their main reasons for leaving, and are being asked other questions in depth about their degree of job satisfaction. Similar enquiries are being made of samples of non-leavers, and will be included in due course in the regular follow-up of new entrants to the Civil Service. This work is being viewed very much as 'action research', leading to positive management action. Results so far indicate that inadequate exploitation of skills and abilities is seen by leavers as an important source of dissatisfaction.

A study has also been made on an experimental basis of the practicability of comparing levels of wastage for specified groups of civil servants with those of employees of other organizations. This work, which has been carried out at the request of the Civil Service Department by the Institute of Manpower Studies with the co-operation of 25 other organizations has produced interesting results, and we are hopeful that this work can be extended gradually over the course of time. (See Institute of Manpower Studies Report, 1972.) We would expect the usefulness of this work, like a great deal of other statistical monitoring, to become progressively more obvious as trends over time became apparent.

We would hope at some future date to be able to evaluate relationships between wastage and such internal factors as recruitment selection tests and procedures, assessed potential, perceived promotion opportunities, and changes made as a result of job satisfaction studies; and such external factors as the levels and distribution of unemployment, and the labour market situation for particular categories. But at this stage not all the data needed to support such studies is available, and it is at least questionable whether available research techniques can deal satisfactorily with the very mixed bag of variables which need to be taken into account. However, work will be done as soon as resources are available and if the chances of a successful outcome are deemed to be sufficiently high.

Other studies

There is other relevant work which could be described. For example, in the medical field there have been studies of sickness absence which may well have a bearing on job satisfaction and wastage (see C.S.D. Management Studies No. 1 (1971)); of occupational health; of the relationship between age, health and efficiency amongst middle-aged women; longitudinal studies of the health of a large sample of executives; and so on.

Some work is being done by Operational Researchers in C.S.D. which relates recruiting and wastage rates, and age distributions, to other factors like posting and promotion procedures, training and the mixture of skills required for the proper performance of particular tasks. Most of this work is in its early stages. It makes an assumption (as yet unproved) that administrators currently operate policies more or less as rules of thumb of the kind 'every candidate for promotion must have experience in at least three specialities', or 'fast stream people should spend no more than three years and not less than two years in any given job', and attempts to simulate the working of the system under these assumptions, in such a way that the balance between the short term requirements of getting the job done today and the longer term objective of building up the level of skill available to the organization can be assessed.

In conclusion

We have discussed briefly a fairly wide range of topics under the umbrella provided by the title of this paper, with a view to illustrating the interest of the Civil Service Department in applications which are thought likely to improve the quality of personnel management, or manpower systems management, in the Civil Service. The object of all this work is to improve efficiency in the broadest sense—not in the narrow short-sighted sense in which the word efficiency is sometimes thought to be interpreted by management, but in the sense in which the recognition of the reasonable aspirations of individuals, and adequate development and utilization of skills and abilities, are seen to be essential ingredients in any prescription for efficiency because of the assumed relationships between morale, motivation and feelings of justice on the one hand and work organization and performance on the other.

Manpower planning begins with the more obvious tasks of trying to establish the best possible relationships between work to be done and people to do the work, in aggregate quantitative terms, looking to the future because skilled human resources cannot be acquired, developed or discarded at will and cannot be overstretched or under-utilized for long without serious consequences for both management and staff. The statistical and computer information-systems input needs for this type of work in an organization as large and complex as the Civil Service are substantial, and necessary if useful application of the other kinds of work we have mentioned is not to be handicapped by avoidable aggregate mismatch between demand and supply.

Manpower planning in the wider sense embraces all the kinds of work we have discussed. Improvements in classification will improve the quality of the statistics in terms of accuracy and homogeneity and ability to reflect qualitative aspects in statistical descriptions of people and jobs. Effective work on selection criteria, performance assessment and assessment of potential, besides having obvious value in aiding efficient matching at the individual level, also generate better information for manpower planning of aggregates, and can be viewed as another aspect of classification. Job satisfaction studies, too, are relevant to both individual matching and aggregates matching, and may lead to changes in the assessments of numbers and kinds of people needed to do the work which needs to be done, and hence to the planning of recruitment, deployment, career structures, and reward systems. Studies of recruitment and wastage, and pay research, provide a bridge between the behavioural and economic aspects of our manpower system, and between this internal Civil Service manpower system and the external national manpower systems with which it has to maintain a dynamic equilibrium.

In short, the Civil Service is a dynamic manpower system, interacting with its environment. All the kinds of work we have mentioned can be viewed as means of measuring or assessing aspects of the workings of this system and as aids to management control engineering. In this sense everything we have discussed is manpower planning: ramifications of the framework of information within which we hope that better decisions will be taken.

Acknowledgements

We are grateful for the help given to us in preparing this paper by colleagues who are playing a major part in developing the kinds of work described in this paper, and in particular Professor D.J. Bartholomew, Mr. J.A. Rowntree and Mr. R.F.A. Hopes (Statistics Divisions—Manpower Planning); Mr. C.P.H. Marks (Statistics Division—Personnel Information Systems); Dr. E. Anstey (Behavioural Sciences Research Division); Mr. Keith Robertson (Job Satisfaction Studies Unit); Mr E.K.G. James (O.R. Division); and Mr. J.P. Charkham (Pay Divisions).

References

ANSTEY, E., 1966, The Civil Service Administrative Class and the Diplomatic Service: A Follow-up. *Occupational Psychology*, **40**.

ANSTEY, E., 1968, Follow-up Surveys. Memoranda 4 and 5. *Fulton Report*, Vol. 3(2) (London: H.M.S.O.).

ANSTEY, E., 1971, The Civil Service Administrative Class: A Follow-up of Post-War Entrants. *Occupational Psychology*, **45**.

ANSTEY, E., FLETCHER, C. and WALKER, J., 1971, *Job Appraisal Review Training Manual* (London: H.M.S.O.).

BRIDLE, J.W., and GREGERSEN, R.J., 1971, The Central Management Staff Record—A Personnel Information Retrieval System. *O. & M. Bulletin—Journal of Government Management Services* **26** (2).

CIVIL SERVICE DEPARTMENT, 1970, *First Report of the Civil Service Department, 1969* (London: H.M.S.O.).

CIVIL SERVICE DEPARTMENT, 1971, *Second Report of the Civil Service Department, 1970–71* (London: H.M.S.O.).

CIVIL SERVICE DEPARTMENT, 1970, 1971, 1972, *Civil Service Statistics* (annually) (London: H.M.S.O.).

CIVIL SERVICE DEPARTMENT, 1971, Sickness Absence in the Civil Service, 1967. *C.S.D. Management Studies No.* 1 (London: H.M.S.O.).

COMMITTEE ON THE CIVIL SERVICE, 1968, (*Fulton*) *Report of the Committee*, Cmnd 3638 (London: H.M.S.O.).

FLETCHER, C. (in press), Interview Style and the Effectiveness of Appraisal. *Occupational Psychology*.

HOPES, R.F.A., 1973, Some Statistical Aspects of Manpower Planning in the Civil Service. *Omega* **1** (2).

INSTITUTE OF MANPOWER STUDIES, 1972, Comparative Wastage Studies: Reports *CN 27 et seq* (Sussex: I.M.S.).

MARKS, C.P.H., 1972, The U.K. Civil Service Personnel Record System for Management—PRISM. *I.B.I.–I.C.C. World Conference Papers* (Rome: I.B.I.–I.C.C.).

ROYAL COMMISSION ON THE CIVIL SERVICE, 1956, *Report* (*The Priestley Report*), Cmnd 9653 (London: H.M.S.O.).

SMITH, A.R., 1972, Aspects of Manpower Planning. *Company Practices in Manpower Planning* (London: I.P.M.).

WISHART, D., 1972, Computers in Personnel Management. *Personnel Review*, **1** (2).

Further relevant reading concerned with the U.K. Civil Service may be found in:

BARTHOLOMEW, D.J., and SMITH, A.R. (Eds.), 1971, *Manpower and Management Science* (London: E.U.P. and Lexington: Heath).

CIVIL SERVICE DEPARTMENT, 1971, The Employment of Women in the Civil Service: the report of a departmental committee. *CSD Management Studies No. 3* (London: H.M.S.O.).

CLOUGH, D.J. (Ed.), 1973, *Manpower Planning Models: 1971*, N.A.T.O. Conference Papers (London: E.U.P.).

GARRETT, J., 1972, *The Management of Government* (London: Pelican).

SMITH, A.R. (Ed.), *Some Statistical Techniques for Manpower Planning*. Civil Service College Occ. Papers No. 15 (London: H.M.S.O.).

Prof. F. Eric Burke was educated in mathematics and mechanical engineering, his career moved from design and project engineering, extended research in the physical sciences and its direction, to operational research on the processes of technical change. For the latter, study of highly qualified manpower and its utilization is an important component.

3:2

An empirical model for Canadian engineers' salaries

F. E. Burke*

Introduction

Secrecy, bias and controversy surround professional salary data. Apart from the confidential files of employers and tax collectors, most data are scattered in publications of professional societies, employers' associations and ministries of labour. The topic seems too important to be entrusted to academic study. The rare inroads made by personnel specialists, economist and sociologists have been illuminating, but have been short on empirical foundations.

This study is intended to be more severely analytical than is common in terms of questions asked.

It is noted, for instance, that engineers move from technical work functions to sales, managerial and executive functions, and also from their field of training to different fields of occupational specialization. These latter moves are of particular interest in a rapidly changing professional environment because they tend to put unrealistic demands on education systems. 'Please provide, next year, 3,000 specialists in *xyz* with 10 years' experience'. This aim may be approached if enough academics were interested in *xyz* before employers were and if they know how to select suitable applicants with 8–10 years' applicable experience to whom a year's special instruction can be given.

Only rarely can even the first condition (of prior pre-occupation by academics) be met adequately; we usually aren't sure what experience will prove applicable; and only rarely do we encounter a really experienced man who is willing, and can afford to take leave for a year's training. Thus the initial demand for new skills, e.g., in computing, is often met by self-generated enthusiasts, and only later do trained personnel become available as a second generation.

In moves to both new functional areas, and to new specialized fields, we are preoccupied with the crude question of whether the move was for the worse (an 'expulsion') or the better (e.g., signalled by an unusual increase in pay). We are aware that interest in the new work and other intrinsic motivators play their part, but we believe it is easier to answer such questions if the extrinsic measures are available. Micro-economically expressed, we wish to distinguish demand

* Valuable help was given by Miss M. Hui in performing many of the computations in this paper during her master's work in this Department. Her financial support from various sources, but particularly from N.C.R. grants to Professor D.J. Clough of this dept., is recorded with gratitude. The readiness of Mr. W.W. Hastings to accommodate many demands on his time is beyond reward.

pull (shortage) from supply push (excess) signified by positive or negative price 'premiums'.

Short and excess supplies are often considered macro-economically, and this seems to have led to questionable decisions about provision of professional education facilities and immigration policies. Such lapses are reinforced by conflicting interests, such as that of employers in excess supply so as to keep salaries low, and the opposite on the part of professional groups. On the other hand, quantitative information on salaries may induce less miserly attitudes among employers favouring high quality and morale of staff, and a knowledge of opportunities may encourage self improvement of professionals as well as providing a basis for counsel toward such goals. Before salary data can be used to measure salary premiums (positive or negative), it is desirable to know how much difference would be significant in a statistical sense. This may be even more important to establish if an instance of 'mobility' is involved in the first place—or if a job change results in no more than a change in verbal title rather than in substance.

Measures of what kind of functions or fields command a premium afford opportunities to enquire if 'successful' movers share some educational experiences that might require special emphasis in curriculum development. This may improve career advice. If academics believe that some low salary field holds intrinsic advantage for his students, he can at least advise how much better than average his student has to be to achieve extrinsic success or alternatively what the real opportunity cost is of a choice toward the intrinsically 'attractive' job.

None of these purposes can be achieved by tabulation, however comprehensive or however detailed the functional and field categories. Unless a model exists on which tests of significance can be carried out, statements of 'more' or 'less' or of taxonomy, are mere qualitative words rather than refutable or debatable propositions.

Salary data and models

Salary data for professional personnel are still being produced in naive forms. For instance, the Canadian Information Processing Society (C.P.S., 1973) published average, high and low salaries for over 35 categories of E.D.P. employees on 28 separate tables without regard to ordinal statistics, size of sample recorded, or age distribution. The relevance of such voluminous data to any conceivable decision is not clear. The source is an enquiry from individuals with a 40% response.

A more common form of tabulation is represented by the surveys of the U.S. Engineers Joint Council. Median, upper and lower quartiles and deciles of salaries as a function of age are published every two years (since 1953, the first interval being three years). Information is obtained from 'representative' employers.

The Canadian department of Manpower and Immigration conducted a survey in 1967 (Atkinson *et al.*, 1970), with about 60% response, broken down in several thousand ways. Analysis is difficult, but see Burke (1970).

The Association of Professional Engineers of Ontario surveys salaries regularly, the series being continuous since 1958 but differing in scope. Individual responses are between 45% and 60%. The more extensive enquiries of the last two years (Hastings, 1972, 1973) are the main basis of the present modelling effort, details are given below. Dodge (1971) and Rosenbluth (1961) have conducted multivariate analyses of a cross-sectional type of some Dept. of Labour and Manpower and Emigration data. They used advanced techniques but significance testing is not promising owing to the arbitrary structure of their complex, additive multivariate regression models. More theoretical static discussions have been given by Blank and Stigler (1957), Shockley (1957), Mandelbrot (1968, 1972 and references in the 1972 Bibliography) and Arrow and Capron (1958, 1959). Some theoretical concepts used in this paper are taken from their work. Dynamic analysis of a rudimentary form is attempted by Frey (1965), Perucci (1969), and Burke (1965a). Here, cohorts are followed over prolonged time periods, but mobility could not be considered. The problems of price index numbers over times are encountered but not dealt with. Jacques (1970) tabulates individual progression of careers, but his discussion of mobility is limited. He corrects to constant (1955) money values, but does not consider the growing proportion of engineers in western labour forces. The proportion of engineers in the labour force, and income/rarity questions, have been considered by Towler (1965) and Burke (1965b). No mobility or model information was provided. A recent review (Folk, 1970) does not add new information relevant to this paper.

In summary, static models have reached closer to significance modelling, and have been more adequately related to data, than dynamic models. Dynamic models hold out great promise for actual career studies, but have not so far been adequately supported by data or by theoretical analysis.

A proposed bivariate non-linear static model

The data are from two annual surveys of the A.P.E.O., (W.W. Hastings 1972, 1973) with over 20,000 replies each in answer to individual enquiry. The ordinals, reported by year, show considerable 'noisyness'. Thus the first step in modelling was to undertake a second order regression of each salary ordinal Y_x recorded (medians, quartiles and deciles) to obtain regression lines $\bar{Y}_x$. We are not aware of any such regressions other than for the median, although the techniques are elementary and standard. Such regression is not formally justified because of ignorance of error distribution about the regression lines. The relatively small relevance of the purported 'longitudinal' lines for our purposes persuades us against formal sophistication on this point.

We use three temporal cross-sections of the regressions obtained (for 1971 data, $x=6$, 16, 26) and note the well established skew distributions of $\bar{Y}_x$ at each x. Clearly, a direct development of a distribution and its characteristic statistics for such a small number of observations would be an unpromising effort. Instead, we drew upon theory and found that many previous workers had favoured a log-normal distribution for the extrinsic rewards of human effort, on both theoretical and (on occasion) empirical grounds, to search for a transformation to a function with a normal distribution. Engineering salaries appear not to have been successfully transformed in this manner so far (Rosenbluth, 1961). We found that the function of

$$\log[\hat{Y}_x-\mu_0]=\log[(\bar{Y}_x)-\mu_0]+\log Z \qquad (1)$$

is distributed normally. Our procedure was to solve, by iteration, for μ_0 so that the average variance ratio for $\delta(\bar{Y}\alpha, x)/\delta(y_x)$ at all four ordinal values α and at all three values of x was close to minimal. As all variance ratios were below the 10% significance level, we did not reject the null hypothesis that all 12 inferred variances were statistics of samples drawn from the population of Y with the average variance (defined as $\sigma(\log Z)$). Furthermore, the three average variances at constant x had F values below 1·05, and we did not reject the null hypothesis that all these variances at all three temporal cross-sections were drawn from a distribution having a single variance independent of time. We show the 1971 model $\hat{Y}_x$, after inverse transformation, on Figure 1, together with the

Figure 1. Proposed model for Canadian Engineers salaries, with regression lines and raw data, 1971 Salary Survey (Hastings, 1972)

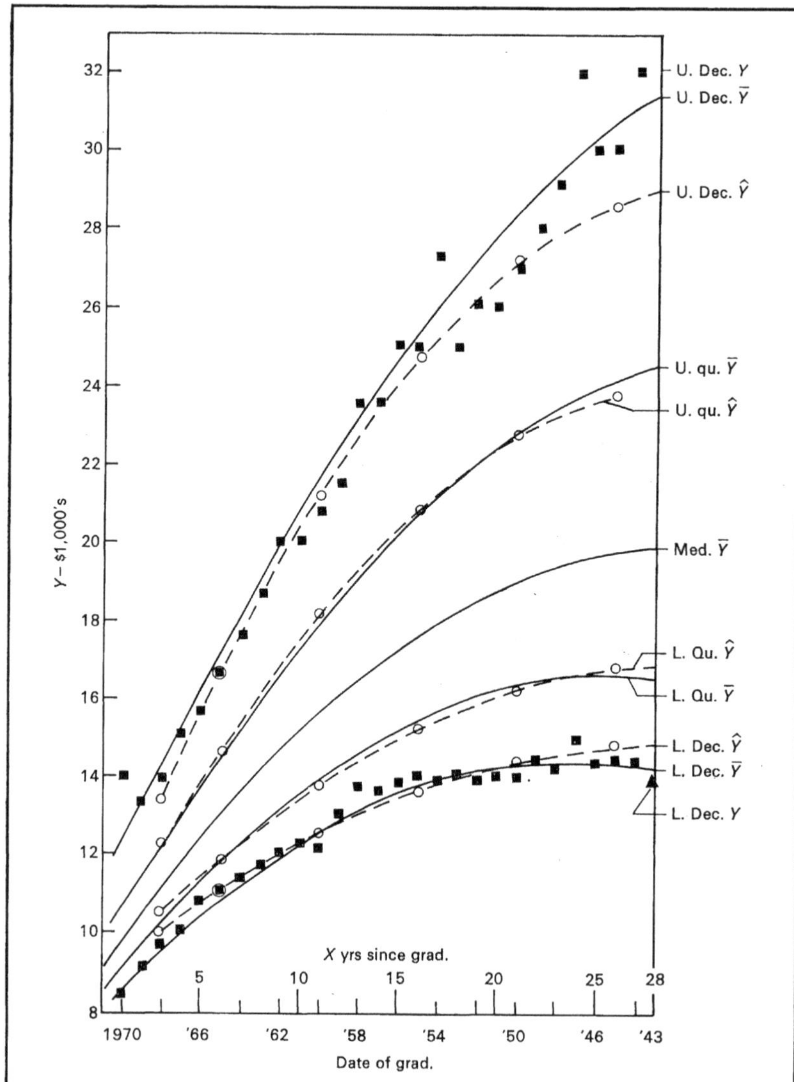

regression lines $\bar{Y}_x$, and actually observed salaries Y_x as distinct points (for the deciles). The remaining raw observations have been omitted as they would make the figure virtually unreadable due to close coincidence.

A departure of $\hat{Y}$ from $\bar{Y}$ will be noted from the upper decile $\bar{Y}$ at $x=26$. Even this apparently large departure is not significant owing to the small sample involved.

We noted that the iterated values of μ_0 were surprisingly close to the reported starting salaries for 1971 and 1972, and that σ log (Z) was the same for both years. A preliminary check showed that μ_0 coincided with the starting salaries back to 1960, and that the same value of σ (log Z) was acceptable in that year. *Neither* was true in the 1952 survey so we concluded that the major changes in the Canadian Engineering population between 1943 and 1950, noted by Rosenbluth (1961), make our model unacceptable in the pre-1955 period.

In summary, we propose a model for Canadian Engineering salaries in the period since 1955.

$$\hat{Y}'_x = (\bar{Y}'_x)x \log^{-1} z \tag{2}$$

where log z is normally distributed with $\mu_z=1$, and where $\sigma(\log z)$ is constant over time and in salary surveys between 1960 and 1972, and $\hat{Y}'_x = \hat{Y}_x - \mu_0$, and where $\mu(\hat{Y}'_x) = \mu(\bar{Y}) - \mu_0$.

Also in the transform equation (1)

$$\log [\bar{Y}_x - \mu_0] = \log [\mu(\bar{Y}_x) - \mu_0] + \log [Z]$$
$$\qquad\qquad\text{(temporal)} \qquad (X = \text{Const.})$$

no interaction term appears between the temporal and the 'vertical' submodels. We tentatively interpret this as consistent with the view that the market has valued engineers as possessing a constant multiplicative spread of ability compounded with a desirable mix of specialities and functions. Thus we would expect an individual, or an employer, or an educator to view any single observation of salary to be drawn at random from this model distribution *except* as modified (*a*) by the temporal regression of the median $\mu(\bar{Y}_x)$ and (b) by either the individual's ability or (c) by the individual belonging to a group differing significantly from $\hat{Y}$ by virtue of function, specialization or location in special areas of Canada.

Applications to apparent taxonomic groups of significance tests of the model in section 3

By application of the standard student t test formula for the significance of departure of the mean μ_s^1 of a sample of size N ($N-1$ degrees of freedom in this case) from the mean μ_z of an infinite population, we have

$$\log \frac{\mu_{s,}^1 g}{\mu(\hat{Y}_x^1)} - \log \mu_z = \frac{^{\alpha}t_{N-1}}{\sigma_z/\sqrt{N}} \tag{3}$$

where $\mu_{s,\,x}^1/\mu(\hat{Y}^1)$ is the normalized mean of the sample at time x (presumed transformed as in section 3), μ_z is the mean of the normal distribution log z, i.e., $\mu_z=1$, log $\mu_z=0$. $^{\alpha}t_{N-1}$ is the student t value for the chosen significance value α and the degrees of freedom corresponding to sample size N for the year in the apparent taxonomic group S.

Thus equ. (3) reduces to

$$\mu^1_{s,\,x} = \mu(\hat{Y}^1)\log^{-1}\left[\frac{{}^{\alpha}t_{N-1}}{\sigma_z/\sqrt{N}}\right] \tag{4}$$

Equation (4) has the dimension of dollars, as $(\hat{Y}^1)$ is in dollars and the right hand term dimensionless. A partial set of values of N, the size of the sample in a given year, and $\Delta\mu_{S,\,x}$, the dollar values of a significant deviation of sample means, for significance levels α of 0·10, 0·05 and 0·01, is shown in Table 1. 'Upper' and 'lower' differences $^{\Delta}\mu_{S,\,x}$, are shown, because of the skew nature of the inverse transformed $\hat{Y}$, equ. (2). It will be appreciated that for well behaved Y_S (over time) a moving average value at X can be inserted to increase the value of N and to sharpen discrimination of the test—but some judgement is, naturally, required.

Illustrations of the use of significance testing

While only medians (transformed to means for test purposes) are used and tabulated, computations can be made by standard, though computationally laborious means for the other ordinals compounded with differences in medians—such work is beyond the scope of this paper.

Only the 0·05 level of significance is referred to:

(*a*) *Comparison of electrical engineering salaries with the salaries of the total engineering population* (Figure 2)

Figure 2. Comparison of electrical Engineers with the total sample of A.P.E.O. (Hastings, 1971)

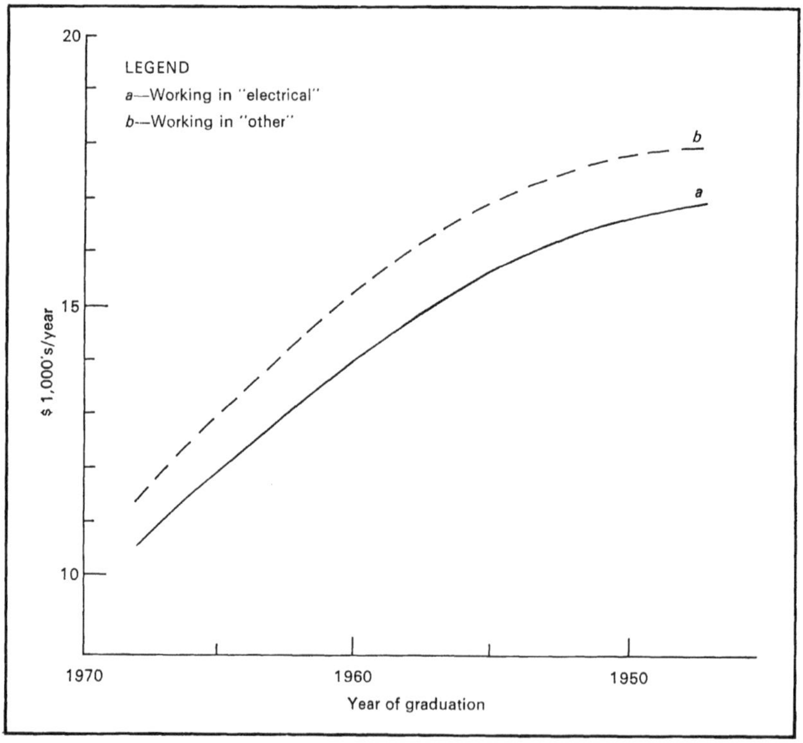

In view of the 'well behaved' nature of both medians (taken from an unregressed interpolation, W.W. Hasting [1971]) five-year moving averages are considered reasonable. We use the 'lower' values, as electrical engineers seems a low paid group. At $x = 5$, this underpayment is highly significant. At $x = 15$, the underpayment is not significant at the 5% level (though it is significant at the 10%–12% level). At $x > 15$, the underpayment must be considered insignificant.

In general, it appears that gross engineering fields do not differ significantly in extrinsic rewards in Canada.

No interpretation of this result is given here, though a number may come to mind to those familiar with Canada's electrical industry. It is claimed, however that the progressive insignificance of the difference (and of like differences, not shown, in specialized functions) cannot be quantitatively discussed without significance tests. For more specialized fields, see section *d*.

Comparison of median salaries of various work functions:

(*b*) *'Executives' 1971 survey* (Figure 3)
With salary differences between $x = 6$ and $x = 26$ rising from $2,300 to $7,500, the differences are between $2\frac{1}{2}$ times and 10 times significance at the 5% level, rising steadily. There is (not surprisingly) a clear taxonomic difference for this function. The case is not so clear for a distinction between 'executives' and 'senior management', which becomes significant only for $x > 12$.

(*c*) *'Senior management'* (Figure 3)
Apart for the confusion with young 'executives', this function is as distinct by significance tests as it looks naively.

(*d*) *'Management'* (Figure 3)
While an astute observer would readily guess the significance results of this function—different from 'senior management' at all ages, different from the total population for young 'managers', it is noteworthy that the difference ceases to be significant around 20 years' experience. Thus an element of certainty can be added to future discussions of this function.

(*e*) *'Specialist' and 'Supervisory'* (Figure 3)
In spite of their great numbers, these functions are not significantly different in rewards. They are different from the total engineering population beyond about 14 years' experience—at an increasing rate.

Their similarity invites behavioural enquiry. Are they given different titular 'functions' to reward the same task performance owing to difference in formal salary schemes? Or do they perform different tasks and seek differing balances of extrinsic and intrinsic rewards?

(*f*) *Median salaries by region* (Figure 4)
This figure shows three regions, of which Ontario may be taken (empirically) to represent the total engineering population in Canada. Again, common sense shows the equality of starting salaries, and tests merely indicate more accurately at what ages differences are worth noting. This may aid any future enquiry into causes of difference, by focusing on the age brackets most clearly concerned.

(*g*) *The salary of engineers in the computer field of specialization—a glance at mobility* (Figure 5)

Figure 3. Various functional groups in the A.P.E.O. population, with model median as reference (Hastings, 1972, this study)

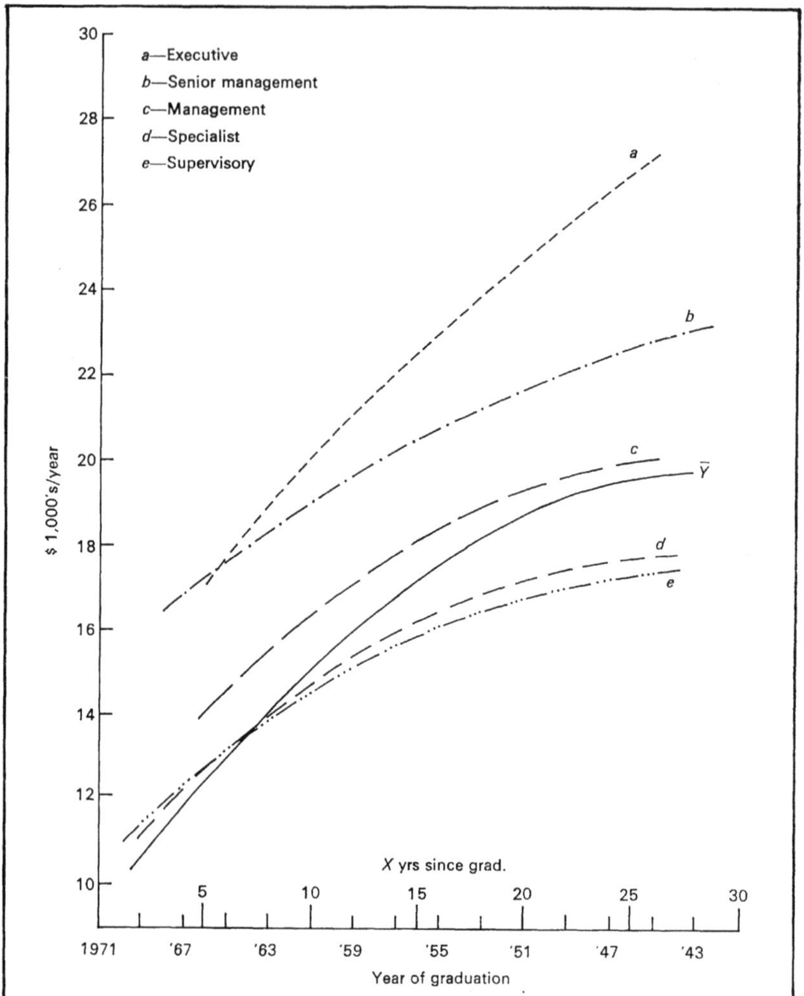

Although our model is static, some comparative statics provide quasi-dynamic information. As no employment for engineers was recordable in this field (the exceptions were too few) in Canada before 1961, all those who graduated in this year and before it (about 40% of the total responses) had to move into the field from an earlier area of specialization. In the case of the highly paid 20% who so moved with 1954 to 1961 graduation dates, we may be observing a case of intelligent and enthusiastic academic and student anticipation of a future market. The even earlier 20% who moved without significant material reward (even some 12 years or more later) may be a fruitful group for later enquiry—did they move because they were not wanted elsewhere? or because the intrinsic

Figure 4. A regional comparison of Engineering Sub-populations (Hastings, 1972)

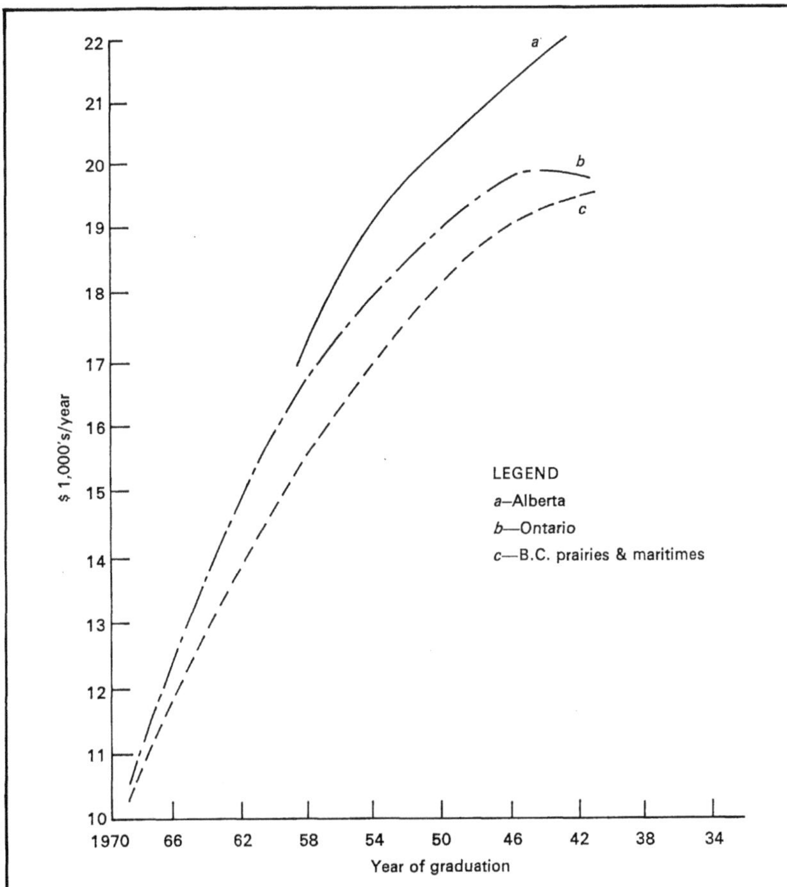

motivation was strong enough? or did they merely turn out to be less competent in their chosen field than their experience may otherwise indicate?

The group graduating between 1964 and 1962 shared in the bonanza of the more prescient colleagues of 1954 to 1961 vintage, probably as they needed foresight at their time of enrolment. Later graduates still fare significantly though not spectacularly well.

Discussion

Our survey of the past literature on engineer's salaries indicated that an adequate taxonomic basis for quantitative enquiry to be followed by behavioural elucidation, does not exist for professionals planning their career, for educators to fit curricula to future employment patterns, or for management interested in optimal upward or inward mobility of their professional staff. We found existing data to begin the task of devising taxonomies of engineers on an empirical basis.

Figure 5. Salaries of the computer Industry's Engineers, and the model regression lines

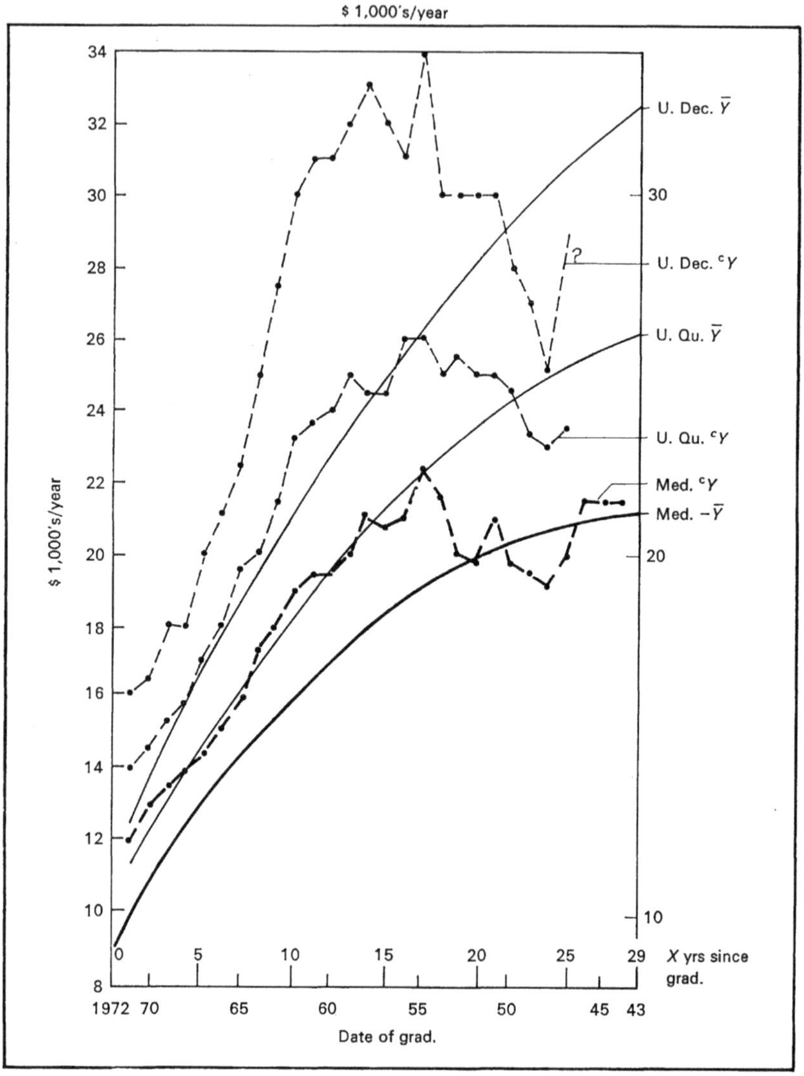

The data used were derived from surveys providing replies from about 50% to 70% of those approached. Thus the question of bias in these samples needs discussion to assess the weight to be attached to any of our conclusions. First, all known salary surveys are incomplete, and rarely exceed this extent of response. There are two basic methods of estimating bias empirically. The apparently most satisfactory method is to sample the 'non-respondents' in follow-up studies. Two weaknesses exist. First, the original population of survey subjects is liable to be biased. Membership of societies excludes not only the non-joiners (by behaviour pattern), but also many whose mobility from their career origin is of greatest concern to us. Lists of professional employees, while ensuring that all those included are reported on (thus obviating any follow-up study) are particularly prone to such population (as distinct from response) bias. Secondly, where 'non-respondents' were studied (Atkinson, 1970 and related private communications) their results have been non-conclusive. A large proportion of 'non-respondents' could simply not be found. Answers of the remainder did not warrant a conclusion of bias.

Another method was applied to the data base in this study. Canadian engineers have been surveyed by five sets of methods: the reports of Hastings (1971, 1972, 1973), an employer listing of major companies, the Canadian Civil Service Pay Research Bureau, the National Professional Register of the Department of Labour—and in addition, a private reconciliation of the National Register and one set of census enquiries. There are reasons to believe that these several surveys had biases (if any) in divergent directions. However, Burke (1965b) and Hastings (1971, as well private communications) showed means and variances whose departure from the null-hypotheses of homogeneous replies or populations was rejected as insignificant. While we are thus unable to give a satisfactory reply to the question of bias, we were not able to establish its existence empirically. A caution remains: even if the data base as a whole may be insignificantly biased, any subset appearing in taxonomic categories may be biased to a greater, and unknown, extent.

The statistical techniques employed were unsophisticated, and in particular, the distinction (important at a technical level) between 'parameters' and 'estimates of parameters' has not been implemented. This implies the assumption that after ad-hoc analysis, a model describing an infinite population could be specified (including the parameter values chosen). This is, in principle, arbitrary. The large data base combined with greater simplicity are an explanation rather than justification. We think that in principle all models are arbitrarily specified, and their status as a hypothesis indicated by subsequent tests. In this, we believe, our procedures are adequate.

What is the value, in the face of these numerous shortcomings, of significance tests to choose between empirically confirmed and empirically rejected taxonomic distinctions? We would assert that, using the cardinal money measure, it is useful to distinguish between an upper decile 'specialist' and a lower quartile 'executive', given our survey instrument and its empirical significance, even if they receive identical salaries. If the categories are not significantly different, no such discussion has empirical content until another taxonomic dimension is devised. Thus the value of significance testing is to establish the dimensional adequacy, or empirical redundancy, of proposed taxonomics, even in cases such as ours where the sub-sets created are far from mutually exclusive by the measure chosen.

Finally, our model is static and its application to mobility is mere 'quasi-statics'. But mobility is dynamic in time, and seems the key problem of manpower utilization. What would a dynamic model answer? Suppose we had a comprehensive, static taxonomy and an experience distribution. Cells could be created for each category, experience interval, and salary ordinal range for year 1. We would then wish to be able to determine the probability of finding a member of *this* cell in any subsequent (longer experience) cell in years 2, 3, . . ., n. This would be a dynamic or career model for the group covered by the taxonomy.

To accomplish this, we would need to create a statistically tractable data set over a time range preferably longer than 5 to 10 years—analogous to the individual records of Jacques (1970), but adding firm to firm mobility and categories. In principle, the best vehicle would be employers' total reports (e.g., E.J.C. (U.S.) as in Frey (1965)). It seems that the cost would be a multiple of the order of 10 of present E.J.C. survey costs. While the memory difficulties of respondents would be eliminated, data quality would not necessarily be high (see above). Further steps could be defined only as experience is gained.

Such large expenses may seem less forbidding if viewed in the context of the costs of such events as the surprise and dislocation created by the sudden transition from a shortage to an excess of engineers recently, the uncertainty about a possible reversal of this situation, the implicit costs of educating for improbable careers—and if one weighs the human damage being done in the absence of fuller knowledge.

Table 1. Significant departure of sample medians from an ideal model population median, in dollars (based on A.P.E.O. 1971 Survey, Hastings [1972])

	1965 Graduates						*1955 Graduates*						*1945 Graduates*					
Level of significance	0·10		0·05		0·01		0·10		0·05		0·01		0·10		0·05		0·01	
Sample difference	High	Low	High	Low	High	Low	High	Low	High	Low	High	Low	High	Low	High	Low	High	Low
Sample size																		
5	4450	1950	5290	2320	6960	3050	8830	4600	10500	3850	13800	6000	11000	4800	13000	5600	17000	7000
7	2580		3060		4030		5100		6050		7970		630		7490		9850	
9	1920		2275		2950		3740		4430		5840		4600		5440		7200	
11	1580		1880		2470		3180		3780		4970		3860		4580		6030	
16	1150	800	1365	1000	1800	1300	2280	1650	2700	1950	3560	2500	2830	2025	3340	2400	4400	3160
25	825		480		1290		1630		1940		2550		2020		2400		3160	
36	650		770		1015		1285		1525		2050		1590		1885		2480	
49	560	500	665	600	875	750	1110	950	1320	1150	1730	1500	1370	1170	1530	1420	2140	1850
+81	410		490		645		820		970		1280		1010		1200		1580	
144	325		390		510		640		760		1040		790		940		1240	
900	115		140		180	176	230		270		360		280		330		440	425
1600	85		100		135	132	170		200		265		210		250		330	320
3600	60		70		90		115		135		180		140		170		220	
6400	40		50		70		85		100		130		105		120		165	
10000	35		40		55		70		80		105		80		100		130	
25600	20		25		35		40		50		65		50		60		80	

Bibliography

ARROW, K.J., ALCHIAN, A.A. and CAPRON, W.M., 1958, *An economic analysis of the market for scientists and engineers*, Rand RM-2190-RC.

ARROW, K.J., and CAPRON, W.M., 1959, Dynamic shortages and price rises: The engineer-scientist case. *Qu. Journal Econ.*, 292–308.

ATKINSON, A.G., BARNES, K.J. and RICHARDSON, E., 1970, *Canada's Highly Qualified Manpower Resources*, Research Branch, Dept. Manpower and Immigration (Ottawa: Information Canada).

BLANK, D.M., and STIGLER, G.J., 1957, *The Demand and Supply of Scientific Personnel* (New York: National Bureau of Economic Research).

BURKE, F.E., 1965a, Measures of demand and utilization. Mimeo, Association of Professional Engineers of Ontario.

BURKE, F.E., 1965b, Are salary surveys useful? *Professional Eng. and Eng. Digest*, March.

BURKE, F.E., 1970, Some statistics on Canadian university trained manpower, Mimeo, Dept. Management Sciences, University of Waterloo.

C.P.S., 1973, 1973 Salary survey, Robert F. Linden (Ed.), *Computer Magazine*, **4**, 4.

DODGE, D.A., 1971, *Structure of Earnings of Professional Engineers in Ontario* (Toronto: Assoc. Prof. Engs. Ontario).

FOLK, N., 1970, *The shortage of scientists and engineers* (Lexington: D.C. Heath & Co.).

FREY, C., 1965, Engineers incomes. *International Science and Technology*, Feb.

HASTINGS, W.W., 1971, Annual Salary Survey—1970. *Prof. Eng. and Eng. Digest.*

HASTINGS, W.W., 1972, Annual Salary Survey—1972. *Prof. Eng. and Eng. Digest.*

HASTINGS, W.W., 1973, Annual Salary Survey—1973. *Prof. Eng. and Eng. Digest.*

JAQUES, E., 1970, *Equitable Payment*, 2nd ed. (London: Heineman).

MANDELBROT, K. 1968, Stable distribution properties. *Amer. Statistical Assoc. Journal*, Sept.

MANDELBROT, K. 1972, Statistical methodology. *Annals of Econ. and Social Measurement*, **1**, 3, July.
PERUCCI, C.C., 1969, In: Perucci, R. and Gerstl, J.E., (Eds.), *The Engineers and the Social System* (New York: Wiley).
ROSENBLUTH, G., 1961, Salaries of engineers and scientists. In: *Conference on Statistics 1960* (Toronto University Press).
SHOCKLEY, W., 1957, Statistics on productivity in research laboratories. *Proceedings, Instit. Radio Engs.*, **45**, 249.
TOWLER, F.H., 1965, The status of the professional engineer. *Chartered Mechanical Eng.* (London), Oct., p. 512.

Dr. Richard V.L. Cooper who took his Ph.D. (1971) under Arnold Zellner and Milton Friedman at the University of Chicago, joined The Rand Corporation's Economics Department in 1971. Before assuming direction of Rand's military manpower research, he worked on problems associated with the management of the Air Force Officer Corps, the effects of removing procurement restrictions on foreign development assistance, and hospital costliness. He teaches econometrics and monetary theory part-time at the University of California at Los Angeles and at Santa Barbara, and at the Rand Graduate Institute for Policy Studies. He is also a consultant to the California Hospital Association.

Charles Robert Roll, Jr. is a Ph.D. candidate at Harvard University and is currently working on military manpower and the Chinese economy at The Rand Corporation, Santa Monica, California.

The allocation of military resources: implications for capital–labour substitution

R. V. L. Cooper and C. R. Roll, Jr.*

I. Introduction

The advent of a volunteer armed force, rising manpower costs and tight defence budgets have all served to make military manpower one of the most important issues in defence planning and budgeting. Manpower costs have risen dramatically in recent years, both in total dollars and in their share of the U.S. defence budget. For example, personnel related costs for defence increased by 100% between 1962 and 1972; in 1962, manpower costs constituted 43% of the total U.S. defence budget; the 1972 figure is 54%† Further, manpower costs are expected to continue to increase, while the total U.S. defence budget is expected to stay roughly constant in real terms for the foreseeable future.‡

These trends have focused attention on the possible alternatives for reducing manpower costs. Manpower planners have traditionally taken manpower requirements as given and have therefore directed their efforts toward more efficient methods for achieving the 'desired' enlistments and re-enlistments.

* The authors are senior members of the research staff at The Rand Corporation in Santa Monica, California. This study has been funded by the Human Resources Research Office of the Defense Advanced Research Projects Agency (A.R.P.A.) as part of an ongoing research programme dealing with Department of Defense Manpower problems. The authors are indebted to A. Alexander, D.S.C. Chu, W. Oi, R. Shishko, J.P. White and C. Wolf, Jr. for helpful comments and suggestions. Any remaining errors are, of course, the responsibility of the authors.

† *Budget of the U.S. Government, Fiscal Year 1972; Budget of the U.S. Government, Fiscal Year 1962.*

‡ Similar trends have been witnessed in much of Western Europe. Between 1962 and 1972 personnel expenditures (and their share of the defence budgets) changed as follows: Italy, from 216 billion lire (30%) to 1,061 billion lire (57%); West Germany, from 4,161 million DM (27%) to 11,236 million DM (46%); Great Britain, from £997 million (51%) to £1,387 million (49%); and France, from 10,370 Fr million (54%) to 16,683 Fr million (47%).

See *Atti Interni* (1963); *Atti Parlamentari* (1972); *Budget of the U.S. Government* (1962, 1972); *Le Budget de 1962, Le Budget de 1972, Statement on Defence, 1962; Statement on Defense Estimates, 1972; White Paper 1970 . . .; White Paper 1971/1972. . . .*

However, the costliness of these options has recently motivated defence planners to consider substituting other, less expensive inputs for manpower. In particular, the notion of substituting non-labour inputs (i.e., capital) for labour in the military has generated considerable interest. The substitution of a fork-lift truck for warehousemen in a base depot is an example. Of course, the substitution between capital and labour is not one-sided: additional men can be used to replace machines.

Besides the pressure from increased military wages, the substitution of capital for labour is encouraged by the type of technological innovations that the American economy has traditionally produced. For a variety of reasons, the direction of innovative activity in the United States has tended to favour inventions that permit the substitution of capital for labour. The most frequently cited examples involve the automation of activities formerly performed by hand, not only for consumer items (e.g., washing machines), but also for industrial activity (e.g., computer-controlled lathes). These innovations are frequently adaptable to military use—in fact, some have been the product of military research and development.

Pressed on the one hand by rising manpower costs and lured on the other by labour-saving technical change, the obvious solution may seem to be the substitution of capital for labour in performing military missions. Unfortunately, the issue is not that straightforward. First, and perhaps most important, we must be concerned not only with the cost of labour but also with the *cost of capital.*

Second, as educational levels advance, training technologies improve, and technical innovations make labour more productive, the quality of military manpower rises. In such a situation, productivity increases may outstrip wage increases, and the rational policy might be to substitute labour for capital—i.e., more (or more highly skilled) men and less (or simpler) equipment. Third, as military wages have increased, so have civilian wages risen—but not as much. The substitution of civilian personnel for uniformed personnel must therefore be considered as well as the substitution of capital for labour. The civilianization of kitchen duties is a case in point. Finally, as wages have risen in general, wages for skilled personnel and unskilled personnel have not increased in the same proportions. As a result, the substitution of unskilled labour, or unskilled labour and capital, for skilled labour must also be examined. The replacement of highly skilled aircraft maintenance technicians by less skilled personnel and replaceable (rather than 'repairable') parts serves as an example.

To properly address these issues, an analytic framework is required. The issues put forth here all relate to the allocation of military resources among various inputs:

Capital and labour.
Military and civilian labour.
Skilled and unskilled labour.

The framework must be sufficiently general to encompass this spectrum of issues, but the same time it must be specific enough to provide guidelines to the actual allocation of resources among these inputs.

In addition to a conceptual framework, the trends mentioned earlier, such as rising manpower costs, should be placed into proper perspective. For example, although both labour and capital costs have risen, which has risen more?

Only then can we hope to establish an appropriate set of policies to deal with the allocation of scarce military resources.

This paper presents, first, a conceptual framework for analysing the efficient allocation of defence resources. Such a framework is necessary for the development of guidelines for more efficient management of military capital and manpower. Second, to put increases in military compensation and procurement costs into the proper perspective, we examine the historical trends in the cost of labour and the cost of capital. These trends can then be used to focus on the possible opportunities for savings.

Our broad purpose is to motivate defence planners to make input cost considerations an integral part of force planning. In each of the Services and in the Office of the Secretary of Defence (O.S.D.), separate organizational entities determine the amount of manpower required (manpower) and how those requirements are to be filled (personnel). As a result of this distinction, manpower costs seldom enter as a criterion for determining the structure of the military force. Only when the individual requirements become aggregated into total Service budgets do planners begin to worry about costs. However, the lack of visibility of costs at the initial planning level results in gross adjustments that cut force structure rather than reallocate resources. To ensure efficient allocation of resources, it is essential to consider costs of inputs in the early stages of force planning.

II. Conceptual framework for military resource allocation

The concept of the *production function* offers a useful analytic device for investigating the conditions for efficient allocation of military resources. In particular, guidelines for efficient manpower utilization can be developed from a careful analysis of the relationships between military inputs and outputs. These guidelines permit us to determine the importance of changes in the prices of inputs and how the military should respond to these changes.

The production function and the optimum allocation of resources

The technological relationship between inputs and outputs is given by the production function—that is, the production function specifies the amount of output resulting from each alternative combination of inputs.* In its simplest form, the production function is commonly written in terms of primary (versus intermediate) inputs. The two-factor production function—with capital and labour as inputs—is a useful representation of the military production process.

The general two-factor production function may be given algebraically as

$$Q=f(K, L) \tag{1}$$

where $Q=$ amount of output produced,
$K=$ amount of capital input, and
$L=$ amount of labour input.†

* For a more thorough discussion of the issues related to the production function, see Samuelson (1947) and Solow (1955–1956).

† In a less aggregated version, the production function could be written in terms of several different types of labour and capital inputs:

$$Q=f(K_1,\ldots,K_n;\ L_1,\ldots,L_m), \tag{1a}$$

where $K_i=i$th type of capital input, $i=1,\ldots,n$,
$L_i=i$th type of labour input, $i=1,\ldots,m$.

The military planner may wish to consider the tradeoffs between highly skilled maintenance personnel and less highly skilled (and, hence, less costly) maintenance personnel. Such an examination follows easily from equation (1a).

Figure 1. A Hypothetical Production Function

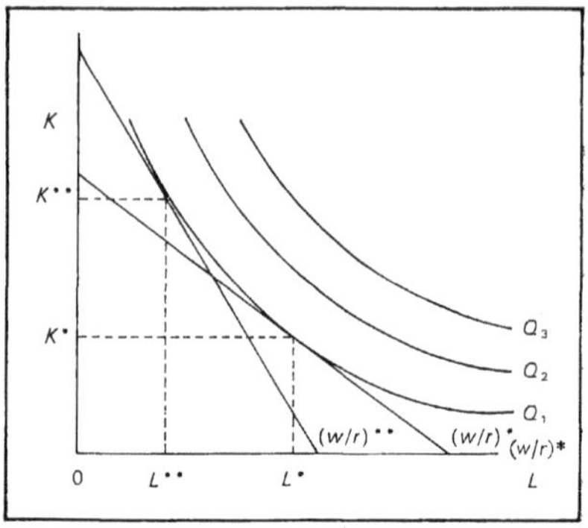

The production function in equation (1) may be represented graphically as in Figure 1. Each of the curved lines in the (K, L) plane is an isoquant—that is, it represents a fixed level of output. Each isoquant shows the various combinations of the two inputs capable of producing the given output. The slope of the isoquant measures the rate at which capital and labour can be substituted for one another. Therefore, the curvature of the isoquants in Figure 1 has the intuitively appealing notion that as less and less of one input is used, it becomes increasingly difficult to further substitute for that input.

The production function, by itself, does not provide guidelines for the allocation of resources; it simply identifies the alternative combinations of technologically feasible inputs that achieve a given amount of output. Instead, guidelines for the efficient allocation of resources are the result of putting the production function into a cost framework. For a given budget, the optimal allocation is the combination of capital and labour that maximizes output.*

In the two input-model, the total cost of using any combination of inputs can be written:

$$C = rK + wL$$

where C = total cost,
w = cost (per unit) of labour services, and
r = cost (per unit) of capital services.

In the simplest case, the cost per unit of labour services is just the wage rate. That is, to purchase a unit of labour services a firm must pay the prevailing wage rate for those services. Although the current wage rate may be a reasonably good approximation of the cost of labour for most private firms, it is not adequate for the military. The cost of labour services to the military includes training costs, payments in kind (e.g., medical benefits), and substantial retirements benefits as well as current wages. Therefore, a better approximation of the true wage rate for the military may be total personnel costs (including all of the above items) divided by the amount of labour services used by the military.

The cost of capital is somewhat more elusive. Further, the issue concerning the cost of capital has been confused considerably by the recent furor over military procurement cost overruns. This is not to say that they are unimportant, rather, the cost of capital includes more than just the cost of procurement.

* It can be shown that the case of minimizing cost for a given output generates equivalent results.

The cost of capital means what would have to be spent to purchase a given amount of *capital services*, not what would have to be spent to purchase a piece of equipment. This distinction is important since capital renders services for many time periods, but procurement of a given piece of equipment occurs in only one period. It is this lack of coincidence between the time periods that causes the difficulty.* Since a piece of equipment is not entirely used during the production process, the costs of using that equipment should reflect the costs of purchasing the services of that equipment, not the total cost of the equipment itself.

An alternative way of viewing the cost of capital is to think of it as what would have to be spent to 'rent' a unit of capital. As procurement costs increase the cost of capital services increases, since a more expensive piece of equipment is being rented. As the cost of borrowing funds (i.e., the interest rate) increases, the rental rate increases, since investors in equipment must be compensated for the forgone interest. As depreciation or obsolescence increases, the rental rate increases, since the cost of the equipment is amortized over a shorter length of time.

Since the military generally does not rent its capital, but instead purchases it, we must impute the rental rate on capital. The cost of capital is given by

$$r_t = (d_t + i_t)P_t, \tag{2}$$

where r_t = cost of capital in period t,
d_t = depreciation rate of capital equipment in period t,
i_t = money cost of borrowing (i.e., the interest rate) in period t, and
P_t = relative price of capital equipment in period t.

Therefore, it is possible for the 'cost of capital' to fall even when the purchase price is increasing. This can happen if either the depreciation obsolescence rate or the interest rate falls sufficiently. Thus equation (2) indicates that the cost of capital includes more than just procurement costs.

Given the cost of labour (w), the cost of capital (r) and the budget constraint (B), it can be shown that the conditions for optimization are

$$\frac{\partial f/\partial L}{\partial f/\partial K} = \frac{w}{r} \tag{3a}$$

$$B - rK - wL = 0, \tag{3b}$$

where $\partial f/\partial L$ = marginal product of labour, and
$\partial f/\partial K$ = marginal product of capital.

Thus, output is maximized for the budget B when the budget is allocated between capital and labour such that the ratio of the marginal product of labour to the marginal product of capital† equals the ratio of the cost of labour to the cost of capital. Since the ratio of the marginal product of labour to the marginal product of capital is a function of the capital-labour ratio (K/L), the optimal capital–labour ratio satisfies equations (3a, b), as shown by the tangency between the isoquant Q and the budget line $(w/r)^*$ in Figure 1.

* Note that this is not generally a problem with labour services, since labour is usually paid for its services at the time those services are performed.

† This ratio is commonly referred to as the 'technical rate of substitution of capital for labour'.

As the cost of labour services rises relative to the cost of capital services, the capital–labour ratio should be increased by substituting capital for labour. *As a result, we should focus our attention on changes (past and expected) in the cost of labour relative to the cost of capital—not just on compensation and procurement costs.*

Military production function

The production function illustrates the relationships between various combinations of inputs and the resultant outputs. In particular, the production function representation of the alternative ways of providing national defence is a useful abstraction of the military manager's problem. Conceptually, we could write down a production function of the type shown in Figure 1 and then apply the optimization techniques to obtain the least costly combination of military inputs to achieve the specified level of national defence (or, alternatively, to maximize defence effectiveness for a given cost). Unfortunately, in the real world, measurements of national defence outputs and military inputs are not easily made. In addition, the precise meaning of a 'military production function' is not clear.

Since the production function relates quantities of inputs used to quantities of outputs produced, inputs and outputs must be given in terms of measurable quantities. Such quantities may be hard to come by in the case of providing national defence. Perhaps the most difficult conceptual problem is the definition of output. The production function framework presented in the last section generally takes output to be measured in physical units. Yet, how does one define units of national defence? 'National defence' is itself vaguely defined, so that it is virtually impossible to measure national defence output. Therefore, a major task in developing criteria for efficient allocation of military resources involves finding measurable quantities that can serve as proxies for national defence.

One method for dealing with the problem of defining national defence would be to categorize defence according to the various military missions that are part of national defence. That is, national defence can be decomposed into its separate military components.* For example, one might think of the capability to destroy 1,000 tanks in a 90-day Central European war scenario, or the capability to deliver a given amount of bomb tonnage in Southeast Asia, or the capability to provide a given number of surveillance steaming hours in the Mediterranean. Therefore, rather than develop a production function for national defence, we can think of military production functions, where the military production function relates military inputs to military outputs (i.e., the 'military mission'). This can be represented algebraically as:

$$Q=f(M_1, M_2, \ldots, M_n), \tag{4}$$

where Q represents national defence and M_i, $i=1$ to n, represent the n different military missions. Each of these military missions can itself be thought of as a function of the capital and labour in that mission:

$$M_i=g_i(K_i, L_i), \qquad i=1, 2, \ldots, n, \tag{5}$$

where K_i = capital used in the ith mission, and
L_i = labour used in the ith mission.

* Presumably, other factors, such as diplomatic skills, would also be a part of the production of national defence. However, our focus here will be on the military components of national defence.

It can be shown that the optimal allocation of defence resources between capital and labour is achieved when each mission is separately optimized with respect to capital and labour usage, per equations (3a, b).* This enables us to examine the allocation of defence resources to capital and labour by way of the individual military missions. In fact, since the production function for national defence is just the combination of production functions for the specific missions, changes in the allocation of defence resources between capital and labour are a result of changing the allocation within the missions.

The production function given in equation (1) is directly applicable to the design of new military systems, for the designer is explicitly confronted by a vast array of alternative configurations of the system, each of which may embody different amounts of capital and labour. For example, in the case of a new naval vessel of some specified capability, subsystems for the ship (including support on shore) can each be designed to incorporate different levels of automation (capital intensity). Therefore, the designer faces the type of capital–labour tradeoffs shown in Figure 1 for the total ship, since the ship is just the sum of the various subsystems—each of which embodies different amounts of capital and labour. The optimum configuration is that for which the capital–labour ratio satisfies equation (3a). In other words, the least-cost solution is obtained when the isoquant in Figure 1 is tangent to the budget line.

The production function is also applicable to a broader range of problems—*the allocation of military resources for existing systems.* Generally, the military uses a variety of different systems in the course of fulfilling a specified mission. Further, different combinations of these systems can be used in the performance of a mission. Since these existing systems incorporate different capital–labour ratios, the capital–labour ratio for the mission can be changed implicitly by explicitly altering the mix of systems used. That is, even if each system has a fixed capital–labour ratio, the usage of capital and labour in the mission can be altered by altering the mix of systems. To illustrate this, consider a hypothetical antitank mission in a 90-day Central European scenario. The mission may be performed by various combinations of close air support, helicopters, tanks, artillery and infantry, among others. Each of these systems most likely embodies a different capital–labour ratio. The capital–labour ratio for the mission can be altered by using different combinations of these systems, even though the capital–labour ratio for each system might be fixed.

Given the production function for the mission, the optimal allocation of that mission's resources between capital and labour is determined by equations (3a, b). Therefore, the mission commander should select the capital–labour ratio for which the ratio of the marginal product of that mission's labour to the marginal product of that mission's capital equals the ratio of the cost of labour to the cost of capital.

Responding to changes in prices, technology and desired output

The preceding discussion has centred on the allocation of military resources between capital and labour for given factor prices, technology, and desired

* The major condition that must be satisfied for this result to hold is that the missions must be aggregated such that the contribution of the capital and labour of one mission to the output of all others must be small. For example, if daytime and night-time reconnaissance were managed as separate missions, then each mission commander would most likely require separate aircraft. However, since the same aircraft could be used for both missions (only requiring different cameras), the rule of aggregation suggests that these two activities would be managed as one mission.

military output. How should the military respond when some or all of these change?

The general response to a change in *relative* factor prices can be seen from a closer examination of equation (3a). Cost is minimized for a specified level of output when the technical rate of substitution of capital for labour equals the ratio of the cost of labour to the cost of capital. Since the marginal products of capital and labour are decreasing functions of the amounts of capital and labour used, the technical rate of substitution of capital for labour is in an increasing function of the capital–labour ratio. Therefore, as the ratio of the cost of labour to the cost of capital increases (decreases), the capital–labour ratio should be increased (decreased) such that the technical rate of substitution of capital for labour equals the ratio of the cost of labour to the cost of capital. For example, if the ratio of the cost of labour to the cost of capital increases from $(w/r)^*$ to $(w/r)^{**}$ as in Figure 1, then the optimum capital–labour ratio increases from (K^*/L^*) to (K^{**}/L^{**})—that is, by *substituting* capital for labour.

The above discussion relates to the amounts of physical units of inputs used. That is, if the cost of labour rises relative to the cost of capital, then capital should be substituted for labour—namely, the amount of physical units of capital used should be increased while the amount of physical units of labour used should be decreased. However, the amount of dollars spent on capital and labour, as a function of the ratio of the cost of labour to the cost of capital depends on the elasticity of substitution of capital for labour.† For example, if the elasticity of substitution of capital for labour is greater (less) than one, the share of the budget spent on labour will increase (decrease) with a rise in the ratio of the cost of labour to the cost of capital. Thus, the share of the budget allocated to labour could actually increase with a rise in relative cost of labour, even though fewer units of labour would be used. It is therefore misleading to focus solely on the share of the budget allotted to various inputs. Instead, our attention should be directed toward the relative costs of capital and labour and the elasticity of substitution of capital for labour.

Second, consider the relationship between the optimum capital–labour ratio and technological innovation. For a given ratio of the cost of labour to the cost of capital, the optimum capital–labour ratio increases with more labour-saving technological innovation, and conversely for capital-saving innovation. Since the American economy has tended to produce capital-intensive (labour-saving) technological innovations, we should expect the optimum capital–labour ratio to increase over time, other things equal.

Finally, how is the optimum capital–labour ratio related to the level of output? That is, should a larger force be more capital intensive or labour intensive than a smaller force? The answer depends on both the ratio of the cost of labour to the cost of capital and the shape of the isoquants at different

† The elasticity of substitution of capital for labour is defined along the production function isoquant as the percentage increase in the capital–labour ratio resulting from a percentage increase in the ratio of the marginal product of labour to the marginal product of capital. If labour and capital are paid their marginal products (e.g., if w and r equal the marginal product of labour and capital, respectively), then the elasticity of substitution of capital for labour is given by:

$$\epsilon = \frac{\Delta(K/L)}{K/L} \frac{\Delta(w/r)}{w/r}.$$

For example, if the efficient capital–labour ratio changes by one per cent as a result of a one per cent change in ratio of the cost of labour to the cost of capital, then the elasticity of substitution equals one.

levels of output. In most analyses, the ratio of the cost of labour to the cost of capital is assumed to be insensitive to the level of output. However, this is not likely to be the case for the military since the supply of capital goods to the military is likely to be much more elastic than the supply of labour to the military. In other words, as the military seeks to purchase both more labour and more capital (to produce a greater military capability), the increased wage rate it will have to pay in order to attract sufficient numbers of additional volunteers is likely to be much larger than the higher price it has to pay for its increased capital purchases. Therefore, the wage-rental rate would be expected to increase for higher levels of output. On the other hand, we know little about the shape of the isoquants for different levels of output. If we assume that the shape of the isoquants is the same at different levels of output, then the optimum capital–labour ratio is likely to be larger for greater levels of military capability, since the ratio of the cost of labour to the cost of capital increases for larger amounts of output.

The production function as a tool for analysis

The analytic framework presented here provides a useful method for examining the issues related to the allocation of military resources among various inputs. In particular, the following have been established:

(1) Military capability is directly related to the inputs used and, therefore, efficient management of military resources is achieved by choosing appropriate combinations of those inputs.
(2) The classification of inputs into two broad categories—capital and labour—is a useful device for examining alternative responses to such changes as rising manpower costs or rising procurement costs.
(3) The relevant costs are the cost per unit of capital services and the cost per unit of labour services. The cost of capital includes not only procurement costs but also the cost of borrowing funds and depreciation or obsolescence costs. The cost of labour to the military includes training costs, payments in kind, etc. as well as wage costs.
(4) The optimum allocation of military resources between capital and labour is then a function of the relative costs of labour and capital. Thus, the optimum capital–labour ratio is an increasing function of the ratio of the cost of labour to the cost of capital.

To determine the appropriate allocation of military resources among inputs, we should focus our attention on changes in the relative prices of labour and capital and on the opportunities for substitution.

The aggregate production function framework developed earlier enables us to examine the evidence on capital and labour costs in a systematic manner and to prescribe general guidelines for more efficient management of defence resources. For example, both manpower costs and capital procurement costs have been rising. If the cost of labour has risen more than the cost of capital, then the appropriate response is to substitute capital for labour, not simply to cut the force size.

III. The costs of military capital and labour: some empirical evidence

Military managers have been confronted with various, and possibly conflicting, pieces of information with respect to the allocation of military resources. For example, the cost of labour to the military has risen markedly in recent years, but so has the cost of military procurement.

A general methodology for examining this allocation was developed in Section II. It was shown that 'military capability' may be thought of in terms of the collection of military missions. Since the product of each mission is a function of the inputs used, 'national defence' (the *aggregate* military production function) may be constructed in terms of the aggregate amounts of these inputs. It was then suggested that the classification of inputs into two categories—capital and labour—offers a useful conceptual tool for the military manager. In other words, an aggregate military production function may be written in terms of the total amounts of capital and labour used in the military. Therefore, if military resources are to be optimally allocated between capital and labour, the capital–labour ratio for the military should be an increasing function of the ratio of cost of labour to the cost of capital.

This framework indicates that the major cost variable of concern to the military manager is the ratio of the cost of labour to the cost of capital, not just manpower costs and procurement costs. Given the considerable confusion that has surrounded the issue of the costs of capital and labour, the true costs of these inputs must be identified to ensure the maximum effectiveness from scarce defence resources.

The cost of capital is an elusive concept that must be imputed since the Department of Defence (D.o.D.) does not rent the services of capital equipment from year to year, but instead purchases its equipment. The method for imputing the cost of capital facing D.o.D. was given by equation (2) and is reproduced here:*

$$r_t = (d_t + i_t)P_t, \tag{6}$$

where r_t = cost of capital in period t,
d_t = the rate at which the capital stock depreciates in period t,
i_t = the money cost of borrowing in period t, and
P_t = relative price index of military procurement in period t.

Equation (6) simply says that the cost of utilizing a dollar of capital equipment in year t (expressed relative to some base year) is a function of the money cost to the government of borrowing, the rate of depreciation, and the rate of inflation in the prices of capital goods. However, each of these components of the cost of capital requires both explanation and estimation.

Our estimate of r_t is the rate of interest on three- to five-year government bonds. This rate of interest is the nominal money cost to the government of long term borrowing in any given year. Our estimate of P_t is the wholesale price index of machinery and equipment published by the Bureau of Labour Statistics (B.L.S.). This index is obviously not a perfect price index for the military sector. However, since no military price index is available, we used this index because we assumed it most closely approximated changes in the prices of

* This definition of the cost of capital measures the cost to D.o.D., and not necessarily the cost to society of forgoing a dollar's worth of consumption or investment in the private sector. There are various concepts that have been proposed to measure the opportunity cost of investing in the public sector. These measures can differ from our definition of the cost of capital. In this paper we have not addressed the issues of society's efficiency versus D.o.D.'s efficiency but have simply undertaken an examination of the factor costs that would influence internal D.o.D. efficiency.

military goods. Other possible price indexes tend to be highly correlated with the machinery and equipment price index but also do not seem to be as suitable for estimating the prices of military goods.

Our estimate of the rate of depreciation is derived from estimates of the military capital stock in 1967 dollars and U.S. budget data on procurement expenditures deflated to constant 1967 dollars with the above B.L.S. wholesale price index used as the deflator.* For each year our estimate of the rate of depreciation was calculated as the following:†

$$\delta_t = 1 - (K_t - I_t)/K_{t-1}$$

where δ_t = the depreciation rate estimate for d_t,
K_t, K_{t-1} = are estimates of the capital stock in years t and $t-1$, and
I_t = the amount spent on procurement.

The details on the various components of the cost of capital together with the actual calculation of the cost of capital are presented in Table 1. With the

Table 1. Cost-of-capital index

Fiscal Year	*Rate of Depreciation*	*Rate of Interest on 3–5 Year Govt. Bonds*	*Price Index (1967 = 100)*	*Cost of Capital*
	(1)	(2)	(3)	(4)
1972	0·083	0·058	119	142
1971	0·117	0·066	115	178
1970	0·114	0·071	111	174
1969	0·121	0·062	107	166
1968	0·115	0·053	103	147
1967	0·067	0·051	100	100
1966	0·071	0·047	97	97
1965	0·069	0·041	95	89
1964	0·096	0·039	94	108
1963	0·097	0·036	94	106
1962	0·084	0·036	93	95
1961	0·102	0·038	93	110
1960	0·091	0·042	93	105
1959	0·144	0·036	92	140
1958	0·104	0·033	90	104
1957	0·088	0·034	86	89
1956	0·108	0·028	80	92

Sources: Col. (1): See text. Col. (2): ***Economic Report of the President***, January 1973, p. 260 (Adjusted to Fiscal Year basis by averaging two adjacent calendar years). Col. (3): U.S. Department of Commerce, Office of Business Economics, *1971 Business Statistics*, Washington, 1971, p. U.S. Department of Commerce, *Survey of Current Business*, Vol. 53, No. 4 (April 1973), p. S-9. Col. (4): Col. (1) + Col. (2) times Vol. (3) with 1967 = 100.

* Details of the capital stock estimate may be found in Cooper and Roll (1973) and with slightly revised figures in a forthcoming paper by the authors. The basic estimating procedure which was followed was to take annual data from *Real and Personal Property of the Department of Defence* and adjust these inventory data on military equipment in use, and supply system inventories for (1) changes in coverage and (2) the valuation of military equipment in use at acquisition cost and thus with a mixture of vintages of historical prices. These results are estimates; nevertheless, we feel that they give a reasonably accurate picture of the year-to-year changes in the level of the military capital stock. We have focused on military equipment; military construction and research and developments are not included.

† Derived from the relationship between the capital stock in two adjacent years and the level of investment:

$$K_t = (1 - \delta_t)K_{t-1} + I_t.$$

exception of the year 1959 the series for the rate of depreciation is entirely reasonable. As we move into the war period the cost of capital rises because both the rate of depreciation (destruction) and the rate of inflation increase. The general rise in the interest rate is a function of both monetary policies designed to check the rate of inflation and expectations about further price inflation. Nevertheless, this increases the money cost of capital to the government.

The cost of labour is conceptually somewhat simpler than the cost of capital as far as estimation procedures are involved. We define the cost of labour—the cost of military labour—as the average cost per effective military labour unit. We have taken the total U.S. Budget category (Military Pay and Allowances) for the active duty force and divided this by an estimate of effective labour units.* Our focus is entirely on active duty personnel; we have excluded reservists and their associated costs. The measure of effective labour units was derived by weighting the number of personnel in each age cohort (from 17 to 55) by the relative wage of white fully employed males in the same cohort for male military personnel. Female military personnel were weighted by the relative wages of white high school and college graduates for officers and enlisted women, respectively.†

To accurately reflect effective labour units, the yearend numbers of personnel engaged in training were subtracted from the total labour force figure. The result was then averaged and divided into the total labour cost and the figure expressed in terms of a 1967 base as shown in Table 2. This calculation effectively accounts for training costs. Most training costs are personnel related, and the salaries and allowances of the trainers are the bulk of the costs. By removing these individuals from the denominator we have counted the cost of training.

Figure 2a draws together the calculations of Tables 1 and 2 to present our estimate of the trend in the cost of labour relative to the cost of capital. There are two striking features evident in Figure 2a. First, the series is not a nice, smooth curve. The nature of our cost of capital is such that the continuous process of depreciation is divided into discrete time periods. However, our interest is not in the estimate for any particular year but in the broad trend that may be apparent from the data. Second, and more obvious, is the decline in the ratio during the years 1968 and 1971. As we have noted above, the cost of capital increases considerably during this period, primarily because of the shift in the rate of depreciation during the war. Tables 1 and 2 make it quite clear that costs of both labour and capital are rising over this period, but that the cost of labour did not rise in proportion to the cost of capital. However, if we ignore the heavy war years and concentrate on what may be termed the peace-

* Our measure of average labour costs does not include retirement costs or medical costs. The true measurement of retirement involves imputing the average discounted present value of retirement benefits (estimated over length of service), assigning portions to service years, and adjusting for the probability of retention. That is, we need to compute the (expected) retirement costs for today's force, not current retirement expenditures. Very rough estimates of these numbers indicate that they vary in a fashion similar to average labour costs. The same is true of medical costs. The lack of these two items makes our index of labour costs less than all-inclusive; nevertheless, these costs are closely linked to wages, and thus the presentation of average labour costs in index number form would tend to correct for the lack of medical and retirement costs because the proportionality factor would cancel out in both the numerator and the denominator.

† Further details of the calculations and sources of data may be found in Cooper and Roll (1973), and in a forthcoming paper by the authors.

Table 2. Index of the average cost of labour (1967 = 100)

Fiscal year	*Index of average labour cost*
1972	163
1971	140
1970	128
1969	111
1968	103
1967	100
1966	93
1965	84
1964	81
1963	73
1962	83
1961	82
1960	79
1959	75
1958	72
1957	70
1956	71

Source: See text.

time trend in costs, the long-term trend in the ratio of the cost of labour to the cost of capital has been increasing.† Such a measure is depicted in Figure 2b. The cost of capital underlying the index of relative costs indicated in Figure 2b is calculated using the average peacetime rate of depreciation of about 9·3 per cent, instead of the rate of depreciation calculated for each year in Table 1. The upward trend in the cost of labour relative to our estimate of the peacetime cost of capital is unmistakable.

The evidence we have presented above indicates that the current interest in manpower costs is warranted. Despite past concern over the price of capital goods and our finding that capital costs have indeed increased, *the price of capital has fallen relative to the price of labour.*

What trends are likely in the near future? It is impossible to use historical data and assumptions to project future trends since the abolition of the draft and the move to the all-volunteer force is a large institutional change and produces many uncertainties with respect to the labour supply. It does not seem unreasonable, however, to advance the speculation that the immediate future will see a further increase in the cost of labour relative to the cost of capital. If the cost of capital rises with inflation and there are no large changes in the depreciation rate or interest rate, then the adjustment in terms of the

† A method of examining the hypothesis that the ratio of the cost of labour to the cost of capital has increased over time is to regress the index of relative costs on time and test whether the coefficient on time is significantly greater than zero. The problem with this approach is that the cost of capital shifts up during the war years because the rate of depreciation shifts up. To control for this effect a dummy variable can be inserted in the regression for the war years. The results of the regression are presented below.

$$\text{C.C.L.} = 61{\cdot}32 - \underset{(-4{\cdot}44)}{29{\cdot}70^{*}D} + \underset{(4{\cdot}86)}{2{\cdot}82^{*}T} \quad R^2 = 0{\cdot}66, \quad n = 17$$

C.C.L. = cost of labour/cost of capital ratio: $D = 1$ in 1968, 69, 70, 71 and zero otherwise; T = time (1 = 1956, 2 = 1957, . . ., 17 = 1972). t statistics in parentheses. * significantly different from zero at 99%.

The coefficient on time is significantly greater than zero at the 99% level of significance, confirming the hypothesis that the peacetime cost of capital has decreased relative to the cost of labour.

Figure 2. Indexes of the Cost of Labor Relative to the Costs of Capital (1967 = 100).

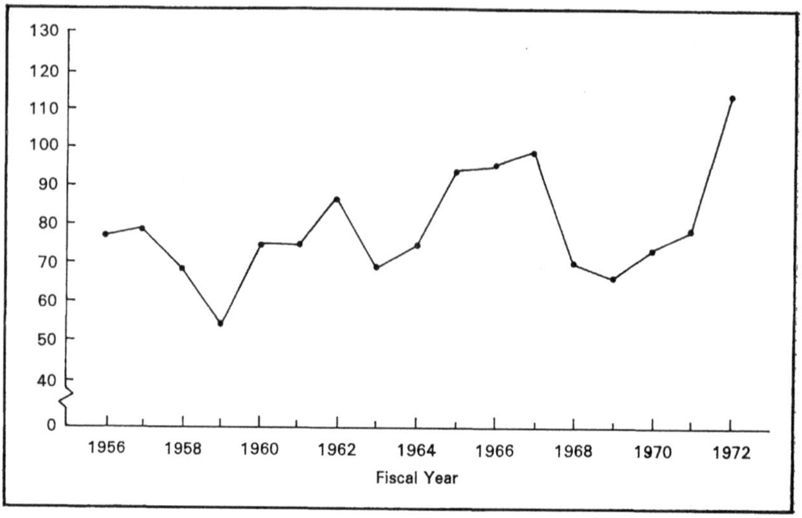

military wages necessary to compete with the civilian sector would almost certainly seem to lead to an increase in the price of labour relative to the price of capital. Once this adjustment process is over we could expect changes in the relative price to match (more or less) those changes occurring in the civilian economy. Thus, we can probably expect to see further relative increases in the cost of labour during the near future before a general levelling off in the relative costs of capital and labour.

IV. Implications for resource management

We have identified the empirical course of the past (and the immediately expected) upward trend in the cost of labour relative to the cost of capital. The questions to ask, then, become those of adjusting to changes in prices, defining the opportunities for the substitution of capital and labour, and erecting organizational structures for carrying out the substitution possibilities. There are, of course, alternative ways of answering these questions, and we present some of these alternatives below.

Adjusting to changing relative prices

In our previous discussion we presented the changes in input usage in response to changes in relative input prices as if the process were instantaneous. Such an analogy may be valid for very small firms with limited amounts of capital, but it is obviously not correct for such a large institution as the Department of Defence. The manner in which the Department of Defence can respond to a rise in the cost of labour is, in fact, two-fold and may be divided into the short-run and the long-run response.

In the short run, the only variable input is labour. Conditions for efficiency suggest that the amount of labour employed should be reduced in response to a relative increase in the cost of labour. With the capital stock fixed, this seems to imply a lower level of output. However, military capability need not be reduced if the decrease in the amount of labour employed occurs in the maintenance of capital equipment, rather than in the use of the equipment. Of course, the capital would be used up more rapidly, which is one way of substituting capital for labour. At the same time, this increases the cost of capital because it increases the rate of depreciation. Consequently, if one desires to maintain the same level of capability, the process of adjustment to the rising cost of labour entails the raising of the cost of capital. This effect is due to the endogenous nature of the rate of depreciation.

If we consider the long run, the capital stock can be increased through the procurement process. As older elements of the capital stock are retired, the newer elements that replace them can embody more capital and require less labour. Moreover, new methods of maintenance and operations that employ less labour and more capital can be implemented. Indeed, the principal area that needs exploring is the determination of significant substitution possibilities.

Our initial impression of the capital intensities embodied in the various missions carried out by the Department of Defence is that the weapons systems themselves are relatively capital intensive when viewed from the mission operations standpoint. There may, of course, still be areas where substitution of capital for labour could take place. For instance, the automation of ship propulsion plants seems to be both feasible and cost effective. However, the major possibilities for extensive substitution of capital for labour probably lie in the weapons support area, including both maintenance and logistics. Weapons systems today are highly sophisticated, and the existing practice of repairing and supplying these systems requires vast amounts of manpower. An alternative to repairing these systems is to have a large inventory of spare parts on hand and replace, rather than repair, defective components. Inventories are capital goods, and such a procedure not only would increase the stock of capital but also would reduce the labour force. The reduction would come about in two ways. First since replacement rather than repair is carried out, fewer maintenance personnel would be required. Second, replacement would not entail the skill level required by the ability to repair; the average skill level of the force could be less, and fewer effective labour units would be needed. Similarly, there may be substantial opportunities to substitute capital for labour in the logistical support of weapons systems. For example, base depot operations can be automated. Alternatively, technological innovations, such as precision guided munitions (the so-called 'smart bombs'), may require much less manpower for warehousing and supply and are, thus, a form of capital–labour substitution.

Changing the conceptual viewport somewhat, divide the force into two components: front-line and support. The front-line forces require certain levels of support. This derived demand should be restructured toward a higher capital intensity. That is, we should look for alternatives to make the support forces more capital intensive. At the same time, alternatives to substitute the more capital-intensive front-line forces for the more labour-intensive support forces should be explored. The construction of equipment with replaceable parts and the subsequent reduction in maintenance requirements is an example of such a substitution.

Methods for ensuring efficient resource allocation

Military resources are optimally allocated between capital and labour when the technical rate of substitution of capital for labour equals the ratio of the cost of labour to the cost of capital. Moreover, the past and projected increases in the cost of labour relative to the cost of capital suggest that the military should become more capital intensive. The principal questions before us now are:

Do current institutional arrangements promote efficient resource management?

If not, what alternatives might encourage more efficient resource management?

Before answering these questions, we should first consider what is meant by efficient resources allocation over time, particularly with respect to adjustments to changes in the conditions for efficiency. That is, although equations (3a, b) dictate the conditions for efficient resource allocation between capital and labour, there are both short-run and long-run implications for adjusting to changes in input costs. In the short run, the response to changing costs should encourage substitution of resources rather than a lessening of force capability. In the longer run, we should be especially concerned with the general trends in the relative costs and utilization of inputs. That is, since the costs of labour and capital are partly endogenous, we should direct our attention more to the long-run—and anticipated—trends in these costs rather than just to the yearly changes. For example, we have indicated that the ratio of the cost of labour to the cost of capital is expected to remain significantly higher in the peacetime environment of the 1970s than it was in the peacetime environment of the late 1950s and early 1960s. Will current methods of allocating resources motivate a reallocation of resources toward the more capital-intensive force suggested by this change in costs?

There are, in fact, two reasons why the military would not be expected to respond efficiently to changes in the optimum capital–labour ratio. First, the method of budget submission required by Congress results in an asymmetric treatment of capital and labour services. The budget should be structured in terms of the cost of labour and the cost of capital, but it is actually structured in terms of the cost of labour and capital procurement costs. This method of budgeting can result in serious misallocations of funds for capital equipment.

Second, the method for determining manpower utilization in the military tends to promote inefficiencies. In each of the Services and in O.S.D., separate organizational entities are responsible for determining manpower requirements (manpower) and for fulfilling those requirements (personnel). The demand for manpower therefore tends to be constructed independently of personnel costs. Only when individual requirements for manpower and capital are aggregated into total Service budgets is there a general concern for costs. The lack of visibility of costs at the lower planning echelons results in the types of gross adjustments that cut force structure rather than reallocate resources within the given force structure. Methods for avoiding these problems must be developed if D.o.D. is to be expected to allocate resources efficiently. Three possibilities are explored here: (1) centralized military planning; (2) decentralized resource allocation; and (3) civilian contracting.

The military currently uses a method of centralized planning. However, if this method is to result in efficient resource allocation, then manpower planners must be brought into the early stages of force planning, including both the design of new systems and the use of existing systems. That is, we must move away from the input–output type of manning tables encouraged by the separation of manpower 'requirements' and 'personnel' and instead recognize in the early planning stages that there are genuine opportunities to substitute capital for labour, or labour for capital, as conditions for efficiency warrant. Second, and equally important, the budget should be restructured to include the cost of capital, not just procurement costs.

An alternative method of allocating resources is to rely on decentralized decision-making. Under this option, the manager of each military mission would be responsible for allocating his budget so as to maximize output from that mission. If missions are aggregated such that the marginal contribution of additional capital and labour of any one mission to another is relatively small,* then permitting each mission commander to maximize his output will result in a maximization of overall defence output and, hence, the optimum allocation of resources. This option then places the major share of responsibility of resource allocation upon the individual mission commander rather than upon a central planning authority.

An alternative way of carrying out decentralization of resource allocation is to contract for certain services in the civilian economy. This may be particularly appropriate for many support functions with direct counterparts in the civilian sector. The military has made good use of this option, even during wartime, but further use may produce greater efficiencies.

Implications for manpower utilization

The results of Section II provide a conceptual framework for more efficient utilization of military resources. At the same time, the empirical results presented in Section III make it clear that the cost of labour has risen considerably relative to the cost of capital and that alternatives for a more capital intensive military should be explored. In certain cases it may be desirable to develop equipment with throw-away parts, rather than with repairable parts, thus enabling the military to replace highly skilled technicians with less highly skilled—and less costly—individuals. This would have major implications for the types of individuals acquired by the military and their training. In other instances, it may be worthwhile to replace many less skilled individuals with a few highly skilled individuals. In a more aggregate sense, the occupational mix of the military might be substantially altered by moving to a more capital intensive course. It is clear that these shifts would have major effects on the general training base, as well as on the organizational structure of the military. *Since the direction for change is clear, it is essential that manpower planners take an active role in investigating the possible alternatives for more efficient resource utilization.*

Bibliography

ARROW, K.J., CHENERY, H.B., MINHAS, B. and SOLOW, R.M., 1961, Capital-Labour Substitution and Economic Efficiency, *The Review of Economics and Statistics*, **43**, 3, August, pp. 225–250.

Atti Interni, 1963, Disegni di legge, Vol. XXX, dal N. 1901 al N. 2000 (Roma: Tipografia del Senato).

Atti Parlamentari, 1972, Resoconti Stenografici, Delle Sedute Delle, Commissioni Permanenti, Vol. Unico (Roma: Tipografia del Senato).

Budget of the U.S. Government, Fiscal Years 1974, 1972, 1962.

COOPER, R.V.L., and ROLL, C. R., Jr., 1973, Rand's ARPA Manpower Programme: Some Tentative Findings, *Analysts Workshop: Sustaining the Volunteer Force*, O.A.S.D. (M. & R. A.), April 13, 1973.

Economic Report of the President, 1973, Washington, D.C., January.

Le Budget de 1962, Ministere de l'Économie et des Finances, Paris.

Le Budget de 1972, Ministere de l'Économie et des Finances, Paris.

* See footnote, p. 281.

Real and Personal Property of the Department of Defense, O.A.S.D. (Comptroller), Directorate for Information Operations. Annual Reports for FY55 through FY72.

SAMUELSON, P.A., 1947, *Foundations of Economic Analysis* (Harvard University Press).

Selected Manpower Statistics, 1972, Department of Defense, O.A.S.D. (Comptroller), Directorate for Information Operations, April 15.

SOLOW, R.M., 1955–56, The Production Function and the theory of Capital, *Review of Economic Studies*, **XXIII**, 101–108.

Statement on Defence, 1962, The Next Five Years, Presented to Parliament by the Minister of Defence by Command of Her Majesty, February (London: H.M.S.O.).

Statement on Defence Estimates, 1972, Presented to Parliament by the Secretary of State for Defence by Command of Her Majesty, February 1962 (London: H.M.S.O.).

U.S. DEPARTMENT OF COMMERCE, OFFICE OF BUSINESS ECONOMICS, 1971. *Business Statistics*, Washington D.C.

U.S. DEPARTMENT OF COMMERCE, OFFICE OF BUSINESS ECONOMICS, 1973, *Survey of Current Business*, **53**, 4, April.

White Paper 1970 on the Security of the Federal Republic of Germany and on the State of the German Federal Armed Forces, Federal Minister of Defence on behalf of the German Federal Government.

White Paper 1971/1972, The Security of the F.R.G. and the Development of the Federal Armed Forces, 1971, Federal Minister of Defence on behalf of the German Federal Government.

Dr. Uebe did his undergraduate work at Bonn University (1959–64, Diplomvolkswirt) and his graduate work with the University of California at Berkeley (1964–1966, M.S. in operations research) and with the University of Bonn (1966–1969, Ph.D. in economics). At present he is an assistant with Institute of Applied Mathematics Technical University of Munich, and a 'Privatdozent' in economics with the University of Bonn. His research interests are in econometric model building and manpower planning.

3:4

Manpower planning within a major Federal department*

G. Uebe

The paper discusses two related approaches of formal manpower planning, which have been applied within a major German Federal department. Both models rest on a simplified, yet sufficiently detailed description of the department.

I. The framework

1. *The network of jobs*

A minimum objective of the department is to maintain a satisfactory performance of a set of activities, i.e., there is a certain amount of work to be done. These jobs have been classified by a catalogue† and due to this classification they can be analysed as a set of project network activities.

Considering the qualifications a person has to satisfy in order to fulfil satisfactorily a job k, for each job there is only a limited number of predecessor jobs and a limited number of successor jobs (see Figure 1). The total work of the department can be described as a network of jobs (see Figure 2).

Figure 1. Context of present job

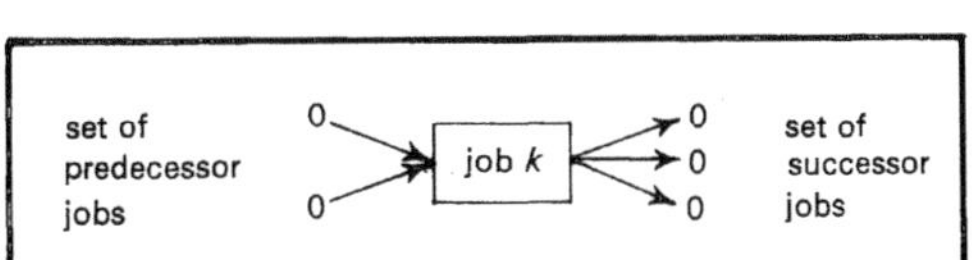

By choosing properly the qualification requirements and by designing the lines of responsibility within the department correspondingly, the total network of jobs of the department can be naturally decomposed into loosely

* A progress report written by the above author reporting on a project on manpower planning with collaborators Prof. Dr. Martin J. Beckmann, Erwin Bihlmayer and Erika Marwitz, all Technische Universität München, Germany.

† For this analysis we assume the catalogue to be given, actually, however, the job classification problem is of paramount importance, see e.g., the papers of the WEMA-symposium. See also the papers of Gagné, Miller, Fleishman and Singleton of this volume.

Figure 2. An example of an office of eight jobs

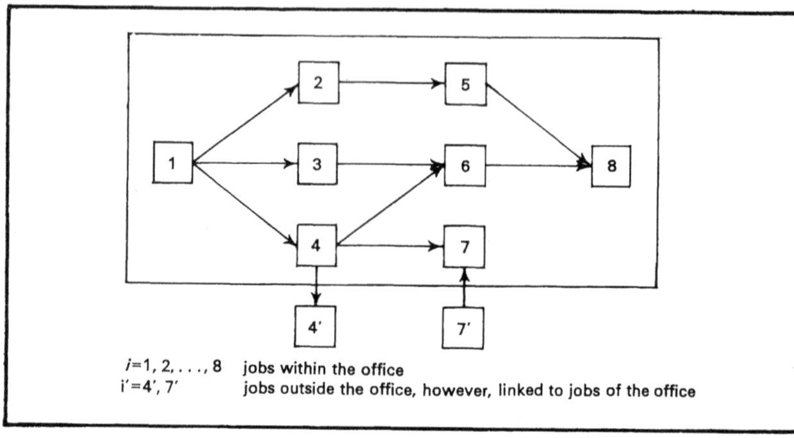

connected subnetworks of offices*† (see Hitch, 1965). Representing the linkage by an incidence matrix (0_{ij}) with

$$0_{ij}=\begin{cases}1 & \text{if a job of office } i \text{ precedes a job of office } j,\\ 0 & \text{otherwise}\end{cases}$$

we have a sparsely occupied matrix such as

Figure 3. An example of eight offices and four agencies

	1	2	3	4	5	6	7	8
1	1	1	1					
2		1	1					
3	1		1					
4				1				
5				1	1			
6						1	1	
7							1	
8								1

Aggregating finally those offices which are related into agencies, each agency is a completely independent network of jobs. (These ideas of aggregation are obviously borrowed from the analysis of equations, see, e.g., Steward, 1973 or Uebe, 1971.)

* These 'offices' do not necessarily agree with the exact institutional set up of the department, but they are used in our analysis.

† Some bureaucratic institutions decompose naturally following the process by which they were set up, see, e.g., the re-shuffling of government agencies among cabinet members. This is not the case here.

2. *The bureaucratic hierarchy*

The hierarchy is defined by a sequence of paylevels (grades) (Figure 4).

Figure 4. A sequence of paylevels of an office

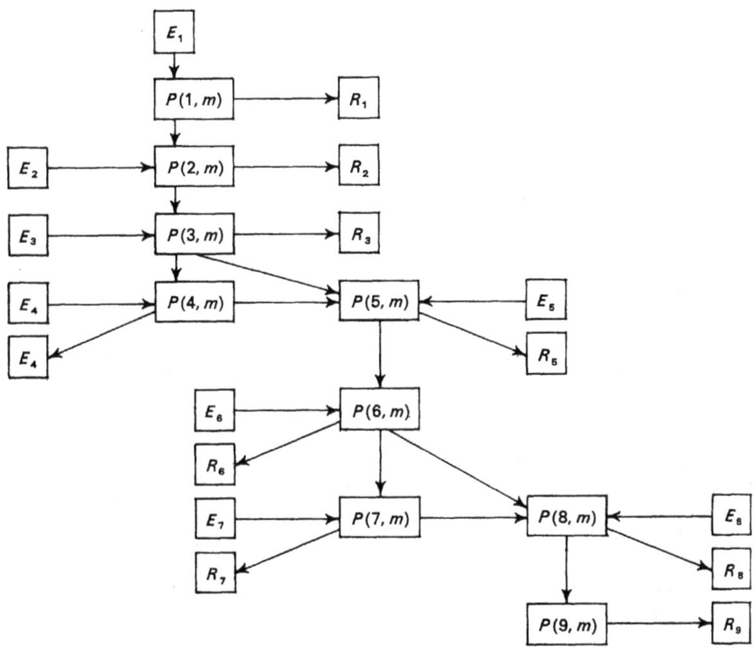

$P(i, m)$=number of position of paylevel i of office m (i=1, 2, . . . , 9)
E'=entry from outside the office
R =retirement, respectively departure for another office

(1) Considering each office separately, there is a fixed hierarchy of paylevels in a unidirectional sequence, i.e., there are no demotions. A person can either stay, or move up, and for the movement up in each case there is only one or two possibilities, i.e., at most one level can be skipped. In addition to the internal movement, there are external links, E and R, people entering and leaving the office.

(2) This scheme is an outline only. Generally there are significant differences among the different offices.

- (i) Not all of those external links exist, e.g., a certain office may have only E_1 and R_9.
- (ii) Not all of those possibilities of promotion may exist, e.g., the link $P(4, .)\rightarrow P(5, .)$ does not exist, i.e., paylevel 4 of that office is a dead end.
- (iii) The hierarchy of a particular office may be truncated from below or above or both, i.e., there may be offices, beginning with $P(1)$ and

ending with $P(5)$; beginning with $P(3)$ and ending with $P(9)$; and beginning with $P(3)$ and ending with $P(8)$.

(iv) The hierarchy of a particular office need not be connected, e.g., it only contains $P(1)$, $P(2)$, $P(3)$ and $P(6)$. Obviously such hierarchies can only be viable by external promotions.

The connection of the offices via the paylevel structure occurs

(i) by the possibilities of external promotions (E, R), i.e., the intra office placement of persons

(ii) by the budget process, i.e., the allocation of the budget of resources to the positions to be assigned to an office.

3. *The influence of time (dynamics).*

The influence of time shows twice:

(i) Trivially, the persons who perform the jobs and occupy the levels of the hierarchy become older. This presents the well known problem of the age structure.

(ii) All the components of the department, the network of jobs and the hierarchy change over time. The changes may be slow, but nevertheless they are essential ingredients of the departmental description.

4. *The diffuseness of the decision problem (the objective function).*

Summarizing the descriptive part of the analysis, we can characterize the institution by a set of people, who are interrelated by a network of jobs, a hierarchy of positions and their change over time, i.e., for any point of time, a member of the institution is a point of a state space $A \times B \times C$, where A is *a set of ages*, B a *set of pay-levels* and C a *set of jobs*. Formalizing the departmental manpower problem in the framework of the general decision problem (Nemhauser, 1966) we have a flow of persons over time through a changing network of jobs

Figure 5. Process through job network

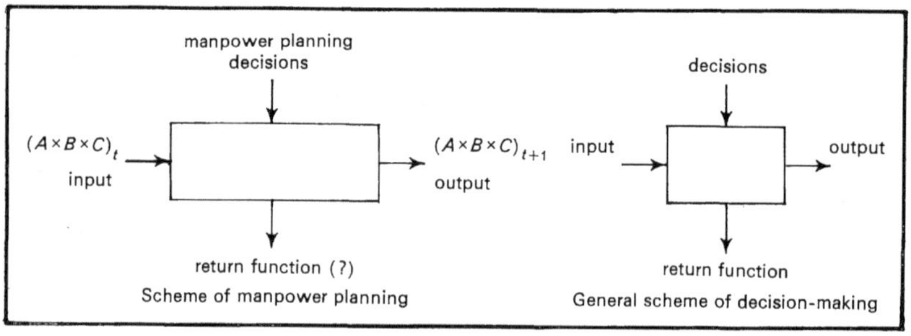

and positions, which represents the transition function and manpower planning decisions. A most difficult problem is to identify the role of the objective (return) function, hence the question mark. Due to the size of the institution—about 500,000 people and about 20,000 of those in the position of at least partial decision-making—with many members which have partial control of different decisions, one single well defined objective function cannot exist (see e.g., Hanssmann and Ramer, 1972). Any model with such a single valued objective function such as a linear programming of non linear programming type objective function must be an extreme simplification. (Nevertheless with such rigorous simplification we can obtain useful results, see below.)* Having sketched the four relevant items, the structure of jobs, the hierarchy of positions, the problem of time and the diffuseness of the objective function, we are now able to specialize into our two models: Summarising the basic properties of the two models against these requirements, we have Table 1.

Table 1. The basic properties of the two models

	Model 1	*Model 2*
The network of jobs	has been neglected	has been used completely and in extenso
The bureaucratic hierarchy	has been modelled in detail	is tied implicitly to the network of jobs
The time	has been eliminated by attainment of a stationary solution	has been used by two points (arbitrary initial and terminal points of time)
The objective function	is missing and is approximated by an iterative approach	is approximated by a sequence of linear sub-optimizations

Model 1 presents a detailed analysis of the hierarchy and Model 2 is a detailed analysis of the job structure.

II. Model 1

1. *The Markov chain representation*

The hierarchy is presented as a set of states, each of which is characterized by two properties, the age of a person and the paylevel a person occupies. A state of S is an entry $P(k, l)$, $k = 1, 2, \ldots, l = 1, 2, \ldots k, L$ of the following table (Figure 6).

Figure 6. Progress hierarchy

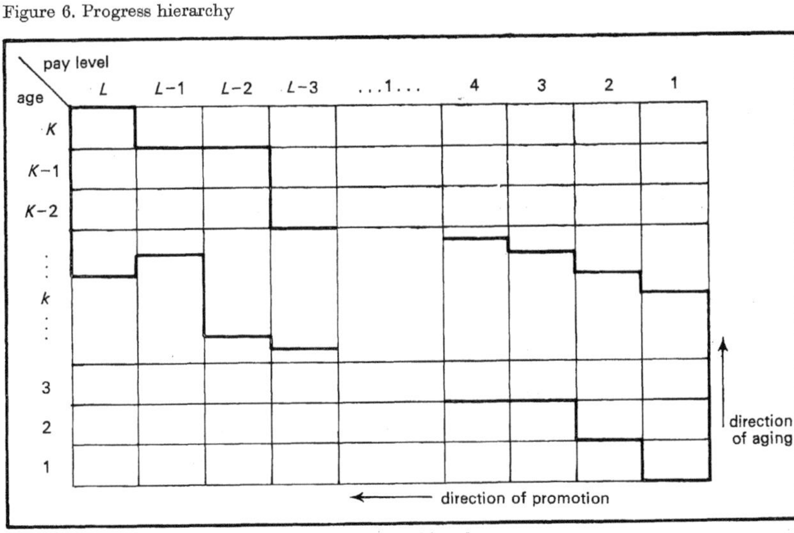

* See also the work of Smith and collaborators in this volume.

The states outside the heavy lined cells are not attainable. The states of one paylevel, i.e., the non-zero entries of a column of table P will be denoted by $S(l)$, i.e., $S \simeq (S(1), S(2), S(3), \ldots, S(L))$. The 'natural' counting of states will be from below and to the left, the total number of positions of level l of hierarchy P are

$$\sum_k P(k, l) \equiv P(l)$$

Listing the admissible states of table P, i.e., the states of S by their natural order, by a vector p, the problem of the optimal (desired, stationary, ideal) hierarchy is defined as *to find a matrix T of constant transition (promotion) probabilities* such that

$$p_t = p_{t-1}T$$

I.e., we have a Markov chain approach. Since the matrix T has triangular structure due to the unidirectional set up of the hierarchy (see Figure 4) a non-zero stationary solution of p does only exist if there are constant entries π into the hierarchy,

$$p_t = p_{t-1}T + \pi$$

with a stationary solution

$$p = (I - T)^{-1}\pi$$

These constant entries are in fact the underlying assumption.

2. *The comparison of desirable versus actual hierarchy*

Describing the actual organization we don't have a table $P(k, l)$ $k = 1, 2, \ldots, K$, $l = 1, 2, \ldots, L$, but there is a table $Y(k, l)$ $k = 1, 2, \ldots, K$, $l = 1, 2, \ldots, L$, with a total number of people of level l

$$Y(l) \equiv \sum_k Y(k, l) \quad l = 1, 2, \ldots, L$$

Usually neither

$$P(k, l) = Y(k, l)$$

nor

$$P(l) = Y(l)$$

and the states of P and Y do not match in general. Hence the model postulates a two step procedure.

Step (i) Construction of a desirable hierarchy,
Step (ii) Adaptation of the actual hierarchy to the desired one.

Both steps are defined algorithmically, i.e., by two programmes.

3. *The construction of a desirable hierarchy*

Dividing the total span of time assigned to any one level schematically

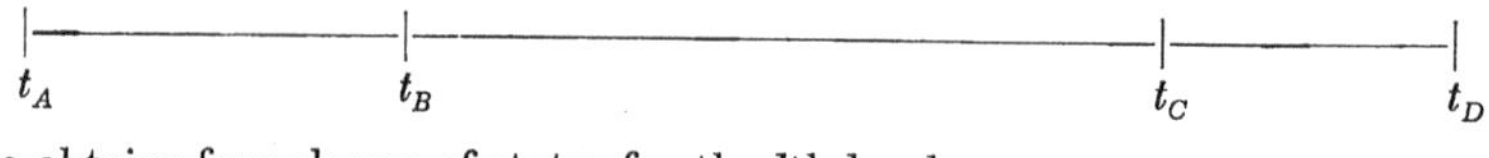

one obtains four classes of states for the lth level.

$S_1(l)$ the set of states corresponding to the years before promotion, the interval $[t_A, t_B]$,

$S_2(l)$ the set of states corresponding to the time at which the member can be promoted, the interval $[t_B, t_C]$,

$S_3(l)$ the set of states corresponding to the time in which the member cannot be promoted any more and is waiting for retirement, the interval $[t_C, t_D]$.

$S_4(l)$ a retirement state.

I.e., $S(l) = S_1(l) \cup S_2(l) \cup S_3(l) \cup S_4(l)$.

With any state s of $S(l)$ there are at most four transition possibilities with respect to the level.

(1) P_0 to stay at the level,
(2) P_1 to get promoted to a first successor level,
(3) P_2 to get promoted to a second successor level,
(4) P_R to get retired.

Depending on $S_q(l)$, $q = 1, 2, 3, 4$ the promotion process, i.e., matrix T, will be determined as follows:

Case 1. If $s \in S_1(l)$ (before promotion), then the person just gets older, $P_0 = 1$, $P_1 = P_2 = P_R = 0$.

Case 2. If $s \in S_2(l)$ (the time span of promotion), then a four-step promotion process is used:

(1) *Decide on the distribution over time.*
If $S_2(l)$ contains $(n+1)$ years $[t_C - t_B = n]$, then the promotions are distributed according to the binomial

$$B(n, i) = \binom{n}{i-1} b^{i-1}(1-b)^{n-(i-1)} \quad i = 1, 2, \ldots, n+1$$

where i denotes the ith year of the span of promotion. Result is a first preliminary set of probabilities:

$$P_0^{(1)} = 1 - P_1^{(1)},\ P_1^{(1)} = B(n, i),\ P_2^{(1)} = 0,\ P_R^{(1)} = 0$$

The binomial parameter b is given for each level.

(2) *Scale* $(P_0^{(1)}, P_1^{(1)}, P_2^{(1)}, P_R^{(1)})$ *down to those eligible for promotion.*
Not all of those people distributed over time by (1) are eligible for promotion, only c_1, $0 \leqq c_1 \leqq 1$, hence

$$P_0^{(2)} = 1 - P_1^{(2)}$$
$$P_1^{(2)} = P_1^{(1)} \quad c_1 \qquad (c_1 \text{ is a constant for each level})$$
$$P_2^{(2)} = 0$$
$$P_R^{(2)} = 0$$

(3) *Assign the promotions to the successor level.* (Preference among alternative possibilities of promotion.)

Subcase 1. There is only one successor level

$$P_0^{(3)} = P_0^{(2)},\ P_1^{(3)} = P_1^{(2)},\ P_2^{(3)} = P_2^{(2)},\ P_R^{(3)} = P_R^{(2)}$$

(The probabilities are taken over from step (2) without change.)

Subcase 2. There are two successor levels

$$P_0^{(3)} = 1 - P_1^{(3)} - P_2^{(3)}$$
$$P_1^{(3)} = P_1^{(2)} \quad c_2 \qquad (c_2 \text{ is a constant for each level})$$
$$P_2^{(3)} = P_1^{(2)} \quad (1 - c_2)$$
$$P_R^{(3)} = 0$$

Total promotions are partitioned corresponding to c_2, $0 \leqq c_2 \leqq 1$.

(4) *Adjust the promotion probabilities for early retirements.*

$$P_0 = P_0^{(4)} = P_0^{(3)} c_4(i)$$
$$P_1 = P_1^{(4)} = P_1^{(3)} c_4(i)$$
$$P_2 = P_2^{(4)} = P_2^{(3)} c_4(i)$$
$$P_R = P_R^{(4)} = 1 - P_0 - P_1 - P_2$$

Depending on age i, a fraction of the persons will retire early, $0 \leq c_4(i) \leq 1$.

Case 3. If $s \in S_3(l)$, then there is only the possibility to wait for retirement, i.e. $P_0 = c_4(i)$, $P_1 = 0$, $P_2 = 0$, $P_R = 1 - c_4(i)$. (Possibly Cases 1 and 3 agree.)

Case 4. If $s \in S_4(l)$, then the person leaves the hierarchy, i.e., $P_0 = P_1 = P_2 = 0$, $P_R = 1$.

Given the list of inputs:

(i) the set of ages, i.e.,
t_A = the earliest age at which one can enter a paylevel,
t_B = the earliest age at which one can leave a paylevel by being promoted (t_B is implied by t_A, t_C, t_D),
t_C = the latest age at which one can leave a paylevel by being promoted,
t_D = the compulsory retirement age of a paylevel;
(ii) the coefficients describing the promotion process c_1, c_2, b, c_4 (the stochastic specification);
(iii) the list of possible successor paylevels (the hierarchy);
(iv) a fixed pattern of entries into the hierarchy $P(k, l)$;

the model will generate a hierarchy $P(k, l)$. The hierarchy is called desirable if it satisfies the management. This definition of optimality sounds rather empty. The true objective of the institution however, is rather obscure and does not appear to be analysable on this level of abstraction. Not only the output pattern, i.e., the hierarchy ($[P(k, l)]$) and in particular ($P(l)$) determine the desirability, but in addition most items of the input list are figures of merit which enter the evaluation of a hierarchy.

Hence the basic philosophy of the model has been:

(i) to make explicit any changes of the hierarchy due to changes of the input list
(ii) to leave the evaluation to the user of the program, i.e., to management
(iii) to aid the heuristic evaluation by the computation of additional figures of merit such as, average ages and aggregated hierarchies and by simple re-runs of the model (ceteris paribus analyses).

The approach is completely heuristically guided. The model is re-run with changed input data, until the manager is satisfied with the resulting hierarchy. Due to the insight of management where and what to change these re-runs are rather modest in number opposite to what one might expect. This is an interactive approach (see e.g., Steward, 1973).

4. *A first set of rules of adaptation*

Given any such desirable hierarchy $P(k, l)$ and comparing it with the actual one, $Y(k, l)$, two kinds of adaptation rules are distinguished.

(1) A first set of rules of adaptation,
(2) A second set of rules of adaption.

The first set of rules flow from a first check: For each paylevel the entries of $P(k, l)$ and $Y(k, l)$ are compared, i.e., the two tables are compared column-wise. Considering one column we have three regions:

$\bar{S}(l)$ — the actual hierarchy has entries above the desirable hierarchy (too old)

$S(l)$ — the states of P and Y match

$\underline{S}(l)$ — the actual hierarchy has entries below the desirable hierarchy (too young)

Since the desirable hierarchy only applies to $S(l)$, there must be short term adjustments for those persons too old ($\bar{S}(l)$) and those too young ($S(l)$).

Case 1. $s \in \underline{S}(l)$ (A person is too young.) By plain waiting the person moves up into the hierarchy proper, from where on the ordinary promotion policy applies.

Case 2. $s \in \bar{S}(l)$ (A person is too old.) Depending on the hierarchical position of the level, three subcases are distinguished.

Subcase 1. The level is the top of the hierarchy. Any person older than the highest age of the desirable hierarchy will be retired.

Subcase 2. The level is not the top of the hierarchy. Depending on the existence of a positive retirement span, i.e., if $S_3(l) \neq \varnothing$ $(\Rightarrow S_4(l) \neq \varnothing)$, there are two subcases:

Subcase 2.1. $S_3(l) \neq \varnothing$. The retirement span from t_C to t_D is extended in order to cover those persons above. The persons above the regular retirement age t_D are retired increasingly with age, i.e., the older those persons the more are retired:

Figure 7. Retirement span

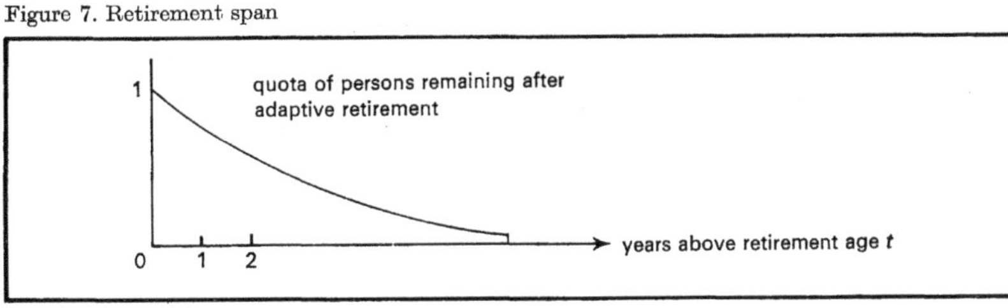

(This adaptive retirement policy corresponds to what is called in optimal replacement theory an I.F.R.-policy: The older the person, the less his performance, hence his retirement corresponding to this performance profile, see Barlow *et al.* 1965.)

Subcase 2.2. $S_3(l) \neq \varnothing$. The level has no retirement span, since it is one of the few levels which feed the hierarchy from below. If a person is too old for such a level he will be promoted, each year at most one level, until a level is attained, from which retirement can occur.

5. *The second set of rules of adaption*

A second set of adaption rules comes from the comparison of $P(l)$ and $Y(l)$, a comparison which is made from top to bottom of the hierarchy.

Case 1. If $P(l)-Y(l)<0$, i.e., if the actual number per level exceeds the desirable one, then one retires the oldest as far as possible, i.e., in $\bar{S}(l)$. Below t_D there is no retirement by fiat of management.

Case 2. If $P(l)-Y(l)>0$, i.e., if the actual number per level falls short of the desirable one, then additional promotions occur. Among the predecessor level(*s*) $l-1$ resp. $l-2$, one promotes proportionately over a possibly enlarged span of promotion into paylevel l with its deficit. The possible enlargement of the span of promotions $S_2(l-1)$, $S_2(l-2)$ is due to the exceptional situation. Checking prior promotions into $l-1$ and $l-2$, duplicate promotions per year are excluded.

6. *Summary*

The two sets of adaption rules are derived from the matching of $P(k, l)$ and $Y(k, l)$ (set 1) and of a comparison of $P(l)$, versus $Y(l)$ (set 2).

The basic motivation is to obtain a gradual change from the actual hierarchy to a hierarchy considered to be optimal.

If such a transformation fails, then one has to reconsider either the desirable hierarchy or the adaption rules.

Hence the total model is a simple and interactively linked sequence of two programmes, one producing a desirable hierarchy and one adjusting the actual hierarchy.

III. Model 2. A linear programming model of a network of jobs

The network of jobs is used in full detail. The hierarchy is tied to these jobs, since all jobs can uniquely be partitioned into sets $S(r)$, $r=1, 2, \ldots, R$, such that $S(r)$ denotes the set of jobs which corresponds to level r, $r=1, 2, \ldots, R$. For each job there is a set of successor, respectively predecessor jobs $N(k)$, respectively $V(k)$, $k=1, 2, \ldots, K$.

Beginning with an initial performance of the jobs, i.e., number of persons filling job k, y_{0k}, $k=1, 2, \ldots, K$, and beginning with an initial hierarchy, i.e., number of positions at level $r=1, 2, \ldots, R$, P_{0r}, the problem is to find a flow of people from the initial situation y_{0k} to a terminal situation y_{1k} and to find a change of hierarchy from P_{0r} to P_{1r} $r=1, 2, \ldots, R$. Both set of changes are interrelated and constrained.

First we have two fundamental balance equations.

$$y_{1k}=y_{0k}-s_{0k}+n_{0k}+\sum_{l\in V(k)} z_{lk}-\sum_{l\in N(k)} z_{kl} \qquad k=1, 2, \ldots, K \tag{1}$$

$$P_{1r}=P_{0r}+P_r^+-P_r^- \quad r=1, 2, \ldots, R \tag{2}$$

(1) describes the flow of people, and (2) describes the flow of positions to be filled by these people.

In addition to the variables y_{0k}, y_{1k}. P_{0r}, P_{1r}, we have variables z_{lk}, n_{0k}, P_r^+ and P_r^-.

z_{lk} is the number of people which move from job l ($l=1, 2, \ldots, K$) to job k ($k=1, 2, \ldots, K$), i.e., the movement inside the network of jobs. A subset of these are obviously the promotions P_{rs}, i.e.,

$$P_{rs}=\sum_{l\in S(r)}\ \sum_{k\in S(s)} z_{lk} \qquad r\neq s \tag{3}$$

n_{0k} and s_{0k} ($k=1, 2, \ldots, K$) denote the persons which enter from outside the network of jobs (outside the agency s.a.), respectively leave.

Hence (1) can be phrased verbally: The new stock of people on job k is equal to the old one minus departures from the office plus arrivals from other offices plus transfers from other jobs minus transfers to other jobs.

Since P_r^+ respectively P_r^- are the increase respectively decrease of positions, then (2) can be phrased correspondingly. The new stock of positions is equal to the old one plus changes. For linear programming reasons de- and in-creases are denoted separately.

Since for reasons of size of the LP we only discuss a one period problem—the transitions from an initial situation to a final situation—the temporal distribution of the flow of people will be bounded by a maximum time in job k, $\bar{M}_k$, and a minimum time in job k, $\underline{M}_k$

$$\bar{M}_k \geq \underline{M}_k \geq 0$$

Linking these bounds to the initial stock y_{0k} we obtain

$$\frac{y_{0k}}{\bar{M}_k} \leqq \sum_{l \in N(k)} z_{kl}$$

$$\frac{y_{0k}}{\underline{M}_k} \geqq \sum_{l \in N(k)} z_{kl}$$

respectively

$$y_{0k} \leqq \bar{M}_k \sum_{l \in N(k)} z_{kl} \quad \forall k \tag{4}$$

$$y_{0k} \geqq \underline{M}_k \sum_{l \in N(k)} z_{kl} \quad \forall k \tag{5}$$

Since the status quo (y_{0k}, P_{0r}) can only be changed slowly the flows have to be bounded, i.e.,

$$\sum_{k \in S(r)} s_{0k} \leqq \alpha \sum_{k \in S(r)} y_{0k} \quad \forall r \tag{6}$$

$$n_{0k} \leqq \beta \, y_{1k} \quad \forall k \tag{7}$$

$$P_r^+ + P_r^- \leqq \gamma P_{1r} \quad \forall r \tag{8}$$

where $0 \leqq \alpha \ll 1$, $0 \leqq \beta \ll 1$, $0 \leqq \gamma \ll 1$.

The choice of how to bound the changes s_{0k}, n_{0k}, P_r^+, P_r^- permits various other formulations, e.g.,

$$s_{0k} \leqq \alpha' y_{0k} \quad \forall k \quad 0 \leqq \alpha' \ll 1 \tag{6'}$$

$$n_{0k} \leqq \beta' y_{0k} \quad \forall k \quad 0 \leqq \beta' \ll 1 \tag{7'}$$

$$\sum_{\forall r} P_r^+ + P_r^- \leqq P \quad P \geqq 0 \tag{8'}$$

(6)–(7)–(8) (or alternative versions) are to enforce the essential requirement of a slow change of the status quo and to maintain essentially the hierarchy. There are only marginal changes of positions (8) and the system has essentially to be fed from within (6), (7). The external flows must be relatively small.

Finally the interrelation of the flow of people and the flow of positions is given by

$$\sum_{k \in S(r)} y_{1k} \leqq P_{1r} \quad \forall r \tag{9}$$

At the end each person must be on a duly appropriated position of the hierarchy.

2. *Various objective functions*

The choice of an objective function has been a major problem.

Following and generalizing the work of Charnes *et al.* (1969) for the equations (1)–(9) different objective functions are explored.

First a list of objective functions is presented:

01 $$\text{Max} \sum_k l_k y_{1k},\ l_k > 0$$

respectively

$$\text{Min} \sum l_k y_{1k},\ l_k < 0$$

Either a linear function of the final stock of people is maximized (l_k a positive figure of merit) or minimized (l_k a cost figure). Both cases require to clamp down in y_{1k}, i.e., in either case we need bounds on the final stock of persons, in order to avoid nonsensical results such as the shifting of all people into a few jobs, while the majority of jobs will not be fulfilled. Hence we need additional constraints either

$$y_{1k} \leqq r_k,\ 0 < r_k \text{ given},\ \forall k$$

or

$$y_{1k} \geqq r_k,\ 0 < r_k \text{ given},\ \forall k$$

02 $$\text{Min} \sum_k |y_{0k} - y_{1k}|$$

The change of the flow of people is minimized or equivalently

$$\text{Min} \sum_k (y_k^+ + y_k^-) \text{ subject to}$$

$$y_{1k} - y_{0k} = y_k^+ - y_k^- \quad \forall k$$

Usually this objective function neglects the importance of (4)–(5), and in addition the set of requirements r_k (not yet formalized by (1)–(9)) is disregarded. Hence the next formalization:

03 $$\text{Min} \sum_k (c_k^+ y_k^+ + c_k^- y_k^-)$$

subject to

$$y_{1k} - r_k = y_k^+ - y_k^- \quad \forall k$$

I.e., the more appropriate function than (*02*) is to minimize the deviations with respect to given requirements r_k. Depending on the choice of the coefficients c_k^+, c_k^- we have subcases:

c_k^+, c_k^-	
(i) $\geqq 0 \geqq 0$	arbitrary weights of the deviations
(ii) $= 1 = 1$	equal weight to deficiencies and excesses
(iii) $= 0 = 1$	only deficiencies matter
(iv) $= 1 = 0$	only excesses matter

04 Minimize a maximum deviation (The Tchebychef-criterion). The deviations of (*03*) are bounded, e.g.,

$$y_k^+ \leqq \delta^+$$
$$y_k^- \leqq \delta^-$$

(i) Min δ

$\delta \equiv \delta^+ \equiv \delta^-$ (The maximum deviation overall is minimized)

(ii) Min δ

$$\text{Either} \begin{cases} \delta^+ = \infty \\ \delta^- = \delta \end{cases} \text{or} \begin{cases} \delta^+ = \delta \\ \delta^- = \infty \end{cases}$$

(Only a one-sided deviation is of significance)

A corresponding comparison of objective functions involving P_{1k}, respectively P_r^+ and P_r^- can be presented. Each of these objective functions either in terms of y_{1k}, respectively y_k^+, y_k^-, or in terms of P_{1k}, respectively P_r^+, P_r^- use a minimum of comparison of utilities which—as we know from model 1—are involved in the consideration of the different relevant items.

What we try to do is to approximate a nonlinear objective function by a linear one* and hopefully improve the performance of the institution. Hence the approach is not strictly optimizing but suboptimizing due to its approximate validity. As in model 1 the approach of model 2 is of the satisfaction seeking type behaviour. The objective function we have adopted is (*03*, ii), i.e., to postulate a minimum performance level r_k, $k = 1, 2, \ldots, K$, and to minimize the deviation from these requirements.

3. *Summary—Results*

Reporting on work in progress we arrive at the following conclusions

(1) The factual background, i.e., the four items of the decomposable network of jobs, the bureaucratic hierarchy, a limited view of time and an approximate objective function permit a reasonable and computable linear programming formulation. [A typical problem of about 40 jobs and seven paylevels has about 250 equations and 500 variables including slack variables.]

(2) The present state is that of experimental runs with real data.

(3) Provided each of the agencies of the department can be modelled along these lines—as we think—we plan to link these agency models by Dantzig Wolfe decomposition. The natural links are the external flows n_{0k} and s_{0k} and the positions P_r of the hierarchy. However, since our trial runs have not fully been evaluated, we do not want to claim more than can be documented now.

References

BARLOW, R., PROSCHAN, F. and HUNTER, L.C., 1965, *Mathematical Theory of Reliability* (New York: Wiley).

BECKMANN, M.J., Theoretisches Modell des Kegels der Berufsoffiziere im stationären Gleichgewicht in Die Personalstruktur.

CHARNES, A., COOPER, W.W., NIEHAUS, R.J., STEDRY, A., 1969, Static and Dynamic Assignment Models with Multiple Objectives and Some Remarks on Organizational Design. *Management Science*, **15**, 8, B 365–B 375.

DANTZIG, G.B., 1963, *Linear Programming and Extensions* (Princeton: Princeton University Press).

FERSCHL, F., Markovketten, 1970, *Lecture Notes on Operations Research and Mathematical Systems, No. 35* (Heidelberg and New York: Springer-Verlag).

* Obviously a careful analysis of the validity of this approach is necessary, see, e.g., Rao.

HANSSMANN, F. and RAMER, S., 1972, Die Programmierung sozioökonomischer Entscheidungen. *Analysen und Prognosen*, **4**, 3, 17–21.
HITCH, C.J., 1965, *Modern Defense Planning, in Military Defensive Planning and Operations Research* (Bonn: The Federal Minister of Defence).
KEMENY, J.G. and SNELL, J.L., 1960, *Finite Markov Chains* (Princeton, N.J.: Von Nostrand Corp.).
NEMHAUSER, G., 1966, *Dynamic Programming* (New York: Wiley).
STEWARD, D.V., 1973, The Analysis of the Structure of Systems (forthcoming).
UEBE, G., 1971, On Partitioning Large Systems of Sparse Linear Equations. *M.R.C. Technical Summary Report 1126*, August (The University of Wisconsin).
WEISSBUCH, 1969, Zur Verteidungspolitik der Bundesregierung, Bonn.
WEISSBUCH, 1971/1972, Zur Sicherheit der Bundesrepublik Deutschland und zur Entwicklung der Bundeswehr, Bonn.
WEMA-SYMPOSIUM, 1973, Internationaler Workshop: Systemtechnik und Personalstruktur (Cologne: Wema-Institut).
RAO, M.R., 1973, Some comments on 'Linear' Programming with absolute-value functionals. *Operations Research*, **21**, 1, January-February, 373–374.

Upon receiving his Ph.D. degree in 1970 from the University of Cologne, Professor Meinolf Dierkes was managing director of the Research Centre in Empirical Economics of Cologne University. Dr. Dierkes joined the Battelle staff on April 1, 1971, as a Fellow at the Battelle Seattle Research Centre. While at the Seattle Research Centre, Dr. Dierkes served as an affiliate Associate Professor at the University of Washington. At present Dr. Dierkes is responsible for the Research Centre for Applied Behavioural and Social Science at Battelle's laboratory in Frankfurt, Germany.

Mr. Coppock holds degrees in general studies, physical sciences and in public administration. After working briefly in state and local government, he joined the research staff of Battelle Memorial Institute where he contributed to work on social indicators, corporate social accounting and the analysis of world-wide problems. He is currently a member of Battelle's Applied Social and Behavioural Research Centre in Frankfurt where he concentrates on social change and organizational management.

3:5

Human resources accounting: A tool for measuring and monitoring manpower utilization in a business environment

M. Dierkes and R. Coppock

Introduction: The perception

There is probably no other area of social change in the economically highly developed countries in which people's aspirations are rising as fast as with regard to the work environment. After the basic needs for income, security and stability of employment have been satisfied, an increasing number of the working population is turning its interest toward the higher-order needs hypothesized in Maslow's scale: such as self-actualization, participation and self-development. In short exactly those dimensions of work which have traditionally been characteristics of highly rewarding professional activity.

This growing recognition of the role 'higher order' needs play in the structure of work accompanies the broadening of business goals and responsibilities in other areas. Business and government alike are being called upon to acknowledge their responsibilities in the physical environment, in consumerism and equal opportunity issues, as well as other areas of major social concern (Coppock *et al.*, 1973). Organizational responsibilities are changing as well in other ways not so directly tied to specific social demands and pressures. Employing organizations increasingly assume the responsibility for the education of their employees, both in terms of formal education and additional specific training and 'updating'.

It has been argued that the quality of the work environment has seen substantial improvement over the long range (Wilson, 1969). We discover, however, at a far greater pace new areas of dissatisfaction and fields of impact of a poor working environment. One of the results of this development is the widening of the gap between the perceived quality of working life and the expectations of the majority of the population regarding how the work environment should be designed to meet their needs.

Furthermore, it can be expected that this gap will become wider—as survey results indicate—with the further increase of personal income and the upgrading of the educational level of our population (O'Toole *et al.*, 1972). A steadily increasing proportion of our population backed by growing political power will demand a significant enhancement of the quality of their working environments to increase the basic prerequisites of their overall social and mental well-being. It can be stated, therefore, in accordance with the main report on *Work in America* prepared last year by a special task force to the U.S. Secretary of Health, Education and Welfare, that there has never been a more widely discussed and broadly supported concern for the negative consequences of present day work environment. This broad concern includes issues like:

Alienation of workers as a result of the extreme taylorization of work (Wilson, 1969),

Obsolescence of skills resulting from the abuse of specific human resources and the lack of both planning and investment in human resources (Wilson, 1969 and *Life*, 1972).

Diseases due to psychic strains and stresses (Levi, 1971).

High accident rates and diseases due to physically monotonous, poisonous or otherwise damaging work environments (Schmidt, 1973).

Development of the need/work situation gap

How can it be that this gap between people's needs and capabilities on one side and organizational job requirements and designs on the other side could have occured without significant preventive actions of the major employing institutions in our society, business and government?

Without claiming to have an absolutely comprehensive list of causal factors, our hypotheses to explain this development are the following:

(1) An over-emphasis on narrowly defined economic efficiency without taking the social costs of actions and organizational concepts into consideration;

(2) A lack of preparedness among the decision-makers and planners to measure, monitor and forecast social trends, especially the expectations of people relevant to those decisions which design organizational concepts;

(3) At least up to very recent years but from our point of view still today, a lack of empirically tested knowledge of the impact of the quality of the work environment on people's overall social well-being;

(4) The individualistic philosophy, i.e., the belief in an absolutely efficient functioning of the labour market and the definition of labour as just another input factor into the economic process like raw material, land, machinery etc.;

(5) The neglect of social and human factors in the formal information systems of the two major employing institutions, business and government, as a basis for decision-making and appraising management performance.

With regard to the full list of items, there are some encouraging trends regarding items one, three and four. We have already discussed, as have several others, the need for a new social forecasting function in addition to the traditional field of predicting technological and economic trends; therefore, we would like to focus on item five (Coppock *et al.*, 1973; Dierkes, 1972; Bauer and Fenn, 1972; Likert, 1967). This represents neglected dimensions in the institutionalized feedback systems regarding the utilization of our human resources: the social and human factors. Since the concept we would like to discuss has been developed primarily for the business corporation, mainly due to the greater innovativeness of this institution, we will describe the advantages and problems when applying it to a business environment. However, we would like to point out that it easily can be applied to the government as an employing institution too, and it is our conviction that the need for introducing this concept in government is at least as great as in the business environment.

To help clarify what is meant by item five, the neglect of social and human factors in institutional systems, we have modified Porter and Lawler's performance satisfaction model (Wilson, 1969, after Porter and Lawler) to include the functioning of rewards (and lack of rewards) in the area of the utilization of human resources within the organization. Important aspects are that both profitability and decreases or damage to human resources are ignored in the reinforcement scheme while short term costs of human development and profit resulting from short term conerns are included. The model portrays a situation biased against the considered development of human capabilities.

The traditional approach: Chain of intervention

What has been the traditional approach to match human needs and capabilities with the organizational job requirements?

The traditional, and still predominantly used approach is a chain of interventions mainly characterized by the following five-step-process:

(1) A problem is recognized by specific sub-groups in the society,
(2) It gains recognition in other parts of the population and the mass-media,
(3) It increasingly becomes a major concern of the political decision-making body (there has only recently been a development of pressure outside the government forcing the institution under consideration to solve the problem without involvement of the political decision-making institutions),
(4) Legislation is passed setting legal standards and regulations, and administrative structures, and
(5) The standards are generally applied.

All the milestones in the improvement of our working lives (abolishment of child labour, reduction of working hours, establishment of basic safety standards, etc.) have been introduced and enhanced the quality of our environment following more or less exactly this pattern. Thus, the chain of interventions, especially at the macro-institutional level, has proven to be an effective approach to dealing with necessary changes in our society and forcing decision-makers to consider human and social factors.

The effectiveness of this concept, however, is increasingly questioned with respect to those personal needs for self-actualization and human development.

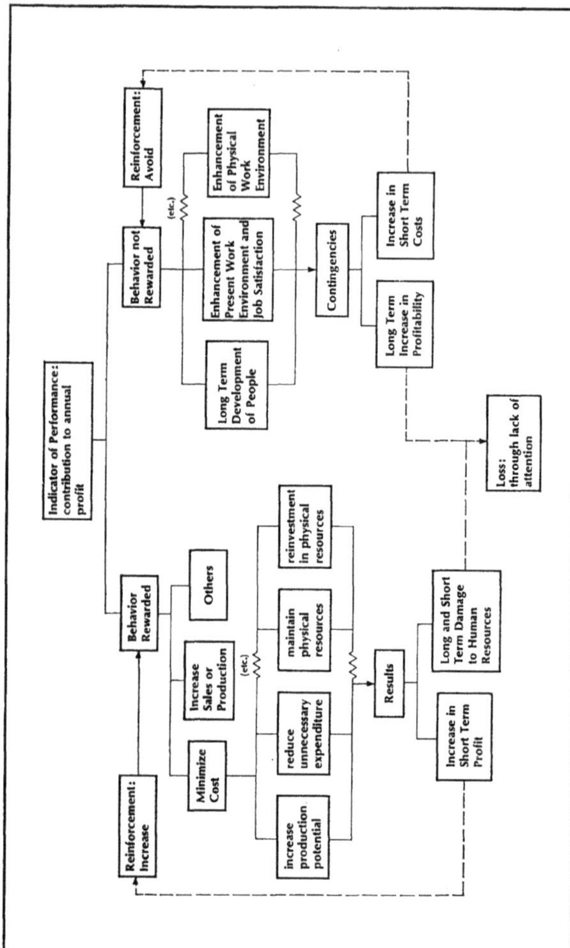

Figure 1. Performance criteria within the system

Together with health aspects, self-actualization and individual development are the main focuses of the newly emphasized personal needs. Since these are considered to be highly diversified, specialized and characteristic of various subgroups of the labour force, and therefore not easily identified, the chain of interventions seems to have the following major deficiencies when applied to our present-day problems:

(1) Its lack of flexibility and adaptability to specific situations. For example, the assembly-line, which still seems to be an adequate working situation for approximately 10–15% of this labour-force (according to empirical studies), should not be abolished by law, putting all people immediately into jobs requiring within the work-job concept a high degree of responsibility when some are not yet prepared nor willing to take on this responsibility.

(2) With the increasing speed of new demands regarding the quality of the work environment the organizational and political decision-making process is—as the already mentioned growing gap between expectations and perceived reality emphasizes—increasingly incapable of handling these problems with the speed necessary to efficiently meet people's needs.

(3) the bureaucratic structure administrating these problems quite often places unnecessary constraints and delays on the decision-making process of the employing organization.

The chain of intervention approach therefore cannot be considered to be exclusively the valid and efficient concept to handle our future problems (Cassell, 1971; Chaplin *et al.*, 1971). This is especially valid when taking into account the improved understanding of the functioning of our social institutions as dynamic systems as well as the important role of feed-back information in guiding and directing organizational behaviour. These new sets of theories and hypotheses allow for a quite different and more effective approach. Without interfering with decision-making by setting new constraints, the process itself will be altered in the sense that the input-data for the decision-making process will be changed together with the establishment of new criteria for the measurement of performance. This approach attempts to set up a new or redesigned self-regulating system capable without further interference, of meeting people's needs for personal development, human growth and an enhanced work environment. Such a new self-regulating system would be capable of meeting these challenges

- With the necessary speed,
- Without creating bureaucratic structures,
- Taking into account the specifics of different situations.

Human Resources Accounting (H.R.A.) is suggesting as such a system meeting these new needs of our working population. The basic concept has been developed by Likert (1967); Brummet *et al.* (1969). The total accounting of work systems suggested by Davis is similar in its effect (Wilson, 1969, p. 19).

Let us start with an example to help understand the H.R.A. concept: Suppose a manager has approval for expenditures of $100,000 on new equipment during the next year. This capital outlay will be recognized on the balance sheet as an asset with benefits to be expected over an extended period of time. Therefore, it is not included or added to the projected costs which will be subtracted from revenue to determine the net income for the year. In this manner conventional accounting practice helps the manager to compete for the scarce financial resources of the business by demonstrating that these expenditures are expected to generate revenue over an extended period of time and need not be justified in relation to this year's income alone. Now assume the manager plans to invest this money in training and developing human assets or in upgrading the quality of work environment. Under conventional accounting practice this $100,000 would be included in the costs of this period to be charged against this year's revenue rather than amortized over the expected life of the expenditure. Thus, it is quite difficult for the manager to compete for financial resources to develop long term human capabilities or to enhance the work environment.

A taxonomy of human resources accounting

H.R.A. is developing as a tool to aid managers in their decision making. As has been indicated, the most widely used measure of overall organizational efficiency matches the revenue from the sale of the firm's product or services with the costs required to produce that revenue. H.R.C. grows out of the recognition that traditional accounting and management information treat costs associated with the development of long-term human capabilities as expenses which understate revenue in the short term. This new accounting concept is designed to correct this distortion in the measures of business efficiency (Pyle, 1970a).

As inputs to these measures of efficiency, accountants have provided information on the acquisition, development, maintenance and utilization of certain capabilities employed by the firm. When physical capabilities, to continue the prior example, expire prematurely, the increased write-off becomes an expense against revenue in the current year. Reported profitability is reduced and the responsible manager is held accountable. Unfortunately, the protection afforded physical assets has not traditionally been accorded to human capabilities. One focus of human resources accounting is to extend this protection.

The initial focus: Investments in human capability

The initial focus of human resource accounting has been to determine investments in human capabilities and develop appropriate accounting procedures. The primary effort has been in business with large contributions from human capabilities. The major objectives have been:

(1) providing information pertaining to human resources,
(2) providing feedback on manager's performance with respect to human assets in the organization,
(3) providing a more accurate accounting of the return on total assets employed (Woodruff, 1969).

Approaches to these objectives include:

- Human resources inventories,
- Determination of outlay costs,
- Determination of replacement costs,
- Determination of the economic value of the human resources employed in the organization.

Constructing an *inventory* is in some ways the simplest of these approaches, and probably the most sensible first step in approaching the utilization of human resources in the firm. The following are typical questions that might be used in developing an inventory of human resources classes and their importance (Pyle, 1970b).

What human assets are most crucial to the success (or failure) of the business?

To what degree can each have positive or negative impact on the enterprise?

Does the firm have special competitive advantage (disadvantage) in a particular human resource area that it wishes to preserve, develop or remove?

Has the firm ever been surprised by an unanticipated exodus of capable employees?

To what degree has the firm's growth or profitability been enhanced (impaired) by unpredictable changes in relationships with those outside the organization?

The answers to these questions will suggest others as well as stimulate thinking about the role of human resources in the particular organization.

Outlay costs are associated with the actual cash outlays for obtaining, maintaining and developing the organization's human assets. Large sums are spent each year recruiting, familiarizing and developing people with the expectation that they will be of benefit beyond these costs (see page 319 for a discussion of outlay costs as they are being developed at the R.G. Barry Corporation). Capitalization of these outlay costs with amortization over the expected employment of the individual will provide a more accurate picture of the firm's overall return on investment than charging them all in the year incurred (Woodruff, 1969, p. 19). (See Figure 2 as an example.)

Replacement costs represent the outlay costs that the firm would have to make to replace its employees or to provide a certain level of human resources. This concept introduces the fluctuations of the job market as well as the general increases in cost of living, etc. Replacement costs provide better guidelines for forecasting, budgeting and planning extensions (Woodruff, 1969, p. 19). However, since actual outlays are not involved, the values must include some estimation. Therefore, determination of replacement costs are both more difficult to develop and less reliable than outlay costs.

Both outlay costs and replacement costs of human resources point toward the concept of the *economic value* of human resources. This value may be defined as 'the present discounted value of their future contributions less the costs of acquiring, maintaining and utilizing those resources in the organization' (Pyle, 1970a, p. 29). The concept obviously involves a large measure of estimation and therefore would be difficult to measure reliably. However, in a sense, every time an employee is hired that value is estimated, at least in terms of whether it is expected to be greater than zero.

The first extension: Health and safety

Once the value of human resources has been acknowledged in ways that recognize their impact on overall return on investment and enter into regular management decision-making, consideration should be given to those actions and conditions that reduce or impair those resources. The emphasis in this and the next section is on the nature of the position and how the conditions the individual finds in his job can affect his capabilities. Health and safety are the aspects of the job most easily measured and integrated into the scheme outlined in the last section. A similar series of approaches to those described for determining human resources investments may be used:

- Inventory of accidents and illnesses,
- Costs of reduced production,
- Rehabilitation costs.

As is the case with investments in human capabilities, the concepts of costs

Figure 2. The initial focus of human resources accounting: investment in human capabilities (outlay cost system)

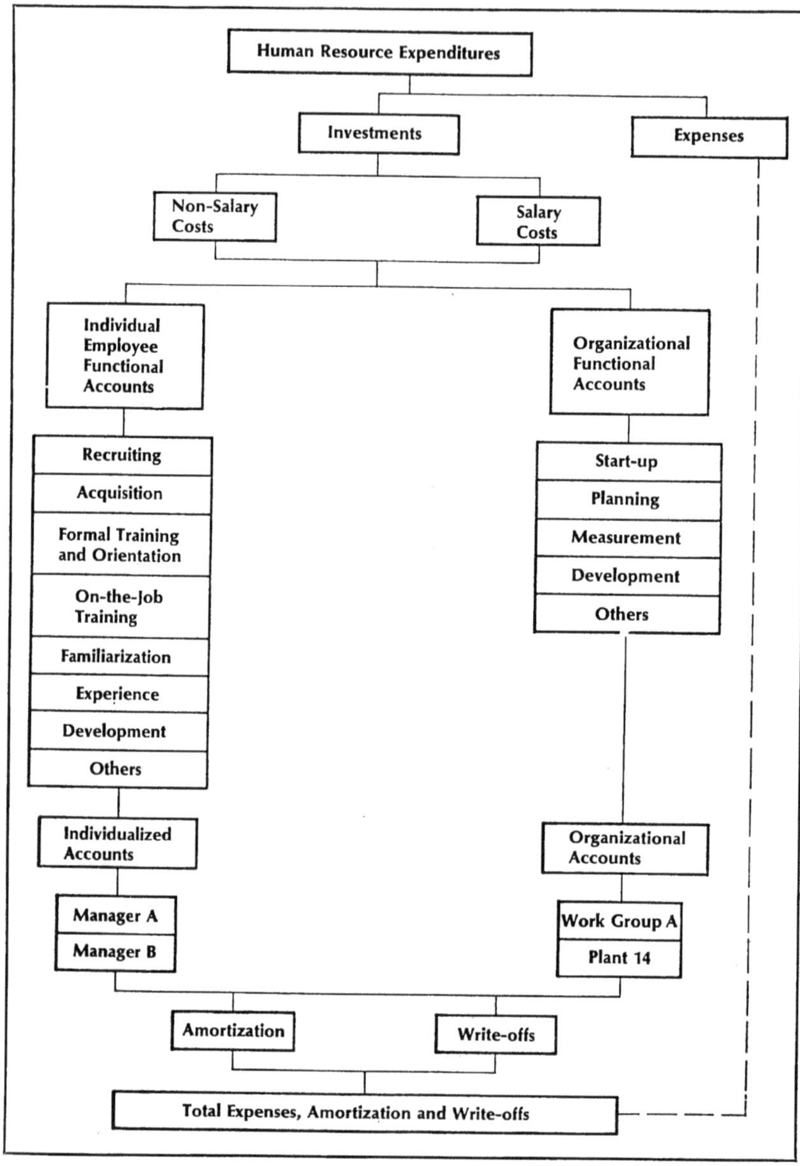

of reduced production and rehabilitation contribute to the idea of economic value of human assets (Schmidt, 1973, p. 13).

An inventory of accidents and illnesses of the firm personnel appears to be the logical first step. Workmen's compensation laws already require the

Figure 3. The first level of extension: health and safety measures. (*a*) Analysis of losses due to accidents and diseases

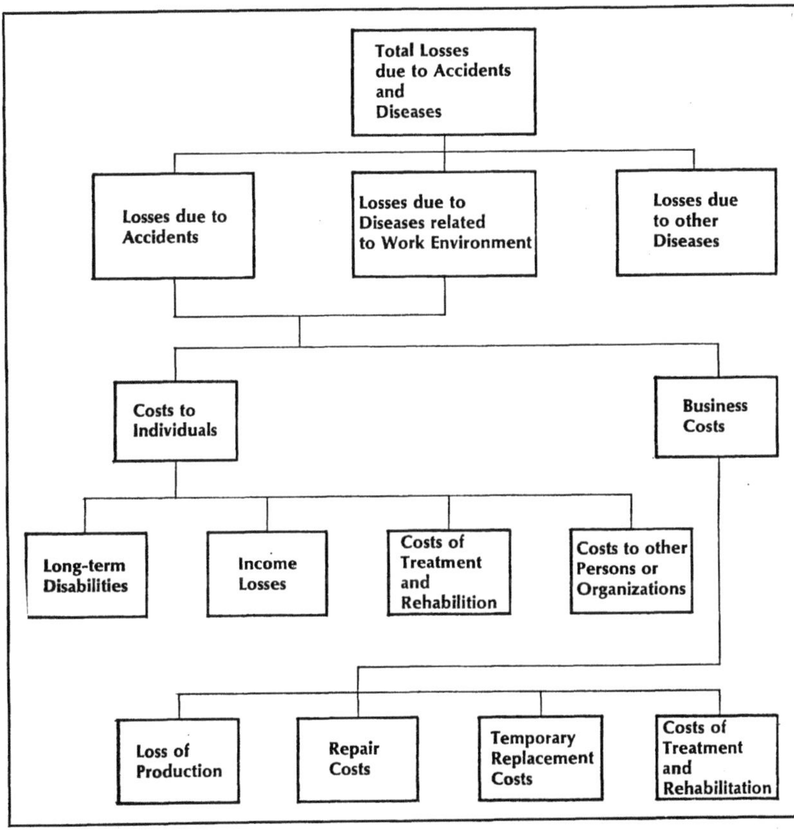

collection of much information in this area, of course, but it is seldom used in relation to the value of human resources. Appropriate questions for such an inventory might be:

What are the accidents and illnesses the firm's personnel have?

To what degree do such illnesses and accidents interfere with the operation of the business?

Do accidents or illnesses occur in cycles, either weekly, or seasonally?

To what extent does the absence or reduced productivity of individuals restrict the productivity of others?

Such questions can suggest the importance of the health of an organization's employees.

Direct and indirect costs are incurred when employees are absent due to accident or illness as well as any other reason. Substitutes are likely to be less efficient than the regular employees. Sometimes the absent worker's part of the production process stays idle or is picked up by those around him—in either case production slows. In those cases in which the employee is hospitalized or must consult a doctor, costs fall on the firm. These expenses and the costs of reduced production attribute to accidents or illnesses.

During or following an illness or accident rehabilitation costs may occur. As a minimum these will reflect decreased production when the employee returns to work. They range from this minimum all the way to considerable amounts in terms of medical treatment, therapy or pensions.

Costs can easily be monitored and compared with investments in health and safety measures. Figure 4 illustrates a framework for dealing with such investments in equipment, training and information and manpower.

Figure 4. The first level of extension: health and safety measures. (*b*) Monitoring investments for improvement

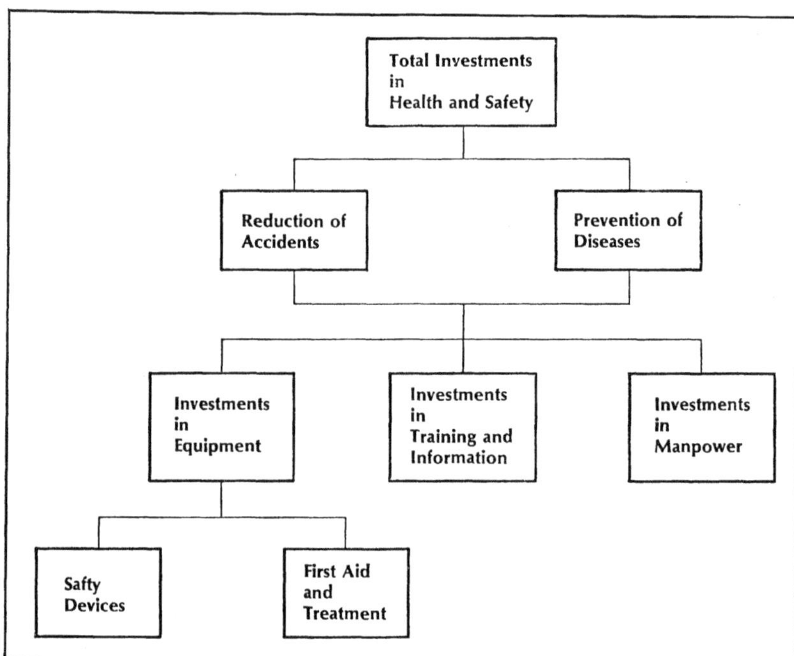

Accidents and illnesses detract from the overall efficiency of the organization by removing or impairing employees and by causing direct costs in terms of rehabilitation and medical expenses. The value of health (lack of accident or illness) on the part of the employee would be the expected benefit of the employee less costs attributable to illness or accident. This value cannot be calculated of course, but estimates can be made for expected costs of illness and accident, as well as actual expenditures collected. Such information can be used both to inegrate with other information on human assets and to evaluate safety programmes.

The second extension: Quality of the psychological work environment

The quality of the psychological work environment also has impact on the different dimensions of manpower utilization in a work environment. More and more studies are addressing the way the organization and pace of modern industrial life affect the individual (Levi, 1969). Other studies deal with the effects of social change and industrial progress (Schwab, 1971; Wilson, 1969). The ways the psychological work environment influences mental and physical health are not yet always clear. However, many examples can be found that demonstrate some kind of impact.

The automobile industry has the most automated assembly process in the U.S. The assembly is broken down into the simplest and fastest possible motions. Seventy-five percent of the workers on automobile assembly lines are unskilled compared with 10% in other parts of the industry. The General Motors Vega assembly plant in Youngstown, Ohio turns out 101 cars an hour. The pressure on this assembly line has already led to a strike protesting against the work conditions. Job boredom is blamed for poor workmanship and absenteeism rates as high as 13% throughout the industry, this compared to 3% a few years ago. Strikes were once called on grounds of pay and job security. Increasingly discontent with the job is becoming the key issue (Assael and German, 1970; National Clearing House for Mental Health Information, 1972; and Wright, 1968).

Discontent with working conditions in the automobile industry is probably more extreme than is commonly the case. Yet this same discontent is widely found in manufacturing (Wilson, 1969, pp. 30–38) and the automobile industry can serve as an example of the impact the work environment can have on production and therefore on return on investment. The saying 'don't buy a car built on Monday' (because of the poor workmanship following the weekend) is a sad comment on this impact. In attempts to deal with absenteeism both Ford and General Motors are developing programmes where workers are permitted planned absences. Both use counselling to deal with instances of excessive absenteeism.

Absenteeism and poor workmanship can be integrated into calculations of overall efficiency in straightforward ways. But in work which depends more on the human capabilities of the employee, the impact of the psychological work environment is more difficult to assess, even though it may be more important. Shoddy work on the part of an executive will probably be much more costly than that of an assembly worker. Generally, the more the nature of the work done depends upon human capability the more important the result of any single 'failure'. But, it also appears that the less the work involves human capabilities the greater the discontent.

Both, the work situation and the characteristics of the employee must be considered in discussing the psychological work environment. Efforts in the modification and design of work with the goal of improving production have increasingly taken into account ego needs of the employee like his desire for self esteem, control of his immediate environment and sense of development. Much recent work has concentrated on the measurement and improvement of employee satisfaction, morale, etc. (Wilson, 1969; Lawler, 1973). The use of self-report measures is one way of taking individual differences into account, however, their fakeability varies, and they provide subjective data. An alternative is focusing on behavioural outcomes such as turnover rates, absenteeism,

Figure 5. The second level of extension: quality of the psychological work environment

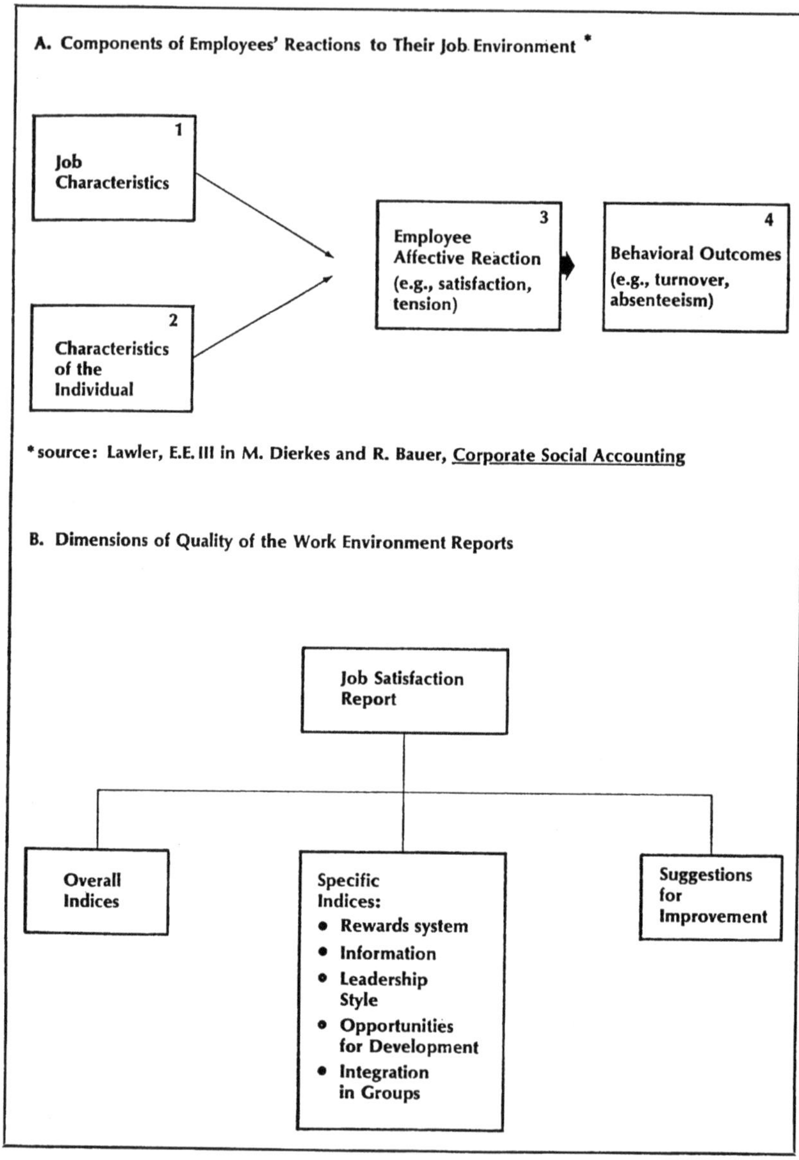

mental illness rates, etc. A disadvantage of such a strategy is that they reflect unacceptable situations after they occur rather than predict their coming about. A second alternative to self-report measures is to measure directly the actual working conditions. The capability is being developed for measuring conditions like how stressful and how challenging the working environment actually is. (For an excellent summary, see Lawler (1973).)

If the firm is serious about assessing its overall efficiency in a way that recognizes the long-term value of the human capabilities in the organization, then it will consider both the impact of health and safety and of the psychological work environment in its assessments of human assets.

The experience: An analysis of experiments with human resources accounting

The best known and most extensive experience with H.R.A. focused primarily on investments in human capabilities in the R.G. Barry Corporation of Columbus, Ohio. A similar effort is called 'force loss cost analysis' and has been applied at New Jersey Bell. This analysis is a management tool designed to reflect the costs of work turnover. Hiring, training and on the job development are treated as capital investments rather than operating expenses and are amortized over time.

After a long series of attempts to develop evaluations of manager performance, the Barry Corporation undertook late in 1966 the development of an H.R.A. system. A working relationship was established with the Institute for Social Research at the University of Michigan, and a team was formed to begin the first stages of the system.

The basic objectives of a human resource accounting system were defined as:

(1) To provide Barry managers with specific feedback information on their own performance in managing the organizational assets and customer loyalty assets entrusted to their care so that they can make the proper adjustments in their pattern of operation to correct adverse trends or further improve the condition of these assets.
(2) To provide Barry managers with additional information to assist in their decision-making and in evaluating the performance of their subordinates.
(3) To provide the organization with a more accurate accounting of our return on total assets employed, rather than just the physical assets, and to enable us to analyse how changes in the status of the assets employed affect the achievement of corporate objectives. (Internally we will show organizational assets on the balance sheet.) (Woodruff and Whitman, 1970, p. 11.)

The first stage was the accounting for managerial organizational assets. Three approaches were considered in treating managerial organizational assets: (Woodruff and Whitman, 1970, p. 11): (1) Outlay costs, (2) Replacement costs and (3) Economic value.

Outlay costs were selected for the initial approach because:

(1) it requires less 'intuitive' judgement and more of the necessary information is readily available,
(2) since the information is solely related to expenditures and not returns it is not threatening to the members of the organization, and
(3) it is the approach most consistent with the conventional accounting system (Woodruff and Whitman, 1970, pp. 14–15).

Figure 2 is illustrative of the concept as applied at Barry. Accounts were set up both for each individual and for the functional accounts within each organizational unit. It should be emphasized that only the debit side of the ledger is shown here, and, due to the amortization of the human investments in his unit over their expected span of contribution to the organization, the manager will normally reflect a positive balance of human resource assets to expenses.

Seven functional accounts were established for accumulating those direct or allocated outlay costs considered to be investments in organizational assets with worth beyond the current accounting period (Woodruff and Whitman, 1970, pp. 16–17):

(1) *Recruiting outlay costs* are associated with locating and selecting new (management) personnel, including: search fees, advertising, travel, internal screening and interviewing and testing and evaluation.
(2) *Acquisition costs* are incurred in bringing a new man to his job. This category includes placement fees, moving costs, physical examination and departmental time in placing him on the payroll and providing him with the equipment to do his job.
(3) *Formal training and familiarizing costs* are those incurring immediately after hire or transfer such as formal orientation programmes, vestibule training, etc.
(4) *Informal training costs* are associated with teaching a person to adapt his existing skills to the specific requirements of his new job. Such costs are normally only salary allocations and vary with each position depending on level in the organization, number of subordinates, interaction patterns, etc.
(5) *Informal familiarization costs* are associated with the complex process of integrating a new manager into the organization so that he can be an effective member of that organization. Such costs include learning the company's philosophy, history, policies, objectives, communication patterns, etc, and may be sizable depending on the level and scope of the position.
(6) *Investment building experience costs* are associated with on-the-job learning following the initial familiarization. An example might be the first union organizing campaign in which a personnel manager is involved.
(7) *Development costs* are investments increasing a manager's capabilities in areas beyond the skills required by the position, i.e., management seminars, college courses, etc.

The outlay cost system including the seven functional accounts is obviously dependent upon the accuracy of salary allocations made, for they make up the bulk of the entries. Information for development costs is much more accurate than for the other accounts. A form has been derived to analyse the allocations of time for each function associated with each position. This form serves to standardize judgements, but at the same time reduces confidence in the allocations.

Each operating manager receives a quarterly report of the outlay costs associated with the organizational assets in his care. The report shows the investments in each of the seven accounts for each manager in his group. Account balances are amortized annually based on the expected working life of the individual, or in the case of development costs, a shorter period. Each operating manager reviews the accounts quarterly and indicates the appropriate write-offs to training, experience, or the obsolescence of the investment. Total write-off to the individual's account occurs upon his departure from the company.

The cost outlay system is virtually separate from the conventional accounting system both in terms of process and reportage. The only real interaction between the two is in the form of adjustment to income statements and other conventional reports for internal consumption. In 1969, the firm prepared what is believed to be the first capital budget for human resources (Pyle, 1970a, p. 26). The 1969 Annual Report contains the first published financial statements to include human resources. This information is contrasted with conventional financial statements in a special section (Pyle, 1970a, p. 27).

The primary purpose for developing human resource accounting at R.G. Barry Corporation was to improve internal management. It reflects, in part, the recognition of the firm's ability to borrow more than the 'cold figures' would indicate, the fact that the personnel of the firm were a valuable and real asset. In reality, it was felt, managers did not make decisions about people separate from other resources and information about human resources should be provided as is that about physical resources. The company president says, 'In evaluating a project; we take the physical assets into account as everyone else does, but we also add to that the investment to be made in the human resources required to support the activity' (Pyle, 1970a, pp. 26–27). The comptroller adds, 'Human resource accounting data provide still another tool to evaluate the allocation of resources among profit opportunities to maximize the return on all corporate resources' (Pyle, 1970a, p. 27).

Future developments

Human resources accounting is one of a growing number of techniques that can assist in the recognition and sensible utilization of human resources in today's organizations. It contributes to the integration of individual employee and corporate goals, and helps show why it is in the organization's self-interest to do so. Furthermore, human resources accounting appears at a time when business and government alike are increasingly being called upon to account for their human and social costs, both within and outside the organization (Flamholtz, 1973). This paper focuses on human resources accounting as a tool in monitoring manpower utilization in a business environment. As such, it combines with other techniques presented in this volume to assist the better utilization as well as the continuous development of people in a work environment.

References

ASSAEL, M. and GERMAN, G.A., 1970, Changing Society and Mental Health. *Israel Annuals of Psychiatry and Related Disciplines*, **8**/1, 52–54.

BAUER, R., and FENN, D., 1972, *The Corporate Social Audit* (New York: Russell Sage Foundation).

BRUMMETT, R.L., FLAMHOLTZ, E.G. and PYLE, W.C., 1969, *Human Resources Accounting: Development and Implementation in Industry* (Ann Arbor: Found. for Research on Human Behaviour).

CASSELL, F., 1971, Manpower Administration: a New Role in Corporate Management. *Personnel Administrator*, **34**/6, Nov.–Dec. 33–37.

CHAPLIN, E.H., *et al.*, 1971, Report of the Committee on Behavioural Science Content of the Accounting Curriculum. *The Accounting Review*.

COPPOCK, R., DIERKES, M., SNOWBALL, H. and THOMAS, J., 1973, Social Pressure and Business Action. In: Dierkes, M. and Bauer, R. (Eds.), *Corporate Social Accounting* (New York: Praeger).

DIERKES, M., 1972, Corporate Social Accounts. *Research Futures*, Battelle-Institute, Fourth Quarter.

FLAMHOLTZ, E., 1973, The Role of Human Resources Accounting in Social Accounting. In: Dierkes and Bauer, *Corporate Social Accounting*.

LAWLER, E.E. III, 1973, Quality of Working Life and Social Accounts. In: Dierkes and Bauer, *Corporate Social Accounts*.

LEVI, L., 1969, Society, Stress and Disease. Institute of Biology, Scottish Branch, 'Consequences of Affluence', *Nature*, 742.

LEVI, L. (Ed.), 1971, *Society, Stress and Disease*, Vol. 1 (London: Oxford University Press).

LICKERT, R., 1967, *The Human Organization, its Management and Value* (New York: McGraw-Hill).

LIFE MAGAZINE, 1972, Boredom on the Assembly Line, *Life*, 73/1, September.

NATIONAL CLEARING HOUSE FOR MENTAL HEALTH INFORMATION, 1972, Influences of Industrialization on the Health of Workers in the Community of Ivangrad (Yugoslavia), *Occupational Mental Health Notes*, April, 2–3.

O'TOOLE, J., *et al.*, 1972, *Work in America, Report of a Special Task Force to the Secretary of Health, Education and Welfare* (Cambridge, Mass.: M.I.T. Press).

PYLE, W.C., 1970a, Monitoring Human Resources—On-line. *Michigan Business*, **22**/4, 19–32.

PYLE, W.C., 1970b, Human Resources Accounting. *Financial Analysts Journal*, September/October, 75.

SCHMIDT, H., 1973, Relations Between the Quality of the Work Environment and Corporate Human Accounting. In: Dierkes, M., and Bauer, R., *Corporate Social Accounting* (New York: Praeger).

SCHWAB, J.J., 1971, Psychosocial Medicine and the Contemporary Scene. *Comprehensive Psychiatry*, **12**/1, 19–26.

WILSON, N.A.B., 1969, On the Quality of Working life. *Report to the N.A.T.O. Committee on Challenges of Modern Life* (Mimeographed).

WOODRUFF, R.C., Jr., 1969, What Price People? *The Personnel Administrator*, **14**/1, 17.

WOODRUFF, R.C., Jr., and WHITMAN, R.G., 1970, The Behavioural Aspects of Accounting Data for Performance Evaluation at the R.G. Barry Corporation (with special relevance to human resource accounting). In: Burns, T.J. (Ed.), *The Behavioral Aspects of Accounting Data for Performance Evaluation*, College of Administrative Science Monograph No. AA-4, The Ohio State University, Columbus, Ohio.

WRIGHT, B., 1968, Stress. *Observer, June 16*, pp. 19–25, 29.

Section 4

Summary Papers

Prof. F. Eric Burke was educated in mathematics and mechanical engineering, his career moved from design and project engineering, extended research in the physical sciences and its direction, to operational research on the processes of technical change. For the latter, study of highly qualified manpower and its utilization is an important component.

4:1

Notes on taxonomies for interdisciplinary communication

F. E. Burke

Introduction

As this conference closes, there is some regret that more bridges did not emerge between the several discipline authorities who condensed their approaches into taxonomies. Here is an attempt to understand this difficulty from historical examples and logical and pragmatic analysis. This paper makes several suggestions in outline. Full discussion relating these to the major contributions of the conference, or to the source of the suggestions, is beyond my scope.

As we have heard and read in the key papers, there is a large literature on the construction of taxonomies. Most such efforts are viewed in isolation. I will focus on two problems that generally remain peripheral.

Any new taxonomy represents a change from an earlier one. Either it details more finely to obtain more nearly homogeneous categories, or it demonstrates that unification and simplification retains precision while improving generality. Change is pervasive because perception itself implies earlier taxonomies, even those embedded in common language.

Further, a new taxonomy is useful only if adopted: the more widely in terms of users, and the more extended over time, the richer its influence. Even if pursued by those eminent in their discipline bent on increasing their power of problem solving, if peers do not accept or numerous apprentice scholars prefer a changed taxonomy, it will be found sterile in any broad perspective. Change and adoption, then, are of the essence of work on taxonomies, and can be viewed as extrovert communication processes rather than introvert theoretical —linguistic discoveries or learning.

The history of western modern science, in the unfolding of its unprecedented successes, has left us many examples for instructive study. Dr. Miller has already referred to the periodic table of chemical elements as an important instance. Only relatively recently has the history of science become sufficiently developed to influence the philosophy of science, and the philosophy of science powerful enough to enrich the analysis of what scientists actually do. In Section I we shall draw a few sketchy implications from these fields for our topic.

Also in the current generation, developments in mathematics (e.g., statistical inference, preference theory) have reached the level where they can be applied, if in a preliminary way, to criteria for the communication of taxonomies. We shall attempt illustrations in Section II.

An incomplete but suggestive discussion for future taxonomic work is the aim of Section III. In these concluding remarks, some of the work reported in the conference is viewed in a perspective so broad as to permit, nay invite, the constructive disagreements of my readers.

Section I. Developments of taxonomies in the history of science

The most ambitious aims for a taxonomy in this conference is, I believe, the first half of Dr. Miller's contribution. My use of terms is a subset of his, or I would not be able to distinguish taxonomy, theory and the content of a discipline.

Sufficient for a taxonomy, to me, is to have elements, rules that group these elements into sets and subsets, and a minimal set-theoretic structure relating sets and subsets. Often, even the form of such structural relations goes well beyond taxonomy. Thus Newton's mechanics concerned itself with mass points of matter, gravitation, distance and time, and from their relations (outside his taxonomy) designated momentum, inertia and force. It seems important to me that while all his elements had empirical referents, his notions (e.g., that of matter) were far more restrictive or, indeed, invisible (e.g., force, gravitation) than was at all comfortable for his contemporaries. To work out the implications of his view of mechanics took well over 100 years. His taxonomy, however, survived though it was elaborated. From a communications point-of-view it was a model success, influencing the thinking of each of us probably far more than we know. Thus we are apt to think of mechanics as far more mathematical than is useful for conceptual clarity. For if any of the element had, in time, turned out to be empirically lacking in communication tasks—they would have long been replaced. This, of course, happened when Boyle attempted to found a mechanical theory of chemical molecules (using, he thought, the most successful taxonomic elements of Newton's teaching): chemistry, sad to say, did not co-operate empirically.

The change from the chemistry of the alchemists, with their taxonomy of substances (base and noble, phlogiston etc.) to that of Lavoisier and Dalton and their colleagues was accompanied by the communications problems I am most concerned with. So was the evolution of the taxonomy of electrical physics between 1600 and Maxwell's days. In both fields, there was very intensive scientific activity for dozens of years before an ultimately comprehensive, predictive taxonomy evolved from the earlier notions. The whole process took some $2\frac{1}{2}$ centuries in electricity (longer before electrons could be counted as 'one potato, two potatoes . . .' by Millikan), over one century until 'the table' succeeded the 'substances' in post Lavoisier chemistry.

I can now propose the extremes of a progressive set of empirical properties for elements of taxonomies (the structure will have to wait till Section II).

One extreme may be called labelling or coding: think of people passing a gate, or books arriving one by one, and simply being numbered. For some purposes, this is the perfect taxonomy (we use it in library catalogues and dictionaries, the alphabet serving as a large number base): We obtain order, identity, retrievability. But if we lose the labels, we start from scratch. If we wish to communicate *how* we labelled, we have to transmit enough of the context to regain the original label—object correspondence, that is to give a unique description of each empirical object. As this full description has nothing to do with the label in lexicographic order, we conclude that at this extreme, our taxonomy has no communicable empirical content at all! For this grave defect, we obtain a number of logical advantages I explore in Section II—and we have heard on several occasions in this conference that without these advantages, a taxonomy is not really acceptable.

The other extreme is a taxonomy of categories based on cardinal, conservative, additive measures (often found in the well established physical sciences) such as height, volume, etc. Here, only the measurement method needs to be communicated if we want to repeat (reproduce) the classification, and we can compare classes at different points at the slight cost of transporting reference standards etc. Clearly, information processing for taxonomic purposes has, in principle, been carried as far as possible, and the full empirical information of interest has been embodied in the taxonomy.

The cost is, however, a loss of uniqueness. In the extreme, we cannot tell one element from another (e.g., electrons), and in the continuous case, there will be large fractions about whose categories we are in doubt—e.g., for height, given the compressibility of humans and their cussedness in slouching, most people within 3 to 4 mm. are indistinguishable.

Now, I would like to proceed from these examples to some of the more systematic findings of history and of research on research, as it bears on my topic.

The work of Sir Karl Popper (1935) is a natural starting point, as it has aroused wide attention, without suffering substantial defeat, in over 30 years. For my purpose, it is sufficient to paraphrase Sir Karl with the propositions that a hypothesis in science is never proved. It is useful if it can be *dis*proved. It advances to the status of a theory after surviving concerted attempts at disproof, including those which cause it to confront, through appropriate relationships, other well tested theories and their associated bodies of empirical observation.

Note that theories in science are thus viewed as highly dependant on being communicated; not only sent out via publication, but received seriously enough to be progressively tested by attempts at disproof. As I tried to illustrate earlier, such communication and any change based on acceptance has taxonomic change as a vehicle. I conclude that most of the taxonomies we heard about here do not meet Sir Karl's criteria: they are not directly susceptible of disproof; they propose to be useful for a purpose (implying that meeting that purpose will, in some sense, validate them), or they are presented because they have been useful. With reference to the spectrum between labelling and classifying according to empirical measures, they seem close to labelling—and this implies that they are less communication oriented than scientific taxonomies in the fields discussed by Popper.

The next major contribution to such systematic views of the growth of science is Thomas S. Kuhn's *Structure of Scientific Revolutions* (1962). This work has had great impact, aroused deep disputes, and it is fair to say has been rejected by the most competent historiographers of science as a bad prescription how they should do their work. But the problems it raises for us has not been dented by the controversy L.M. (1970), and later work on the sociology of science (Hagstrom (1965), Mullins (1972)) has tended to increase rather than decrease its relevance. As we find in the conference report L.M. (1970), one may view Kuhn as extending the propositions of Popper. Kuhn's notion of the 'paradigm' (a favourite target of his critics) has more direct bearing on taxonomies than Popper's hypotheses and theories. To this notion he adds the distinction between 'normal' science operating with and within a paradigm (or taxonomy), and a scientific 'revolution' which implies paradigm (or taxonomic) change. Popper tended to dismiss 'normal' science as hack work unfit for his attention, but has softened this position (L.M., 1970).

In Kuhn, we first encounter the problem that a paradigm is an entity focusing the work of a group of people with two properties—close agreement on taxonomy, and strongly limited in the number of active contributors at any one time. The latter notion is more explicit in de Solla Price (1963), and has been explored by a more formal mathematical model of F. Adler (1960). Both draw attention to the difficulty of keeping up-to-date in professional work. Thus they suggest that invisible colleges form to maximize scientific advance. They balance the benefits from adopting peers' contributions (at a cost in reading or listening and travel time) and the time remaining for active research and its publication in the most spare language that will still result in acceptance. The pressure of both forces (reading economy and economy of understanding) are harsh constraints on the quality of taxonomies as the language of the groups, and stresses their communication economy as a condition of scholarly advance. Strangely (until one remembers that human capacities for language processing have changed little, Zipf (1935)) the sizes of invisible colleges have been invariant, to the accuracy with which we know them, for about 200 to 250 years. It seems reasonable to conclude that the linguistic desiderata of taxonomies have also retained great regularity.

Section II. Structure and communication of taxonomies

The last section has explored elements of taxonomies with minimum attention to structure. Structure is viewed here in the traditional sense of the hierarchy of measures, from the nominal, ordinal, ratio(nal), to the cardinal. I have noted that communication, or the transmission of information from locked room to locked room for the purpose of scientific reproducing or disproving on the basis of taxonomies, emphasizes the distinction between their logical and empirical properties.

At the logical extreme of labelling, coding, lexicography and nominality, our elements conform to Shannon's (1949) notion of the completely shared vocabulary. On this and (to our purpose irrelevant) other foundations, 'information theory' has been erected and stands as the only formalization of communication which we have. All other quantifications should be viewed as its elaboration. It is clear that the completely shared vocabulary begs our fundamental question, how does it get shared? As language, both professional and common, changes constantly, there is clearly a need to determine how many Shannon 'words' may be needed to introduce one new word from the status of noise to a place in shared vocabulary, now enriched by one unit. Unpublished research indicates that such an information content is large and related both to the size and structure of the original information space. It also shows that a new invisible college is characterized by new vocabulary, and in those we studied only a few dozen (often less) new words were found. Thus the spectrum of taxonomic elements is paralleled by one of measures as well as by a spectrum of departure from the shared vocabulary information theory. The very great information load implied by vocabulary additions may hint at a quantification of the principle of parsimony in theories—and taxonomies.

At the cardinal end of the spectrum, we noted the close tie of elements to physical measures. Whether the elements are continuous (e.g., length) or discrete (e.g., elements, nuclear particles), the measurement procedures always involve reference standards as well as methods of comparison. Mathematically the reference standard is the physical or empirical interpretation of the expected value or the mean of an adequately large set of measurements carried out. The dispersion (e.g., the variance) of the measurements is, in empirical terms, an interpretation of the method of comparison with the reference standard. This clarifies an important methodological issue: in principle, neither non-parametric analysis nor the analysis of variance even of empirical observations can legitimize any mean value, or even compare two different mean values, without the independent existence of a reference standard.

At the cardinal extreme, to sum up, we are dependent on the empirical existence of a conservatively and additively metric space. Given this, we can communicate by transmitting the measure, reference standard and measurement method, and with descriptions of the objects to be measured, which can be identified in the receiver's locked room.

The structures determined by the spectrum of measures described above can best be understood in terms of the orderings to which they lead. Labelling or nominal measure will always produce strong order (for a particularly clear exposition of the formalism see (Fishburn (1970), part I). It is always possible to tell the order of names in a telephone book.

Ordinal measures are perhaps most clearly exemplified by utility or preference notions. For decades, stronger measures of preference have been investigated and their logic is well developed. No cardinal utility measures have been found to have empirical meaning, but ratio (substitution) measures are at the basis of 'marginal' analysis in economics. I suggest that methodologists in applied psychology might find the history of this part of economics instructive, and its length and evident difficulty encouraging in the light of present frustrations.

The major new feature of these measures is the existence of indifference among subsets of elements—that is, order is weak. The logic is clearly more difficult, and empirically the assignment of items to subsets may not be unique, nor the subsets mutually exclusive. Yet this may represent taxonomies superior, at least from the viewpoint of communication economy (and hence, as we saw possible rates of progress) to the strong order measures with their distinct and themselves strongly ordered subsets.

Lastly, we find that the cardinal measures and their conservative empirical metrics are veritable logical horrors. Instead of the indifference subsets of weak order, we find classes of observations (measurements) that are not *significantly* different, though they may appear to have order. Thus we end up with a need for the whole, as yet contentious apparatus of statistical inference. It is clear that if we set our categorical classifications too narrowly, almost all objects would be classified with uncertainty, and our locked room receiver would be quite rude about itemized reproducibility—though he should end up with reasonably similar estimates of statistics. If we set the category interval in relation to the power functions arising from our observations, the above class of errors can be minimized, but all our conclusions have become statistical.

The notion of a 'conservative metric' has been mentioned freely. Most physical quantities have such a metric, few others have. A water tank contains all the water that ever flowed into it, diminished by all that flowed out (or evaporated). Many convenient mathematical tools apply in such cases, but break down when conservation in this sense does not hold. This distinction is probably more fundamental, and leads to more confusion between logical argument and empirical consequences, than the open versus closed systems distinction in General Systems Theory. Attention to conservation is, I believe, one of the most fruitful additions that can be made to the methodological tools of the social scientist.

Observe that some quantities are what I would call 'locally conservative'. Distances and mass in Newton's mechanics are: if you move far and fast enough, relativistic effects causes other taxonomic elements to be conservative. Engineers, however, would be foolish to abandon the Newtonian simplicity as long as they are aware of its 'locality'. Similarly, money in any closed economy and at a given time is conservative; the accounting equations work, to great benefit, in these conditions. Note that money is not conservative if you compare the U.S.A. and India. Apart from more serious theoretical consequences, many people are getting wealthy from this, only mildly illegally. Nor is money conservative over long time periods, so that comparisons in economics over decades or longer are beset with great difficulties. There are examples in individual differences of human resources, but their discussion would be too lengthy.

For practical purposes, we may repeat that without conservative metrics, comparison of means usually becomes invalid; and that any technique (e.g., non-parametric analysis) which discards means, reduces communication power if valid means could be obtained.

Discussion

The material of this paper suggests that more attention needs to be paid to empirical considerations of the elements of taxonomies, compared to the logical and mathematical hierarchies erected on them. A number of the desiderata of Dr. Miller may, unfortunately, be recognized to demand the logical nicety only available with strong order, at the same time as the invariant soundness only available with conservative metrics and less than weak order.

In the conference, most taxonomies fell well between the extremes of the spectrum discussed. Starting from those most solidly founded empirically, ergonomics and psychophysical applications are nearly cardinal. They are subject (shades of Hawthorn) to what is recalled, and perceived, and to what has to be inferred from intervening variables. Perhaps closest to the nominal, as yet, appear task categorizations (for nonmanual training and selection purposes and goals).

Compared with early science, there is more clarity about the crucial role of taxonomies, but perhaps an undue sense of hurry to become more like the older sciences at a pace that may be unrealistic.

Particularly, there appeared an absence of agreement on paradigm-like notions, and the conference seemed to show the resulting information overload, and uncertainty of what contributed to endeavours outside the source discipline, that the physical sciences escaped some time ago.

It is known that scientists often believe that laboratory understanding is the origin of progress. Others have pointed out, and given many examples, that the artifacts of the doers have in many cases provided something more simple for scientific investigation than millennia of natural phenomena (Pierce (1961)). This conundrum has no solution yet. Clearly, Drs. Miller and Fleishman represented both views. I believe technology should (indeed must) be pursued before all the understanding is in—but logical programmes have, in history, often slowed technologies rather than accelerated them. On the other hand, the laboratory has, in the history of science, been second only to the thought experiment as a fount of those taxonomic elements and structures that have been most fruitfully adopted—clearly some should be left unfettered by demands of pre-specified application.

Non-parametric methods, almost the preserve of the social scientists, have merits and pitfalls. Perhaps these have been best combined by biologists and chemical engineers who used the hypotheses generated as objects for attempted disproof in experiments with conservative metrics.

The considerations of communicability of taxonomies are offered as links with history and logic. They won't do the work.

Bibliography

ADLER, F.P., 1960, Organization Size and Efficiency. *Management Science*, **VII**, 1, October.

FISHBURN, P.C., 1970, *Utility Theory for Decision Making* (New York: Wiley).

HAGSTROM, W.O., 1965, *The Scientific Community* (New York: Basic Books).

KUHN, T.S., 1962, The Structure of Scientific Revolutions (2nd ed., 1970) (Chicago: University of Chicago Press).

L.M., 1970, *Criticism and the Growths of Knowledge*, edited by Lakatos, I. and Musgrave, A. (London: Cambridge University Press).

MULLINS, N.C., 1972, The Development of a Scientific Speciality. *Minerva*, **X**, 1, January, pp. 51–85.

PIERCE, J.R., 1961, *Symbols, Signals and Noise* (New York: Harper Brothers).

POPPER, K.R., 1935, *Logik Der Forschung* (Vienna). Transl. to: *The Logic of Scientific Discovery* (London: Hutchinson, 1959).

PRICE, D.J., de SOLLA, 1963, *Little Science, Big Science* (New York: Columbia University Press).

SHANNON, C.E., 1949, *The Mathematical Theory of Communication* (Urbana: University of Illinois Press).

ZIPF, G.K., 1935, *The Psycho-Biology of Language* (New York: Houghton Mifflin).

Professor Wallis trained as a psychologist and practised in the field of Occupational Psychology after graduating. He was engaged on research in personnel assessment, ergonomics and vocational training, whilst working as a research psychologist in the British Navy. Recently he has been Chief Psychologist of the Department of Employment; and he has very recently moved to Cardiff to occupy the chair in Applied Psychology at the University of Wales Institute of Science and Technology.

4:2

A concluding commentary on the conference papers

D. Wallis

Introduction

We have all seen from the Preface to the collection of abstracts that the Conference '. . . is concerned with efficient use of human resources'. Now the word 'efficient' can be an emotive one; so it was comforting to read that it was '. . . being used in its true sense as the best possible utilization of a resource and not with the concomitant aspects of robotic control and impersonal manipulation of individuals'. I think all our speakers have followed this line. Their concern, from whatever disciplinary standpoint, has been with production and conservation rather than impersonal exploitation of a very special economic resource. That resource consists of people and their occupational skills.

I don't suppose any of us needed persuading of the range and difficulty of strictly technical problems in this field. We have heard plenty of evidence for this. But I think it has been reassuring to find that neither the difficulty nor the intrinsic interest of these technical problems has deflected proper attention from the strictly human needs and values which in the long run confer meaning and justification for our applied work in the real world.

Now Professor Singleton warned us yesterday that at the world level, at any rate in the N.A.T.O. countries, we are faced with:

(*a*) an increasing rate of using up the world's natural wealth and resources;
(*b*) a disturbing tendency to take insufficient account of human assets, which after all are the sole creators of new wealth.

He also pointed out in his final paper that a number of different scientific disciplines are preoccupied with the question of how to employ these human resources, i.e. people, sensibly and productively yet with a regard to their own well-being. Here are the disciplines: Education; Training; Selection and Placement; Vocational Guidance; Work Design and Ergonomics; Manpower Studies and Manpower Planning.

We have been fortunate to have all of these represented at the Conference. This has faced us with a wide span of topics, and the relations between them may not always have seemed self-evident. Before the conference assembled last Monday, Professor Singleton pointed out to some of us what he perceived these relations to be. I think it will be helpful if I pass on to you now what he suggested were points to note in contemplating inter-disciplinary relationships. Each main discipline contributes to the utilization of human resources. But, perhaps as a consequence, they also share the following features:

(i) Conflicts sometimes arise between their ostensible objectives and/or respective techniques. Educational and Training objectives may be a case in point.

(ii) Trade-offs between them may often be necessary in the context of the total system of manpower resources, e.g., between Selection and Training to meet specified job requirements.

(iii) Each discipline is deeply concerned with appraisal or measurement of individual human performance.

(iv) They have all relied to some extent on ideas and methods of assessment modelled on the physical and biological sciences. Yet there is commonly a realization that these ideas and methods are not always appropriate.

(v) For each discipline there are persistent and basic problems to be solved in the areas of *taxonomy*, and *analysis* of data.

The relevance of this last feature was explicitly recognized in the Conference programme. I think the others too were abundantly revealed as the proceedings unfolded.

Actually, our first day was taken up not so much with 'taxonomies', in the strict sense of that term, as with *classification*, i.e. with relationships between categories into which we try to fit the various kinds of data we happen to be working with. The second day concentrated on *analysis*, though here too the classification problem was conspicuous. And then on the third day we moved away from grappling with topics which underpin the refinement of all approaches to human resources utilization, and turned to *application*. You may have been struck, as I was, by the evidence of effective application to real problems despite the uncertainties about fundamental scientific issues. Even though we may not fully understand what we are up to, we do seem from time to time to achieve moderate success in getting something done.

Let me now turn to some personal observations on what we have learned from our speakers. I shall follow the pattern of the preceding three days and pick out some highlights appertaining first to scientific problems and then to practical applications.

Classification and analysis

I shall refer to these topics together because they are closely interwoven, as was clearly recognized by our main speakers. Let us first see what they had to tell us about the nature of the elemental data we all have to deal with in one form or another in our work on manpower utilization. From what we have heard this week, I think we can identify various ways of describing the data and breaking it up into manageable units.

Tasks. I am inclined to regard 'tasks' as the first order data in our field. In an occupational setting, tasks are the stuff of behaviour. They are what people actually do. At least, tasks are what people are supposed to do! They consist perhaps at an elementary level of what work study practitioners call 'therbligs'. (Notice that behaviour in a working environment can rarely, if ever, be usefully broken down by applied scientists into even more elementary, even if less variable, categories.)

Alternatively, units of work are sometimes described as 'operations', like turning a knob, pulling a lever, or measuring a diameter, on a machine tool. When a number of operations hang necessarily together—as in setting a machine tool, or diagnosing a fault in it, or perhaps monitoring the displays on the control panel of a continuous process plant—they can sensibly be put together to define a 'task'. I think it is helpful to regard a group of tasks which any one person has to undertake as adding up to a 'job'. Pursuing this principle of classification, we can speak of jobs which are more or less similar as defining an 'occupation'. And from the standpoint of vocational and careers guidance, we can envisage a series of occupations which confer meaning on the concept of a 'career'.

I suppose this kind of classification of occupational data into tasks and their subordinate or superordinate categories is an approximation to a taxonomy; though it is still far from being strictly a taxonomy. Moreover, we should remember Dr. Miller's insistence that we cannot in fact describe tasks fully, if by a full description we imply an equivalence between our descriptions of tasks and what people actually do. In practice we pick out selected features which seem to us important and relevant to the objectives we are trying to achieve.

Demands. Related to the above principle of classification, but certainly not the same, is an ordering of data according to the 'demands' upon human operators which tasks impose. This is how specialists in training, like Dr. Duncan, Dr. Gagné and Dr. Miller, prefer to look at things. So too, I think, does Professor Rohmert whose approach to manpower utilization starts from work design and egonomics. It has to be admitted that a classification of tasks concentrates attention upon the effects an operator is supposed to produce in his working environment. A task description does not of itself reveal just what these effects require in behavioural terms. A classification of 'demands' therefore i.e. of the behavioural requirements which arise from specified tasks is arguably more meaningful psychologically. It should help us to judge, as Dr. Duncan has stressed, how difficult the tasks are: whether they demand special skills for which training may have to be provided.

Abilities or Skills. This leads me to another level of classification which Dr. Fleishman featured in his presentation. Abilities, or 'skills' as they are more commonly conceived nowadays, are whatever it is that people possess in order to cope with the demands which tasks impose. In order to make proper use of the facilities in an electronic repair shop, say to mend a television set, a maintenance engineer must have some technical knowledge and the ability to use certain tools, coupled with skill at diagnosing faults.

Let us stick to the term 'abilities' for a moment. Both in the United Kingdom and the United States, a preoccupation with the classification of abilities goes back a long way. We recall such names as Spearman, Godfrey Thomson and Sir Cyril Burt, in Britain; they were struggling with the problem fifty years ago. From the United States, Thurstone, Guildford and Dr. Fleishman himself, have been equally prominent and perhaps more influential still. The earlier psychologists were all seeking something approaching a true taxonomy of human abilities. They sought a structure of categories ordered according to a hierarchical principle, and inferred after applying the technique known as factor analysis to correlations between measures of performance. One of the objects of striving for a hierarchical system was that to say of an individual that he possessed a high degree of a certain higher-order ability, verbal reasoning ability for example, would be also to predict relatively high performance in a whole range of tasks demanding subordinate abilities. These might perhaps involve knowledge of vocabulary, awareness of grammatical rules, assimilation of meaning from verbal material, and a flair for inferring logical relationships between concepts.

Rather little of all this classificatory work on abilities has taken root in basic psychology or ergonomics, I would think. But it has been highly influential, though not always recognized as so, for applied studies in every one of the six major disciplines I mentioned at the beginning. Dr. Fleishman's work has contributed conspicuously to its recent and continued influence. We heard from him of success he has achieved in identifying some basic categories of an abilities classification. I think it is particularly interesting to note how Dr. Fleishman's studies of perceptual-motor abilities and physical proficiency are helping to close what used to be an uncomfortable gap between the positions of the 'human abilities' schools of applied psychology, and those of a more ergonomic persuasion. The latter have tended to speak of 'skills' rather than 'abilities' and to be wary of clustering elementary skills into higher-order ones. But the real as well as logical distinctions between what Dr. Fleishman calls 'abilities' and Professors Singleton and Rohmert would probably call 'skills' are scarcely perceptible; and both groups of scientists rely alike on experimental and correlational methods of deriving and analysing their raw data.

Acquiring Abilities and Skill. Now it is very obvious that of the skills which are exercised by people to meet the demands of tasks, very few if any are innate. Since they are learned instead, we have to pose the question of how this happens. Another kind of data classification is therefore needed, having to do with the acquisition of skill. Dr. Gagné talked about this in the context of his theme about the derivation of educational objectives. I refer here to the learning processes (or, more strictly, to the conditions of learning) when various kinds of skill have to be acquired. Dr. Gagné described five different levels of learning process with concomitant optimal conditions for learning. Even though some of us may point out that his classification was not exhaustive—for example, where do perceptual and social skills fit in?—we can readily appreciate that it takes us another step forward in the direction of identifying the essential similarities and differences among our data.

Before passing on from the subject of learning, I should draw your attention to the associated topic of instructional techniques or teaching methods. After all, it is these techniques which largely give expression to Dr. Gagné's 'optimal conditions for learning'. We heard very little about these during the conference. Yet they are certainly an important factor in the utilization of human resources. And there is a critical problem of classification which faces us when we try to decide what instructional techniques are appropriate for the acquisition of particular skills in the context of particular tasks. We need two-way or even three-way classificatory models here. Dr. Duncan and I were struggling with this problem some years ago in connection with military training (Table 1). Our attempt at a two-way classification of tasks and methods of instruction for them was scarcely more than a first shot at the target, but it at least illustrated the difficulties (Wallis, Duncan and Knight, 1966). I don't think we have moved much further along the path since that time.

Ergonomics. I think it is only fair to say at this point that there is an underlying assumption behind the approaches we have mentioned so far. It is that 'utilizing human resources' generally means adjusting people, through selection and training, for example, to meet the demands of tasks which are more or less 'given'. Ergonomists, however, look upon tasks from the complementary angle of designing them to meet human capabilities and limitations in the first place. This is the perspective from which Professor Rohmert delivered his address. He dealt comprehensively with the classification and analysis of ergonomic factors in work design.

There is more than one principle according to which ergonomic factors can be grouped. It all depends, to remind you again of Dr. Miller's dictum, on what your objectives are. I was interested to note that Professor Rohmert started from 'job demands', just as our speakers who represented a 'training' viewpoint did. He went on to speak of 'stresses and strains' imposed by jobs and of 'skills and aptitudes' required to meet the demands. You may have discerned some similarities between features picked out by Professor Rohmert as a basis for classifying skills and those which cropped up in other classifications. One should expect such overlapping features, of course; fundamentally, we are all trying, selectively, to make sense of the same data about people at work. However, I think it is also fair to say that ergonomic classifications are distinctive in having to show where there is a correspondence between aspects of human performance and the characteristics of working environments.

Manpower Studies. Finally, we come to grips with classification of data at the level where specialists in manpower planning operate. Here we are dealing with 'whole people' rather than with aspects of their performance. We heard from Mr. Smith how the statisticians are able to work with real personnel problems, impersonally perhaps, but treating people as individuals who can be grouped in meaningful ways and certainly not as mere numbers. Mr. Smith's example from the British Civil Service illustrated a classification of 'whole' persons into categories such as occupational groups, grades (or ranks) within these groups, employing departments, and so on. It is easy to see how much in the context of manpower forecasting and planning hangs upon accurate and meaningful classification of the people who make up an organization's human resources.

I have tried to pick out enough from the information and ideas presented to us to assess the importance of continued research upon analytic and taxonomic problems. Let me just underline three aspects. For me, the principal issue remains as a problem of moving from one classification of data to another. This is not a serious problem for us as theoreticians; because theoretically we shouldn't have to make such moves. But as practising professional workers, I don't see how we can escape the need to 'think' our way across from one set of categories to another. Let me remind you of Professor Singleton's example, where he showed that the practical problems of occupational guidance are very largely born of difficulties in translating skills and abilities into jobs and occupations. In my Department, which has responsibility for national job-seeking and vacancy-filling services, we are constantly aware of the imperfections in our classificatory systems for matching up the occupational demands of jobs and the needs and characteristics of people.

We heard too from Dr. Fleishman that he is trying to devise a classification of Task Demands which will correspond closely with his classification of

Table 1. Towards a Technology of Training: A Classification of Training Areas and Instructional Methods (modified

Training area \ *Instructional method*	*Self instructional/student-centred methods*			
	Pro-grammed instruction (*a*)	*Correspon-dence courses workbooks and private study* (*b*)	*Learning 'on the job'* (*c*)	*Role-playing and group dynamics* (*d*)
1. Physical Fitness *a.* in normal climates; *b.* in extreme climates.				
2. Procedural and Routine Skills Sequences of fixed, discrete, 'open-loop', actions. E.g., switching-on drills for equipments; clerical and supply routines; manual handling procedures; dismantling and assembly operations.				
3. Perceptual Skills Operator tasks involving mainly perceptual activity, e.g., radar, sonar and other monitoring tasks; photographic interpretation; aircraft recognition.				
4. Control Skills Serial tasks, involving continuous non-repetitive, error-actuated ('closed-loop'), actions. *a.* Craft: using hand/machine tools for production. *b.* Operating: tracking, guiding, piloting, or driving in a man-machine system. *c.* Coding: typing: shorthand; teleprinting.				
5. Acquisition of Information Learning 'theory', facts or background knowledge, about equipments or operations, including those covered by other categories.				
6. Intellectual Skills Exercise of reasoning, judgement, inferential thinking, e.g., electronic fault-finding, navigation.				
7. Character-Building. Development of self-reliance, initiative, resourcefulness.				
8. Managerial Skills *a.* Leadership: persuasion of others to action, by means other than direct orders. *b.* Decision-making: deployment of physical resources and personnel. *c.* Committee Activity: evolution of policy; administrative control.				
9. Identification with the Group Emergence of positive attitudes towards aims and conditions of the organization at many different levels.				
10. System Activities Co-ordinated operational work undertaken in small 'man-machine' groups, where (by definition) there is no redundant member, e.g., working teams.				

from Table 1 of Wallis *et al.*, 1966)

Instructor-centred methods						*Equipment-Centred Methods*		
							Simulators	
Expedition training (*e*)	*Classroom teaching with directed activity* (*f*)	*Supervised activity and practical work in labs./workshops* (*g*)	*Learning in the occupational setting with formal instruction* (*h*)	*Illustrated lectures and closed-circuit TV* (*i*)	*'Guidance' training* (*j*)	*Procedural trainers and synthetic devices* (*k*)	*Using 'real' equipment* (*l*)	*Using synthetic devices or computers* (*m*)

Abilities. However imperfectly, we have to look for corresponding categories from one set of data to another, or within the same set classified in different ways. It happens whenever we make decisions about guidance, selection, work design or training; particularly so for individuals, but also for groups of people. Depending upon how freely and precisely we can move from one classification to another, there is not only a limit upon practical action but also upon validity of whatever action seems possible. Moreover, you may be disposed to feel, as I do, that without some understanding and appreciation of the distinctive classificatory schemes used in other specialized disciplines than our own, we can scarcely hope to communicate with each other as freely as our common interests will incline us.

A second practical issue, for me, is whether we really take enough pains to examine and use our data from as many complementary points of view as possible. Are there important classifications we have heard too little about here? I think there is always a danger of personnel and manpower planning systems (and of ergonomic systems too) concentrating upon cognitive/intellectual characteristics and excluding, for example, personality factors. Certainly we have to be cautious about arousing misdirected enthusiasm for personality studies in areas where there has been a singular lack of success in the past. Dr. Fiedler's presentation of his 'contingency model' contained sufficient material to deter us from undue reliance on personality characteristics as predictors of suitability among 'leadership' resources. As he argued, it seems that leadership tasks can be performed effectively by just about anyone who is motivated to be a leader. However, I think we have to acknowledge that in practical occupational guidance and placement, and in work design too, we neglect personality characteristics at our peril.

And secondly, I wonder how we stand now on the issue of whether or not to strive for classifications of data which are more truly taxonomic. Dr. Miller told us roundly that he sees no need for concern about classifications providing they are useful. He argued that utility, relevance and cost are the over-riding considerations in practice. So long as our classifications take account of these criteria, they need not abide by other constraining principles. Dr. Duncan also urged that applied scientists must pay more attention to costs. He demonstrated very convincingly that by taking deliberate account of costs we can arrive at sensible and acceptable guidelines for when to cease the process of task analysis as the necessary precursor to recommendations about training needs.

Dr. Duncan did, however, also stress the importance of a classification which related superordinate to subordinate categories. And Dr. Fleishman identified a number of strictly taxonomic features, such as mutually exclusive categories which allow for exhaustive coverage of the data, among his criteria for judging the effectiveness of any classificatory system.

Application

Yesterday we turned from Analysis and Classification to Application. Examples were given from each of our six contributory disciplines. They represented a formidable, not to say bewildering, array of practical applications. Let me just remind you of the spread. We heard from Mr. Cassie and Mr. Killcross of novel developments in the field of personnel selection. Mr. Shepherd showed us how the task analysis and classification ideas we learned about from Dr. Duncan have been put to fruitful use in the petro-chemical industry. Mathematical models were illustrated, by Dr. Cooper and by Dr. Uebe, in the service of manpower planning; and we heard how Professor Burke's model of engineers' salaries in relation to economic influences has inter-disciplinary theoretical applications as well as relevance to real-life educational and manpower planning issues. It was also a measure of the breadth of our conference theme that we were able to receive from Mr. Bowen an intriguing account of industrial relations problems arising from employee participation in systems of work control.

No doubt we shall differ widely among ourselves in our reflections on the conference and its theme as a whole. I should like to leave you with three broad questions which surfaced during my own preliminary reflections last night. They are particularly apposite to the applications side of our work, and I suggest that we all have to answer them at least to our own personal satisfaction.

Here is the first question. In the real world of advanced socio-technical organizations, where there are human as well as technological and economic objectives to reconcile, what are the criteria we employ in judging how adequate is the utilization of human resources? To be pragmatic about it, what are the symptoms which lead us to assess a situation as being so inadequate as to demand rectification or improvement? After all, we have to make personal decisions about using ourselves as resources for scientific study and application.

Perhaps I could point out some instances we have encountered this week. Dr. Bates and Mr. Moore told us of a problem in New South Wales where the observable symptoms were of unrest among doctors and nurses. I'm not sure what practical problem may have prompted Dr. Fiedler's work in the U.S. Navy and elsewhere; but from what he said I assume someone had diagnosed that leadership and management training courses were not producing the desired results. And according to Mr. Smith, the manpower studies programme in the British Civil Service was triggered off by the not uncommon symptoms in an organization of impending failure to match supply with demand for human resources. I suppose my question invites the response that we either tackle symptoms which our employers insist are important; or, if we are free agents in the matter, we choose those which we find interesting. Well, I don't know that such a response takes us far enough, or whether it would reflect a majority opinion among us.

My second question has to do with decisions about trade-offs among the many and various approaches we might adopt to improve the use of resources. You may remember that Dr. Cooper was concerned about this in the military context he described. Let us suppose we have determined to our own satisfaction what the underlying nature of a problem really is—will this automatically inform us as to which approach to back in tackling it? Should we go for selection, work design, training, manpower modelling, guidance or whatever? Should we always think of more than one approach in tandem? And if so, how do we estimate the trade-offs between them in terms of costs and benefits to the organization or system as a whole?

Finally, I believe we ought to take more account of the 'consumer' in all this; or, as some of us may prefer to call him, of the 'client'. In this context, I seem to recall a remark of Professor Lawrence Stolurow to the effect that Education is probably the only industry in which the consumer does not actually determine the choice of what he will consume. This was a good while ago, and things have changed latterly. For example, Professor Butcher argued for consideration of students' views in setting educational objectives. However, there is a problem we have to face here. Are we always clear who the consumer or client is, whose interests we are fostering in an applied study? Is there sometimes more than one client? And if so, how do we manage to balance what may be conflicting interests among several clients? Questions of value and commitment cannot be brushed aside in our particular field, where the resources we are seeking to deploy more effectively are people with aims and aspirations of their own, as well as needs, which organizations cannot afford to neglect. I was encouraged at the evidence of concern for the consumers' views which came through conspicuously in Professor Verhaegen's study of unemployed persons, in Dr. van de Sandt's investigation into objectives in a military academy, and in Mr. Watson's survey of job appraisal and job enrichment developments in the British Civil Service. Perhaps consumer reaction, or forecasts of it on the basis of consumers' views and attitudes, will play an increasing part in the strategy of applied research, as a relevant criterion for judging the likely success of one approach to manpower utilization rather than another.

Reference

WALLIS, D., DUNCAN, K.D. and KNIGHT, M.A.G., 1966, *Programmed Instruction in The British Armed Forces* (London: H.M.S.O.).

Dr. Gunderson received degrees in psychology. He has conducted basic and applied research in psychiatric disorders, extreme environments and organizational stresses and health. He is Head, Epidemiology and Operational Psychiatry Division, Navy Medical Neuropsychiatric Research Unit, San Diego, California and Adjunct Professor of Psychiatry, University of California, San Diego.

4:3

Utilization of human resources: Summary and comment*

E. K. Eric Gunderson

Introduction

Concepts and patterns of work appear to be undergoing fundamental changes in our society. Dissatisfaction with work is purported to have increased in recent years, although comparative data appear to be lacking on this issue. In any case, motivational factors appear to be increasing in importance. Boredom probably impairs work performance more often than lack of technical skills. Changing social values, perceptions and practices undoubtedly extend into the world of work and may affect job stability and performance in unforeseen ways.

In focusing on utilization of human resources, it is implied that work activities can be made more efficient and productive and that opportunities for personal fulfilment through work can be enhanced. The approaches presented here indeed hold promise for increasing both efficiency and personal satisfaction in the world of work.

Robert M. Gagné emphasizes the dependence of educational objectives on national and societal goals. This suggests a need for constant review of national priorities and to discern insofar as possible how these affect educational aims. Broad educational goals tend to be vague and ambiguous, and, happily, debate on this subject was avoided at this Conference. However, the value of attempts to define and categorize educational aims, if only to encourage critical examination and achieve better conceptualization, is recognized. In Herbert Spencer's famous essay on 'What Knowledge Is of Most Worth?', he proposed usefulness in everyday life as the criterion for what should be taught in the schools. Accordingly, he divided life activities into several broad categories and rank-ordered these in terms of relative importance. The relative worth of various items in the curriculum is perhaps an even more controversial issue today than it was in Spencer's time, and the problem of relating educational objectives to broad social values remains a fundamental concern.

Dr. Gagné presents a general conceptualization of educational goals and

* Report Number 74–14, supported by the Bureau of Medicine and Surgery, Department of the Navy, under Research Work Unit MF51.524.002-5015DX5F and partially supported by the Office of Naval Research under Project RR042-08-01 NR170-743. Opinions expressed are those of the author and are not to be construed as necessarily reflecting the offical view or endorsement of the Department of the Navy.

objectives in terms of an hierarchical ordering with nine levels of specificity. This scheme is very useful for a variety of purposes and includes recognition of the basic dichotomy of societal goals versus individual needs and aspirations. He proposes five major categories of learned human capabilities—motor skill, verbal information, intellectual skill, cognitive strategy and attitudes—and suggests differentiating characteristics. Use of such taxonomic classes at appropriate levels of specificity can reduce the labour involved in curriculum planning and reduce ambiguity in denoting categories of human performance.

Robert B. Miller outlines a technology of training as a basis for a taxonomy of training. He sees a taxonomy as more than a descriptive classification. Rather, it should relate to a theoretical model and provide a conceptual structure, guidelines for decisions and actions, and predictions of outcomes. Miller examines a number of taxonomic approaches, most of them of a practical common-sense variety and typically ambiguous. He noted Guilford's taxonomy of intelligence but sees little possibility of relating these concepts to task descriptions or training procedures. In fact, he questions whether factor analytic taxonomies in general can be meaningful matched with task requirements or specific training operations. He sees little hope of deriving useful guidance for training efforts from the many and diverse taxonomies that have been offered. He states: 'No mere array of names of functions, processes, entities, can produce a discipline or technology of training. Only a model of decision alternatives, supported by rationales and strategies for the selection and combination of alternatives, can produce such a discipline.' Miller contrasts 'cognitive' or holistic learning methods with the conditioning model of learning and characterizes the latter as 'most appropriate for students whose cognitive abilities were relatively low and whose capabilities for self-motivation were neutral or low'. He sees the conditioning approach as tending to limit flexibility, generalization and initiative. Miller urges that motivation be acknowledged as a fundamental variable in learning and competent performance and emphasizes the dynamic role of the student in learning: 'A massive resource for training technology is being forfeited by default: the potential capability of human learners to participate actively in strategies for their own learning.' He places cost-effectiveness analysis in the context of refining objectives, examining alternatives and differentiating the essential from the trivial in order to reduce human costs. Miller describes the basic elements of an effective training system design and points to recent applications in the U.S. military services. A generally accepted, comprehensive training model does not yet exist, but Miller believes that one might be created with intensive effort during the next decade.

E.A. Fleishman's work on measurement of psychomotor skills and physical fitness and proficiency over the past 15 years is well known and in his current paper he extends the scope of his task classification system to new areas of performance research. He evaluates the validities of associated measurement and scaling techniques and the generalizability of research findings when tasks are described in terms of performance classification systems.

The contributions of Gagné, Miller and Fleishman represent the most advanced state of the art with respect to defining and classifying educational objectives, training methods and human performance skills.

K.D. Duncan addresses a number of major questions: for example, what levels of description are appropriate to various tasks and how are molecular units of performance organized into larger molar units? He argues that flexibility or adaptability is the most important characteristic of skilled performance. For Duncan task analysis consists of redefining superordinate operations in terms of subordinate operations (progressive redescription), and training consists of mastering subordinate operations which are selected and ordered so that they complete the next superordinate unit of skilled performance. Task analysis should not only define task contents or components but also should determine the kinds and amounts of training required. The most important advantage of part-task training over whole task training is that part-task training allows concentrating on those elements of the task that are most difficult and most susceptible to rapid learning. At some point whole task training is essential, however, because isolated components must be co-ordinated. Duncan in his detailed example of a complex task analysis (control of an acid purification process) illustrates the many alternatives that are possible in training design and how training design is a hypothesis testing activity. Solutions to operational problems may involve equipment design and personnel selection, placement and development as well as specific training strategies.

Walter Rohmert describes the application of ergonomic methods to work design problems. Ergonomics, narrowly conceived, is concerned with the relations of human inputs to work outputs, but Rohmert extends the concept of work design to include all important influences on man's work performance. One of the most important factors in work design is the evaluation of stress and strain. Limiting strain to tolerable levels is of major concern, and detailed analysis of sources and effects of stress is basic to work design efforts. In this approach measurement of strain by physiological, psychological and biochemical methods is used to evaluate the effects of job demands and working conditions. Rohmert notes that suitable standards are lacking in the area of evaluating individual job satisfaction.

Fred E. Fiedler's contingency model of leadership is an outgrowth of more than 15 years of systematic research. The theory postulates that leader effectiveness (measured as group performance) depends upon leader motivation or style (task-oriented vs. relations-oriented as measured by the Least Preferred Co-worker Index) and the degree to which the situation is favourable to the leader in terms of leader-member relations (liking and trust), task structure and leader power or influence. In an impressive series of studies Fiedler shows that leadership training may enhance performance under certain conditions but may impair performance under others. New approaches are suggested for utilizing leaders and achieving maximum performance, that is, matching task-motivated leaders with either favourable or unfavourable situations and matching relationship-motivated leaders with moderately favourable situations. Higher level management can increase leader effectiveness by rotating assignments, training and changing the favourableness of situations.

A.R. Smith and G.W. Watson are concerned with all aspects of manpower planning in a large organization, the British Civil Service. A basic objective is to match manpower need with manpower supply over a period of time in order to maintain a balanced organization and meet management goals. In other words, manpower planning serves as a control mechanism to maintain stability and permit orderly development. Smith and Watson recognize important constraints on manpower planning in the Civil Service but emphasize the need and opportunity for realistic and flexible planning within these constraints. It is significant that they are concerned with many aspects of personnel management simultaneously—selection, training, placement, performance appraisal, job satisfaction, promotion and retirement. Presumably, better decisions can be made when the functioning of the whole system as a dynamic process is understood. It is of special interest that systematic analysis of the wastage of human resources is proposed, including turnover, illnesses and accidents, etc. Such monitoring of organizational subunits can help locate trouble spots where management intervention is most needed.

W.T. Singleton presents a clear and concise task analysis of the guidance process and differentiates the roles of counsellor, client and computer in gathering and evaluating relevant career information. Meaningful matching of people and jobs depends upon adequate classifications systems for both people and jobs. Some sort of standard matrix of individual capabilities and job requirements would greatly facilitate the matching process, but existing taxonomies are not precise enough conceptually or empirically to be of much help. This is an important area for future investigation, and Singleton has identified a number of specific research areas worth pursuing. He points out the desperate need for vocational guidance services, which bridge the gap between the educational system and the world of work, but notes the very high cost of providing such services.

A. Shepherd, in describing problems of matching a task taxonomy with training needs, recommends that initially task taxonomies be restricted in scope to a particular industry or setting. More general taxonomies can be created as similarities become apparent from one setting to another.

Paul Verhaegen reminds us that there are important personality or characterological determinants of being a stable worker. Attitudes toward authority figures were most important, and such psychological factors probably play a significant part in marginal work histories.

A. Cassie and M.C. Killcross discuss an interesting contribution to the technology of selection and placement called 'tailored testing'. This alternative to mass standardized testing purports to achieve greater efficiency in classification by matching interests and abilities to military needs on an individual basis. The method would appear to work best when integrated with career guidance counselling.

The study reported by B.N. Moore and E. Moore on the adverse effects of job role conflicts points to an important but often neglected source of human resources wastage, that is, organizational stresses.

A number of recent studies have linked various forms of life stress, particularly job stress, to specific psychosomatic diseases and psychiatric disorders (Gunderson and Rahe, 1974). The role that organizational stresses play in ill health is not well understood at this time, but many medical investigators support the view of Moore and Moore that psychosocial stresses on the job represent definite health hazards for many workers.

Selection, training and placement, the traditional areas of personnel research, are indispensable in large organizations but do not in themselves provide techniques for dealing with other major perennial work force problems, such as recruitment, retention, job satisfaction, group morale and efficiency of the organization as a whole. Increasing attention is being given to the organizational context in which the individual works in efforts to make full use of manpower resources at all levels. Organizational theory is still in its infancy, and behavioural science has not yet come to grips with the diverse problems of management. Administration remains more of an art than an integrated body of concepts and practices. Research on organizations is largely uncharted, and probably because of the expense and complexity of the methodological problems involved, only a few major exploratory studies have been initiated. Multivariate research methods provide powerful new approaches to the analysis of the relative importance of individual characteristics, environmental variables and organizational stresses in determining illness and accident rates, job dissatisfaction, absenteeism, turnover and other indices of manpower wastage. One large scale U.S. Navy study seeks to identify environmental and organizational conditions that are associated with high illness rates and poor morale (Gunderson and Sells, in press). It has been recognized for many years that motivational problems, mental disorders, physical illnesses and accidents, represent a major drain on human resources in the military services. At one level in this research effort the organization (ship or shore station) will be treated as the unit of analysis. Organizational differences in environmental quality, crew abilities and training, leader behaviour, organizational climate, mission, operational schedules and other aspects of overall functioning will be related to illness and accident rates, disciplinary problems, re-enlistment rates and evaluations of organizational efficiency. A long-range major goal is to develop a methodology for organizational analysis that might be applicable to both military and civilian organizations.

Typically, organizations do not compile information on the cost and value of their human resources. Meinolf Dierkes outlines the philosophy and some of the problems of 'human resources accounting'. He sees this method as a potentially valuable tool for measuring human resources and monitoring manpower utilization. Managers are expected to develop and utilize human resources fully, but no information is gathered on how well human resources actually are used or whether human assets, like profits, sales and physical assets, are increasing in value. Knowledge of human assets, as well as responsibility for their development and utilization, could have a profound effect upon manager behaviour. In one case history, human resources data apparently had a strong impact on investor behaviour (Rhode and Lawler, 1973, p. 155).

> On August 8, 1968, C. Lester Hogan, executive vice-president and general manager of Motorola's semi-conductor division, resigned his position and took seven of his division's top executives with him to Fairchild, where he became president and chief executive officer. Investor reaction was immediate. During the 24 hours following Hogan's resignation, the price of Fairchild's stock rose from \$59 to \$67 per share, and Motorola's stock dropped from \$138 to \$130 per share. The market value attached to the personnel changes may be estimated by multiplying the price change per share by the company's average number of common stock shares outstanding. Fairchild's 1968 average of 4,327,578 shares outstanding times \$8 per share reveals an increase in market value of \$34,620,624. Motorola's 1968 average of 6,133,470 shares outstanding times \$8 per share decrease indicates a market devaluation of \$49,067,760. Within a short period, the shareholders of Fairchild and Motorola demonstrated their ability to assess the value of human resources. While common stock prices change for a variety of reasons, the primary cause is the investors discounting the organization's future earning flows. Other, unknown factors

may have influenced the stock price changes in the Motorola–Fairchild case, but price movements for both companies were relatively stable before and after the day of announced personnel changes.

It may be that human resources will only be fully utilized when they are measurable and managers are held accountable for their development and use. The technical knowledge and valuable insights provided by the contributors to this Conference should stimulate and aid managers to utilize human resources more effectively.

References

GUNDERSON, E.K.E. and RAHE, R.H., Ed., 1974, *Life Stress and Illness* (Springfield: C.C. Thomas).

GUNDERSON, E.K.E. and SELLS, S.B., 1974, Organizational Stresses and Health. *Naval Research Reviews*, in press.

RHODE, J.G. and LAWLER, E.E., 1973, Auditing Change: Human Resource Accounting. In: Dunnette, M.D. (Ed.), *Work and Nonwork in the Year 2001* (Monterey, Calif.: Brooks/Cole Publishing Co.).

Overview

Overview

W. T. Singleton and P. Spurgeon

The twin theses of the Conference were the importance of using practice as a stimulus for the development of theory and the need to consider problems as unitary regardless of traditional academic boundaries.

Both of these make great demands on the individual investigator. Each research worker must be prepared to sustain challenge from others of much narrower outlook, he must work enormously hard to attain an adequate breadth and depth of knowledge. Simultaneously he must be able to move to and fro across the boundary between theory and practice. It is understandable that there are not many such people but we did succeed in attracting some of them to the Conference.

The taxonomic issue was enjoined by Gagné, Miller and Fleishman. All three were concerned with fundamental aspects of human resource, notably in developing ability and monitoring performance. A successful, well planned education system is absolutely vital in utilization of human ability. The potential of each individual must be identified, nurtured and developed in an efficient system. However, in total human resource terms an element of appropriateness in this process is essential. That is the output of an education system must combine two apparently conflicting demands. It must meet the needs of its society in terms of the qualities and abilities required in that social system, but it must continue to question and be an agent of potential change within society. Gagné accepted this link between society's goals and setting educational objectives. His proposed taxonomy of educational objectives should help in the measurement and understanding of what we attempt to do in the educational processes. However, societal goals must still be imposed upon the educational system and the problem of how these are to be determined and who shall be responsible for this decision remains. Fleishman was concerned with the output end of the educational process. While the system is primarily concerned with fostering individual capacities, effective resource utilization entails the development of a suitable system for evaluating capabilities. The taxonomy of human performance provides a useful beginning to the development of such an evaluative component. If efficient utilization is to occur, we must be able to measure the capacity of the resources available and therefore we must have a taxonomy to identify the relevant performance criteria. Miller's contribution is concerned with a further stage in the process. Human potential must be developed but for effective utilization it must be directed, it must be trained. If educational objectives and performance criteria were settled the problems of the training practitioner would be much reduced. However, given the flexibility at either end of his task he too is inevitably directed to the taxonomy problem. Can the relevant aspects of training programmes be identified and can we hope to measure these components?

The relevance of the taxonomic issue emerged again in Duncan's description of analytic techniques needed to devise a training programme. Although a specific task analysis was described the detailed analysis highlighted the need for a comprehensive taxonomy. This was illustrated by Duncan's references to the potential importance of other sub-areas in devising such a training taxonomy. The functioning of educational programmes, selection criteria and work design are all relevant to the training sphere. Analytical problems in work design itself were represented by Rohmert. In addition to putting forward analytical techniques useful in work design he also made observations on the place of ergonomics within a wider societal context. The operation of work design should be carried out with some acknowledgement of the place of the occupation within society. The need for extended scope in the design of work is also evidenced in the development of aims such as job satisfaction, job enrichment and job enlargement (Davis and Taylor, 1972).

Manpower planning is a central component in the utilization field and Smith and Watson describe a significant contribution in a complex occupational setting. Although their paper developed particular statistical tools that might be used in manpower planning they were at pains to point out that statistics alone were insufficient. The impact of selection, guidance and training in particular on manpower planning ought to be considerable but this is not yet true in practice.

Fiedler's contribution demonstrated the considerable width of academic expertise involved at the conference. His paper illustrated that we were a long way from making the most efficient use of leadership potential and consequently we are ineffectively utilizing a valuable resource.

Butcher focused on the practice of higher education in Britain and illustrated the inadequacy of taxonomies within the educational sphere. For both selection and assessment the weakness of current taxonomies is such that suitable criteria for these processes are not available. This results in expensive wastage of human ability. Furthermore, the impact of manpower planning on the operations of higher education has been ineffective and is susceptible to a dangerous time-lag.

The guidance process examined by Singleton may be seen as meeting two major objectives. It must attempt to provide an efficient link between the educational sphere and the world of work. It must also on many occasions help individuals to overcome inadequacies in earlier selection and allocation procedures. Guidance is by its nature a problem-solving exercise and it was shown to be in need of a comprehensive and sensitive taxonomies.

The remainder of the conference consisted of a series of papers from investigators currently engaged in tackling problems within this range of disciplines. Many of the issues raised by the theoretical speakers were exemplified and new issues were raised. Cooper and Roll examined the operation of manpower planning in a military setting and as economists raised the important issue of cost. They were principally concerned with the trade-off between capital and labour and the marginal cost attached to such decisions. Although the cost factor must play an important part in any programme of resource utilization it received little attention except from Miller and Duncan on the setting up of training programmes.

Bainbridge gave us a glimpse of the enormous complexity of the human operator at work even on such a relatively low level task as process control. She also illustrated the importance of understanding how a worker achieves his objectives if we are to make any kind of effective approach to designing training or a work space which provides the optimum display of information relevant to the task. The various levels of sequences, routines and operations have implications also for learning theory. This intensive study of the process operator reveals on the one hand how much we are underusing people in getting them to do jobs such as assembly and on the other hand how far we have to go before we approach any understanding of human tasks involving aspects such as social interaction, management and creativity. Shepherd proposed a model to examine fault locating techniques operating within a specific industry. The importance of such behaviour in the chemical industry is obvious and the need for an improved taxonomy and training scheme was clearly illustrated. The interaction between man and machine is further discussed in the paper by Caille and Kessler, with particular emphasis on problems of 'fatigue' and vigilance. Caille and Kessler suggest that by monitoring the physiological reactions of the subject, using for example E.E.G. patterns, the subject can be made aware of his arousal state and therefore act on his own initiative to reduce further error.

Inefficiency in terms of inadequate job performance was also considered. Bates and Moore were attempting to measure job stress and make some recommendations as to how the situation might be remedied. Verhaegen *et al.* were concerned with workers who might be termed unstable and therefore not contributing effectively in terms of their capacity.

Aspects of pre-employment behaviour was also considered by Tan and in the context of army personnel allocation by Cassie and Kilcross. Tan reported the development of a novel form of interest measure which may be useful in guiding future career choice. Cassie and Kilcross focused upon the individual, arguing against group testing of any capacity, and suggesting instead a suitable test situation to meet the needs of the individual and the characteristics of the 'future' situation. Although individual testing has been considered too expensive the argument that the improved accuracy of measurement is worthwhile deserves consideration. Also within a military context the role of academic education in army training was discussed by van de Sandt and Daniels. The difficulty in defining objectives within a specific context parallels problems for the educational system at a broader level.

Bowen extended the scope of our attention to focus upon the wider social organization and its implications for effective utilization of manpower. The form of control system imposed upon workers in an industrial setting may well impinge upon their willingness to work effectively within that situation.

The overall problem of human resource utilization was examined by Spurgeon in the context of the education system. The problems of devising an effective teacher training scheme without an accepted taxonomy of educational objectives was illustrated. The absence of accepted taxonomies is a constant impediment to applied work. It imposes upon the researcher the need to create arbitrarily defined performance criteria.

Finally Dierkes and Coppock examined a directly relevant area of human asset accounting. Perhaps human resources have been inadequately considered due to the lack of suitable measuring tools. Dierkes and Coppock demonstrated that it might be possible to make some quantitative statement about the value of human components in an industrial setting. Similarly intangible concepts such as 'goodwill' have been the subject of attempts at quantification (Likert, 1967).

The major concern of the conference was to focus attention on human resource utilization and to examine some current attempts to come to terms with the problem. The concept of human resources and areas in which the social science disciplines can make a contribution have been discussed in the introductory chapter. Many of the problems facing individual societies are potentially soluble with appropriate use of the resources available. In this context resources available entail the capacities, abilities, attitudes and values of the members of the society. As with physical resources this implies that these resources must be used in an efficient manner. However, in contrast with the realm of physical resources, the use of terms such as 'resource utilization' and 'most effective use' have emotive connotations. The implication of a monolithic controlling agent, directing, organizing and manipulating individuals is sometimes envisaged. As has been pointed out earlier such a consequence is not regarded by the authors as inevitable or even likely. Furthermore, efficient use of resources implies no adherence to a particular political value structure. Both capitalist and communist extremes might well advocate effective resource utilization. Indeed so might any admixture of the two systems since unemotively and realistically efficient use of resources is in the common interest of all groups. Individual freedom is a precious commodity and it would seem tenable to suggest that more efficient planning and use of human capacities may well create more rather than less.

The efficient use of human resources does not require an all powerful agent, but it does require an advance in our knowledge and understanding of the welter of components of human resources. We have stressed that a number of problems are 'potentially' soluble, and it is this potential that has provided the conference with its theme. Can we identify the features that may contribute to effective utilization? What is the effective state of knowledge in these relevant areas? How far can one discipline in isolation go in attempting to solve complex multi-faceted problems? These were the issues the conference attempted to explore and we might at this point consider how effective it has been in meeting these objectives.

Progress requires a rapid growth in meaningful interdisciplinary research. The conference encompassed the majority of the relevant disciplines and we might hope for progress from such a gathering. There were hopeful signs. The need for sensitive, readily applicable taxonomies was appreciated, especially in education, training and guidance. It is perhaps not coincidental that these have the widest area of operation and also the most loosely defined taxonomic structure. If comprehensive taxonomies were available in these areas the 'potential' solution might be more realistic. It is essential that these three sub-areas operate in accord with one another and successfully in themselves if human resource problems are to be tackled. The need for interdisciplinary activity was also recognized. Miller and Duncan were aware of the constant cost constraint, while Duncan also pointed out the role of education, selection and guidance in the training field.

The willingness of established academics to attempt to encompass other disciplines where relevant gains may be made was exemplified by Gagné's move as a psychologist into the sphere of education, Smith and Watson as statisticians into a broader manpower planning context and Singleton as an ergonomist into the fields of selection and guidance. However, despite these signs there remain large obstacles to further progress. Each of disciplines represented exhibited an unfortunate degree of independence amounting to isolation. There was less than complete awareness of the problems and usefulness of other disciplines. Obviously a certain degree of communication difficulty is involved. Jargon is inevitably a bar to interdisciplinary work. However, there seems to be little pressure to come to terms with other disciplines or to become aware of the potentialities of cross-discipline activity. This difficulty may be engendered by a fear of academic dilution. It may well be that no discipline within the social science feels powerful enough to encompass other areas without some detriment to its own academic standing. This is an unfortunate but not insoluble situation. Interdisciplinary research is increasing and the development of more applied research will inevitably accelerate this trend. As problems in the field are encountered the need for the tools of other disciplines will become apparent. The problem-solving approach within an applied context contains the greatest spur to the furtherance of interdisciplinary work.

The belief in interdisciplinary research and the optimism that it will develop is tempered somewhat by the knowledge that the problems of resource utilization increase with the delay. Effective utilization of human resources requires considerable advancement in the areas represented here. They are not adequately prepared to meet the task as yet. It is to be hoped that this conference will provide a spur to the vital development of interdisciplinary work and a collective attempt to come to terms with a broad, complex problem. It is also hoped that this will not be in the too distant future.

At the conceptual level we have achieved rather more understanding of why interdisciplinary studies are so difficult. It is not merely a matter of administration and academic politics. It is also to do with context dependence. In the present state of knowledge it is difficult to take any approach out of its own context. It is possible to make progress by considering such procedures as task analysis and taxonomy development within a particular field, say training or guidance. It is not possible at present to devise a taxonomy of human abilities which is equally applicable for both training and guidance. Thus there is some defence for the blinkered attitude which results in pursuit of a narrow objective without taking too much account of related problems. As always the real skill of research is in achieving the optimum balance. Too much scanning of vast problem areas all too easily results in nothing but the acknowledgement that the problems are impossible to solve. On the other hand too narrow an approach will at best be uneconomic and at worst will lead to totally false conclusions.

Here again an applied orientation supports progress. The counsellor with a client in his office, a work designer holding up production, a training officer faced with a group of trainees have got to think of something. This is perhaps the reason why applied workers can sometimes afford the luxury of standing back and surveying macro problem areas, they know that the week after the conference they have to get down to cases again.

The Lisbon Conference did cover a tremendous area of endeavour in the human and social sciences. If there is a conclusion and a forecast it is that the separate disciplines are still too immature to consider losing their separate identities. Nonetheless eventually there must be some coalescence, probably beginning with overlapping groups. It has already been mentioned that education, guidance and training are a conceivable set in a theoretical sense, so also are training, work design and ergonomics. Manpower studies comes into all the others and also overlaps outside these sciences into subjects such as economics.

The point made in the Introduction is sustained, all these topics are primitive and fragmented yet there is no disaster pending. The adaptability of individuals remains the glue which holds society together and provides the basis of all the wealth generated. The first thing we have to develop in relation to Human Resources is a full respect for them.

References

DAVIS, L.E. and TAYLOR, J.C., 1972, *Design of Jobs* (Harmondsworth: Penguin).
LIKERT, R., 1967, *The Human Organization: Its Management and Value* (New York: McGraw-Hill).

Author Index

Subject Index

For Product Safety Concerns and Information please contact our EU representative GPSR@taylorandfrancis.com
Taylor & Francis Verlag GmbH, Kaufingerstraße 24, 80331 München, Germany

www.ingramcontent.com/pod-product-compliance
Ingram Content Group UK Ltd.
Pitfield, Milton Keynes, MK11 3LW, UK
UKHW022008180926
475701UK00003B/251
9780415786034